BIG IDEAS M

Modeling Real Life

Grade 3

Volume 2

Ron Larson
Laurie Boswell

Big Ideas Learning™

Erie, Pennsylvania
BigIdeasLearning.com

Big Ideas Learning, LLC
1762 Norcross Road
Erie, PA 16510-3838
USA

For product information and customer support, contact Big Ideas Learning at **1-877-552-7766** or visit us at ***BigIdeasLearning.com***.

Cover Image:
Valdis Torms, bgblue/DigitalVision Vectors/Getty Images

Printed in the U.S.A.

ISBN 13: 978-1-63708-018-4

2 3 4 5 6 7 8 9 10—25 24 23

One Voice from Kindergarten Through Algebra 2

Written by renowned authors, Dr. Ron Larson and Dr. Laurie Boswell, *Big Ideas Math* offers a seamless math pedagogy from elementary through high school. Together, Ron and Laurie provide a consistent voice that encourages students to make connections through cohesive progressions and clear instruction. Since 1992, Ron and Laurie have authored over 50 mathematics programs.

"*Each time Laurie and I start working on a new program, we spend time putting ourselves in the position of the reader. How old is the reader? What is the reader's experience with mathematics? The answers to these questions become our writing guides. Our goal is to make the learning targets understandable and to develop these targets in a clear path that leads to student success.*"

Ron Larson

Ron Larson, Ph.D., is well known as lead author of a comprehensive and widely used mathematics program that ranges from elementary school through college. He holds the distinction of Professor Emeritus from Penn State Erie, The Behrend College, where he taught for nearly 40 years. He received his Ph.D. in mathematics from the University of Colorado. Dr. Larson engages in the latest research and advancements in mathematics education and consistently incorporates key pedagogical elements to ensure focus, coherence, rigor, and student self-reflection.

"*My passion and goal in writing is to provide an essential resource for exploring and making sense of mathematics. Our program is guided by research around the learning and teaching of mathematics in the hopes of improving the achievement of all students. May this be a successful year for you!*"

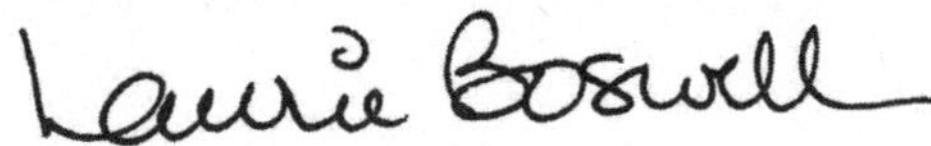

Laurie Boswell, Ed.D., is the former Head of School at Riverside School in Lyndonville, Vermont. In addition to authoring textbooks, she provides mathematics consulting and embedded coaching sessions. Dr. Boswell received her Ed.D. from the University of Vermont in 2010. She is a recipient of the Presidential Award for Excellence in Mathematics Teaching and later served as president of CPAM. Laurie has taught math to students at all levels, elementary through college. In addition, Laurie has served on the NCTM Board of Directors and as a Regional Director for NCSM. Along with Ron, Laurie has co-authored numerous math programs and has become a popular national speaker.

Contributors, Reviewers, and Research

Big Ideas Learning would like to express our gratitude to the mathematics education and instruction experts who served as our advisory panel, contributing specialists, and reviewers during the writing of *Big Ideas Math: Modeling Real Life*. Their input was an invaluable asset during the development of this program.

Contributing Specialists and Reviewers

- **Sophie Murphy**, Ph.D. Candidate, Melbourne School of Education, Melbourne, Australia
  Learning Targets and Success Criteria Specialist and Visible Learning Reviewer
- **Linda Hall**, Mathematics Educational Consultant, Edmond, OK
  Advisory Panel
- **Michael McDowell**, Ed.D., Superintendent, Ross, CA
  Project-Based Learning Specialist
- **Kelly Byrne**, Math Supervisor and Coordinator of Data Analysis, Downingtown, PA
  Advisory Panel
- **Jean Carwin**, Math Specialist/TOSA, Snohomish, WA
  Advisory Panel
- **Nancy Siddens**, Independent Language Teaching Consultant, Las Cruces, NM
  English Language Learner Specialist
- **Kristen Karbon**, Curriculum and Assessment Coordinator, Troy, MI
  Advisory Panel
- **Kery Obradovich**, K–8 Math/Science Coordinator, Northbrook, IL
  Advisory Panel
- **Jennifer Rollins**, Math Curriculum Content Specialist, Golden, CO
  Advisory Panel
- **Becky Walker**, Ph.D., School Improvement Services Director, Green Bay, WI
  Advisory Panel and Content Reviewer
- **Deborah Donovan**, Mathematics Consultant, Lexington, SC
  Content Reviewer
- **Tom Muchlinski**, Ph.D., Mathematics Consultant, Plymouth, MN
  Content Reviewer and Teaching Edition Contributor
- **Mary Goetz**, Elementary School Teacher, Troy, MI
  Content Reviewer
- **Nanci N. Smith**, Ph.D., International Curriculum and Instruction Consultant, Peoria, AZ
  Teaching Edition Contributor
- **Robyn Seifert-Decker**, Mathematics Consultant, Grand Haven, MI
  Teaching Edition Contributor
- **Bonnie Spence**, Mathematics Education Specialist, Missoula, MT
  Teaching Edition Contributor
- **Suzy Gagnon**, Adjunct Instructor, University of New Hampshire, Portsmouth, NH
  Teaching Edition Contributor
- **Art Johnson**, Ed.D., Professor of Mathematics Education, Warwick, RI
  Teaching Edition Contributor
- **Anthony Smith**, Ph.D., Associate Professor, Associate Dean, University of Washington Bothell, Seattle, WA
  Reading and Writing Reviewer
- **Brianna Raygor**, Music Teacher, Fridley, MN
  Music Reviewer
- **Nicole Dimich Vagle**, Educator, Author, and Consultant, Hopkins, MN
  Assessment Reviewer
- **Janet Graham**, District Math Specialist, Manassas, VA
  Response to Intervention and Differentiated Instruction Reviewer
- **Sharon Huber**, Director of Elementary Mathematics, Chesapeake, VA
  Universal Design for Learning Reviewer

Student Reviewers

- T.J. Morin
- Alayna Morin
- Ethan Bauer
- Emery Bauer
- Emma Gaeta
- Ryan Gaeta
- Benjamin SanFrotello
- Bailey SanFrotello
- Samantha Grygier
- Robert Grygier IV
- Jacob Grygier
- Jessica Urso
- Ike Patton
- Jake Lobaugh
- Adam Fried
- Caroline Naser
- Charlotte Naser

Research

Ron Larson and Laurie Boswell used the latest in educational research, along with the body of knowledge collected from expert mathematics instructors, to develop the *Modeling Real Life* series. The pedagogical approach used in this program follows the best practices outlined in the most prominent and widely accepted educational research, including:

- *Visible Learning*, John Hattie © 2009
- *Visible Learning for Teachers*
John Hattie © 2012
- *Visible Learning for Mathematics*
John Hattie © 2017
- *Principles to Actions: Ensuring Mathematical Success for All*
NCTM © 2014
- *Adding It Up: Helping Children Learn Mathematics*
National Research Council © 2001
- *Mathematical Mindsets: Unleashing Students' Potential through Creative Math, Inspiring Messages and Innovative Teaching*
Jo Boaler © 2015
- *What Works in Schools: Translating Research into Action*
Robert Marzano © 2003
- *Classroom Instruction That Works: Research-Based Strategies for Increasing Student Achievement*
Marzano, Pickering, and Pollock © 2001
- *Principles and Standards for School Mathematics*
NCTM © 2000
- *Rigorous PBL by Design: Three Shifts for Developing Confident and Competent Learners*
Michael McDowell © 2017
- *Universal Design for Learning Guidelines*
CAST © 2011
- Rigor/Relevance Framework®
International Center for Leadership in Education
- *Understanding by Design*
Grant Wiggins and Jay McTighe © 2005
- Achieve, ACT, and The College Board
- *Elementary and Middle School Mathematics: Teaching Developmentally*
John A. Van de Walle and Karen S. Karp © 2015
- *Evaluating the Quality of Learning: The SOLO Taxonomy*
John B. Biggs & Kevin F. Collis © 1982
- *Unlocking Formative Assessment: Practical Strategies for Enhancing Students' Learning in the Primary and Intermediate Classroom*
Shirley Clarke, Helen Timperley, and John Hattie © 2004
- *Formative Assessment in the Secondary Classroom*
Shirley Clarke © 2005
- *Improving Student Achievement: A Practical Guide to Assessment for Learning*
Toni Glasson © 2009

Focus and Coherence from

Instructional Design

A single authorship team from Kindergarten through Algebra 2 results in a logical progression of focused topics with meaningful coherence from course to course.

FOCUS

A focused program dedicates lessons, activities, and assessments to grade-level standards while simultaneously supporting and engaging you in the major work of the course.

The **Learning Target** and **Success Criteria** for each lesson focus the learning into manageable chunks, using clear teaching text and Key Ideas.

Learning Target: Compare fractions that have the same denominator.

Success Criteria:

- I can model fractions that have the same denominator.
- I can use the numerators to compare fractions.
- I can explain how to compare fractions that have the same denominator.

Laurie's Notes

Preparing to Teach

In the previous lesson, students learned how to use an Inch Ruler to measure lengths to the nearest inch. In this lesson, they add *foot* and *yard* to their length measurement units. Students will measure objects to the nearest foot and nearest yard. They will also choose among an inch ruler, yardstick, and measuring tape as the instrument for measuring a specific object.

Laurie's Notes, located in the Teaching Edition, prepare your teacher for the math concepts in each chapter and lesson and make connections to the threads of major topics for the course.

Think and Grow: Find Factor Pairs

You can write whole numbers as products of two factors. The two factors are called a **factor pair** for the number.

factor pair

$2 \times 4 = 8$

factor factor

2 and 4 are a factor pair for 8.

Example Find the factor pairs for 20.

Find the side lengths of as many different rectangles with an area of 20 square units as possible.

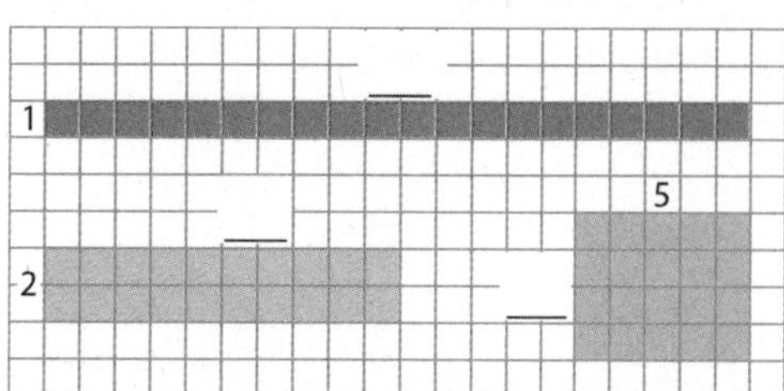

A 4×5 rectangle has the same area as a 5×4 rectangle. Both give the factor pair 4 and 5.

The side lengths of each rectangle are a factor pair.

So, the factor pairs for 20 are ____ and ____, ____ and ____, and ____ and ____.

a Single Authorship Team

COHERENCE

A single authorship team built a coherent program that has intentional progression of content within each grade and between grade levels. You will build new understanding on foundations from prior grades and connect concepts throughout the course.

The authors developed content that progresses from prior chapters and grades to future ones. In addition to charts like this one, Laurie's Notes give your teacher insights about where you have come from and where you are going in your learning progression.

Through the Grades		
Grade 4	**Grade 5**	**Grade 6**
• Create a number or shape pattern that follows a given rule. • Describe attributes of a pattern that are not part of the rule.	• Describe a coordinate system using appropriate vocabulary. • Graph points in a coordinate plane to represent real-world problems. • Explain the value of points in a coordinate plane in relation to a real-world problem. • Analyze patterns based on relationships and operations. • Create numeric patterns using given rules. • Graph ordered pairs in a coordinate plane.	• Graph ordered pairs in all four quadrants of the coordinate plane. • Draw polygons in the coordinate plane. • Graph ordered pairs in all four quadrants of the coordinate plane. • Understand ratios and describe ratio relationships.

One author team thoughtfully wrote each course, creating a seamless progression of content from Kindergarten to Algebra 2.

	Grade K	Grade 1	Grade 2	Grade 3	Grade 4	Grade 5	Grade 6	
Algebra and Functions	Operations and Algebraic Thinking				Operations and Algebraic Thinking		Expressions and Equations	
	Understand addition as putting together and adding to, and understand subtraction as taking apart and taking from. *Chapters 5–7*	Solve problems involving addition and subtraction within 20. Apply properties of operations. Work with addition and subtraction equations. *Chapters 1–5, 10, 11*	Solve problems involving addition and subtraction within 20. Work with equal groups of objects. *Chapters 1–6, 15*	Solve problems involving multiplication and division within 100. Apply properties of multiplication. Solve problems involving the four operations, and identify and explain patterns in arithmetic. *Chapters 1–5, 8, 9, and 14*	Use the four operations with whole numbers to solve problems. Understand factors and multiples. Generate and analyze patterns. *Chapters 2–6, 12*	Write and interpret numerical expressions. Analyze patterns and relationships. *Chapters 2, 12*	Perform arithmetic with algebraic expressions. *Chapter 5* Solve one-variable equations and inequalities. *Chapters 6, 8* Analyze relationships between dependent and independent variables. *Chapter 6*	Write *Chap* Use n expre inequ *Chap*

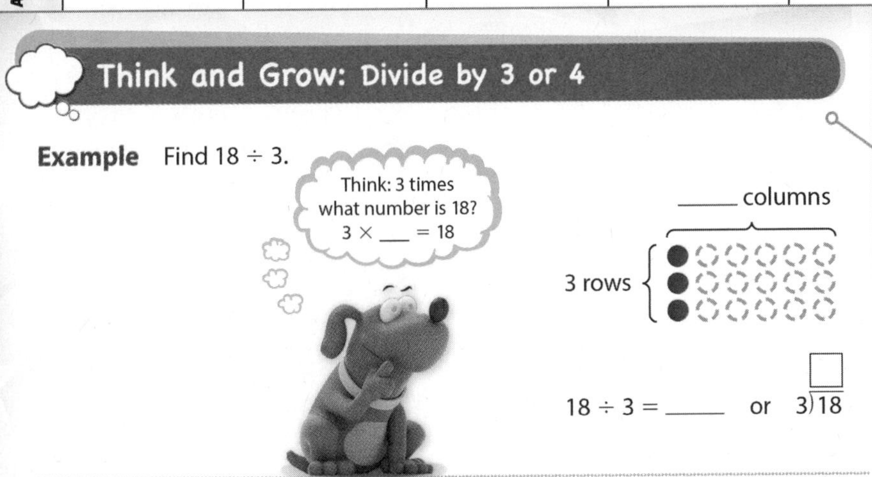

Throughout each course, lessons build on prior learning as new concepts are introduced. Here you are reminded of a multiplication fact, that you already know, to help solve the division problem.

Rigor in Math: A Balanced Approach

Instructional Design

The authors wrote each chapter and every lesson to provide a meaningful balance of rigorous instruction.

RIGOR

A rigorous program provides a balance of three important building blocks.

- **Conceptual Understanding**
  Discovering why
- **Procedural Fluency**
  Learning how
- **Application**
  Knowing when to apply

Conceptual Understanding
You have the opportunity to develop foundational concepts central to the *Learning Target* in each *Explore and Grow* by experimenting with new concepts, talking with peers, and asking questions.

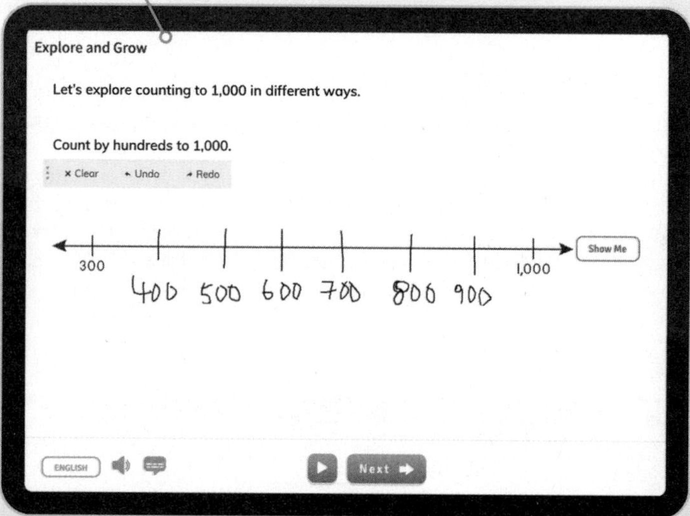

Conceptual Thinking
Conceptual questions ask you to think deeply.

14. MP **Number Sense** A sum has 5 addends. Each addend is a unit fraction. The sum is 1. What are the addends?

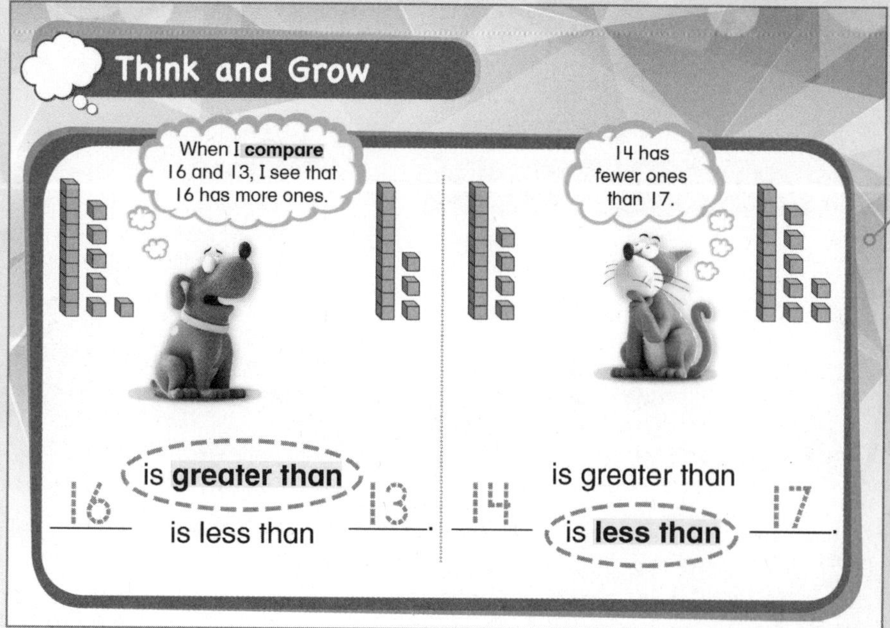

Procedural Fluency
Solidify learning with clear, stepped-out teaching in *Key Ideas* and *Think and Grow* examples.

Then shift conceptual understanding into procedural fluency with *Show and Grow*, *Apply and Grow*, *Homework & Practice*, and *Review & Refresh*.

Connecting to Real Life

Begin every chapter thinking about the world around you. Then apply what you learn in the chapter with a related *Performance Task*.

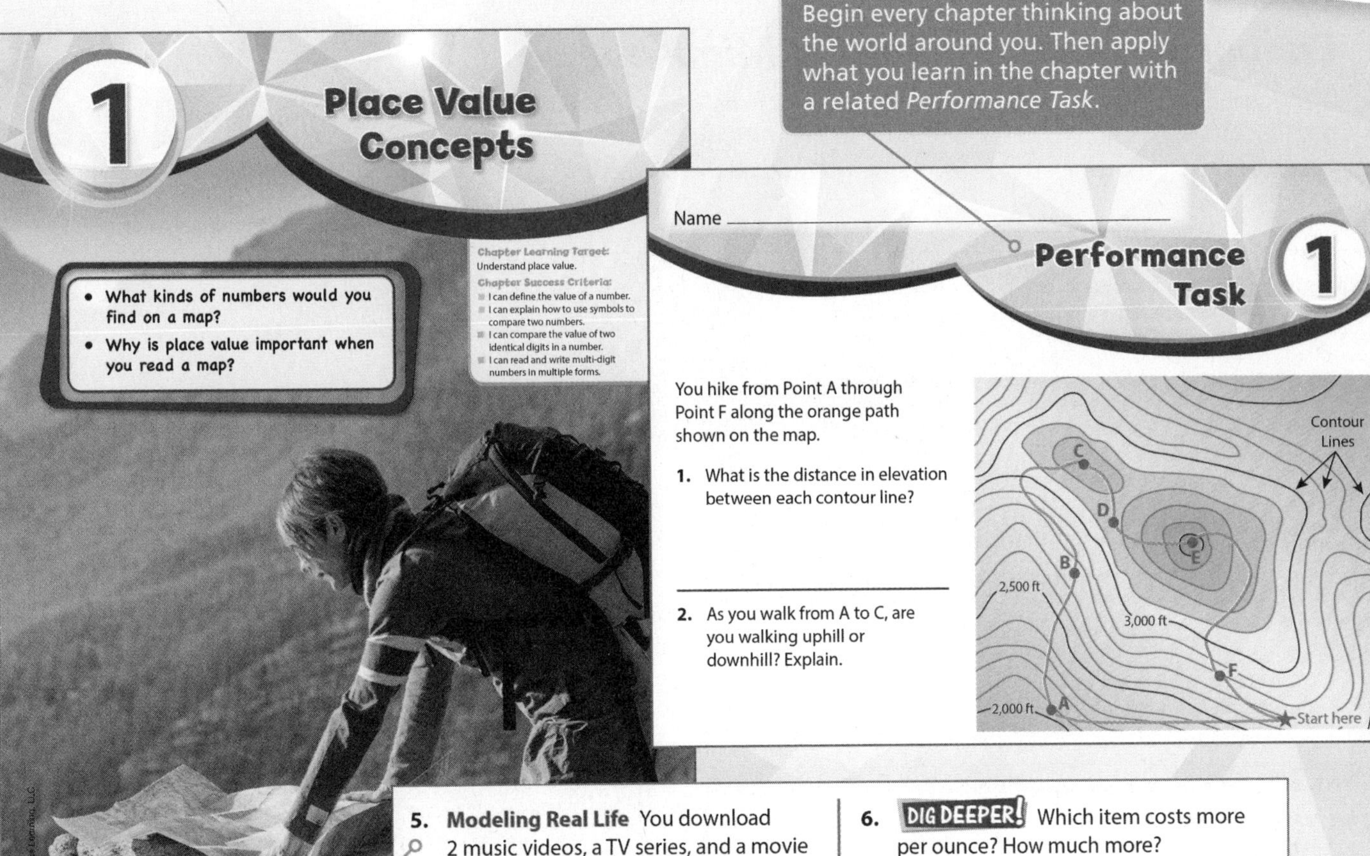

5. Modeling Real Life You download 2 music videos, a TV series, and a movie for $42.95 total. The TV series costs 2 times as much as the movie. How much does each music video cost?

Lost Treasure
Order Confirmation
Total $12.99
WATCH NOW

6. DIG DEEPER! Which item costs more per ounce? How much more?

Glue 1 gal — $23.04
Paste 2 cups — $4.00

Daily Application Practice

Modeling Real Life, *Dig Deeper*, and other non-routine problems help you apply surface-level skills to gain a deeper understanding. These problems lead to independent problem-solving.

THE PROBLEM-SOLVING PLAN

1. **Understand the Problem**
   Think about what the problem is asking, what information you know, and how you might begin to solve.
2. **Make a Plan**
   Plan your solution pathway before jumping in to solve. Identify any relationships and decide on a problem-solving strategy.
3. **Solve and Check**
   As you solve the problem, be sure to evaluate your progress and check your answers. Throughout the problem-solving process, you must continually ask, "Does this make sense?" and be willing to change course if necessary.

Problem-Solving Plan

Walk through the Problem-Solving Plan, featured in many *Think and Grow* examples, to help you make sense of problems with confidence.

Embedded Mathematical Practices

Encouraging Mathematical Mindsets

Developing proficiency in the **Mathematical Practices** is about becoming a mathematical thinker. Learn to ask why, and to reason and communicate with others as you learn. Use this guide to develop proficiency with the mathematical practices.

Example A pet store receives a shipment of 8 boxes of dog treats. Each box is 2 feet high and has 18 bags of dog treats. How many ounces of dog treats does the pet store receive in the shipment?

Understand the Problem

What do you know?
- The store receives 8 boxes.
- Each box is 2 feet high.
- Each box has 18 bags of dog treats.
- Each bag weighs 32 ounces.

What do you need to find?
- You need to find how many ounces of dog treats the pet store receives in the shipment.

Make a Plan

How will you solve?
- Multiply 32 by 18 to find how many ounces of dog treats are in each box.
- Then multiply the product by 8 to find how many ounces of dog treats the pet store receives in the shipment.
- The height of each box is unnecessary information.

Solve

Step 1: How many ounces of dog treats are in each box?

$32 \times 18 = b$

b is the unknown product.

$$\begin{array}{r} \square \\ 3\ 2 \\ \times\ 1\ 8 \\ \hline \end{array}$$

$b =$ _____

Step 2: Use *b* to find how many ounces of dog treats the pet store receives.

$b \times 8 = p$

p is the unknown product.

$$\begin{array}{r} \square \\ \times\quad 8 \\ \hline \end{array}$$

$p =$ _____

1

One way to **Make Sense of Problems and Persevere in Solving Them** is to use the Problem-Solving Plan. Take time to analyze the given information and what the problem is asking to help you plan a solution pathway.

Look for labels such as:
- Find Entry Points
- Analyze a Problem
- Interpret a Solution
- Make a Plan
- Use a Similar Problem
- Check Your Work

2

Reason Abstractly when you explore an example using numbers and models to represent the problem. Other times, **Reason Quantitatively** when you see relationships in numbers or models and draw conclusions about the problem.

Look for labels such as:
- Reasoning
- Number Sense
- Use Equations
- Use Expressions

Example You pick $2\frac{3}{4}$ pounds of cherries. Your friend picks $1\frac{2}{4}$ pounds of cherries. How many pounds of cherries do you and your friend pick in all?

MP **Reasoning**
How do you know your answer is greater than 3 pounds without solving?

3

When you **Construct Viable Arguments and Critique the Reasoning of Others**, you make and justify conclusions and decide whether others' arguments are correct or flawed.

Look for labels such as:

- Construct an Argument
- You Be the Teacher
- Logic
- Make a Conjecture
- Justify a Result
- Compare Arguments

Find an equivalent fraction.

14. $\frac{3}{12}$

17. **Logic** Is ★ greater than or less than ▼? Explain.

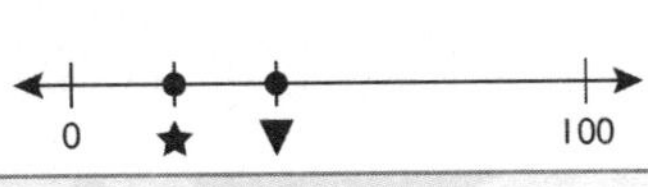

4

To **Model with Mathematics**, apply the math you learned to a real-life problem and interpret mathematical results in the context of the situation.

Look for labels such as:

- Modeling Real Life
- Graph Data
- Analyze a Relationship
- Does It Make Sense?

Modeling Real Life Use the amusement park map to answer the question.

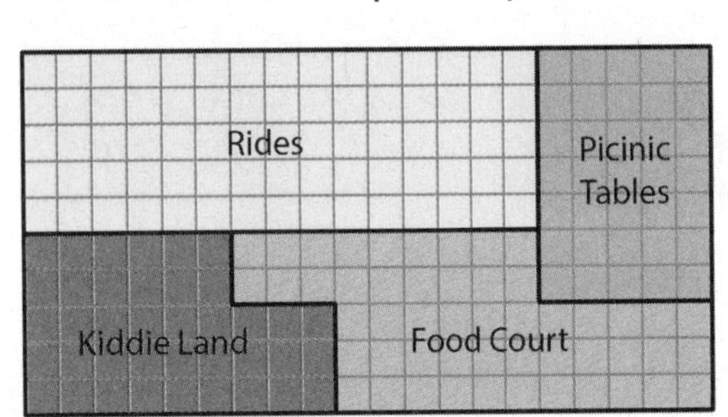

9. What is the area of the food court section?

10. DIG DEEPER! Which area is greater, the kiddie land section or the picnic tables section? Explain.

BUILDING TO FULL UNDERSTANDING

Throughout each course, you have opportunities to demonstrate specific aspects of the mathematical practices. Labels throughout the book indicate gateways to those aspects. Collectively, these opportunities will lead to a full understanding of each mathematical practice. Developing these mindsets and habits will give meaning to the mathematics you learn.

Embedded Mathematical Practices (continued)

5

To **Use Appropriate Tools Strategically**, you need to know what tools are available and think about how each tool might help you solve a mathematical problem. When you choose a tool to use, remember that it may have limitations.

Look for labels such as:
- Choose Tools
- Use Math Tools
- Use Technology

Explore and Grow

Work with a partner. Use an appropriate tool to mark 3 lengths on the floor or in a hallway that are 1 yard, 2 yards, and 3 yards long. Then measure the lengths in feet and in inches.

Think: How do the lengths, in inches, compare to the lengths in feet? How does each length compare to 1 yard?

1 foot is _____ times as long as 1 inch.

1 yard is _____ times as long as 1 foot.

1 yard is _____ times as long as 1 inch.

MP Choose Tools How did you decide which tool to use to draw the 2-yard and 3-yard lengths?

10. MP Choose Tools Choose the best tool to measure each item.

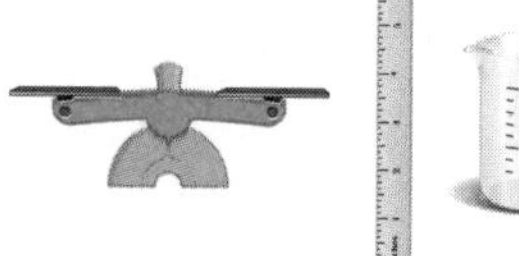

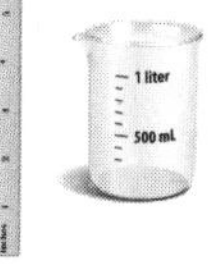

A B C D

The liquid volume of a bowl: _____

The length of a spoon: _____

The mass of an orange: _____

The number of minutes you jog: _____

6

When you **Attend to Precision**, you are developing a habit of being careful in how you talk about concepts, label work, and write answers.

Look for labels such as:
- Precision
- Communicate Clearly
- Maintain Accuracy

Another Way: Use the *make a ten* strategy. Start at 245. Count on to the nearest ten. Then count on by tens and by ones.

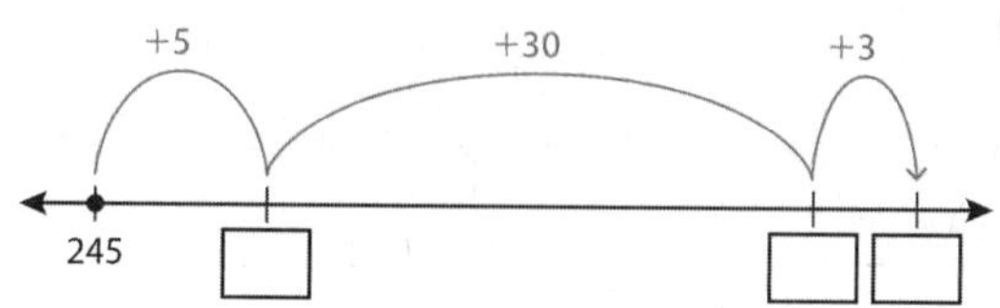

245 + 38 = _____

MP Maintain Accuracy After you add 3, how do you keep track of how much more you need to add?

13. MP Precision How many decimal places are in the unknown factor? Explain.

_____ × 2.8 = 4.48

8. **MP Structure** Write an equation represented by the quick sketch.

Ones	Tenths	Hundredths

Example

Thousands Period			Ones Period		
Hundreds	Tens	Ones	Hundreds	Tens	Ones
2	7	5,	4	4	9

- The number, in standard form, is ________.
- The value of the digit 7 is 7 ten thousands, or ________.
- The value of the digit 4 in the hundreds place is ________.
- The value of the digit 4 in the tens place is ________.
- The value of the digit 4 in the hundreds place is ________ times the value of the digit 4 in the tens place.

MP Patterns What pattern do you notice in the two periods?

7

Look For and Make Use of Structure by looking closely to see structure within a mathematical statement, or stepping back for an overview to see how individual parts make one single object.

Look for labels such as:
- Structure
- Patterns

MP Repeated Reasoning Explain to your partner how you can use expanded form to find 364×8.

Example Create a shape pattern by repeating the rule "triangle, hexagon, square, rhombus." What is the 42nd shape in the pattern?

Create the pattern.

$42 \div 4$ is 10 R2, so when the pattern repeats 10 times,

the 40th shape is a ________. So, the 41st shape is a ________ and the 42nd shape is a ________.

MP Find a Rule Why do you divide by 4?

Example Describe the dot ... re

Figure 1 Figure 2 Figure 3

4 dots, so it has $1 \times$ ____ = ____ dots.

8

When you **Look For and Express Regularity in Repeated Reasoning**, you can notice patterns and make generalizations. Remember to keep in mind the goal of a problem, which will help you evaluate reasonableness of answers along the way.

Look for labels such as:
- Repeated Reasoning
- Find a Rule

Visible Learning Through Learning Targets,

Making Learning Visible

Knowing the learning intention of a chapter or lesson helps you focus on the purpose of an activity, rather than simply completing it in isolation. This program supports visible learning through the consistent use of Learning Targets and Success Criteria to help you become successful.

Every chapter and lesson shows a **Learning Target** and related **Success Criteria**. These are purposefully integrated into each carefully written lesson.

Name ______________________

Measure Elapsed Time within the Hour 12.2

Learning Target: Measure elapsed time, in minutes, within the same hour.

Success Criteria:

- I can identify start and end times.
- I can find the amount of time that passes between two times.
- I can explain how to find elapsed time within the same hour.

Chapter Learning Target:
Understand data.

Chapter Success Criteria:

- Identify a tool to collect data.
- Create a tally chart to make a graph.
- Represent data in different ways.
- Interpret data in different ways.

There are four **Success Criteria** in each chapter.

- indicates surface level
- indicates deeper level which leads to the transfer of learning

Access the **Learning Target** and **Success Criteria** on every page of the Dynamic Student Edition.

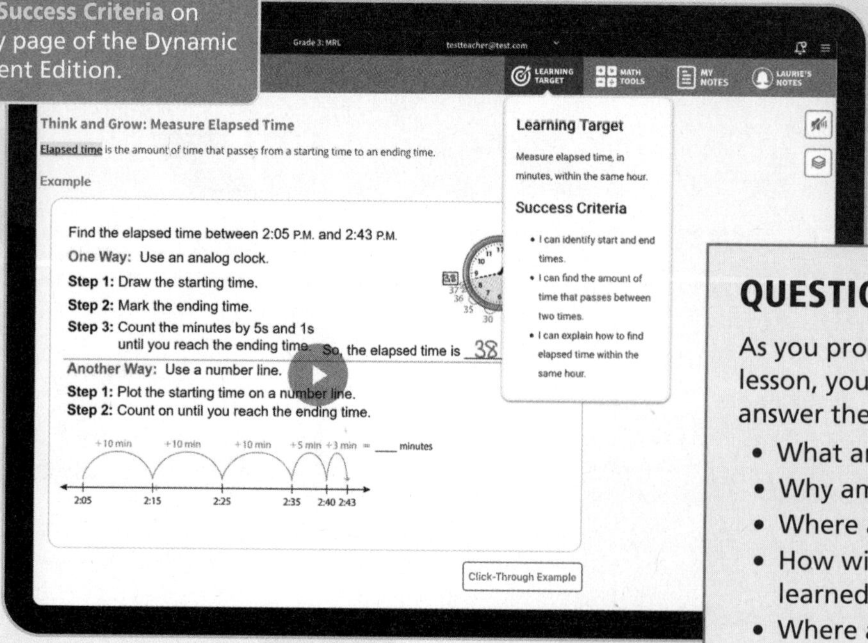

Grade 3: MRL testteacher@test.com

LEARNING TARGET | MATH TOOLS | MY NOTES | LAURIE'S NOTES

Think and Grow: Measure Elapsed Time

Elapsed time is the amount of time that passes from a starting time to an ending time.

Example

Find the elapsed time between 2:05 P.M. and 2:43 P.M.

One Way: Use an analog clock.

Step 1: Draw the starting time.

Step 2: Mark the ending time.

Step 3: Count the minutes by 5s and 1s until you reach the ending time. So, the elapsed time is 38

Another Way: Use a number line.

Step 1: Plot the starting time on a number line.

Step 2: Count on until you reach the ending time.

+10 min +10 min +10 min +5 min +3 min = ___ minutes

2:05 2:15 2:25 2:35 2:40 2:43

Click-Through Example

Learning Target

Measure elapsed time, in minutes, within the same hour.

Success Criteria

- I can identify start and end times.
- I can find the amount of time that passes between two times.
- I can explain how to find elapsed time within the same hour.

QUESTIONS FOR LEARNING

As you progress through a lesson, you should be able to answer the following questions.

- What am I learning?
- Why am I learning this?
- Where am I in my learning?
- How will I know when I have learned it?
- Where am I going next?

Success Criteria, and Self-Assessment

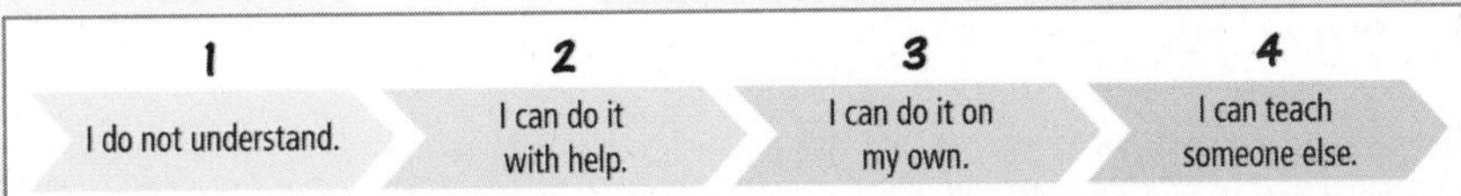

Use a 4-point scale to rate your understanding of each success criterion. Keep track of your learning on paper or online.

3.8 Multiply Three Factors	
Learning Target: Use the Associative property of Multiplication.	1 2 3 4
I can explain the Associative Property of Multiplication.	1 2 3 4
I can change the grouping of factors.	1 2 3 4
I can multiply three factors to find a product.	1 2 3 4

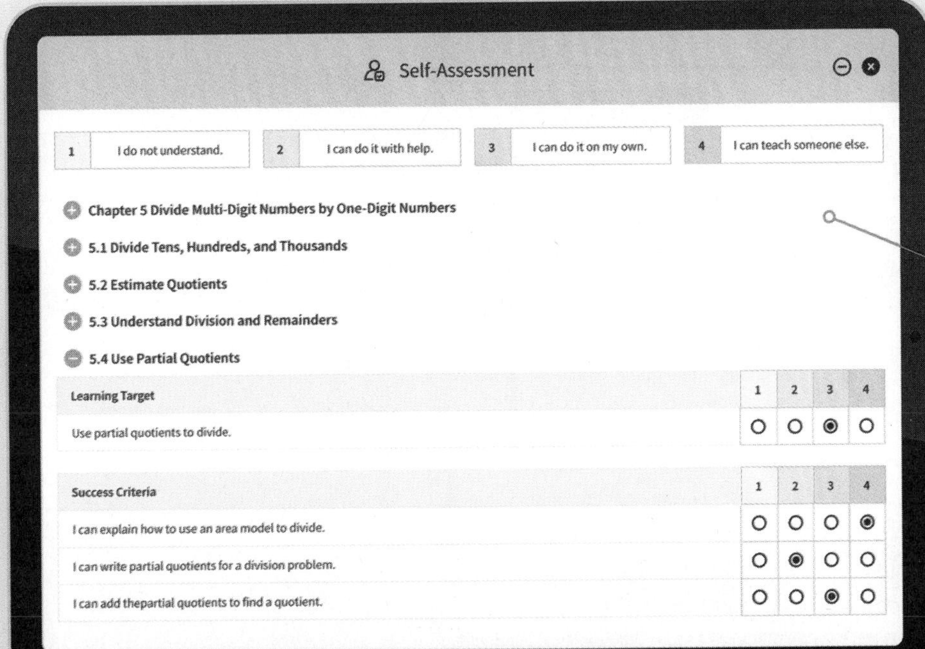

Self-Assessments are included throughout every lesson, and in the **Chapter Review**, to help you take ownership of your learning and think about where to go next.

Ensuring Positive Outcomes

John Hattie's *Visible Learning* research consistently shows that using Learning Targets and Success Criteria can result in two years' growth in one year, ensuring positive outcomes for your learning and achievement.

Sophie Murphy, M.Ed., wrote the chapter-level Learning Targets and Success Criteria for this program. Sophie is currently completing her Ph.D. at the University of Melbourne in Australia with Professor John Hattie as her leading supervisor. Sophie completed her Master's thesis with Professor John Hattie in 2015. Sophie has over 20 years of experience as a teacher and school leader in private and public school settings in Australia.

Strategic Support for Online Learning

Get the Support You Need, When You Need It

There will be times throughout this course when you may need help. Whether you missed a lesson, did not understand the content, or just want to review, take advantage of the resources provided in the *Dynamic Student Edition*.

Use the **Self-Assessment** tool to keep track of your understanding of the lesson's Learning Target and Success Criteria.

Take notes throughout the lesson using the **My Notes** function. These notes will be organized by chapter and lesson.

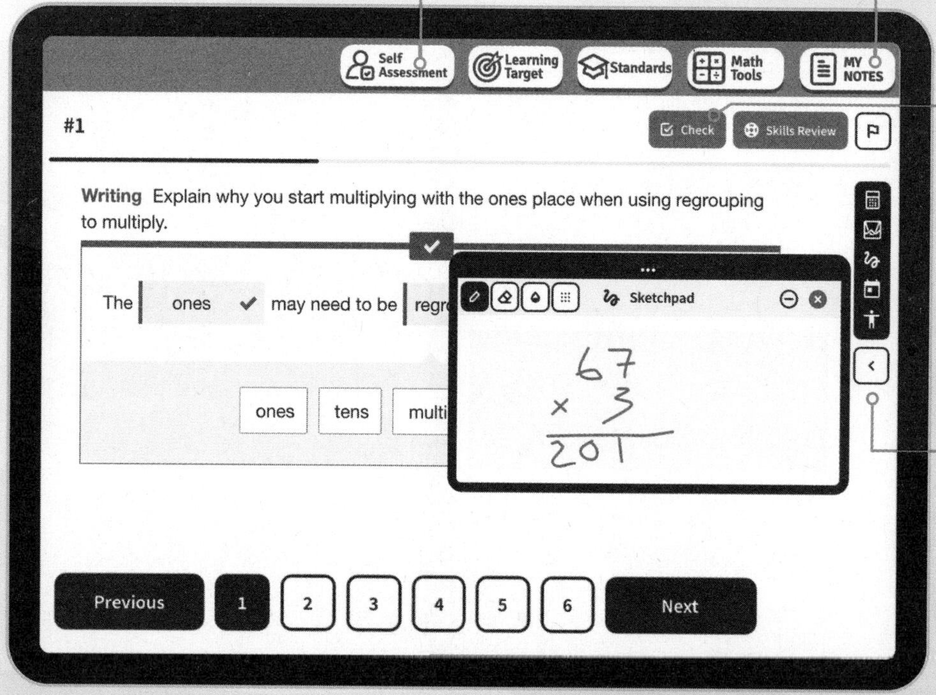

Check your answers to selected exercises as you work through the lesson. Use the **Help** option to view the Digital Example and Tutorial Extra Example videos.

Use the available **tools**, such as the calculator or sketchpad, to help clearly show your work and demonstrate your math knowledge. Tools are easy to use and were created with accessibility and functionality in mind.

USE THESE QR CODES TO EXPLORE ADDITIONAL RESOURCES

Multi-Language Glossary
View definitions and examples of vocabulary words

Skills Trainer
Practice previously learned skills

Interactive Tools
Visualize mathematical concepts

Skills Review Handbook
A collection of review topics

Learning with Newton and Descartes

Who are Newton and Descartes?

Newton and Descartes are helpful math assistants who appear throughout your math book! They encourage you to think deeply about concepts and develop strong mathematical mindsets with Mathematical Practice questions.

MP Check Your Work
How can you use the division facts to check that the products are correct?

MP Precision
Which unit of measure did you use in your answer? Why?

Newton & Descartes's Math Musicals

Math Musicals offer an engaging connection between math, literature, and music! Newton and Descartes team up in these educational stories and songs to bring mathematics to life!

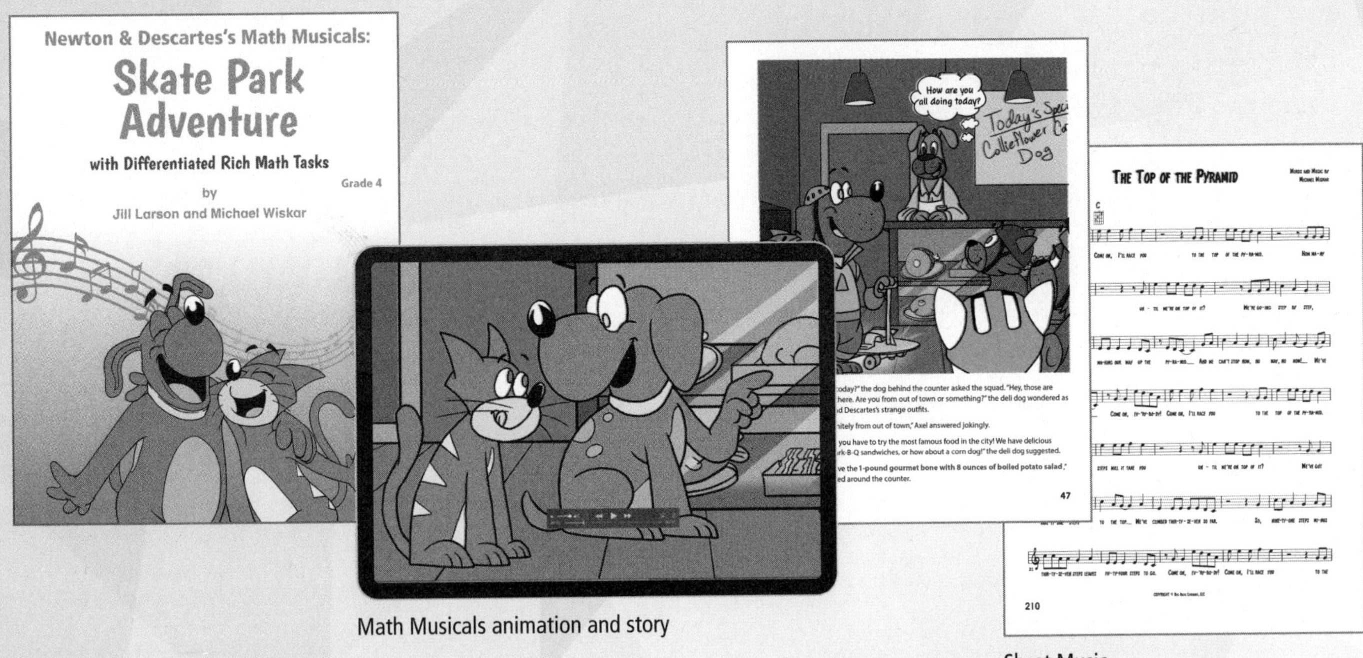

Math Musicals animation and story

Sheet Music

Understand Multiplication and Division

Multiplication Facts and Strategies

- Major Topic
- Supporting Topic
- Additional Topic

More Multiplication Facts and Strategies

Division Facts and Strategies

Patterns and Fluency

6 Relate Area to Multiplication

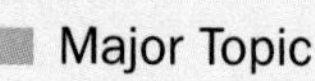

■ Major Topic
■ Supporting Topic
■ Additional Topic

7 Round and Estimate Numbers

8 Add and Subtract Multi-Digit Numbers

Multiples and Problem Solving

10

Understand Fractions

■ Major Topic
■ Supporting Topic
■ Additional Topic

Understand Fraction Equivalence and Comparison

Understand Time, Liquid Volume, and Mass

Let's learn how to understand fractions!

Classify Two-Dimensional Shapes

Represent and Interpret Data

- Major Topic
- Supporting Topic
- Additional Topic

Find Perimeter and Area

Explore and Grow

You have a map with the three side lengths shown. The perimeter of the map is 20 feet. Describe how you can find the fourth side length of your map without measuring.

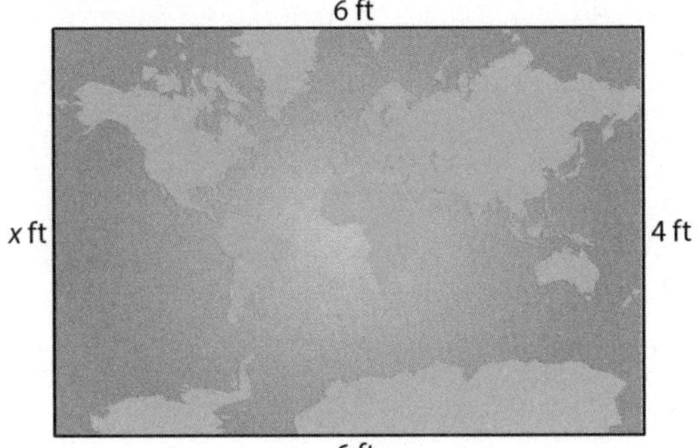

9 Multiples and Problem Solving

- What kinds of books do you like to read?
- You read 10 pages of a book each day. How can place value help you find the total number of pages you read?

Chapter Learning Target:
Understand multiples.

Chapter Success Criteria:
- I can skip count.
- I can describe the pattern when multiplying.
- I can make a plan to solve a problem.
- I can solve a problem.

Name ______________________

9 Vocabulary

Review Words

dividend
divisor
fact family
quotient

Organize It

Use a review word to complete the graphic organizer.

[ ]

A group of related facts that uses the same numbers

$3 \times 2 = 6$ $6 \div 3 = 2$
$2 \times 3 = 6$ $6 \div 2 = 3$

Define It

Identify the review word. Find the word in the word search.

1. The number of objects or the amount you want to divide
2. The number by which you divide
3. The answer when you divide one number by another number

V	R	E	S	K	B	D	Y
A	Z	D	Q	U	W	I	L
T	R	I	P	F	S	V	G
D	J	V	M	V	E	I	D
F	C	I	A	X	O	D	U
N	U	S	R	D	G	E	N
Q	U	O	T	I	E	N	T
E	S	R	O	V	T	D	Q

Name ______________________________

Use Number Lines to Multiply by Multiples of 10

9.1

Learning Target: Use number lines to multiply by multiples of 10.

Success Criteria:

- I can use a number line to skip count by a multiple of 10.
- I can find the product of a one-digit number and a multiple of 10.

Show 5 jumps of 3. Write a multiplication equation shown by the number line.

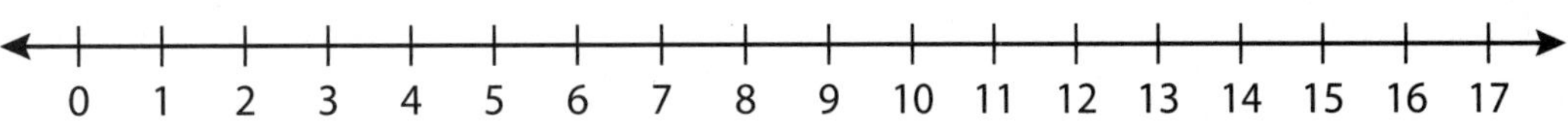

_____ × _____ = _____

Show 5 jumps of 30. Write a multiplication equation shown by the number line.

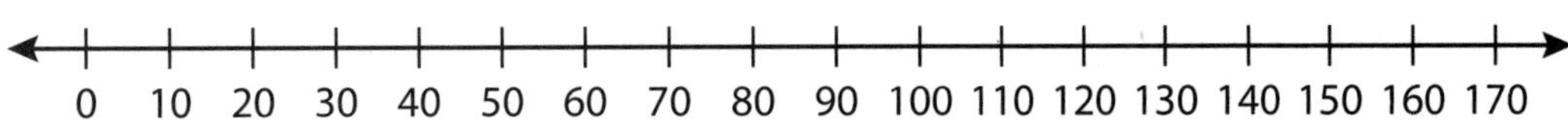

_____ × _____ = _____

Structure Compare the models. How are they the same? How are they different?

Think and Grow: Number Lines and Multiples of 10

Example Find 3×50.

3×50 means 3 groups of 50.

Number of jumps: _____ Size of each jump: _____

Start at 0. Skip count by 50 three times.

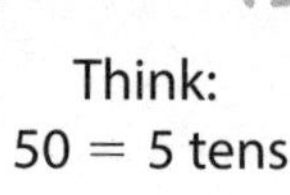

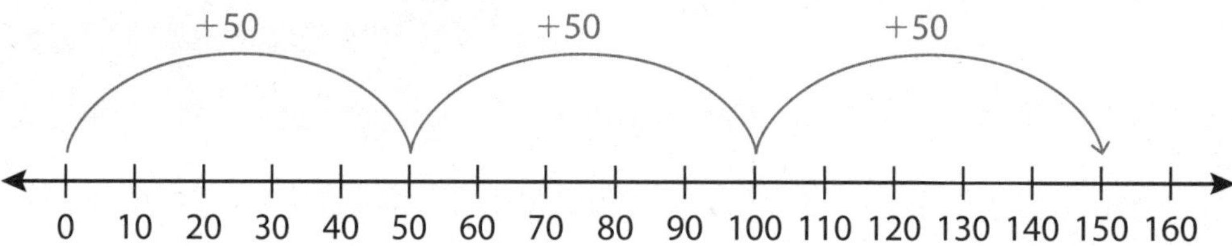

$3 \times 50 =$ _____

MP Use Equations How can you use an addition equation to solve?

Show and Grow *I can do it!*

1. Find 8×20.

Number of jumps: _____ Size of each jump: _____

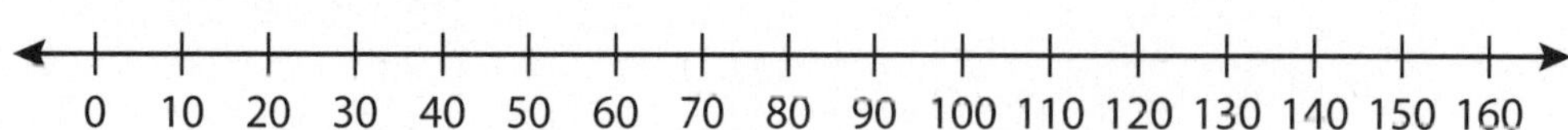

$8 \times 20 =$ _____

---

2. Find 4×30.

Number of jumps: _____ Size of each jump: _____

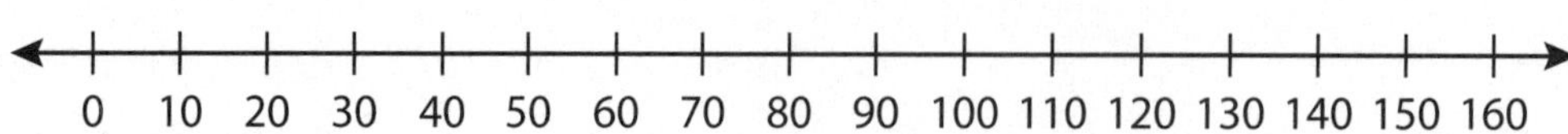

$4 \times 30 =$ _____

Name ______________________________

Apply and Grow: Practice

3. Find 2×60.

Number of jumps: _____ Size of each jump: _____

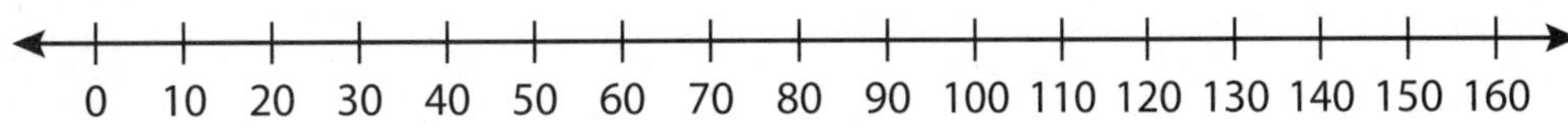

$2 \times 60 =$ _____

4. Find 5×50.

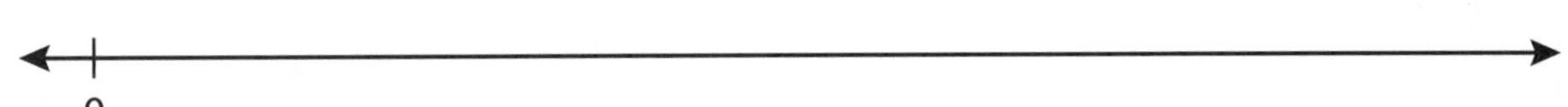

$5 \times 50 =$ _____

5. Find 3×70.

$3 \times 70 =$ _____

6. Find 30×6.

$30 \times 6 =$ _____

7. MP **Structure** Show 2×40 on one number line and 4×20 on the other. What is the same about the number lines? What is different?

Think and Grow: Modeling Real Life

A section of an airplane has 20 rows of seats. Each row has 7 seats. Can the section seat more than 150 people? Explain.

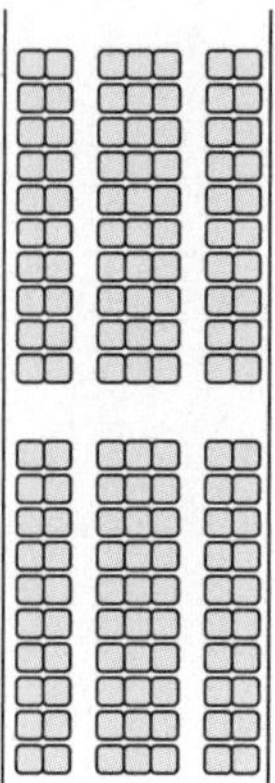

Model:

The section ____________ seat more than 150 people.

Explain:

Show and Grow I can think deeper!

8. There are 9 rows of seats in an auditorium. Each row has 30 seats. Can the auditorium seat more than 250 people? Explain.

9. A mechanic installs new tires on 20 cars and 20 pickup trucks. How many new tires does the mechanic install in all?

10. DIG DEEPER! Newton saves $5 each week for 20 weeks. How much more money does he need to buy a new bike that costs $130? If he continues to save the same amount each week, how many more weeks does he need to save to buy the bike? Explain.

Name ______________________________

Learning Target: Use number lines to multiply by multiples of 10.

Example Find 4 × 50.

Number of jumps: 4 Size of each jump: 50

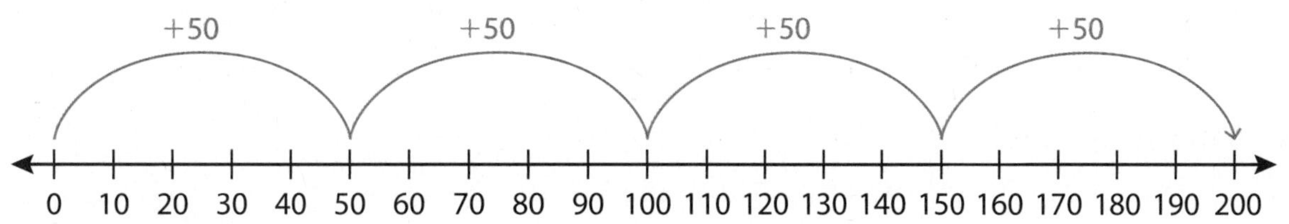

4 × 50 = 200

1. Find 3 × 30.

Number of jumps: _____ Size of each jump: _____

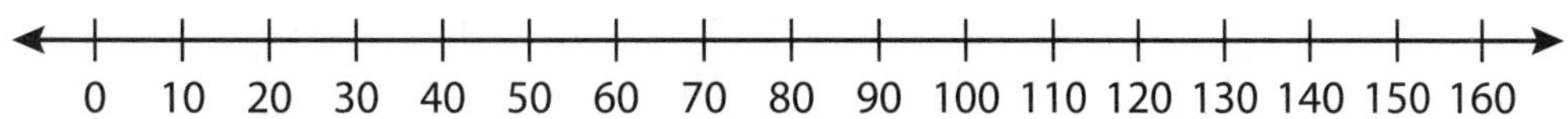

3 × 30 = _____

2. Find 7 × 60.

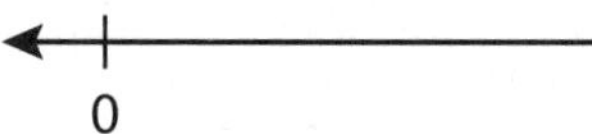

7 × 60 = _____

3. Find 4 × 40.

4 × 40 = _____

4. MP **Structure** Complete the number line. Then write the multiplication equation shown on the number line.

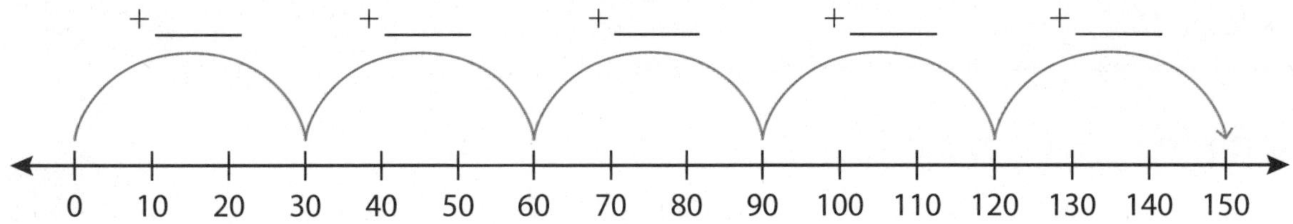

_____ × _____ = _____

5. MP **Modeling Real Life** Ten adults and 20 children fill their bike tires at a public pump. How many tires are filled in all?

6. **DIG DEEPER!** An obstacle course has two climbing walls. The area of the first climbing wall is 400 square feet. Which wall has a greater area?

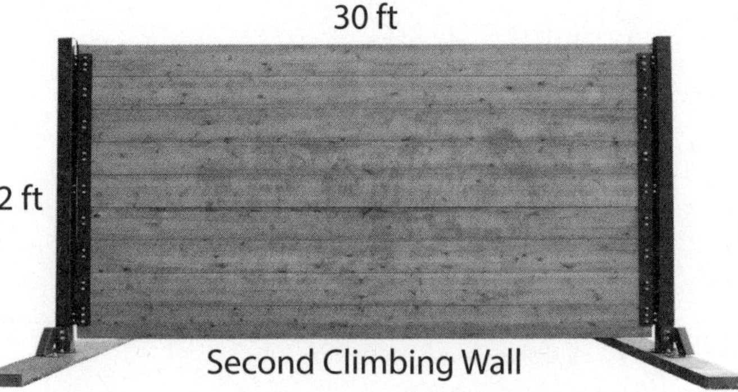

Second Climbing Wall

MP **Construct an Argument** Your friend says the wall with the greater area must be taller. Do you agree? Explain your reasoning.

Review & Refresh

7. There are 35 counters. The counters are in 7 equal rows. How many counters are in each row?

7 rows of _____

$35 \div 7 =$ _____

8. You have 32 counters. You arrange them with 8 counters in each row. How many rows of counters do you make?

_____ rows of 8

$32 \div 8 =$ _____

Name ____________________

Use Place Value to Multiply by Multiples of 10 9.2

Learning Target: Use place value to multiply by multiples of 10.

Success Criteria:
- I can use a model to multiply by a multiple of 10.
- I can find the product of a one-digit number and a multiple of 10.
- I can describe a pattern when multiplying by multiples of 10.

Use models to find each product. Draw your models.

$4 \times 6 =$ _____

$4 \times 60 =$ _____

Structure Compare the models. How are they the same? How are they different?

Think and Grow: Place Value and Multiples of 10

Example Find 4 × 70.

Step 1: Make a quick sketch to model the product. Think: 4 groups of 70, or 7 tens.

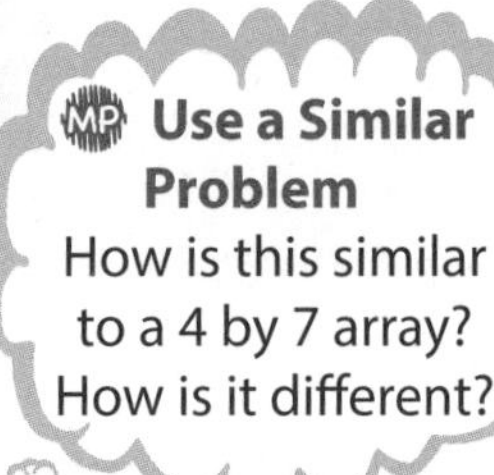

4 × 70 = 4 × _____ tens

4 × 70 = _____ tens

Step 2: Regroup _____ tens.

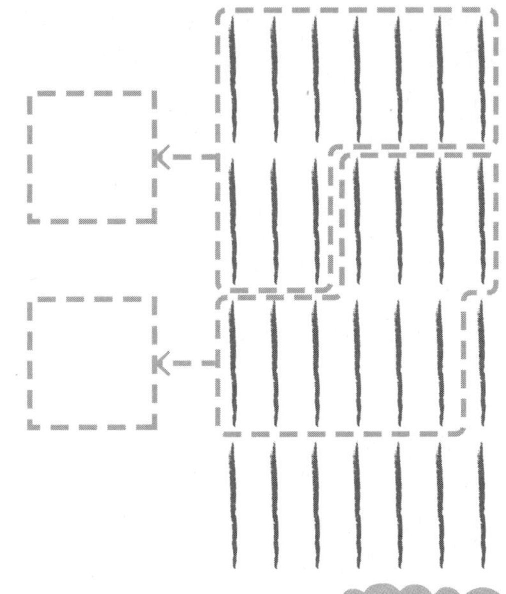

There are _____ hundreds and _____ tens.

So, 4 × 70 = _____.

Show and Grow *I can do it!*

Make a quick sketch to find the product.

1. 3 × 80 = _____

2. 5 × 40 = _____

Name ____

Apply and Grow: Practice

Use place value to find the product.

3. $3 \times 90 = 3 \times$ _____ tens

$3 \times 90 =$ _____ tens

$3 \times 90 =$ _____

4. $6 \times 60 = 6 \times$ _____ tens

$6 \times 60 =$ _____ tens

$6 \times 60 =$ _____

5. $2 \times 70 = 2 \times$ _____ tens

$2 \times 70 =$ _____ tens

$2 \times 70 =$ _____

6. $9 \times 20 = 9 \times$ _____ tens

$9 \times 20 =$ _____ tens

$9 \times 20 =$ _____

Find the product.

7. $3 \times 30 =$ _____

8. $6 \times 80 =$ _____

9. $4 \times 40 =$ _____

10. $7 \times 50 =$ _____

11. $8 \times 70 =$ _____

12. $5 \times 90 =$ _____

13. MP **Communicate Clearly** Explain why the product of 6 and 30 has 1 zero and the product of 4 and 50 has 2 zeros.

14. MP **YOU BE THE TEACHER** Is Descartes correct? Explain.

The product of 3 and 70 is equal to the product of 3 and 7 with a 0 written after it.

Think and Grow: Modeling Real Life

Newton saves $30 each month for 6 months. Does he have enough money to buy the drone? Explain.

Newton ___________ have enough money to buy the drone.

Explain:

Show and Grow I can think deeper!

15. Descartes saves $20 each month for 8 months. Does he have enough money to buy the remote control jeep? Explain.

16. You practice playing the guitar for 40 minutes every day. How many minutes do you practice in one week?

17. A box of snacks has 25 bags of pretzels and 25 bags of peanuts. How many bags are in 9 boxes?

Name ______________________

Homework & Practice 9.2

Learning Target: Use place value to multiply by multiples of 10.

Example Find 2 × 80.

Step 1: Make a quick sketch to model the product. Think: 2 groups of 80, or 8 tens.

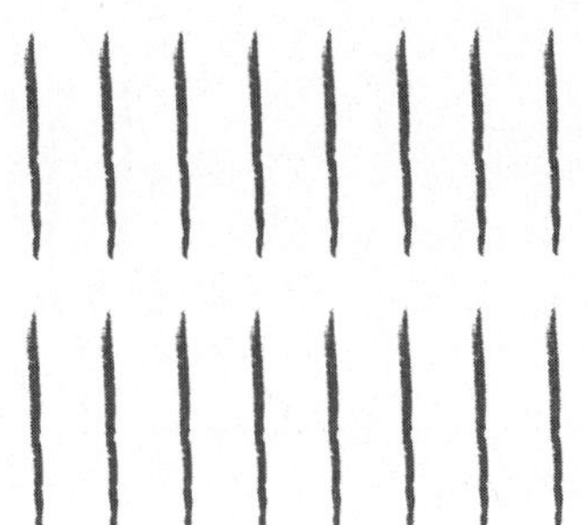

2 × 80 = 2 × __8__ tens

2 × 80 = __16__ tens

Step 2: Regroup __10__ tens.

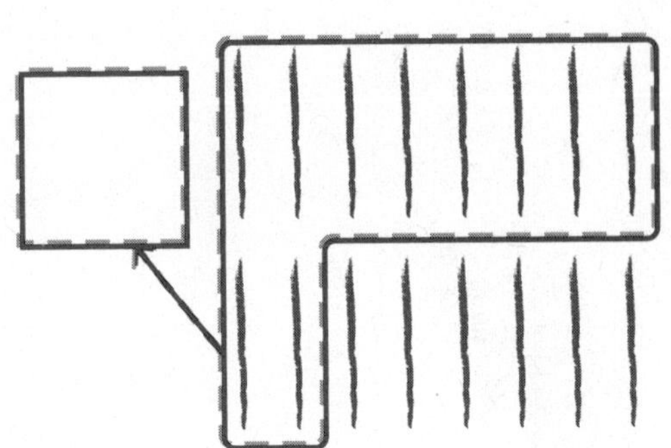

There is __1__ hundred and __6__ tens.

So, 2 × 80 = __160__.

Make a quick sketch to find the product.

1. 5 × 70 = ____

2. 3 × 60 = ____

Use place value to find the product.

3. 8 × 50 = 8 × ____ tens

8 × 50 = ____ tens

8 × 50 = ____

4. 7 × 60 = 7 × ____ tens

7 × 60 = ____ tens

7 × 60 = ____

Find the product.

5. $6 \times 90 =$ ____

6. $8 \times 30 =$ ____

7. $5 \times 40 =$ ____

8. MP YOU BE THE TEACHER Is Newton correct? Explain.

9. MP **Structure** Write an equation for the quick sketch.

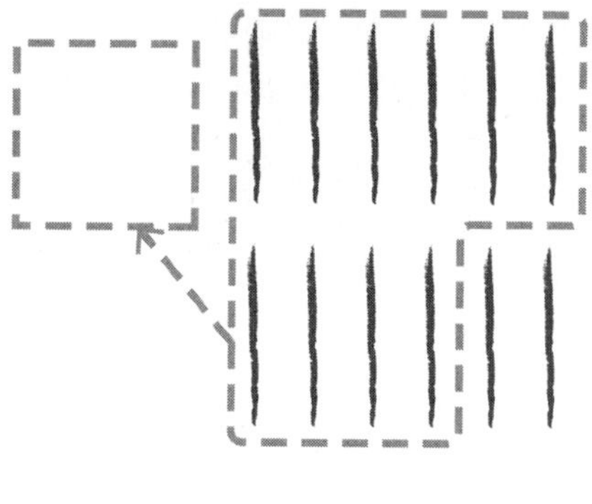

____ $\times$ ____ $=$ ____

10. MP **Modeling Real Life** Descartes saves $50 each month for 5 months. Does he have enough money to buy the game system? Explain.

11. MP **Modeling Real Life** A group of staff members packs coolers for a field trip. Each cooler has 15 peanut butter sandwiches and 15 turkey sandwiches. How many sandwiches are in 7 coolers?

DIG DEEPER! A van holds 4 coolers. How many sandwiches are in 3 vans? Explain.

Review & Refresh

12. Round 282 to the nearest ten and to the nearest hundred.

Nearest ten: ____ Nearest hundred: ____

Name ____________________

Use Properties to Multiply by Multiples of 10

9.3

Learning Target: Use properties to multiply by multiples of 10.

Success Criteria:

- I can use the Associative Property of Multiplication to multiply by a multiple of 10.
- I can use the Distributive Property to multiply by a multiple of 10.
- I can use properties to find the product of a one-digit number and a multiple of 10.

Use the colored rectangles to find 5×30.

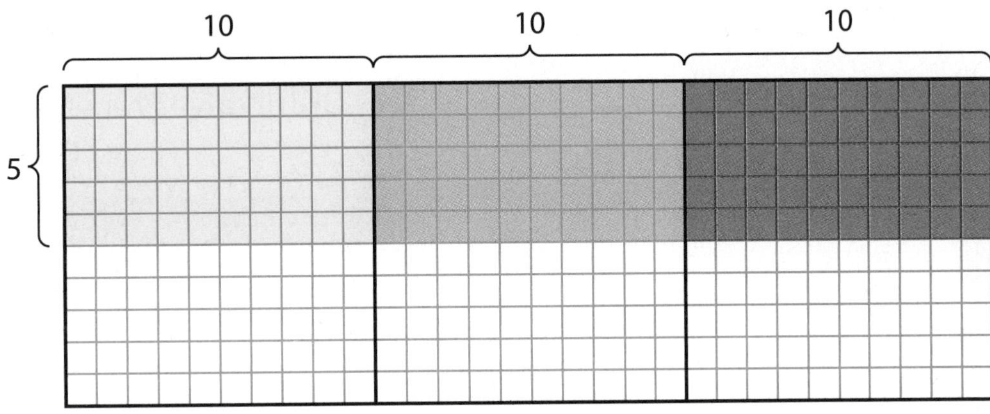

___ $\times$ ___ $=$ ___

___ $\times$ ___ $=$ ___

___ $\times$ ___ $=$ ___

___ $+$ ___ $+$ ___ $=$ ___

So, $5 \times 30 =$ ___.

Reasoning How does this model relate to the Distributive Property?

Think and Grow: Properties and Multiples of 10

Example Find 6×20.

One Way: Use the Associative Property of Multiplication.

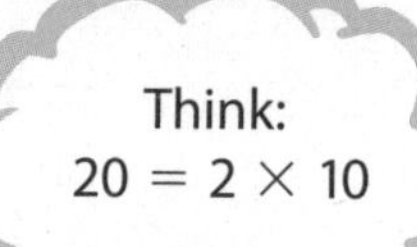

$6 \times 20 = 6 \times (\_\_\_\_ \times 10)$ Rewrite 20 as ____ × 10.

$6 \times 20 = (6 \times \_\_\_\_) \times 10$ Associative Property of Multiplication

$6 \times 20 = \_\_\_\_ \times 10$

$6 \times 20 = \_\_\_\_$

Another Way: Use the Distributive Property.

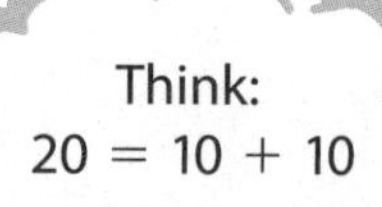

$6 \times 20 = 6 \times (10 + \_\_\_\_)$ Rewrite 20 as 10 + ____.

$6 \times 20 = (6 \times 10) + (6 \times \_\_\_\_)$ Distributive Property

$6 \times 20 = \_\_\_\_ + \_\_\_\_$

$6 \times 20 = \_\_\_\_$

Show and Grow *I can do it!*

1. Use the Associative Property of Multiplication to find 4×60.

$4 \times 60 = 4 \times (\_\_\_\_ \times 10)$

$4 \times 60 = (4 \times \_\_\_\_) \times 10$

$4 \times 60 = \_\_\_\_ \times 10$

$4 \times 60 = \_\_\_\_$

2. Use the Distributive Property to find 9×20.

$9 \times 20 = 9 \times (10 + \_\_\_\_)$

$9 \times 20 = (9 \times 10) + (9 \times \_\_\_\_)$

$9 \times 20 = \_\_\_\_ + \_\_\_\_$

$9 \times 20 = \_\_\_\_$

Name ______________________________

Apply and Grow: Practice

Use properties to find the product.

3. 7 × 30 = _____

4. 5 × 80 = _____

5. 5 × 20 = _____

6. 3 × 90 = _____

Find the missing factor.

7. 8 × _____ = 320

8. _____ × 50 = 300

9. _____ × 30 = 270

10. **Justify a Result** Use the Associative Property of Multiplication to show why 4 × 20 = 8 × 10.

11. **Repeated Reasoning** Write three expressions equal to 240.

12. **Number Sense** Which equations show the Distributive Property?

2 × 20 = (2 × 10) + (2 × 10)

4 × (3 × 10) = (4 × 3) × 10

(7 × 10) + (7 × 10) = 7 × 20

Think and Grow: Modeling Real Life

There are 8 tables in a classroom. There are 5 students at each table. Each student has 10 markers. How many markers do the students have in all?

There are _____ markers at each table.

The students have _____ markers in all.

Make a Plan
How can a drawing help you solve a problem?

Show and Grow *I can think deeper!*

13. Your teacher buys 5 boxes of pens. Each box has 6 bundles of 10 pens. How many pens does your teacher buy in all?

14. **DIG DEEPER!** Newton earns $30 each work shift. He wants to buy Descartes a cat tree. The tree costs $150. After how many work shifts can Newton buy the tree?

Name ______________________________

Homework & Practice 9.3

Learning Target: Use properties to multiply by multiples of 10.

Example Find 8×20.

One Way: Use the Associative Property of Multiplication.

$8 \times 20 = 8 \times (\underline{\ 2\ } \times 10)$ Rewrite 20 as $\underline{\ 2\ } \times 10$.

$8 \times 20 = (8 \times \underline{\ 2\ }) \times 10$ Associative Property of Multiplication

$8 \times 20 = \underline{\ 16\ } \times 10$

$8 \times 20 = \underline{\ 160\ }$

Another Way: Use the Distributive Property.

$8 \times 20 = 8 \times (10 + \underline{\ 10\ })$ Rewrite 20 as $10 + \underline{\ 10\ }$.

$8 \times 20 = (8 \times 10) + (8 \times \underline{\ 10\ })$ Distributive Property

$8 \times 20 = \underline{\ 80\ } + \underline{\ 80\ }$

$8 \times 20 = \underline{\ 160\ }$

1. Use the Associative Property of Multiplication to find 6×70.

$6 \times 70 = 6 \times (\_\_\_\_ \times 10)$

$6 \times 70 = (6 \times \_\_\_\_) \times 10$

$6 \times 70 = \_\_\_\_ \times 10$

$6 \times 70 = \_\_\_\_$

2. Use the Distributive Property to find 3×20.

$3 \times 20 = 3 \times (10 + \_\_\_\_)$

$3 \times 20 = (3 \times 10) + (3 \times \_\_\_\_)$

$3 \times 20 = \_\_\_\_ + \_\_\_\_$

$3 \times 20 = \_\_\_\_$

Use properties to find the product.

3. $9 \times 20 = \_\_\_\_$

4. $5 \times 30 = \_\_\_\_$

Find the missing factor.

5. ____ $\times$ 60 = 180

6. 6 $\times$ ____ = 240

7. ____ $\times$ 80 = 720

8. MP **YOU BE THE TEACHER** Your friend draws a model to find 4 × 20. Is your friend correct? Explain.

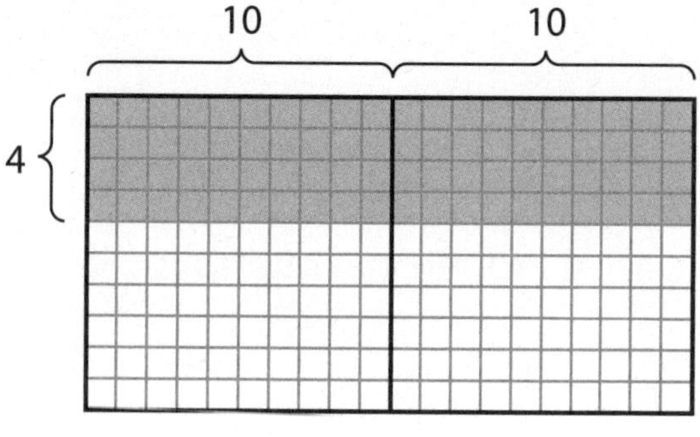

$4 \times 10 = 40$ $4 \times 10 = 40$

$40 + 40 = 80$

So, $4 \times 20 = 80$.

9. MP **Analyze a Problem** How can you tell whether 7 $\times$ 40 or 8 $\times$ 70 is greater without finding the products?

10. MP **Modeling Real Life** There are 9 teams in a math competition. Each team has 6 students. Each student answers 10 questions. How many questions are answered in all?

11. **DIG DEEPER!** A soccer team earns $40 each week washing cars. The team wants to buy an inflatable field for $240. After how many weeks can the team buy the field?

Review & Refresh

Find the quotient.

12. $3\overline{)18}$

13. $4\overline{)32}$

14. $3\overline{)27}$

15. $4\overline{)16}$

Name ______________________________

Problem Solving: Multiplication and Division 9.4

Learning Target: Use the problem-solving plan to solve two-step multiplication and division word problems.

Success Criteria:

- I can understand a problem.
- I can make a plan to solve a problem using letters to represent the unknown numbers.
- I can solve a problem and check whether my answer is reasonable.

Explore and Grow

Use any strategy to solve the problem.

Descartes uses 72 blocks to build ships. He uses 9 blocks for each ship. Each ship has 2 fabric sails. How many sails does Descartes use?

Descartes uses _____ fabric sails.

Structure What equations did you use to solve? How can you write the equations using a letter to represent the number of fabric sails?

Think and Grow: Using the Problem-Solving Plan

Example A box of 8 burritos costs $9. How much does it cost a group of friends to buy 40 burritos?

Understand the Problem

What do you know?

- A box has _____ burritos.
- The box costs _____.
- A group of friends wants to buy _____ burritos.

What do you need to find?

- You need to find how much it costs to buy __________.

Make a Plan

How will you solve?

- Divide _____ by _____ to find how many __________ the group needs to buy.
- Then multiply the quotient by _____ to find the total cost.

Solve

You can use a letter to represent an unknown number.

Step 1: How many boxes does the group need to buy?

b boxes → | 8 | |

40

b is the unknown quotient.

$b = 40 \div 8$ $b =$ ☐

Step 2: Use *b* to find the total cost.

$9	$9	$9	$9	$9

c

c is the unknown product.

$c = 5 \times 9$ $c =$ ☐

It costs $_____ for 40 burritos.

Show and Grow I can do it!

1. You make 9 shots in a basketball game. Each shot is worth 2 points. Your friend has the same number of points. All of her shots are worth 3 points. How many shots does your friend make?

Name ______________________________

Apply and Grow: Practice

Write equations to solve. Use letters to represent the unknown numbers. Check whether your answer is reasonable.

2. You read 3 chapters. Each chapter has 8 pages. Your friend reads the same number of pages. All of her chapters have 6 pages. How many chapters does your friend read?

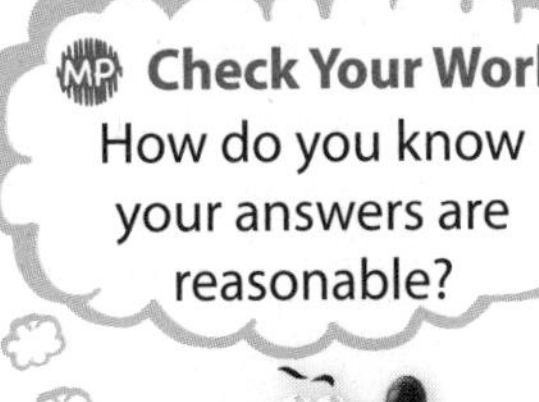

3. There are 42 players in a basketball tournament. The players are divided into teams of 7 players. The teams are divided equally among 3 basketball courts. How many teams are at each basketball court?

4. You have 2 dream catcher kits. Each kit makes 4 dream catchers. You make all of the dream catchers and sell them for $9 each. How much money do you earn?

5. A box of 4 test tubes costs $6. How much does it cost to buy 20 test tubes?

Think and Grow: Modeling Real Life

There are 4 crates of milk bottles. Each crate holds 20 bottles. You hand out an equal number of bottles to 10 tables of students. How many bottles of milk does each table of students get?

Understand the problem:

Make a plan:

Solve:

Each table of students gets _____ bottles of milk.

Show and Grow *I can think deeper!*

6. Six groups of hikers have 2 cases of water to share equally. Each case has 30 bottles of water. How many bottles of water does each group get?

7. **DIG DEEPER!** Newton and Descartes decide to buy 2 pet toys that cost $20 each. Newton saves $5 each week. Descartes saves $3 each week. If they combine their money, how long does it take them to save enough money to buy the toys?

Name ______________________________

Homework & Practice 9.4

Learning Target: Use the problem-solving plan to solve two-step multiplication and division word problems.

Example There are 3 bags of pretzels with 6 pretzels in each bag. The pretzels are shared equally by 2 students. How many pretzels does each student get?

Think: What do you know? What do you need to find? How will you solve?

Step 1: How many pretzels are there?

You can use a letter to represent an unknown number.

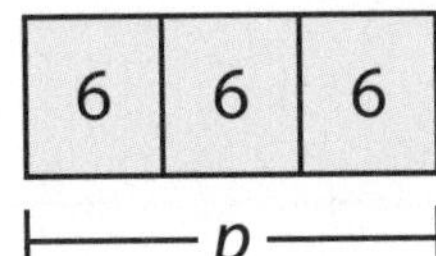

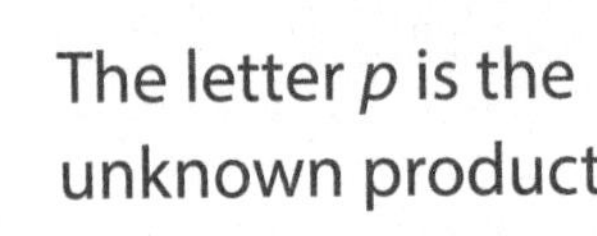

The letter p is the unknown product.

$p = 3 \times 6$ $p =$ 18

Step 2: Use p to find how many pretzels each student gets.

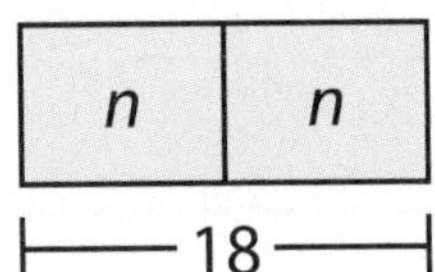

18 pretzels are divided into 2 groups.

The letter n is the unknown quotient.

$n = 18 \div 2$ $n =$ 9

Each student gets __9__ pretzels.

Write equations to solve. Use letters to represent the unknown numbers. Check whether your answer is reasonable.

1. Your friend saves \$5 each week for 8 weeks. He spends all of the money on 4 toys that each cost the same amount. How much does each toy cost?

2. There are 3 trees. Each tree has 2 birdhouses. Each birdhouse has 4 birds. How many birds are there in all?

3. There are 54 students at a field day who are divided equally into teams of 6 students. The teams are divided equally among 3 stations. How many teams are at each station?

4. **Number Sense** Newton runs an equal number of miles 2 days each week. He runs 8 miles each week. One mile is equal to 4 laps around the track. Which equation can you use to find how many laps Newton runs each day?

$r = 8 \div 4$ $r = 4 \times 4$

$r = 4 \div 4$ $r = 2 \times 4$

5. **Modeling Real Life** Ten classrooms have 3 boxes of whiteboards to share equally. Each box has 30 whiteboards. How many whiteboards does each classroom get?

6. **DIG DEEPER!** Newton and Descartes decide to buy 2 amusement park tickets that cost $30 each. Newton saves $2 each week. Descartes saves $4 each week. If they combine their money, how long does it take them to save enough money to buy the tickets?

Review & Refresh

Round to the nearest ten to estimate the difference.

7. $\begin{array}{r} 58 \\ -\ 27 \\ \hline \end{array}$ $\begin{array}{r} \square \\ -\ \square \\ \hline \square \end{array}$

8. $\begin{array}{r} 763 \\ -\ 415 \\ \hline \end{array}$ $\begin{array}{r} \square \\ -\ \square \\ \hline \square \end{array}$

9. $\begin{array}{r} 686 \\ -\ 24 \\ \hline \end{array}$ $\begin{array}{r} \square \\ -\ \square \\ \hline \square \end{array}$

Name ______________________________

Problem Solving: All Operations 9.5

Learning Target: Use the problem-solving plan to solve two-step word problems involving different operations.

Success Criteria:
- I can understand a problem.
- I can make a plan to solve a problem using letters to represent the unknown numbers.
- I can solve a problem using one equation.

Use any strategy to solve the problem.

You are making 6 fruit baskets. Each basket has 3 pieces of fruit in it to start. You buy 18 bananas and divide them equally among the baskets. How many pieces of fruit are in each fruit basket now?

There are _____ pieces of fruit in each fruit basket now.

Structure How can you solve this problem using one equation?

Think and Grow: One Equation with Two Operations

Example Newton buys 3 DVDs for \$4 each. He pays with a \$20 bill. What is his change?

You can write one equation with two operations to solve this problem. The equation is shown.

$20 - 3 \times 4 = c$ ⟵ c is the amount of change.

When solving a problem with more than one type of operation, use the rules below.

- First, multiply or divide as you read the equation from left to right.
- Then add or subtract as you read the equation from left to right.

Step 1: Multiply from left to right.

$20 - 3 \times 4 = c$

$20 - \_\_\_\_ = c$

Step 2: Subtract from left to right.

$20 - \_\_\_\_ = c$

$\_\_\_\_ = c$

His change is ____.

Show and Grow *I can do it!*

1. There are 8 tomato plants. You pick 9 tomatoes from each plant. You give away 35 of them. Use the equation $8 \times 9 - 35 = p$ to find how many tomatoes you have left.

2. A family buys 5 tickets for a musical. Each ticket costs \$9. They spend \$28 at the musical on snacks. Write and solve an equation to find how much they spend in all at the musical. Use a to represent the total amount spent.

Name

Apply and Grow: Practice

Write an equation to solve. Use a letter to represent the unknown number. Check whether your answer is reasonable.

3. Newton buys 2 movie tickets. Each ticket costs \$7. Descartes spends \$23 at the movie on snacks. How much money do they spend in all at the movie?

4. Newton has 28 cards. Descartes has 24 cards. Newton divides his cards into 4 equal stacks and gives Descartes one stack. How many cards does Descartes have now?

5. There are 12 apps divided into 3 equal rows on a smartphone. One row of apps is removed. How many apps are left?

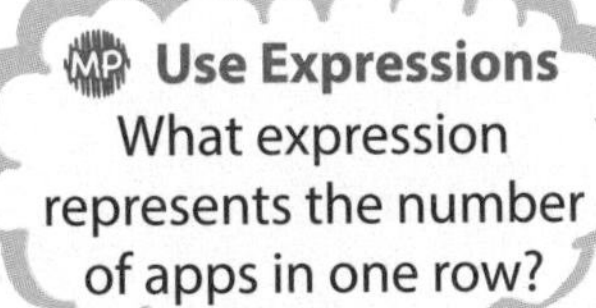

MP Use Expressions What expression represents the number of apps in one row?

6. It costs \$240 each week to rent a car. Newton has a coupon that saves him \$10 each day he rents the car. How much will it cost him to rent the car for a week with the coupon?

7. MP **YOU BE THE TEACHER** Your friend says $24 - 6 \div 2 = 9$. Is your friend correct? Explain.

Think and Grow: Modeling Real Life

Newton has $135. He saves $20 each week for 8 weeks. How much money does he have now?

Understand the problem:

Make a plan:

Solve:

Newton now has ______.

Show and Grow *I can think deeper!*

8. Your teacher buys 3 packages of napkins for a class party. Each package has 50 napkins. The class uses 79 napkins. How many napkins are left?

9. There are 60 seconds in one minute. It takes you 2 minutes and 16 seconds to run from your home to your friend's home. How many seconds does it take you?

10. A store is selling comic books for $5 each. The store sells 33 superhero comic books and 57 science-fiction comic books. How much money does the store earn?

Name ______________________________

Homework & Practice 9.5

Learning Target: Use the problem-solving plan to solve two-step word problems involving different operations.

Example Newton has 36 stickers. He divides the stickers into 9 equal groups and gives Descartes one group. How many stickers does Newton have now?

You can write one equation with two operations to solve this problem. The equation is shown.

$36 - 36 \div 9 = n$ ⟵ n is how many stickers Newton has now.

When solving a problem with more than one type of operation, use the rules below.

- First, multiply or divide as you read the equation from left to right.
- Then add or subtract as you read the equation from left to right.

Step 1: Divide from left to right.

$36 - 36 \div 9 = n$

$36 - \underline{\ 4\ } = n$

Step 2: Subtract from left to right.

$36 - \underline{\ 4\ } = n$

$\underline{\ 32\ } = n$

Newton has __32__ stickers now.

1. There are 20 math problems divided into 4 equal columns on a worksheet. Your teacher has you cross out one column of problems. Use the equation $20 - 20 \div 4 = p$ to find how many problems are left.

2. Newton has 42 blocks. Descartes has 48 blocks. Newton divides his blocks into 6 equal groups and gives Descartes one group. How many blocks does Descartes have now? Use d to represent how many blocks Descartes has now.

3. There are 6 palm trees. An islander gathers 8 coconuts from each tree. She gives away 19 of them. How many coconuts does she have now? Write an equation to solve. Use a letter to represent the unknown number. Check whether your answer is reasonable.

4. DIG DEEPER! Find the number that makes $5 \times$ ____ $- 15 = 5$ true. Explain.

5. MP **Maintain Accuracy** Which equations are true?

$3 + 5 \times 2 \stackrel{?}{=} 13$ $\quad$ $20 - 10 \times 2 \stackrel{?}{=} 20$

$36 \div 6 + 3 \stackrel{?}{=} 4$ $\quad$ $26 - 8 \div 2 \stackrel{?}{=} 22$

6. MP **Modeling Real Life** A school nurse orders 7 packages of bandages. Each package has 20 bandages. The nurse uses 53 bandages. How many bandages are left?

7. MP **Modeling Real Life** There are 60 seconds in one minute. You record a video that is 3 minutes and 48 seconds long. How many seconds long is the video?

Review & Refresh

Estimate. Then find the sum. Check whether your answer is reasonable.

8. Estimate: ____

$$\begin{array}{r} 23 \\ 358 \\ +\ 172 \\ \hline \end{array}$$

9. Estimate: ____

$$\begin{array}{r} 202 \\ 64 \\ +\ 545 \\ \hline \end{array}$$

10. Estimate: ____

$$\begin{array}{r} 21 \\ 15 \\ +\ 837 \\ \hline \end{array}$$

Name ________________________________

Performance Task 9

1. a. You read 120 minutes from Monday through Thursday this week. How many minutes do you read on Thursday? Complete the picture graph for Thursday.

   b. Last week you read 30 minutes each day for 5 days. Your goal this week is to read the same number of minutes as last week. How many minutes do you need to read on Friday to reach your goal? Complete the picture graph for Friday.

Minutes Read	
Monday	★★★
Tuesday	★★★★
Wednesday	★★
Thursday	
Friday	

Each ★ = 10 minutes.

2. **Use Equations** Write equations to solve. Use letters to represent the unknown numbers. Check whether your answer is reasonable.

   a. There are 60 minutes in one hour. Your friend reads 2 hours and 38 minutes during the week. How many minutes does your friend read in all?

   b. Your cousin earns 2 stars on her graph each day for 5 days. How many minutes does your cousin read in all?

3. Use the information above. Order the numbers of minutes you, your friend, and your cousin read from least to greatest. The person with the least number of minutes wants to read the same amount as the person with the greatest number of minutes. How many more minutes does the person need to read?

Multiplication Flip and Find

Directions:

1. Place the Multiplication Flip and Find Cards facedown in the boxes.
2. Players take turns flipping two cards.
3. If your cards show a matching expression and product, then keep the cards. If your cards do not show a matching expression and product, then flip the cards back over.
4. Play until all matches are made.
5. The player with the most matches wins!

Name ______________________________

Chapter Practice 9

9.1 Use Number Lines to Multiply by Multiples of 10

1. Find 8 × 20.

Number of jumps: _____ Size of each jump: _____

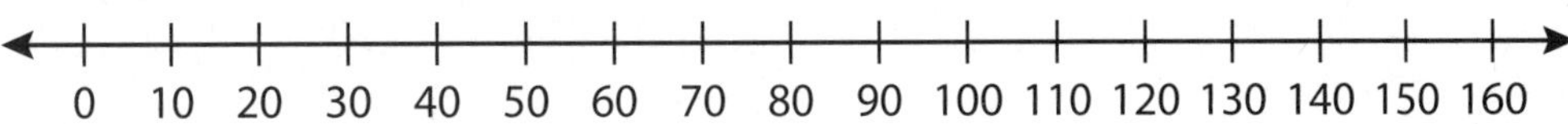

8 × 20 = _____

2. Find 7 × 40.

7 × 40 = _____

3. Find 30 × 9.

30 × 9 = _____

4. MP **Structure** Complete the number line. Then write the multiplication equation for the number line.

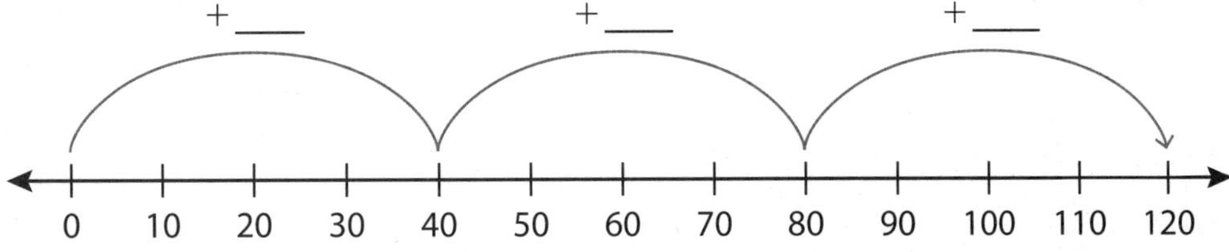

_____ × _____ = _____

9.2 Use Place Value to Multiply by Multiples of 10

Make a quick sketch to find the product.

5. $6 \times 40 =$ ____

6. $5 \times 20 =$ ____

Use place value to find the product.

7. $4 \times 50 = 4 \times$ ____ tens

$4 \times 50 =$ ____ tens

$4 \times 50 =$ ____

8. $3 \times 60 = 3 \times$ ____ tens

$3 \times 60 =$ ____ tens

$3 \times 60 =$ ____

9. $7 \times 70 = 7 \times$ ____ tens

$7 \times 70 =$ ____ tens

$7 \times 70 =$ ____

10. $9 \times 80 = 9 \times$ ____ tens

$9 \times 80 =$ ____ tens

$9 \times 80 =$ ____

Find the product.

11. $2 \times 60 =$ ____

12. $8 \times 40 =$ ____

13. $5 \times 90 =$ ____

14. MP **Modeling Real Life** You practice ballet for 30 minutes every day. How many minutes do you practice in one week?

9.3 Use Properties to Multiply by Multiples of 10

15. Use the Associative Property of Multiplication to find 4×90.

$4 \times 90 = 4 \times (\_\_\_\_ \times 10)$

$4 \times 90 = (4 \times \_\_\_\_) \times 10$

$4 \times 90 = \_\_\_\_ \times 10$

$4 \times 90 = \_\_\_\_$

16. Use the Distributive Property to find 8×20.

$8 \times 20 = 8 \times (10 + \_\_\_\_)$

$8 \times 20 = (8 \times 10) + (8 \times \_\_\_\_)$

$8 \times 20 = \_\_\_\_ + \_\_\_\_$

$8 \times 20 = \_\_\_\_$

Use properties to find the product.

17. $7 \times 20 = \_\_\_\_$

18. $5 \times 70 = \_\_\_\_$

Find the missing factor.

19. $\_\_\_\_ \times 20 = 180$

20. $7 \times \_\_\_\_ = 350$

21. $\_\_\_\_ \times 80 = 240$

---

22. **Open-Ended** Write three expressions equal to 120.

$\_\_\_\_ \times \_\_\_\_$

$\_\_\_\_ \times \_\_\_\_$

$\_\_\_\_ \times \_\_\_\_$

9.4 Problem Solving: Multiplication and Division

Write equations to solve. Use letters to represent the unknown numbers. Check whether your answer is reasonable.

23. There are 2 bookcases. Each bookcase has 3 shelves of 5 books. How many books are there in all?

24. Four veterinarians share 2 boxes of ear wipes. Each box has 20 packs of ear wipes. How many packs of ear wipes does each veterinarian get?

9.5 Problem Solving: All Operations

Write an equation to solve. Use a letter to represent the unknown number. Check whether your answer is reasonable.

25. Newton has 30 beads. Descartes has 22 beads. Newton divides his beads into 3 equal groups and gives Descartes one group. How many beads does Descartes have now?

26. It costs $166 to rent a bounce house for 7 hours. Descartes has a coupon that saves him $5 each hour he rents the bounce house. How much will it cost him to rent the bounce house for 7 hours with the coupon?

10 Understand Fractions

- What games do you like to play?
- How can you use fractions in your daily life? How might a game involve fractions?

Chapter Learning Target:
Understand fractions.

Chapter Success Criteria:
- I can name equal parts.
- I can identify a unit fraction.
- I can write a fraction.
- I can plot a fraction.

Name ______________________________

10 Vocabulary

Review Words

equal shares
fourths
halves
thirds

Organize It

Use the review words to complete the graphic organizer.

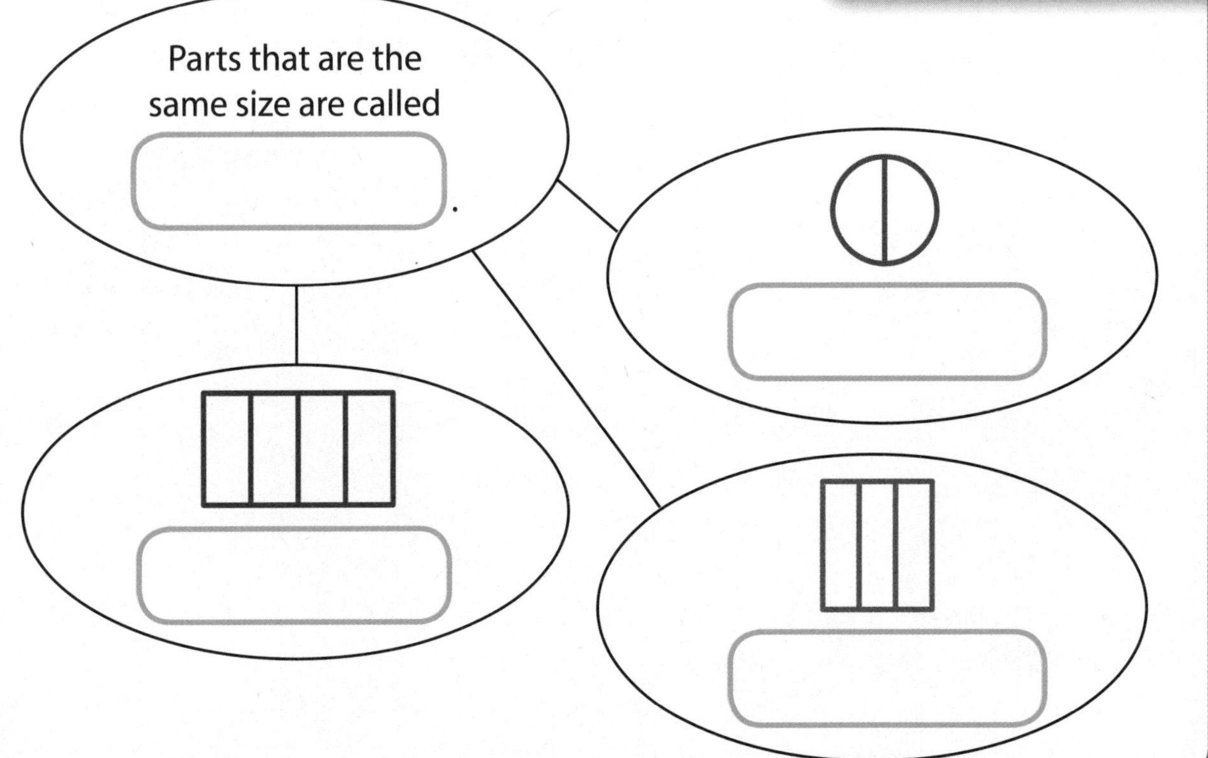

Define It

Use your vocabulary cards to complete the definition.

1. numerator: tells how many ____________ parts are being ____________
2. denominator: tells how many ____________ parts are in a ____________
3. eighths: There are ____________ equal ____________ in the whole.
4. sixths: There are ____________ equal ____________ in the whole.

Chapter 10 Vocabulary Cards

denominator

eighths

fraction

numerator

sixths

unit fraction

whole

whole numbers

The whole is divided into eight equal parts, or **eighths**.

The part of a fraction that represents how many equal parts are in a whole.

$\frac{1}{6}$ ← denominator

The part of a fraction that represents how many equal parts are being counted.

$\frac{1}{6}$ ← numerator

A number that represents part of a whole

$\frac{1}{6}$

Represents one equal part of a whole

The fraction $\frac{1}{6}$ is a unit fraction.

The whole is divided into six equal parts, or **sixths**.

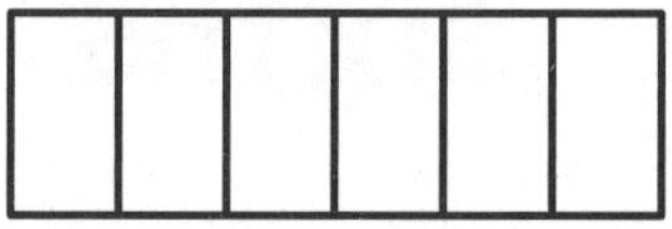

The numbers 0, 1, 2, 3, and so on

All of the parts of one shape or group

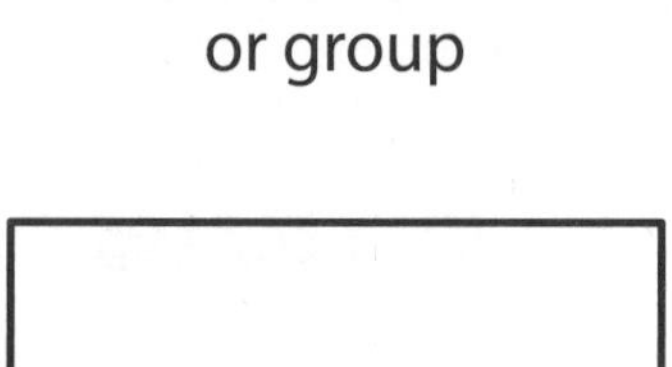

Name ________________________________

Equal Parts of a Whole 10.1

Learning Target: Identify equal parts of a whole and name them.

Success Criteria:

- I can tell whether shapes show equal or unequal parts.
- I can name equal parts.
- I can divide a shape into equal parts.

Use the name of the equal parts to divide each rectangle. Write the number of equal parts for each rectangle.

halves

_____ equal parts

thirds

_____ equal parts

fourths

_____ equal parts

sixths

_____ equal parts

Repeated Reasoning How many equal parts are in a rectangle that is divided into eighths? Explain.

Think and Grow: Equal Parts of a Whole

The rectangle represents a whole. A **whole** is all of the parts of one shape or group.

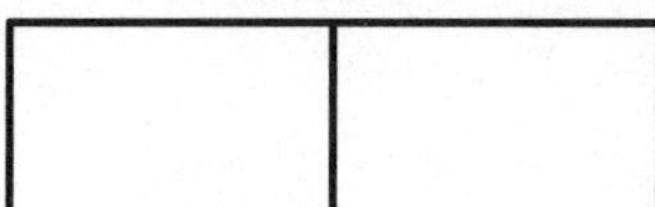

2 equal parts, or halves

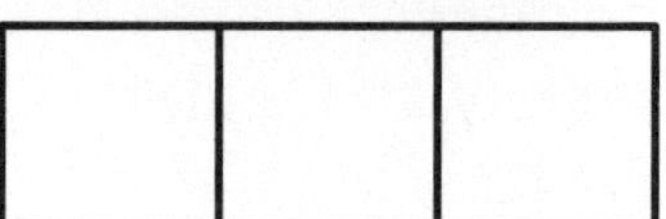

3 equal parts, or thirds

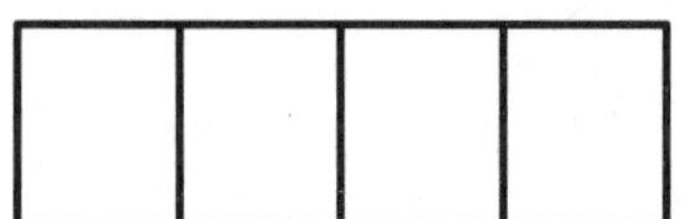

4 equal parts, or fourths

6 equal parts, or **sixths**

8 equal parts, or **eighths**

Example Tell whether the shape shows equal parts or unequal parts. If the shape shows equal parts, then name them.

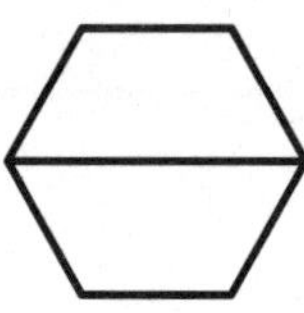

________________ parts

____

________________ parts

____

Show and Grow *I can do it!*

Tell whether the shape shows equal parts or unequal parts. If the shape shows equal parts, then name them.

1.

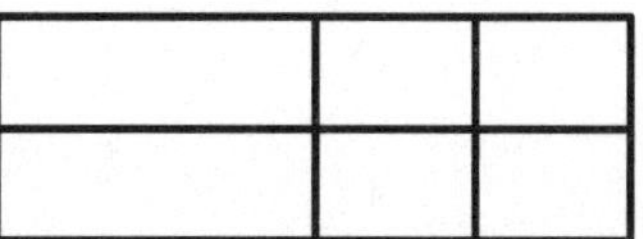

________________ parts

____

2.

________________ parts

____

Name ______________________________

Apply and Grow: Practice

Tell whether the shape shows equal parts or unequal parts. If the shape shows equal parts, then name them.

3.

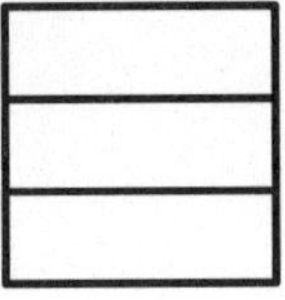

______________ parts

____

4.

______________ parts

____

5.

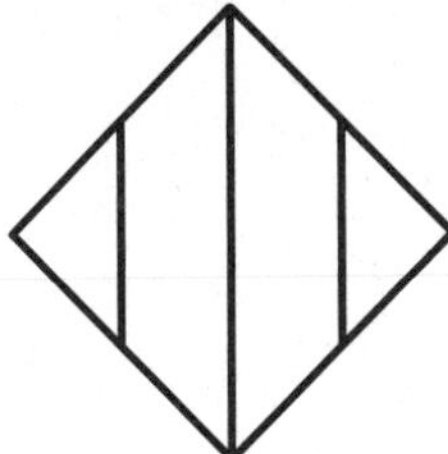

______________ parts

____

6.

______________ parts

____

7. Divide the rectangle into 2 equal parts. Then name the equal parts.

____

8. Divide the square into 6 equal parts. Then name the equal parts.

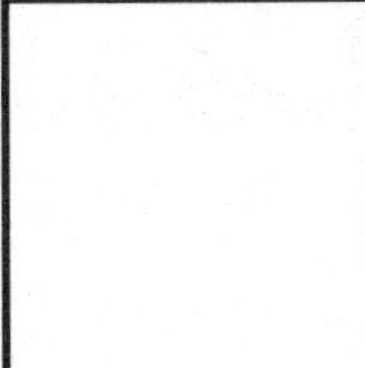

____

9. MP **YOU BE THE TEACHER** Newton says he divided each shape into fourths. Is he correct? Explain.

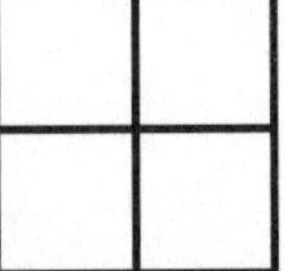

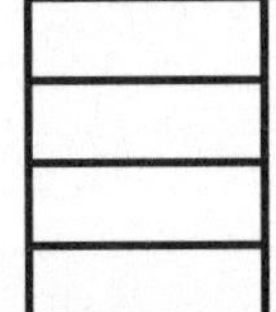

Think and Grow: Modeling Real Life

Three students want to share a whiteboard to solve math problems. Each student wants to use an equal part of the board. Should the students divide the whiteboard into halves, thirds, or fourths?

Draw to show:

The students should divide the whiteboard into __________ .

Show and Grow *I can think deeper!*

10. Six friends want to share an egg casserole. Each friend wants an equal part. Should the friends cut the casserole into halves, fourths, or sixths?

11. Eight students need to sit around two tables. Each student needs an equal part of a table. Should the tables be divided into thirds, fourths, or sixths?

12. **DIG DEEPER!** Ten friends want to share five rectangular sheets of paper. Each friend wants an equal part. Should the friends cut the sheets of paper into halves or thirds? Explain.

Name ___________________________

Learning Target: Identify equal parts of a whole and name them.

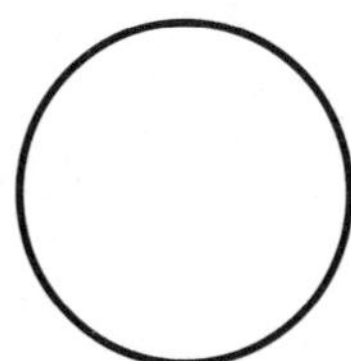

1 equal part, or whole

2 equal parts, or halves

3 equal parts, or thirds

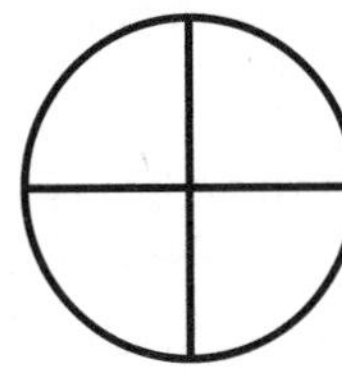

4 equal parts, or fourths

6 equal parts, or sixths

8 equal parts, or eighths

Tell whether the shape shows equal parts or unequal parts. If the shape shows equal parts, then name them.

1. 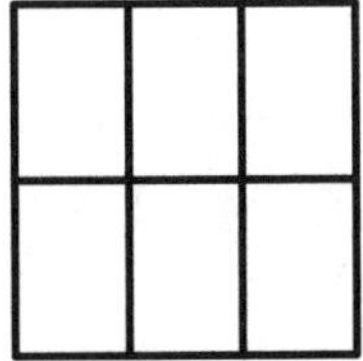

__________ parts

____

2. 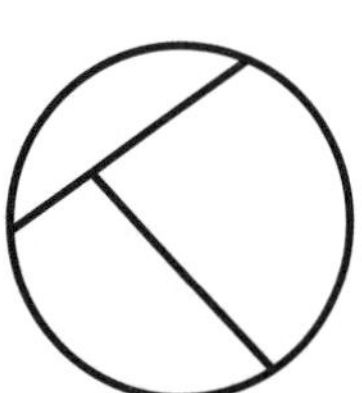

__________ parts

____

3. 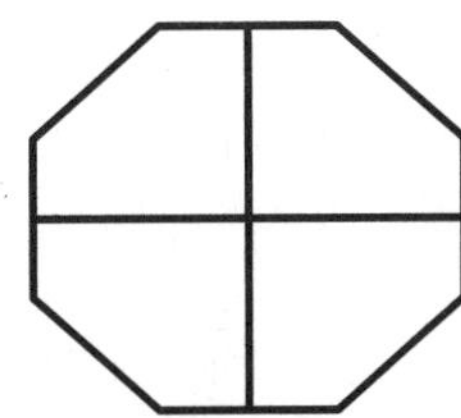

__________ parts

____

4. 

__________ parts

____

5. 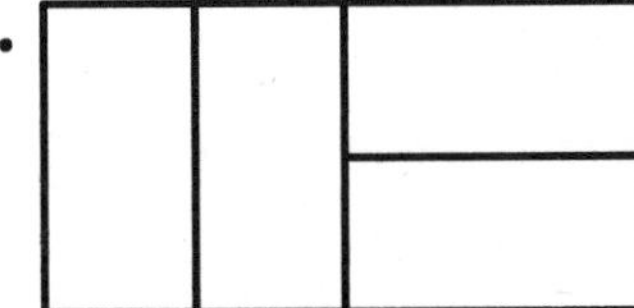

__________ parts

____

6. 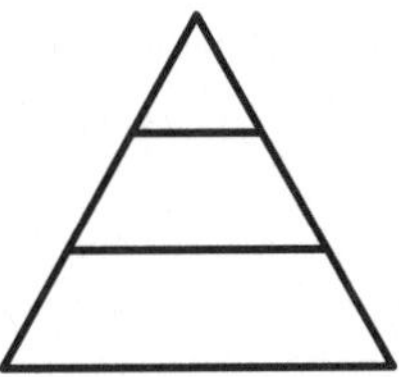

__________ parts

____

7. Divide the square into 3 equal parts. Then name the equal parts.

____

8. Divide the triangle into 2 equal parts. Then name the equal parts.

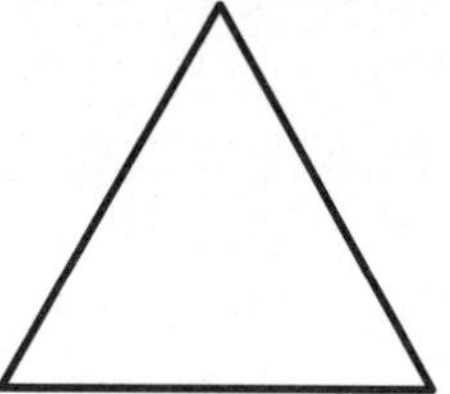

____

9. **MP Patterns** Use the pattern to divide the square into equal parts. Name the equal parts.

   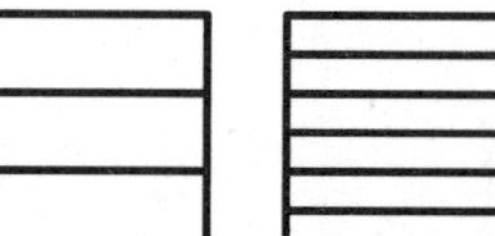 

____

10. **MP Modeling Real Life** Eight friends want to share a lasagna. Each friend wants an equal part. Should the friends cut the lasagna into fourths, sixths, or eighths?

11. **DIG DEEPER!** Twelve friends want to pull weeds from three community gardens. Each friend wants to pull weeds from an equal part. Should the friends divide each garden into thirds, fourths, or sixths?

Review & Refresh

Find the product.

12. $2 \times (3 \times 3) =$ _____

13. $(4 \times 2) \times 9 =$ _____

14. $2 \times (8 \times 5) =$ _____

Name ______________________________

Understand a Unit Fraction 10.2

Learning Target: Identify and write a unit fraction.

Success Criteria:

- I can identify a unit fraction.
- I can write a unit fraction.
- I can explain what a unit fraction is.
- I can explain what the numerator and denominator are in a fraction.

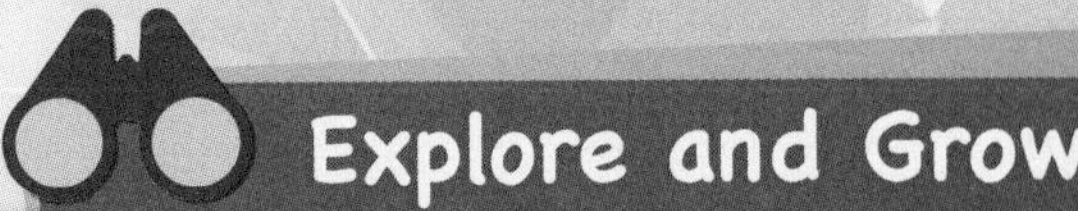

Match each shaded part to its name.

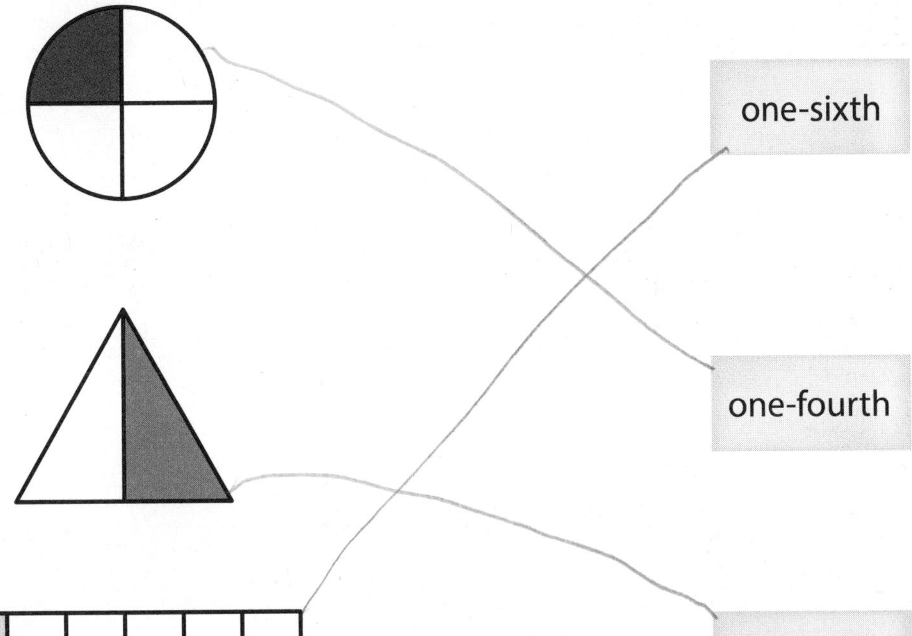

Structure What is the same about each shape? What is different?

Think and Grow: Understand a Unit Fraction

A **fraction** is a number that represents part of a whole.

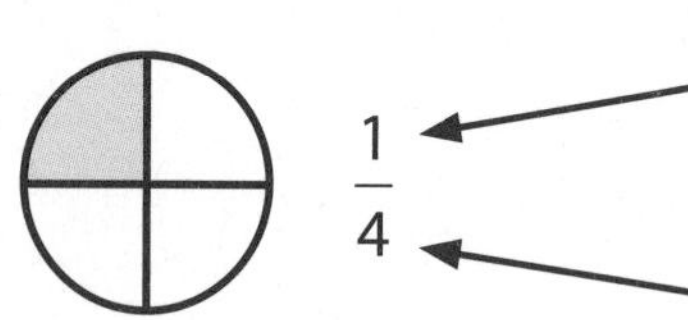

The **numerator** represents how many equal parts are being counted.

The **denominator** represents how many equal parts are in a whole.

A **unit fraction** represents one equal part of a whole.

Example What fraction of the whole is shaded?

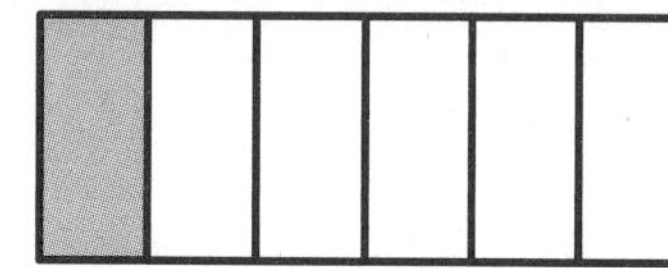

There are 6 equal parts in the whole.

1 of the equal parts is shaded.

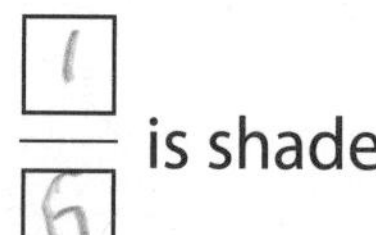

$\frac{1}{6}$ is shaded.

Show and Grow I can do it!

What fraction of the whole is shaded?

1. 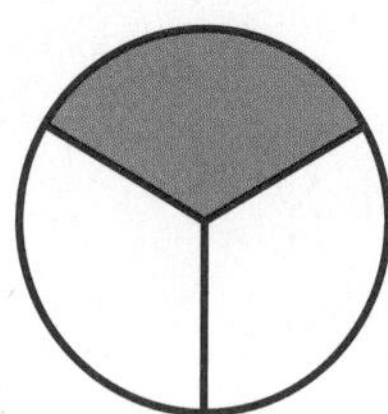

There are 3 equal parts in the whole.

1 of the equal parts is shaded.

$\frac{1}{3}$ is shaded.

2. 

$\frac{1}{8}$ is shaded.

3. 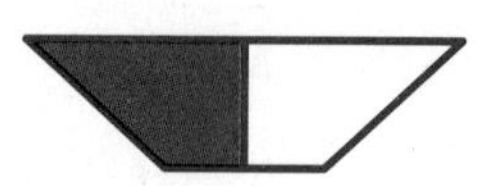

$\frac{1}{2}$ is shaded.

Name ______________________________

Apply and Grow: Practice

What fraction of the whole is shaded?

4. 

$\frac{1}{6}$ is shaded.

5. $\frac{1}{4}$ is shaded.

6. 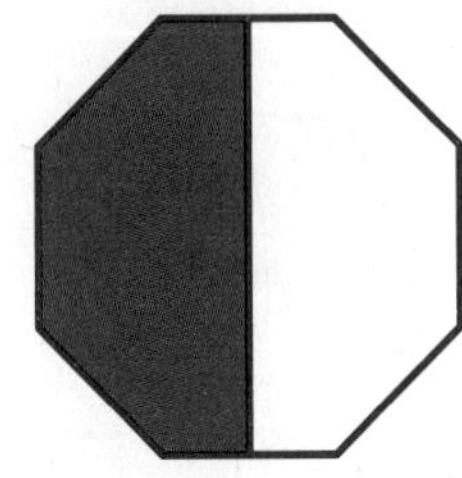

$\frac{1}{2}$ is shaded.

7. 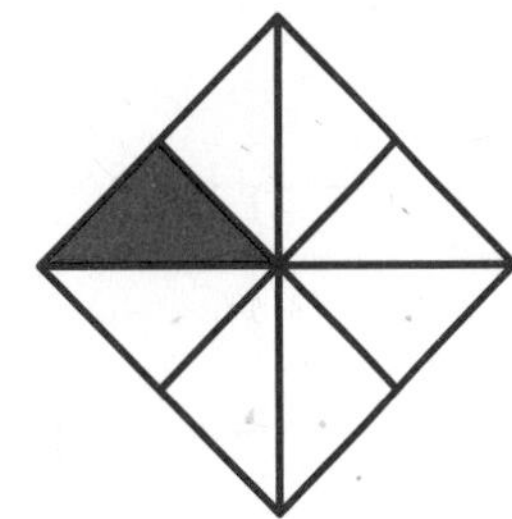

$\frac{1}{8}$ is shaded.

8. 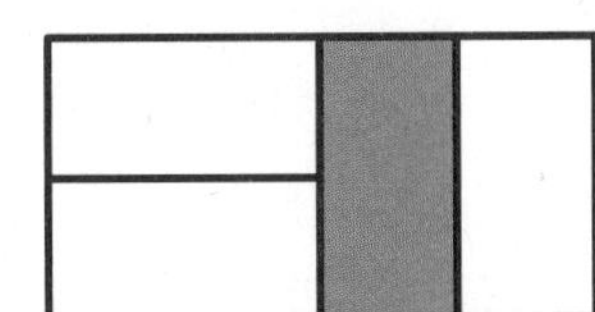

$\frac{1}{4}$ is shaded.

9. 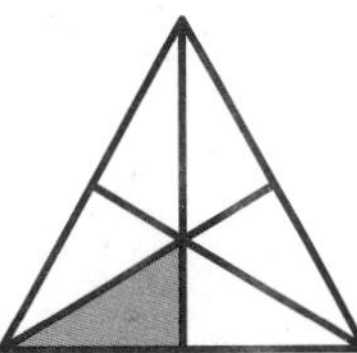

$\frac{1}{6}$ is shaded.

10. Divide the circle into 4 equal parts. Shade one part. What fraction of the whole is shaded?

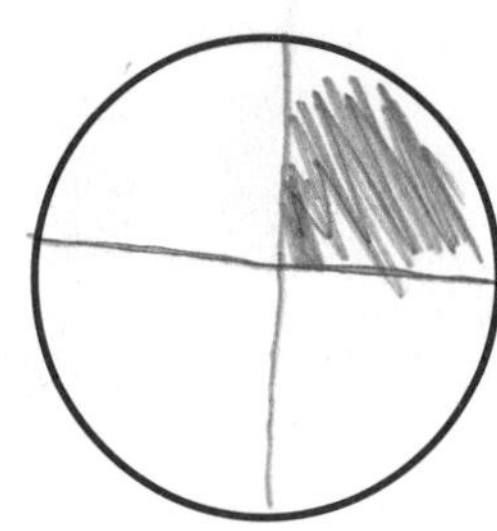

$\frac{1}{4}$ is shaded.

11. Divide the square into 3 equal parts. Shade one part. What fraction of the whole is shaded?

$\frac{1}{3}$ is shaded.

12. MP **YOU BE THE TEACHER** Descartes says the part he shaded can be represented by a unit fraction. Is he correct? Explain.

Think and Grow: Modeling Real Life

For which nation's flag can you use a unit fraction to represent the amount of green? Explain.

Flag of ______________________

Explain:

Nation	Flag
Nigeria	
Mauritius	
Seychelles	

Show and Grow *I can think deeper!*

13. For which nation's flag can you use a unit fraction to represent the amount of red? Explain.

Nation	Flag
Bahrain	
Austria	
France	

14. You paint a plate that has 4 equal parts. You paint two parts orange and one part red. You paint the rest of the plate yellow. What fraction of the plate is yellow?

15. **DIG DEEPER!** Draw a quilt square that has blue, red, and white parts, but only the blue part can be represented by a unit fraction.

Name ______________________

Homework & Practice 10.2

Learning Target: Identify and write a unit fraction.

Example What fraction of the whole is shaded?

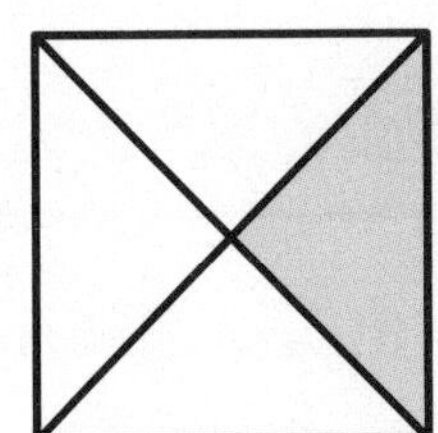

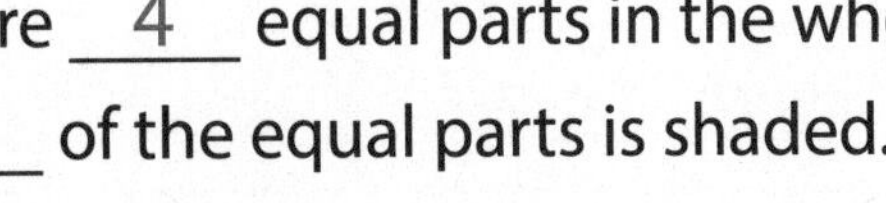

There are 4 equal parts in the whole.

1 of the equal parts is shaded.

$\frac{1}{4}$ is shaded.

What fraction of the whole is shaded?

1. 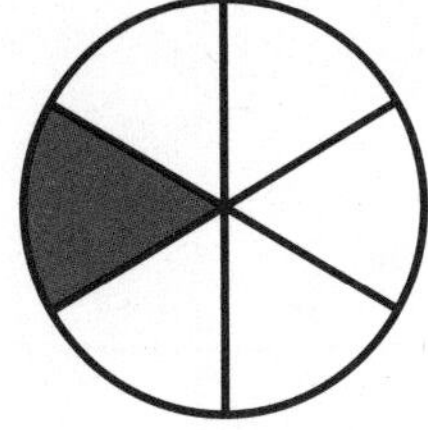

There are ____ equal parts in the whole.

____ of the equal parts is shaded.

$\frac{\square}{\square}$ is shaded.

2. 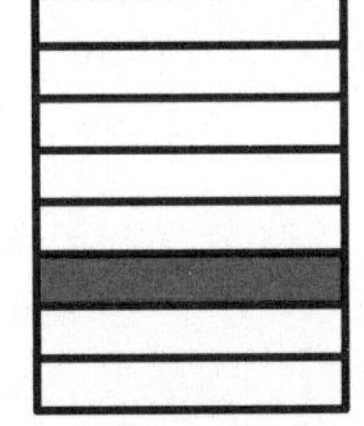

$\frac{\square}{\square}$ is shaded.

3. 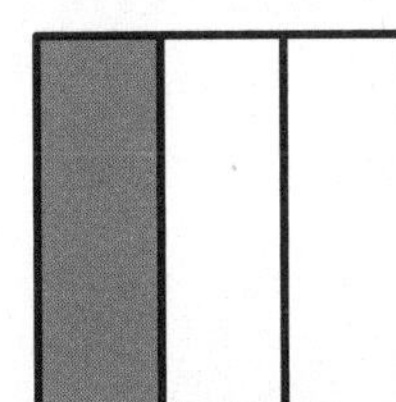

$\frac{\square}{\square}$ is shaded.

4. 

$\frac{\square}{\square}$ is shaded.

5. 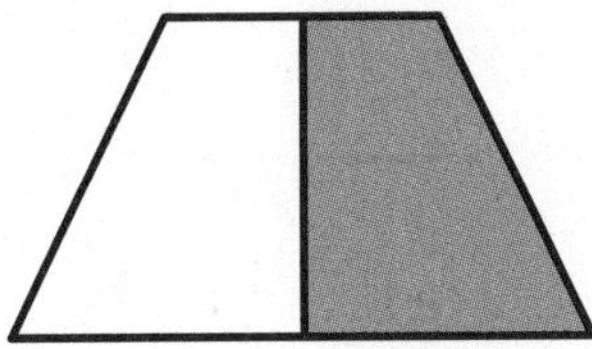

$\frac{\square}{\square}$ is shaded.

6. Divide the square into 6 equal parts. Shade one part. What fraction of the whole is shaded?

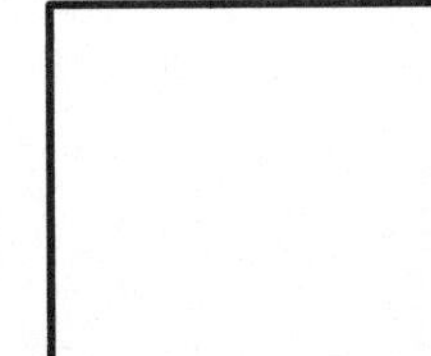

$\frac{\square}{\square}$ is shaded.

7. **MP Construct an Argument** Did Descartes label the shaded part correctly? Explain.

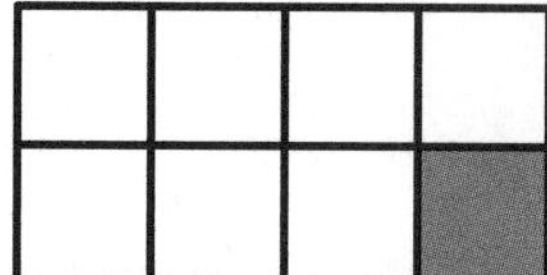

8. **DIG DEEPER!** You want to make a card. You fold a sheet of paper in half, then in half again. What fraction of the sheet of paper represents the front of the card?

9. **MP Communicate Clearly** Explain how you know Newton ate $\frac{1}{3}$ of his taco.

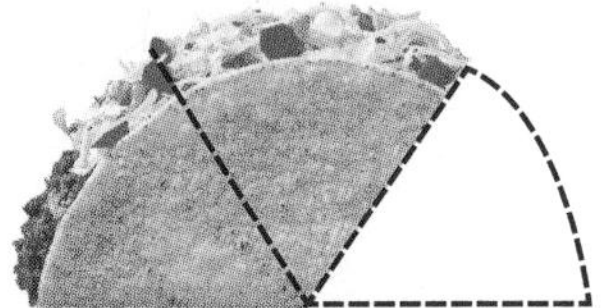

10. **MP Modeling Real Life** For which foods can you use a unit fraction to represent the amount eaten? Explain.

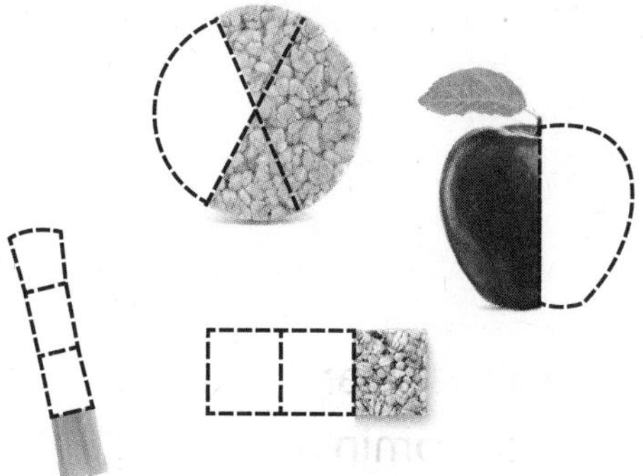

11. **MP Modeling Real Life** You prepare a rectangular dip tray that has 6 equal parts. Three parts are hummus, one part is *queso*, and one part is guacamole. The rest of the tray is salsa. What fraction of the tray is salsa?

Review & Refresh

Compare.

12. 4×6 ◯ 6×6

13. 6×5 ◯ 4×5

14. 42 ◯ 6×7

Name ___________________________

Write Fractions of a Whole 10.3

Learning Target: Identify and write a fraction.

Success Criteria:

- I can identify a fraction.
- I can write a fraction.

Explore and Grow

Write a fraction for the shaded part of each whole.

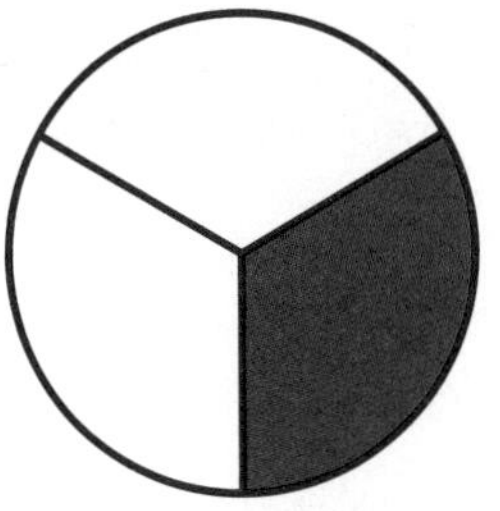

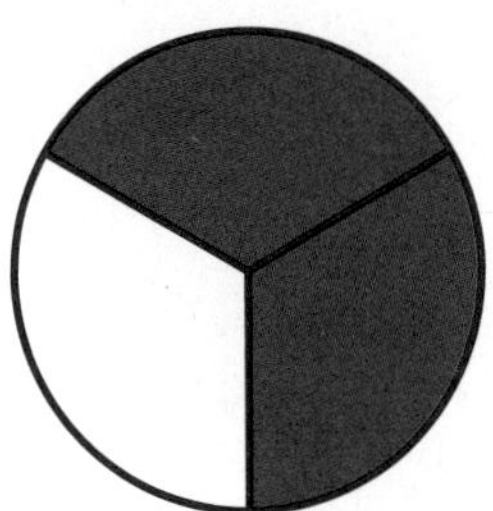

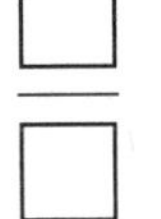

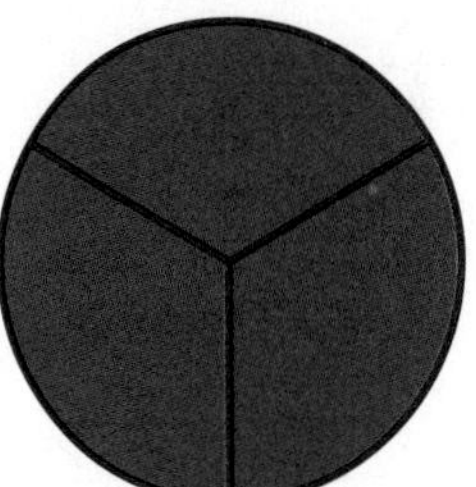

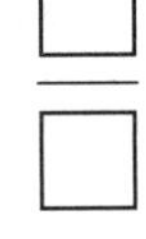

Analyze a Problem All of the equal parts of a shape are shaded. What do you know about the numerator and denominator of the fraction that describes the shaded parts?

Think and Grow: Fractions of a Whole

Example What fraction of the whole is shaded?

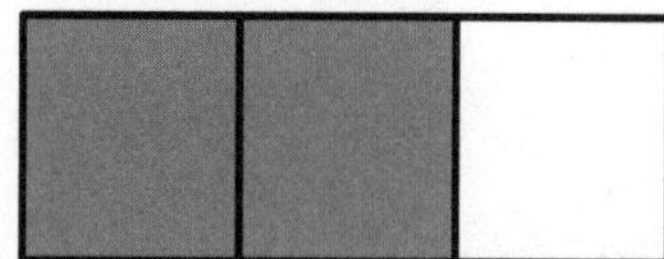

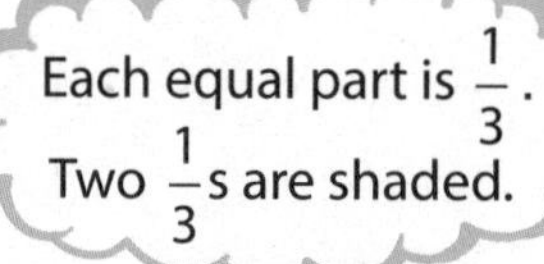

There are 3 equal parts in the whole.

2 of the equal parts are shaded.

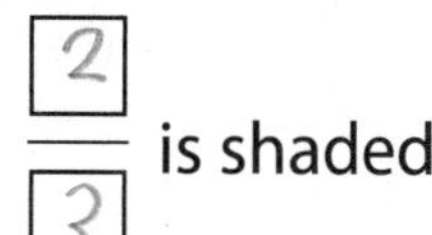

$\frac{2}{3}$ is shaded.

Show and Grow I can do it!

What fraction of the whole is shaded?

1. 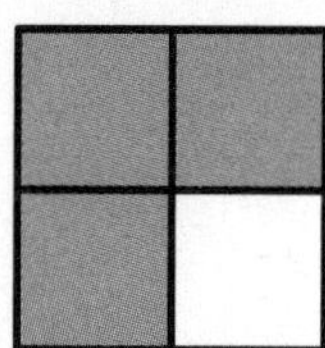

There are 4 equal parts in the whole.

3 of the equal parts are shaded.

$\frac{3}{4}$ is shaded.

2. 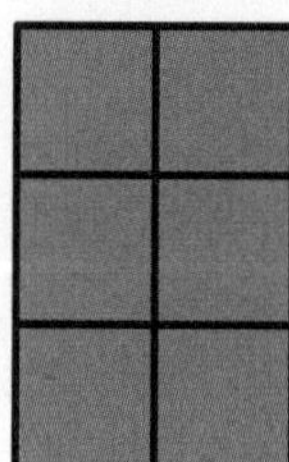

There are 6 equal parts in the whole.

6 of the equal parts are shaded.

$\frac{6}{6}$ is shaded.

3. 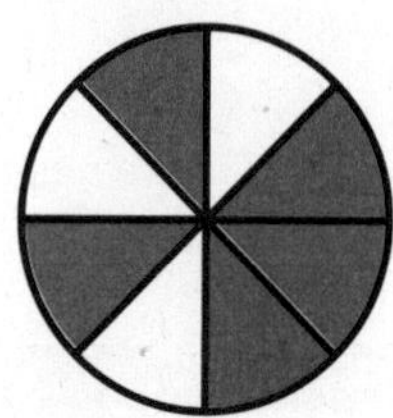

$\frac{5}{8}$ is shaded.

4. 

$\frac{2}{6}$ is shaded.

Name ______________________________

Apply and Grow: Practice

What fraction of the whole is shaded?

5. 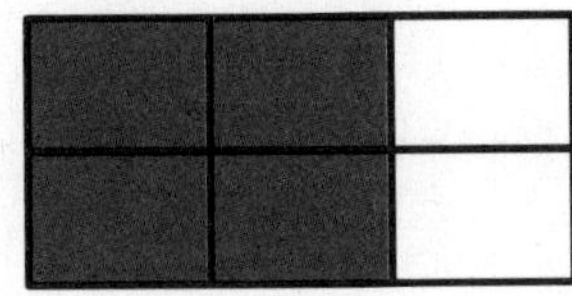

$\frac{4}{6}$ is shaded.

6. 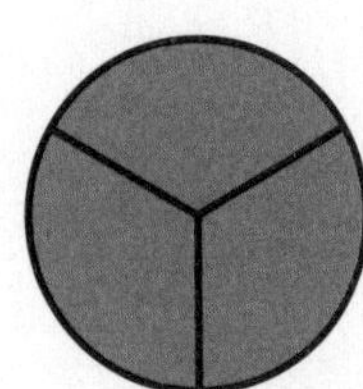

$\frac{3}{3}$ is shaded.

7. 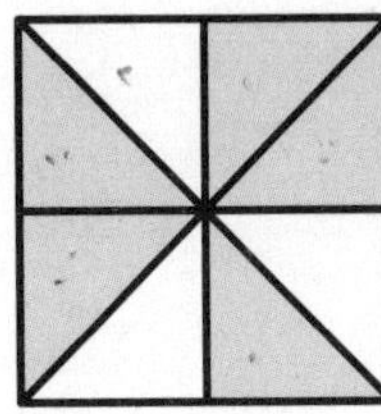

$\frac{5}{8}$ is shaded.

8. 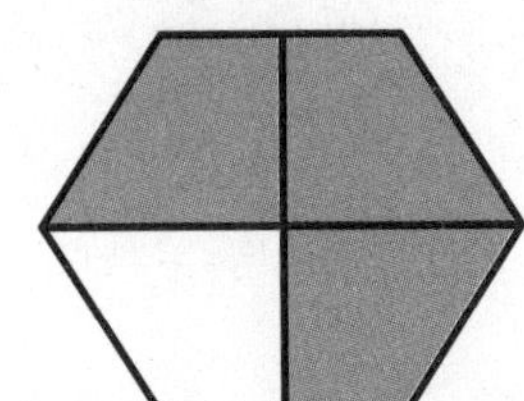

$\frac{3}{4}$ is shaded.

9. Divide the rectangle into eighths. Shade three of the equal parts. What fraction of the whole is shaded?

$\frac{3}{8}$ is shaded.

10. Divide the triangle in half. Shade two of the equal parts. What fraction of the whole is shaded?

$\frac{2}{2}$ is shaded.

11. **DIG DEEPER!** Your friend is thinking of a fraction. What is his fraction?

> The whole is divided into sixths. The numerator of my fraction is an odd number. My fraction is greater than $\frac{3}{6}$.

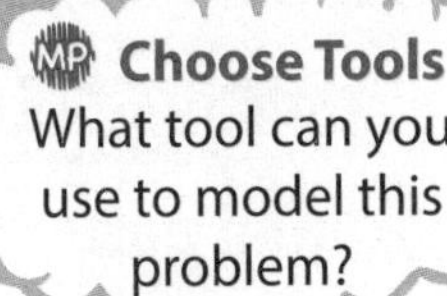

the number is: $\frac{5}{6}$

Think and Grow: Modeling Real Life

You are making a stained glass window that has 6 equal parts. You finish 1 part of the window. What fraction of the window do you have left to finish?

Draw to show:

You have $\frac{\square}{\square}$ of the window left to finish.

Show and Grow I can think deeper!

12. You color 8 equal parts of a banner for a school play. You write the title in 4 of the parts. What fraction of the banner does *not* have the title?

13. A fruit tray has 4 equal parts. One part of the tray has grapes. Another part of the tray has pineapple. The rest of the tray has watermelon. What fraction of the tray has watermelon?

14. DIG DEEPER! You divide a flower bed into equal parts. You plant sunflowers in 1 part. You plant daisies in the other 2 parts. What fraction of the flower bed has sunflowers?

Name ______________________________

Homework & Practice 10.3

Learning Target: Identify and write a fraction.

Example What fraction of the whole is shaded?

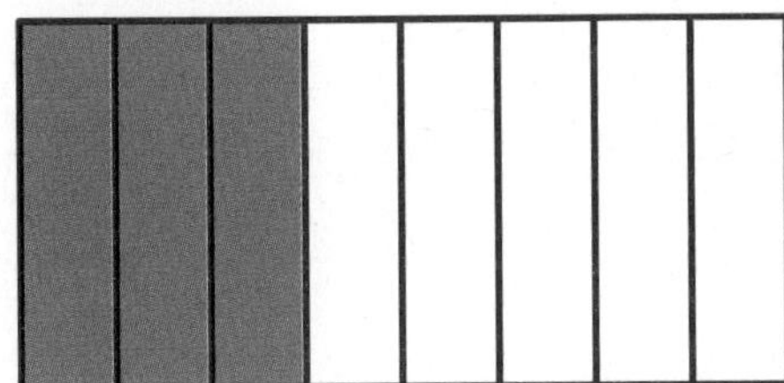

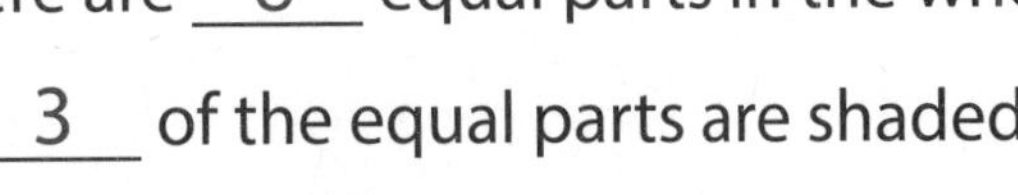

There are 8 equal parts in the whole.

3 of the equal parts are shaded.

$\frac{3}{8}$ is shaded.

What fraction of the whole is shaded?

1. 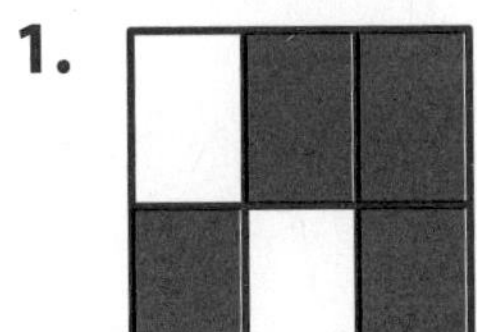

There are _____ equal parts in the whole.

_____ of the equal parts are shaded.

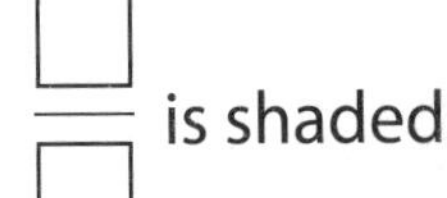

$\frac{\square}{\square}$ is shaded.

2. 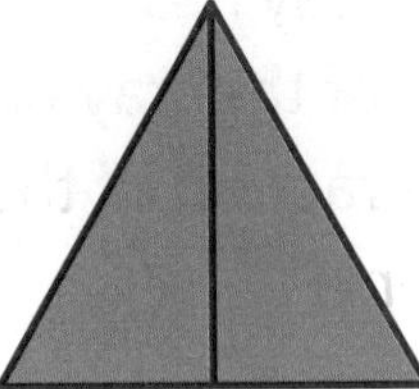

$\frac{\square}{\square}$ is shaded.

3. 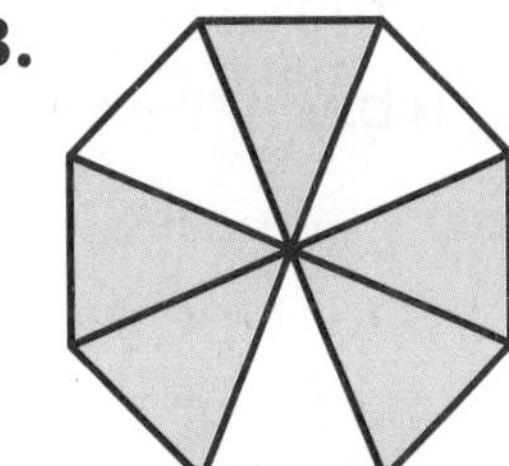

$\frac{\square}{\square}$ is shaded.

4. 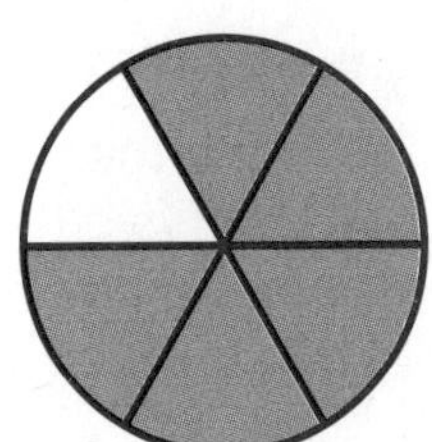

$\frac{\square}{\square}$ is shaded.

5. 

$\frac{\square}{\square}$ is shaded.

6. Divide the rectangle into sixths. Shade 2 of the equal parts. What fraction of the whole is shaded?

$\frac{\square}{\square}$ is shaded.

7. Divide the square into thirds. Shade 2 of the equal parts. What fraction of the whole is shaded?

$\frac{\square}{\square}$ is shaded.

8. **Open-Ended** Divide and shade the square to show more than $\frac{4}{8}$, but less than $\frac{8}{8}$. What fraction of the whole is shaded?

$\frac{\square}{\square}$ is shaded.

9. **MP Reasoning** A pool has 4 swim lanes. Swimmers are using all of the lanes. Draw and shade a model that represents the lanes being used. Then write a fraction for your model.

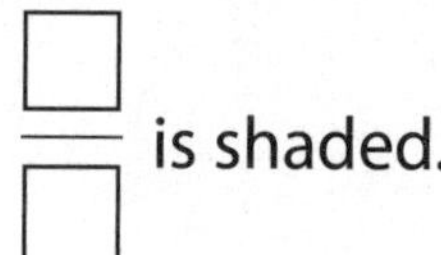

is shaded.

10. **MP Patterns** What fraction of each circle is shaded? Think: What do you notice about the numerators? Model and write the next fraction.

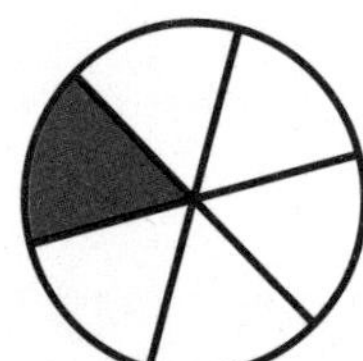 $\frac{\square}{6}$ 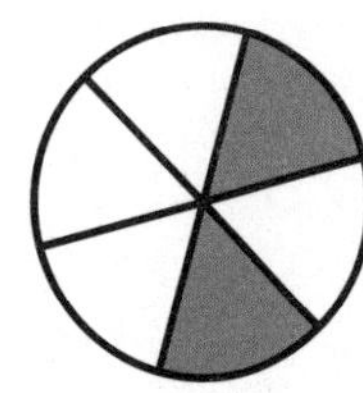 $\frac{\square}{6}$ 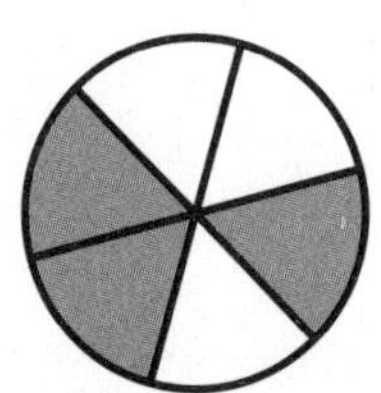 $\frac{\square}{6}$ 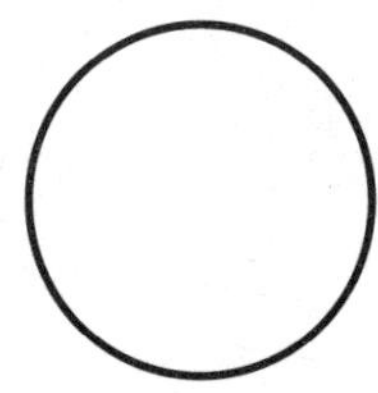 $\frac{\square}{6}$

11. **MP Modeling Real Life** A vegetable tray has 8 equal parts. Three parts have peppers. One part has broccoli. Another part has tomatoes. The rest of the tray has carrots. What fraction of the tray has carrots?

12. **DIG DEEPER!** You divide an art canvas into equal parts. You paint 1 part blue, 2 parts orange, and the last part yellow. What fraction of the canvas is painted orange?

MP Reasoning
Name one other fraction you can use to represent the orange portion of the art canvas.

Review & Refresh

Complete the fact family.

13. $6 \times$ ____ $= 42$ $\quad 42 \div 7 =$ ____

____ $\times 6 = 42$ $\quad 42 \div$ ____ $= 7$

14. $9 \times$ ____ $= 9$ $\quad 9 \div 1 =$ ____

____ $\times 9 = 9$ $\quad 9 \div$ ____ $= 1$

Name ______________________________

Fractions on a Number Line: Less Than 1 10.4

Learning Target: Plot fractions less than 1 on a number line.

Success Criteria:

- I can divide a number line into equal parts.
- I can label fractions on a number line.
- I can plot a fraction.

Use the $\frac{1}{6}$ Fraction Strips to complete the fractions on the number line.

Then plot $\frac{3}{6}$ on the number line.

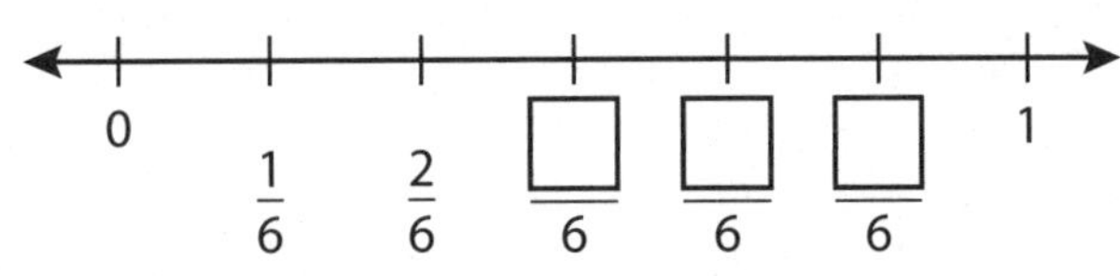

MP Precision Plot $\frac{6}{6}$ on the number line. What do you notice? Explain.

Think and Grow: Fractions on a Number Line: Less Than 1

Every number on a number line represents a distance from 0. The distance from 0 to 1 is one whole. A number line can be divided into any number of equal parts or distances.

Example Plot $\frac{3}{4}$ on the number line.

Step 1: Divide the length from 0 to 1 into _____ equal parts.

Step 2: Label each tick mark on the number line.

Think: One $\frac{1}{4}$ is $\frac{1}{4}$. Two $\frac{1}{4}$s are $\frac{2}{4}$.

Step 3: Plot $\frac{3}{4}$ on the number line.

Think: _____ $\frac{1}{4}$s are $\frac{3}{4}$.

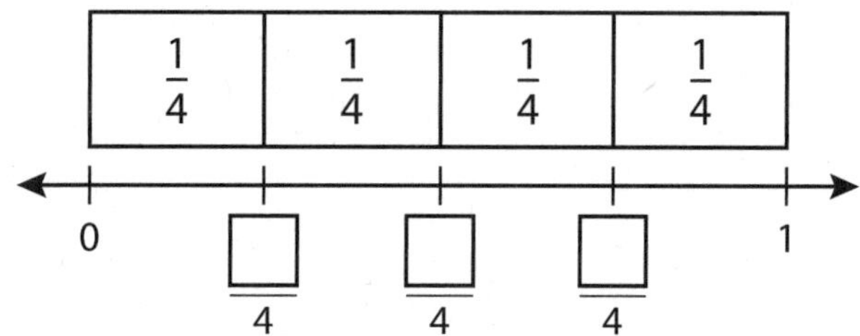

Show and Grow *I can do it!*

Plot the fraction on the number line.

1. $\frac{1}{2}$

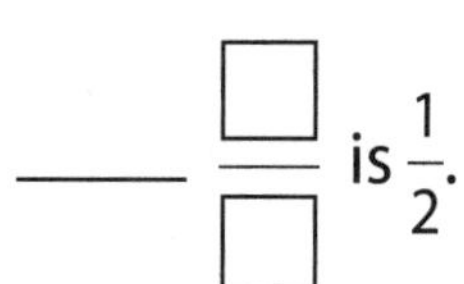

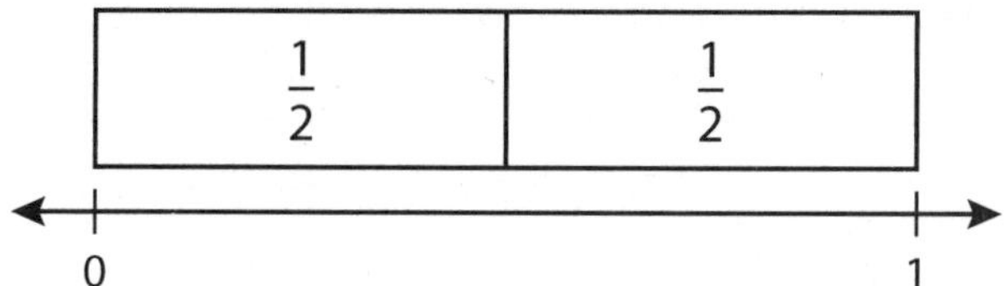

2. $\frac{2}{6}$

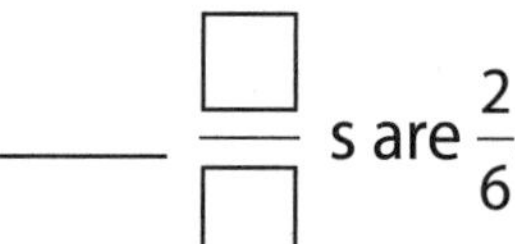

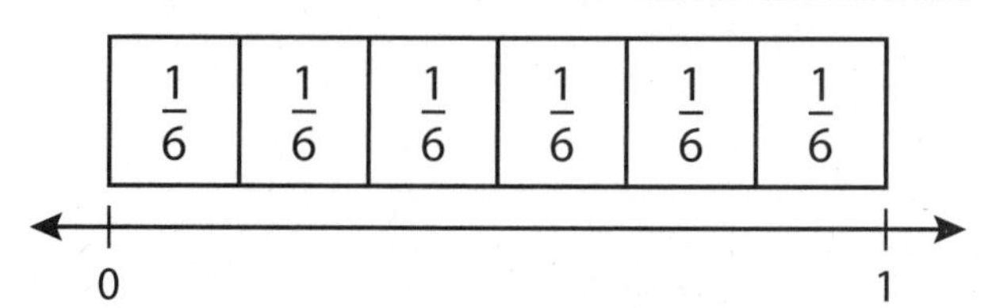

Name ______________________________

Apply and Grow: Practice

Plot the fraction on a number line.

3. $\frac{2}{4}$

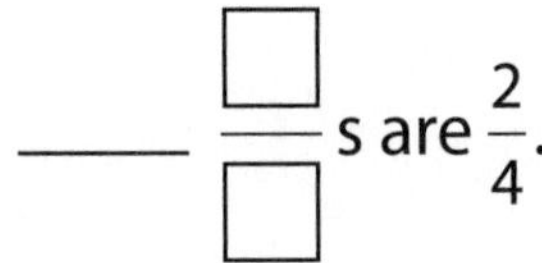

____ $\frac{\square}{\square}$ s are $\frac{2}{4}$.

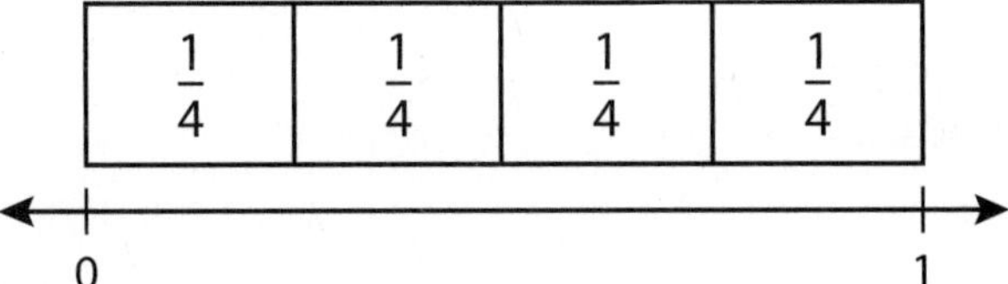

4. $\frac{5}{6}$

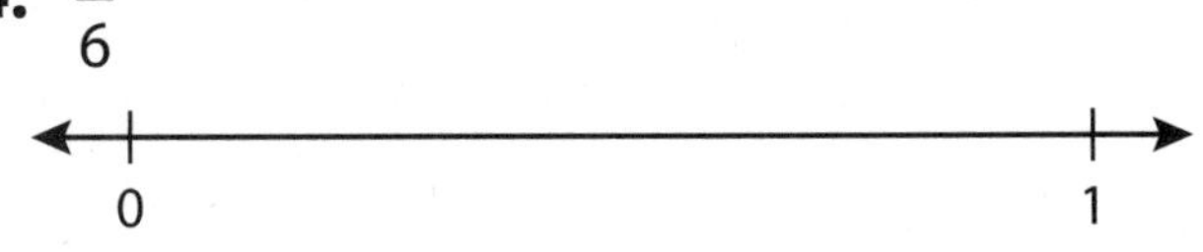

5. $\frac{2}{3}$

6. $\frac{6}{8}$

7. $\frac{3}{4}$

8. **Structure** Complete the number line.

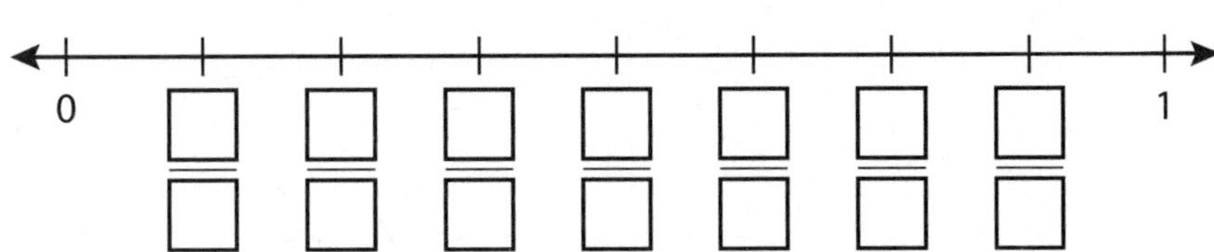

9. **Writing** How are the number lines the same? How are they different?

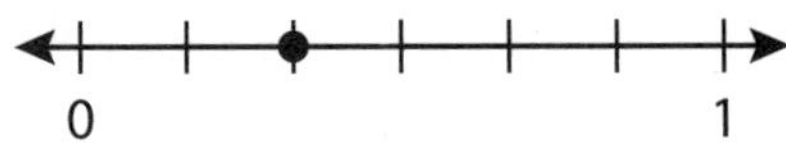

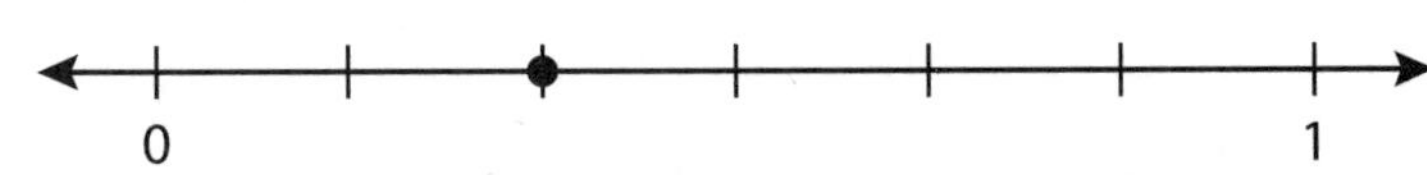

Think and Grow: Modeling Real Life

Three laps around a walking trail is 1 mile. How many laps does it take you to walk $\frac{2}{3}$ mile?

Model:

You need to walk _____ laps to walk $\frac{2}{3}$ mile.

Show and Grow *I can think deeper!*

10. You follow a recipe and make four servings. How many servings can you make using $\frac{1}{4}$ of each ingredient in the recipe?

11. **DIG DEEPER!** A gymnast needs to take 8 equal-sized steps to get from one end of a balance beam to the other. She starts on the left end of the beam and takes 6 steps. What fraction of the beam is behind her? What fraction of the beam is in front of her?

12. **DIG DEEPER!** A tightrope walker needs to take 6 equal-sized steps to get from one end of a tightrope to the other. He starts on the left side of the rope and takes 5 steps. What fraction of the rope is behind him? What fraction of the rope is in front of him?

Name ______________________

Homework & Practice 10.4

Learning Target: Plot fractions less than 1 on a number line.

Example Plot $\frac{2}{3}$ on the number line.

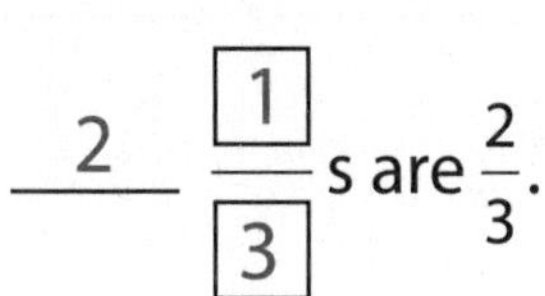

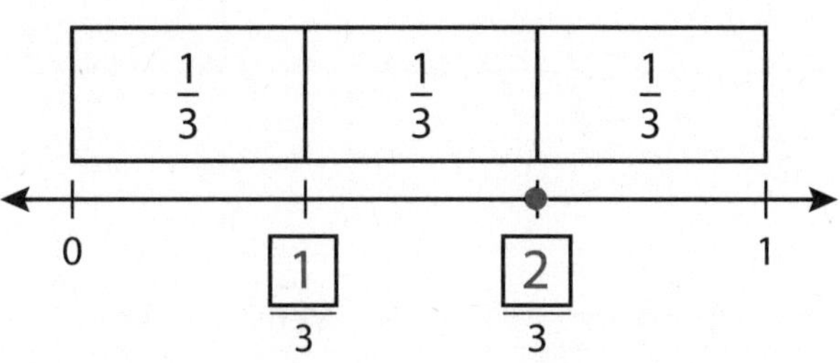

Plot the fraction on a number line.

1. $\frac{4}{6}$

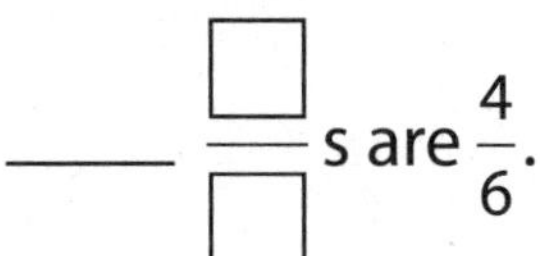

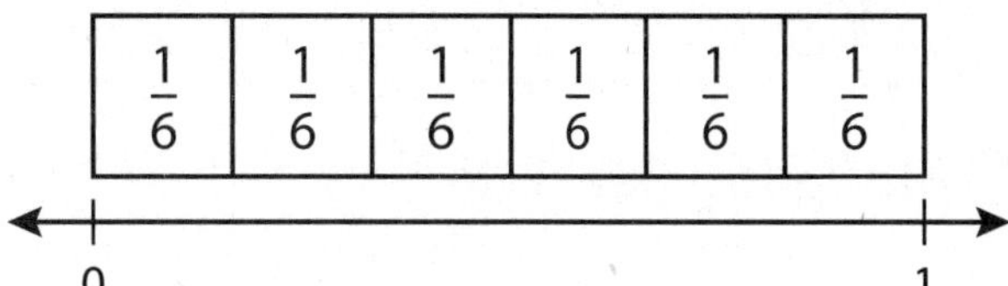

2. $\frac{3}{8}$

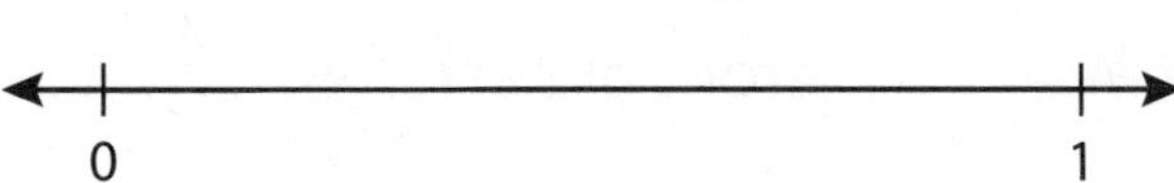

3. $\frac{1}{4}$

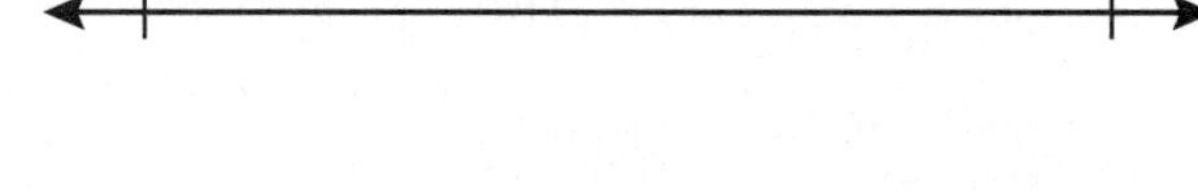

4. $\frac{2}{6}$

5. $\frac{5}{8}$

6. **Logic** What fraction is located halfway between 0 and 1?

7. **YOU BE THE TEACHER** Your friend draws a number line and plots $\frac{2}{6}$. Is your friend correct? Explain.

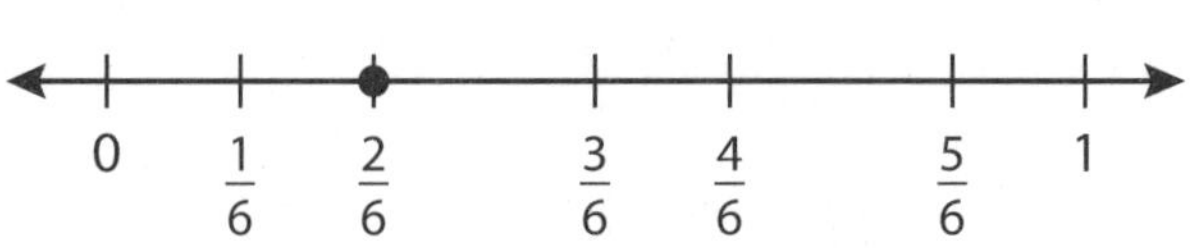

8. **Structure** Which number line shows $\frac{2}{3}$?

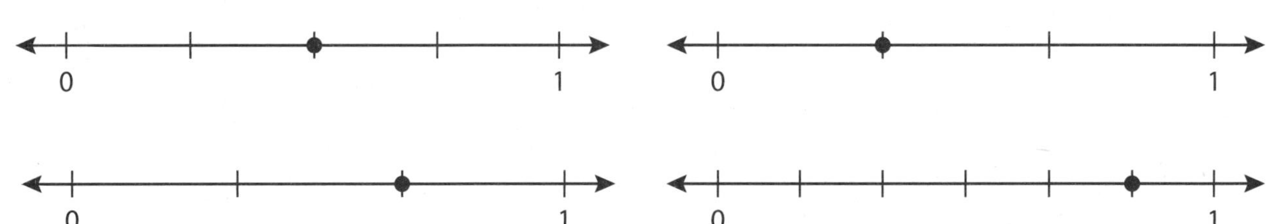

9. **Modeling Real Life** Four laps around a soccer field is 1 mile. How many laps does it take you to run $\frac{3}{4}$ mile?

10. **DIG DEEPER!** A diver needs to take 8 equal-sized steps before diving into the pool. She starts at the beginning of the diving board and takes 6 steps. What fraction of the diving board is behind the diver? What fraction of the diving board is in front of the diver?

Review & Refresh

Find the area of the shape.

11.

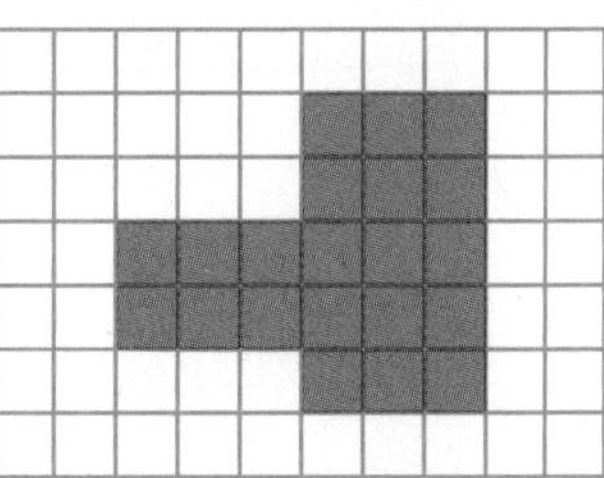

Area = _____ square units

12.

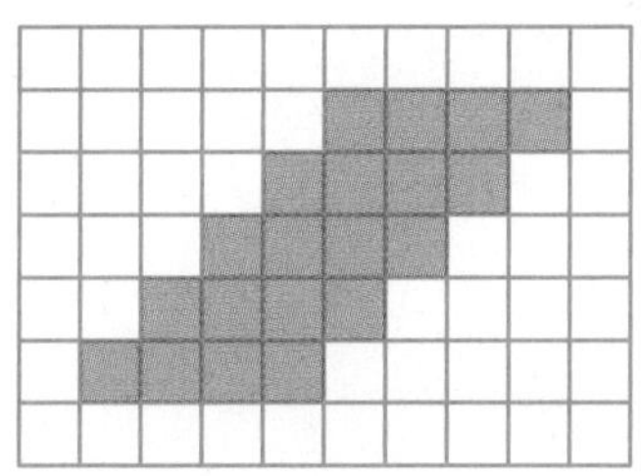

Area = _____ square units

Name ______________________

Fractions on a Number Line: Greater Than 1 10.5

Learning Target: Plot fractions greater than 1 on a number line.

Success Criteria:

- I can divide a number line into equal parts.
- I can label fractions on a number line.
- I can plot a fraction.

Divide each circle into halves. Shade three halves. Write the fraction.

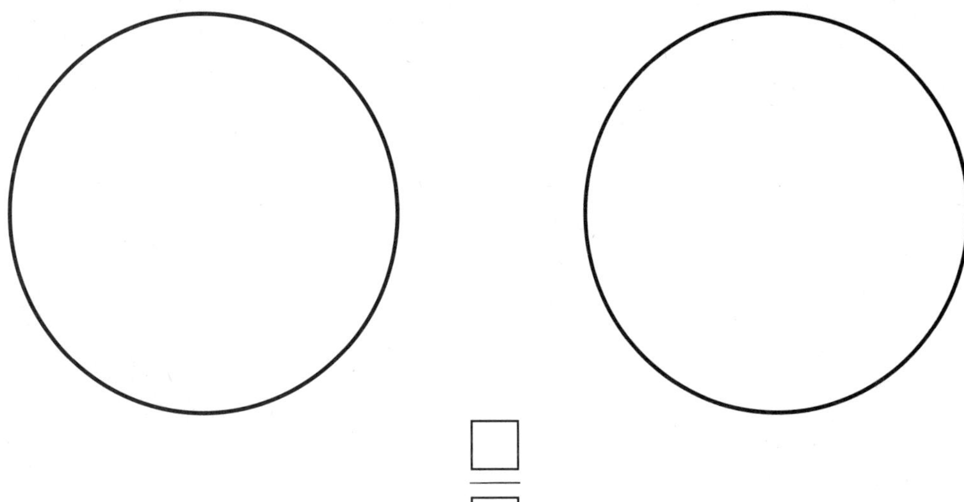

$\frac{\square}{\square}$

Precision Complete the fractions on the number line.

Plot $\frac{3}{2}$ on the number line. What do you notice? Explain.

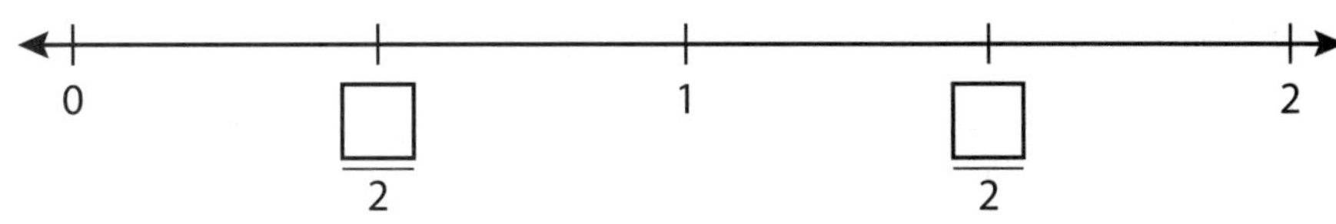

Think and Grow: Fractions on a Number Line: Greater Than 1

When the numerator is greater than the denominator, the fraction is greater than one whole.

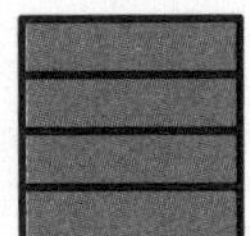 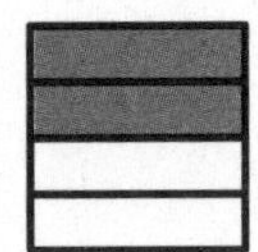

Each square is one whole. Six $\frac{1}{4}$s are shaded. So, $\frac{6}{4}$ is shaded.

You can show fractions greater than one whole on a number line.

Example Plot $\frac{6}{4}$ on the number line.

Step 1: Divide each whole into ______ equal parts.

Step 2: Label each tick mark on the number line.

Think: One $\frac{1}{4}$ is $\frac{1}{4}$. Two $\frac{1}{4}$s are $\frac{2}{4}$.

Step 3: Plot $\frac{6}{4}$.

Think: ______ $\frac{1}{4}$s are $\frac{6}{4}$.

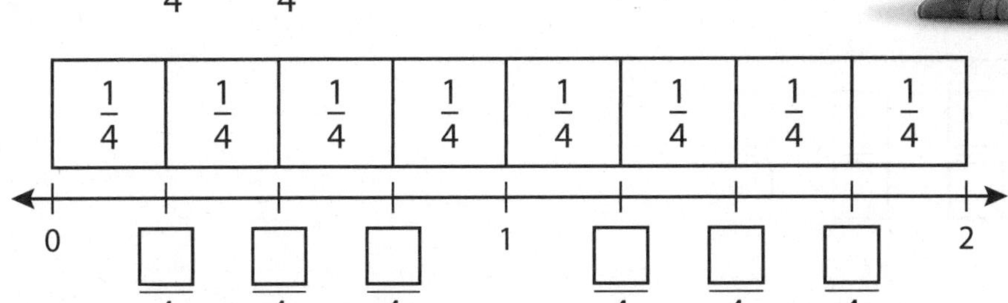

Show and Grow *I can do it!*

1. Plot $\frac{15}{8}$ on the number line.

$\frac{1}{8}$	$\frac{1}{8}$	$\frac{1}{8}$	$\frac{1}{8}$	$\frac{1}{8}$	$\frac{1}{8}$	$\frac{1}{8}$	$\frac{1}{8}$	$\frac{1}{8}$	$\frac{1}{8}$	$\frac{1}{8}$	$\frac{1}{8}$	$\frac{1}{8}$	$\frac{1}{8}$	$\frac{1}{8}$	$\frac{1}{8}$

0 1 2

Name ______________________________

Apply and Grow: Practice

Plot the fraction on the number line.

2. $\frac{7}{4}$

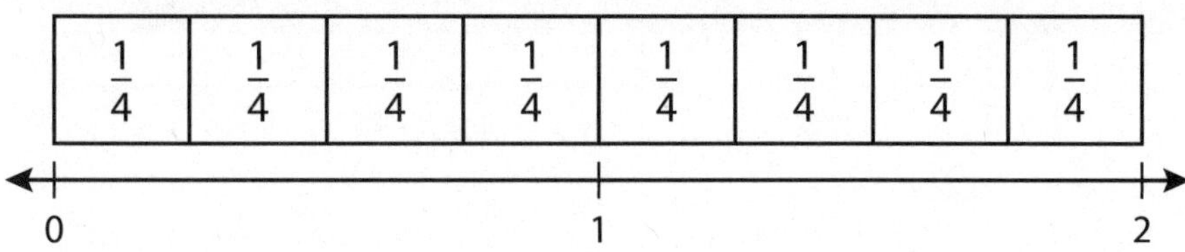

3. $\frac{9}{6}$

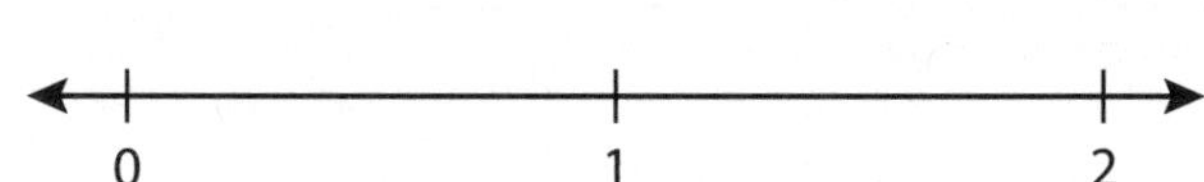

4. $\frac{5}{3}$

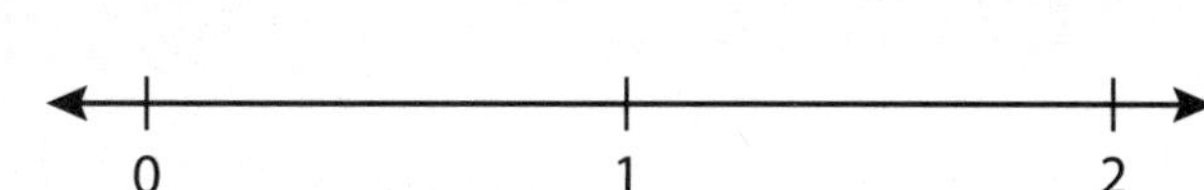

Structure Complete the number line.

5.

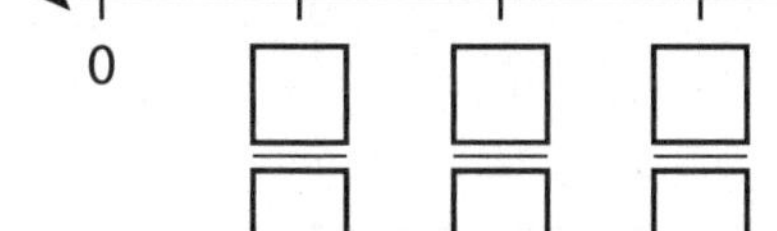

0 1 2

6.

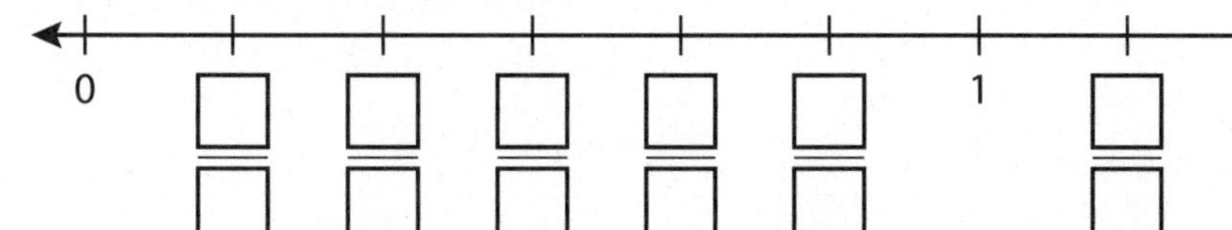

Communicate Clearly
How did you determine the denominator?

Number Sense Draw and shade a model for the plotted fraction.

7.

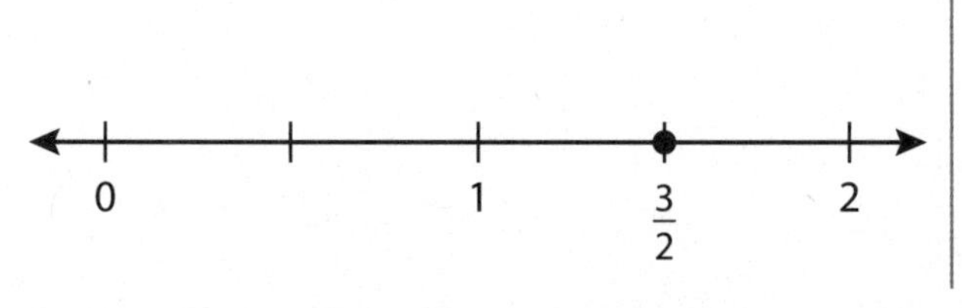

8.

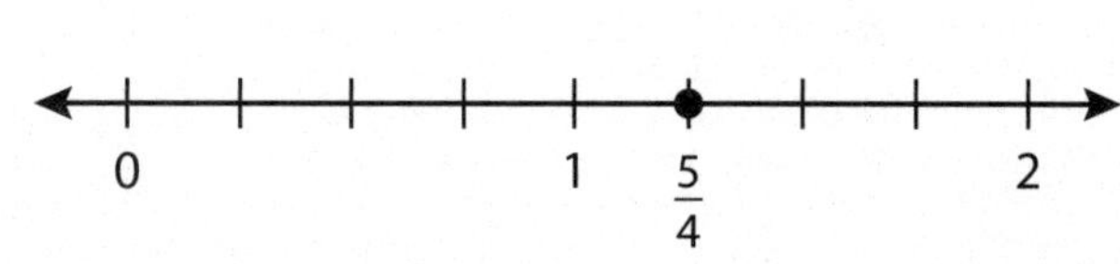

Think and Grow: Modeling Real Life

How far is the aquarium from the bank?

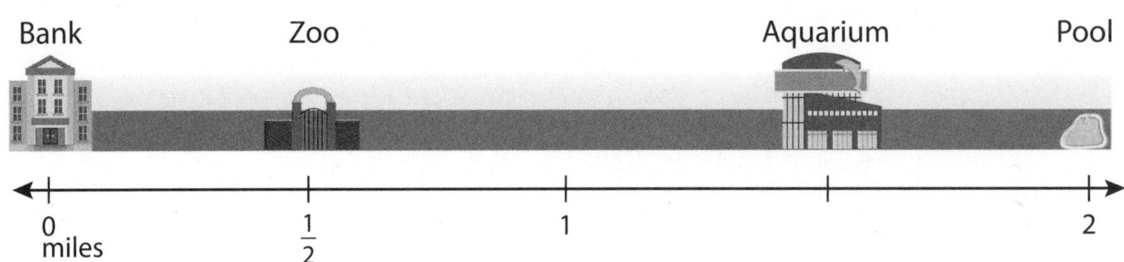

The aquarium is _____ miles from the bank.

Show and Grow *I can think deeper!*

Use the number line to answer the questions.

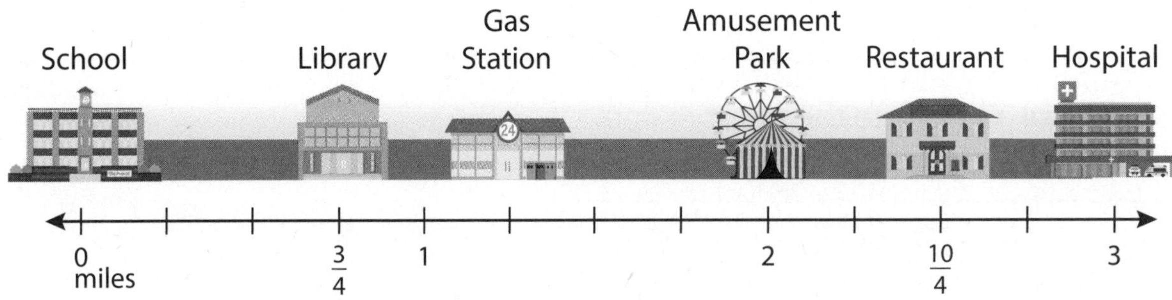

9. How far is the gas station from the school?

10. A post office is the same distance from the restaurant as it is from the hospital. How far is the post office from the school?

11. **DIG DEEPER!** How far is the gas station from the hospital?

12. **DIG DEEPER!** How far is the library from the amusement park?

Name ____________________

Learning Target: Plot fractions greater than 1 on a number line.

Example Plot $\frac{5}{3}$ on the number line.

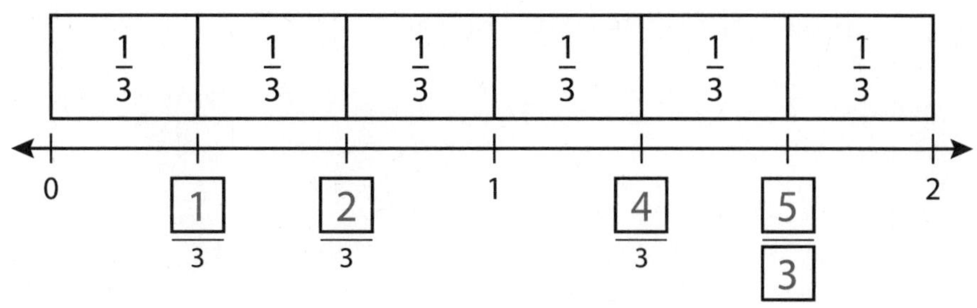

Plot the fraction on a number line.

1. $\frac{8}{6}$

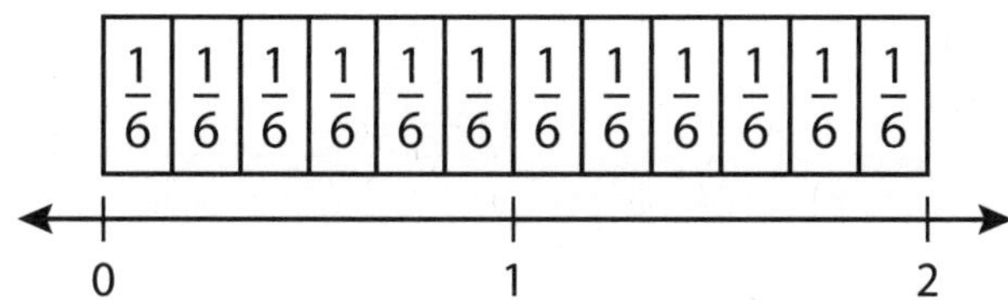

2. $\frac{3}{2}$

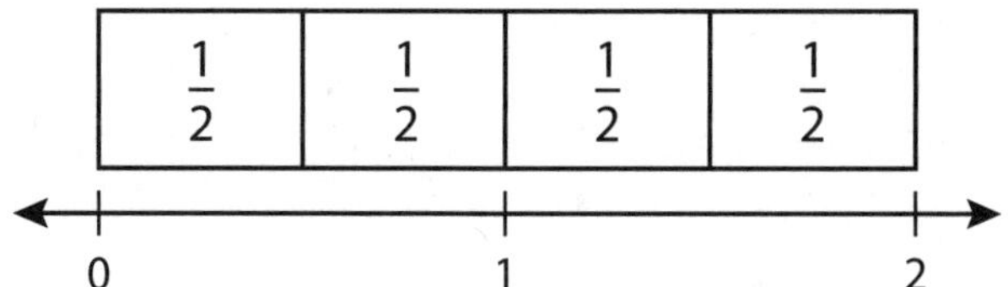

3. $\frac{7}{4}$

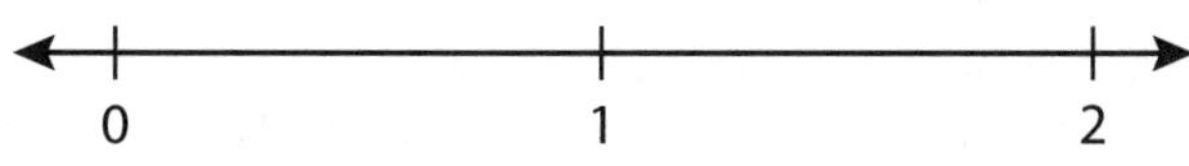

4. $\frac{7}{6}$

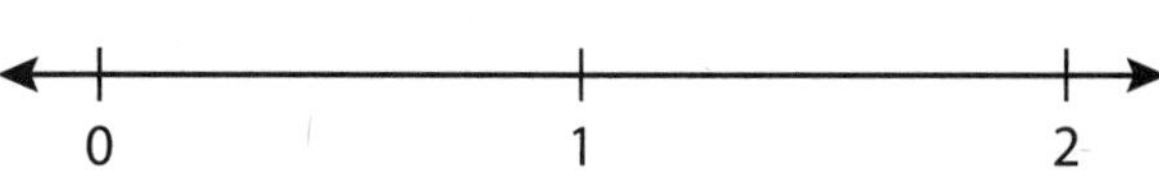

5. $\frac{4}{3}$

6. $\frac{6}{4}$

7. **YOU BE THE TEACHER** Newton says 2 is between 1 and $\frac{9}{8}$ on a number line. Is he correct? Explain.

8. **Communicate Clearly** Explain what the numerator of the fraction $\frac{7}{4}$ represents.

Reasoning What fraction is shaded? Plot the fraction on the number line.

9. 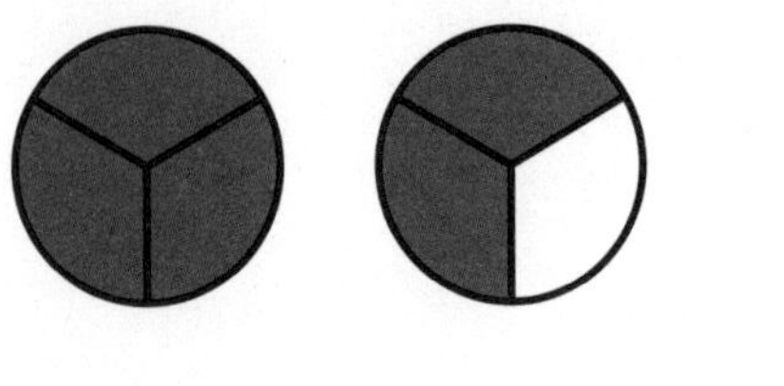

0 1 2

10. 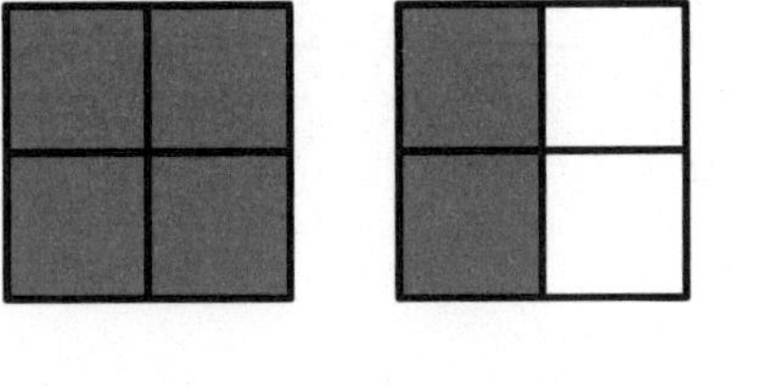

0 1 2

Modeling Real Life Use the number line to answer the questions.

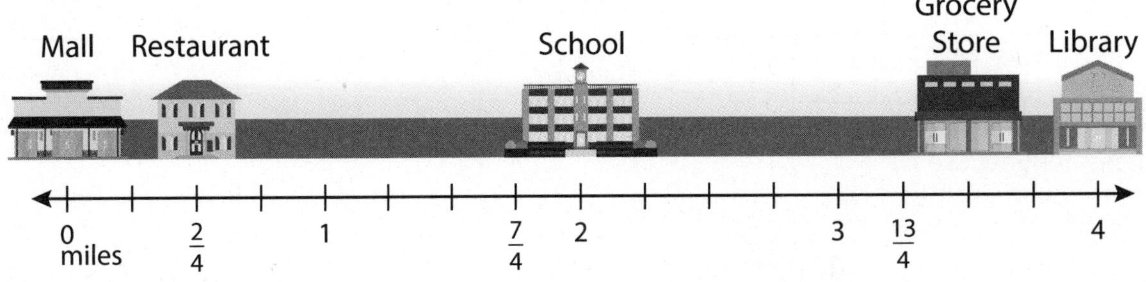

0 miles, $\frac{2}{4}$, 1, $\frac{7}{4}$, 2, 3, $\frac{13}{4}$, 4

11. How far is the grocery store from the school?

12. **DIG DEEPER!** A playground is the same distance from the grocery store as it is from the library. How far is the playground from the restaurant?

Review & Refresh

Round.

13. 25 Nearest ten: ______

14. 182 Nearest hundred: ______

Name ______________________________

Performance Task 10

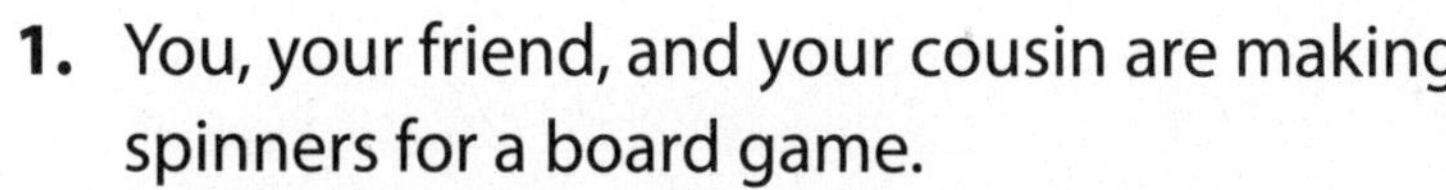

1. You, your friend, and your cousin are making spinners for a board game.

a. You design a spinner with 3 equal parts for your game. Draw the equal parts.

b. Your friend designs a spinner that is split into sixths. Does this spinner work for your game?

Modeling Real Life How else might a game designer use math to create a game?

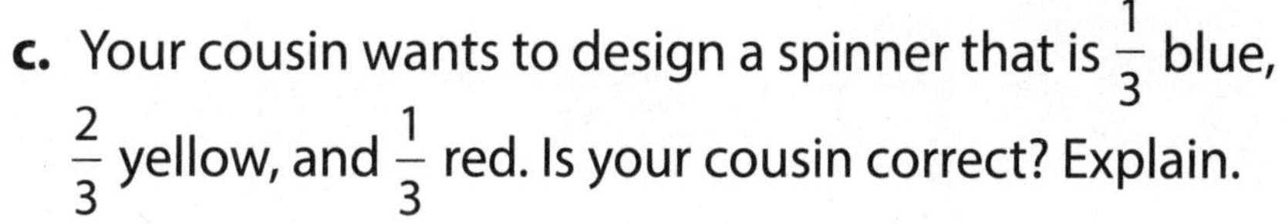

c. Your cousin wants to design a spinner that is $\frac{1}{3}$ blue, $\frac{2}{3}$ yellow, and $\frac{1}{3}$ red. Is your cousin correct? Explain.

2. Use the game board above to find the area of each color in square inches. Which color has the greatest area?

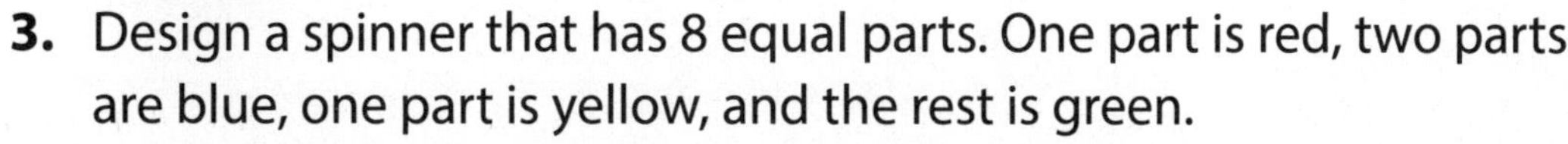

3. Design a spinner that has 8 equal parts. One part is red, two parts are blue, one part is yellow, and the rest is green.

a. What fraction of the spinner is red? blue? yellow? green?

b. Which color are you most likely to spin? Explain.

c. **Reasoning** Compare your answers to parts a and b. What do you notice?

Fraction Spin and Cover

Directions:

1. Take turns using the spinners to find which fraction model to cover.
2. Use a counter to cover the fraction model.
3. Repeat this process until you cover all of the models.
4. The player with the most fraction models covered wins!

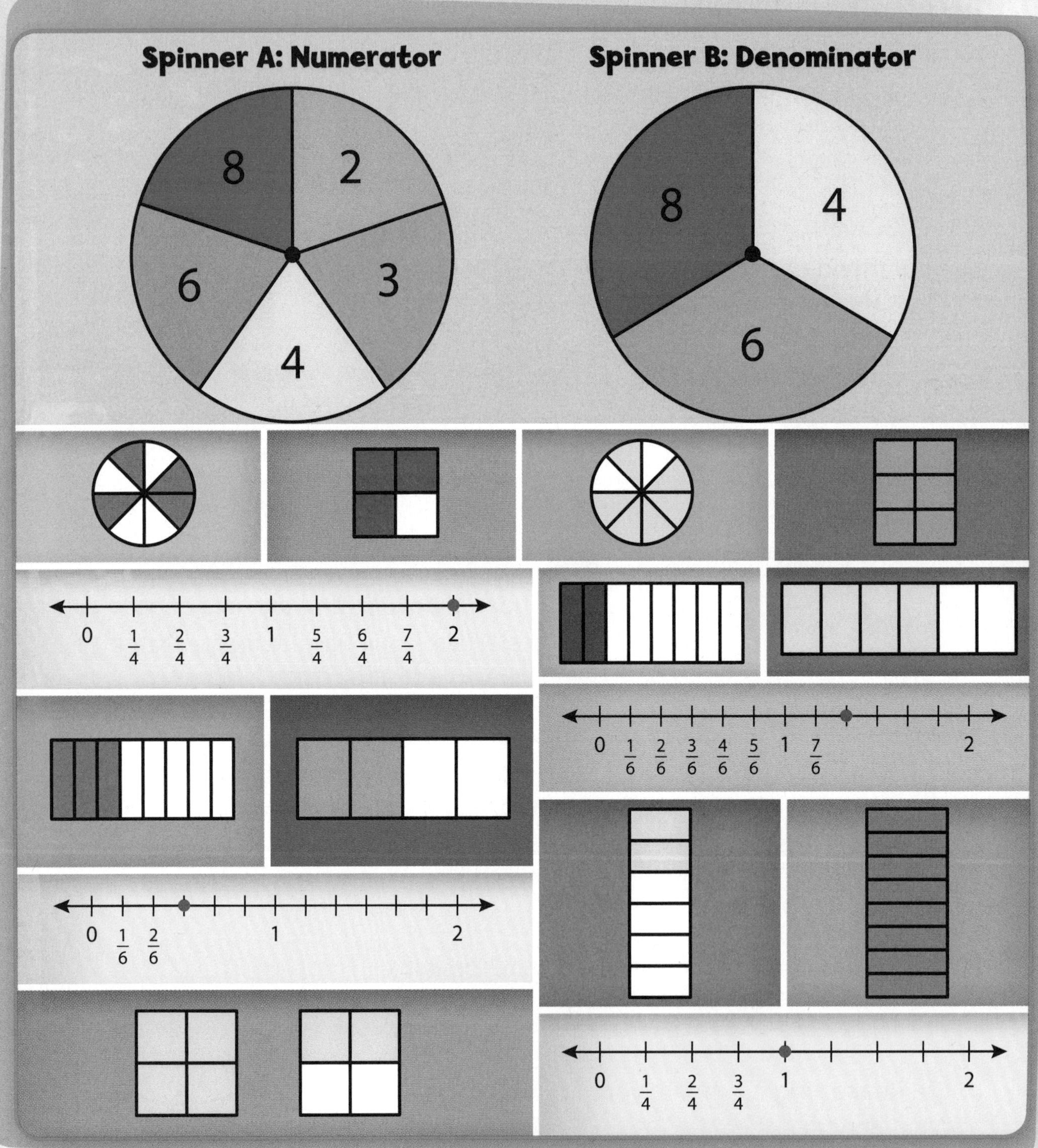

Name ______________________________

Chapter Practice 10

10.1 Equal Parts of a Whole

Tell whether the shape shows equal parts or unequal parts. If the shape shows equal parts, then name them.

1.

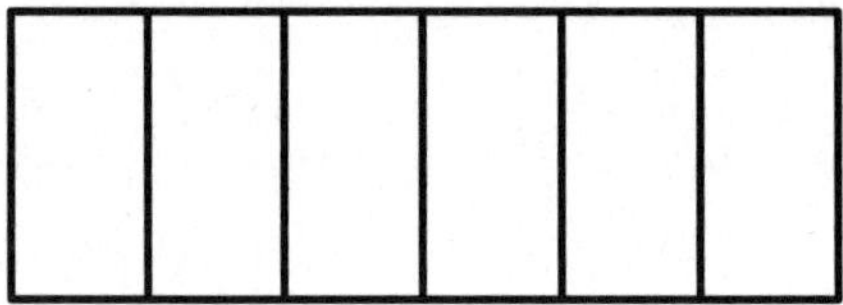

__________ parts

____

2.

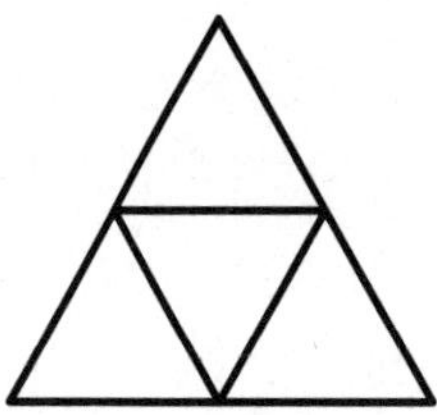

__________ parts

____

3.

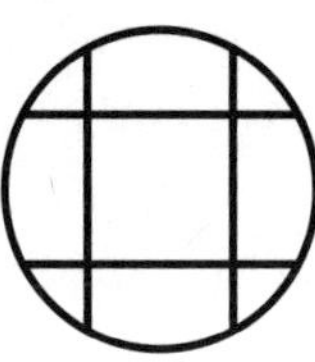

__________ parts

____

4.

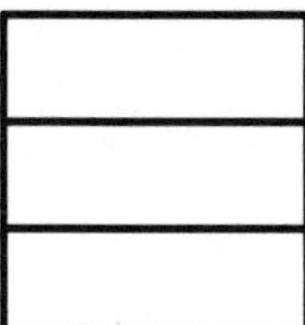

__________ parts

____

5. Divide the triangle into two equal parts. Then name the equal parts.

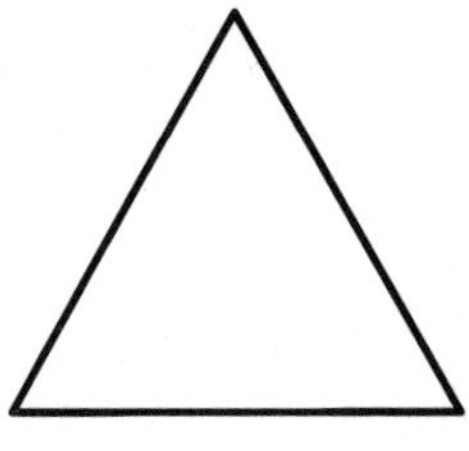

____

6. Divide the circle into eight equal parts. Then name the equal parts.

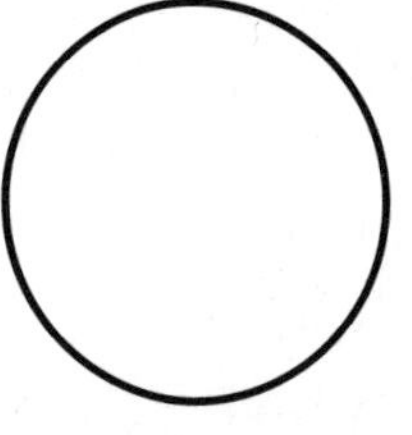

____

10.2 Understand a Unit Fraction

What fraction of the whole is shaded?

7. 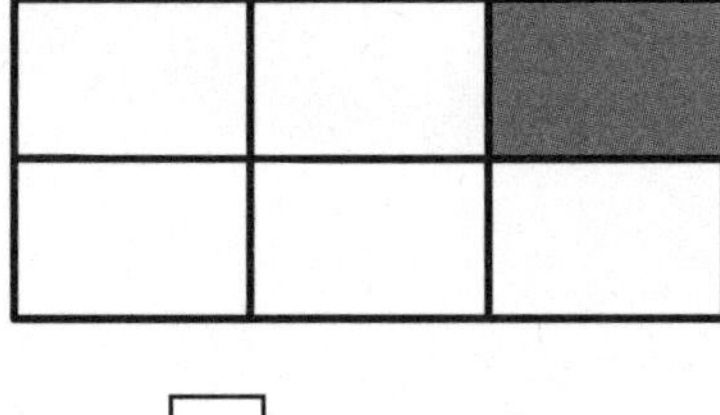

☐/☐ is shaded.

8. 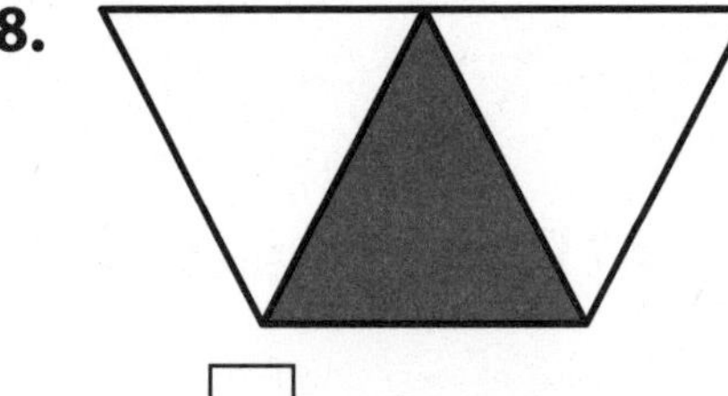

☐/☐ is shaded.

9. Divide the square into four equal parts. Shade one part. What fraction of the whole is shaded?

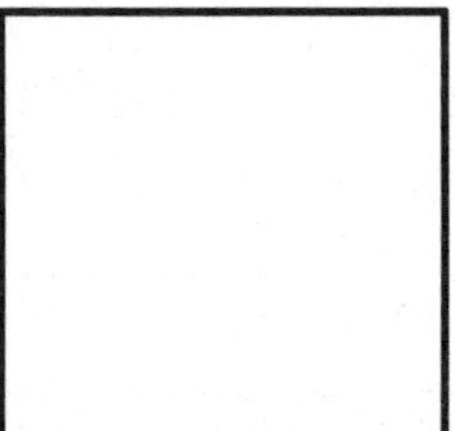

☐/☐ is shaded.

10. Divide the circle into eight equal parts. Shade one part. What fraction of the whole is shaded?

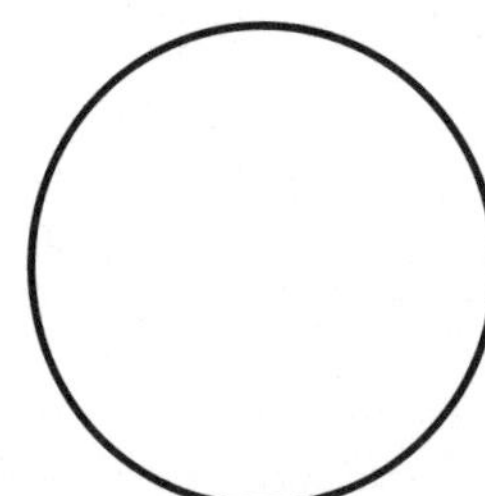

☐/☐ is shaded.

11. MP **Modeling Real Life** Descartes arranges his bedroom into four equal parts. His bed takes up two parts. His dresser takes up one part. The rest of his bedroom is free space. What fraction of Descartes's bedroom is free space?

10.3 Write Fractions of a Whole

What fraction of the whole is shaded?

12. 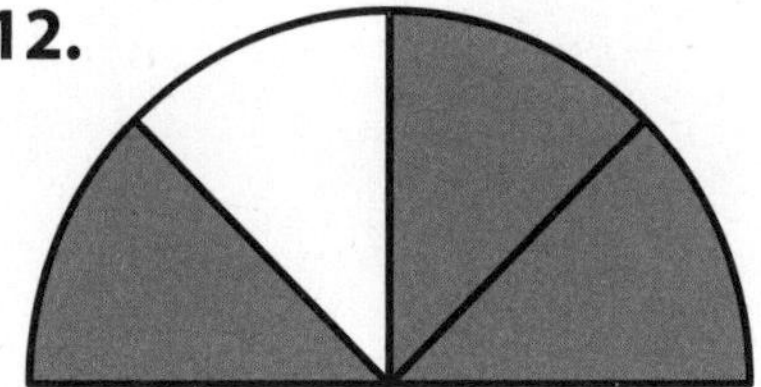

☐/☐ is shaded.

13. 

☐/☐ is shaded.

14. Divide the circle into sixths. Shade 4 of the equal parts. Then write a fraction for the shaded parts.

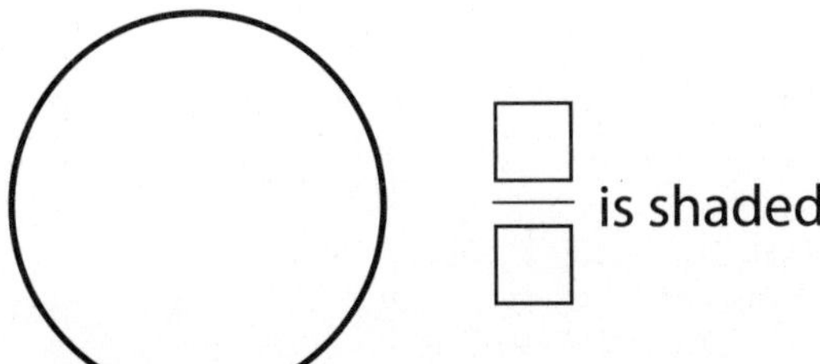

$\frac{\square}{\square}$ is shaded.

15. Divide the square into thirds. Shade 2 of the equal parts. Then write a fraction for the shaded parts.

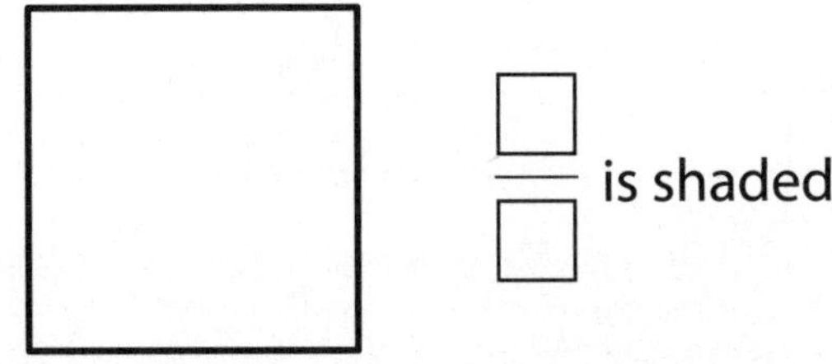

$\frac{\square}{\square}$ is shaded.

16. **MP Modeling Real Life** A circular mandala poster is divided into eight equal parts. You color one part red, three parts green, and two parts yellow. What fraction of the poster do you have left to color?

10.4 Fractions on a Number Line: Less Than 1

Plot the fraction on the number line.

17. $\frac{3}{4}$

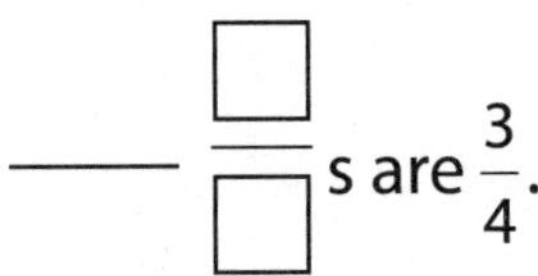

____ $\frac{\square}{\square}$ s are $\frac{3}{4}$.

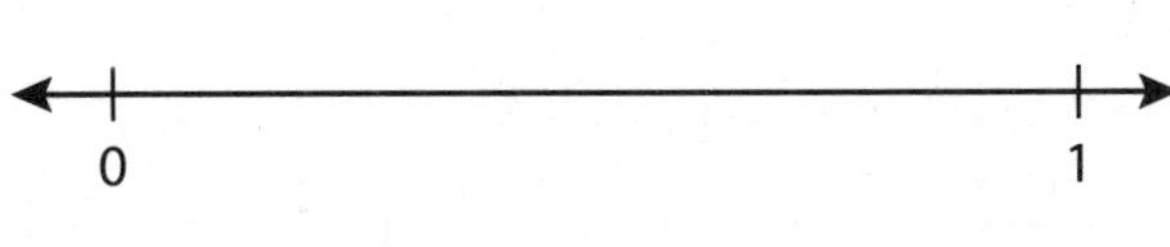

18. $\frac{5}{6}$

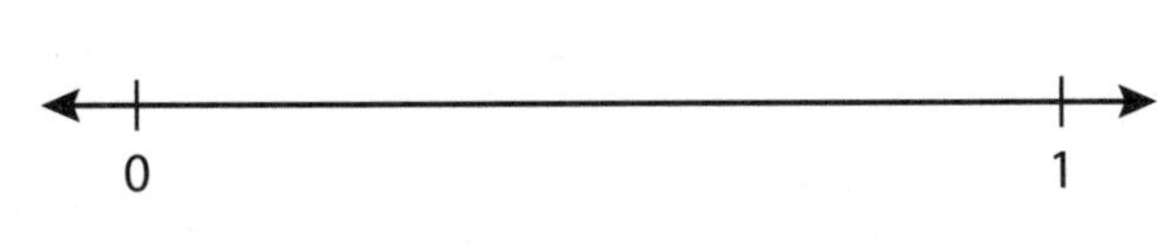

19. $\frac{2}{3}$

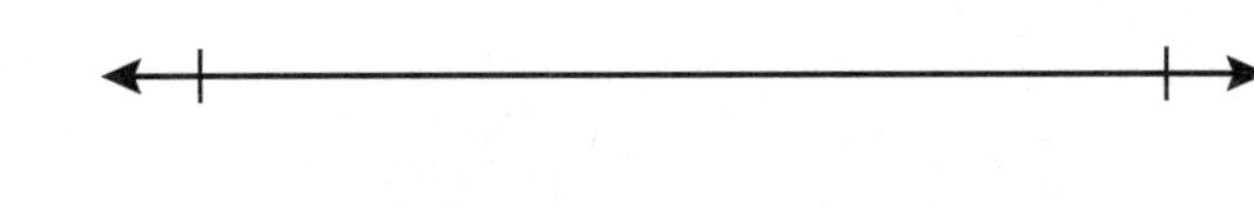

Plot the fraction on a number line.

20. $\frac{3}{6}$

21. $\frac{5}{8}$

22. **Modeling Real Life** You follow a recipe and make three servings. How many servings can you make using $\frac{1}{3}$ of each ingredient in the recipe?

10.5 Fractions on a Number Line: Greater Than 1

Plot the fraction on the number line.

23. $\frac{4}{3}$

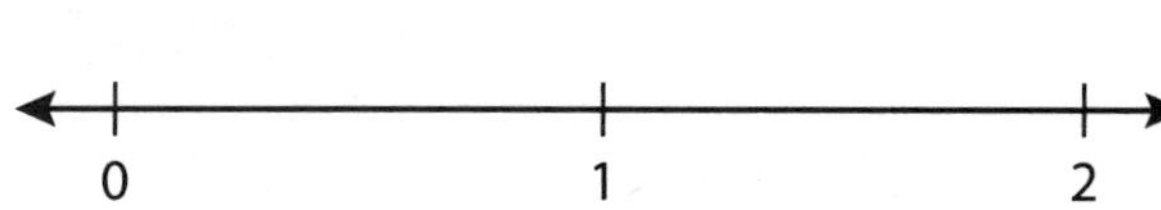

24. $\frac{9}{6}$

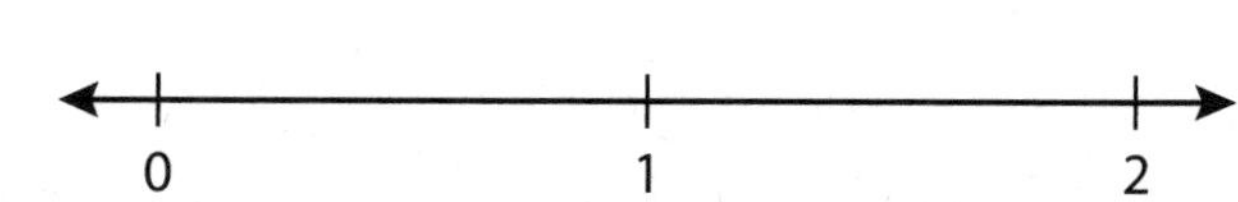

25. **Structure** Complete the number line.

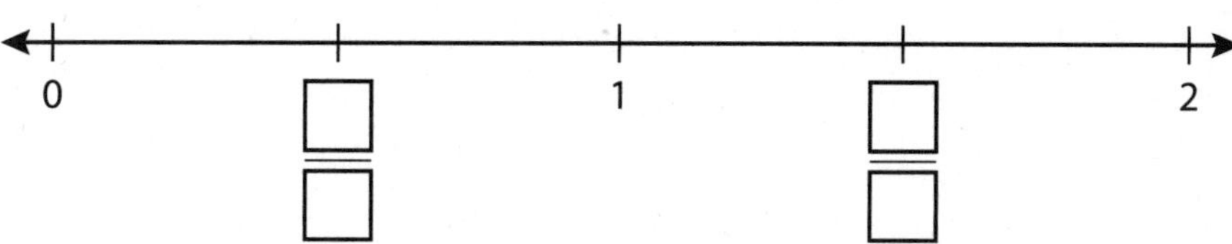

26. **Number Sense** What fraction is shaded? Plot the fraction on the number line.

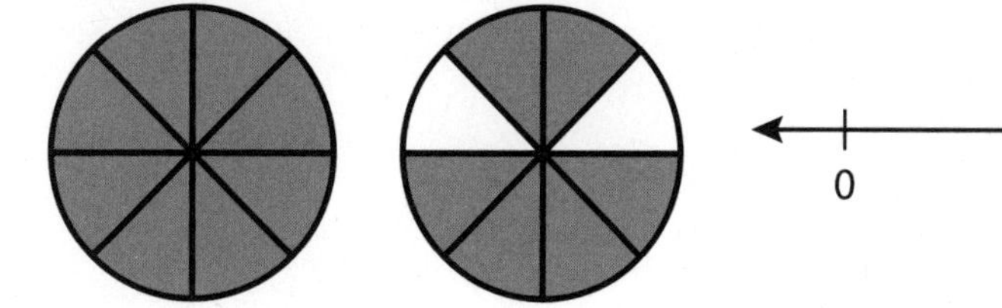

0 1 2

11 Understand Fraction Equivalence and Comparison

- Do you like to cook? What is your favorite recipe?
- How do you use fractions when cooking? Why is it important to understand fractions when following a recipe?

Chapter Learning Target:
Understand fractions.

Chapter Success Criteria:

- I can define a fraction.
- I can find fractions on a number line.
- I can explain how to use a number line to find fractions.
- I can compare fractions on a number line.

Name ______________________________

11 Vocabulary

Review Words
eighths
sixths
unit fraction
whole

Organize It

Use the review words to complete the graphic organizer.

Fraction
A number that represents part of a ______

  $\frac{1}{3}$

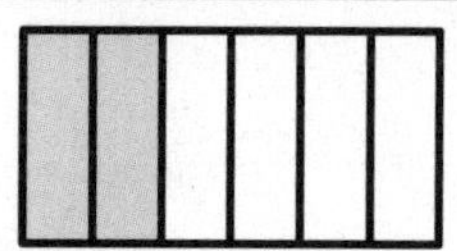 $\frac{2}{6}$

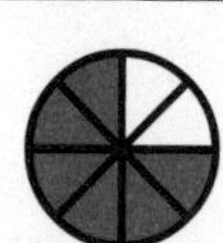 $\frac{6}{8}$

Define It

Use your vocabulary cards to complete the definitions.

1. equivalent: Having the same ____________

2. equivalent fractions: Two or more ____________ that name the same ____________ of a ____________

Chapter 11 Vocabulary Cards

equivalent

equivalent fractions

Two or more fractions that name the same part of a whole

$\frac{2}{3} = \frac{4}{6}$

Having the same value

$\frac{8}{8} = 1$

$3 = \frac{3}{1}$

$2 = \frac{4}{2} = \frac{6}{3}$

Name ______________________________

Equivalent Fractions 11.1

Learning Target: Model and write equivalent fractions.

Success Criteria:

- I can model equivalent fractions.
- I can write equivalent fractions.

Explore and Grow

Use the model to write fractions that are the same size as $\frac{1}{2}$.

<table>
<tr><td colspan="24" align="center">1 whole</td></tr>
<tr><td colspan="12" align="center">$\frac{1}{2}$</td><td colspan="12" align="center">$\frac{1}{2}$</td></tr>
<tr><td colspan="8" align="center">$\frac{1}{3}$</td><td colspan="8" align="center">$\frac{1}{3}$</td><td colspan="8" align="center">$\frac{1}{3}$</td></tr>
<tr><td colspan="6" align="center">$\frac{1}{4}$</td><td colspan="6" align="center">$\frac{1}{4}$</td><td colspan="6" align="center">$\frac{1}{4}$</td><td colspan="6" align="center">$\frac{1}{4}$</td></tr>
<tr><td colspan="4" align="center">$\frac{1}{6}$</td><td colspan="4" align="center">$\frac{1}{6}$</td><td colspan="4" align="center">$\frac{1}{6}$</td><td colspan="4" align="center">$\frac{1}{6}$</td><td colspan="4" align="center">$\frac{1}{6}$</td><td colspan="4" align="center">$\frac{1}{6}$</td></tr>
<tr><td colspan="3" align="center">$\frac{1}{8}$</td><td colspan="3" align="center">$\frac{1}{8}$</td><td colspan="3" align="center">$\frac{1}{8}$</td><td colspan="3" align="center">$\frac{1}{8}$</td><td colspan="3" align="center">$\frac{1}{8}$</td><td colspan="3" align="center">$\frac{1}{8}$</td><td colspan="3" align="center">$\frac{1}{8}$</td><td colspan="3" align="center">$\frac{1}{8}$</td></tr>
</table>

MP **Reasoning** Can you write a fraction with a denominator of 8 that is the same size as $\frac{3}{4}$? Explain.

Think and Grow: Model Equivalent Fractions

Two or more numbers that have the same value are **equivalent**. Two or more fractions that name the same part of a whole are **equivalent fractions**.

Example Use the models to find an equivalent fraction for $\frac{2}{3}$.

Both models show the same whole.

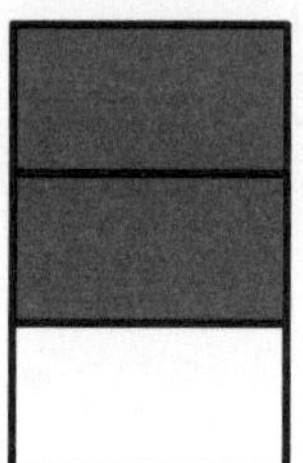

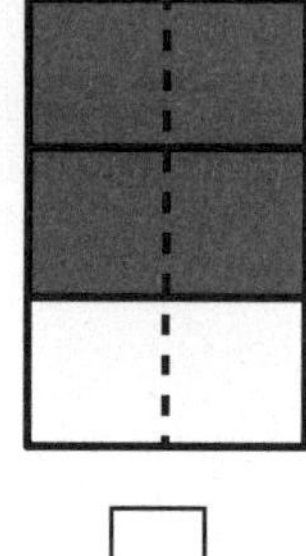

The shaded parts show the same part of the whole.

$\frac{2}{3}$ $\frac{\square}{6}$

$\frac{2}{3}$ and $\frac{\square}{6}$ are equivalent fractions. So, $\frac{2}{3} = \frac{\square}{6}$.

Show and Grow *I can do it!*

Use the models to find an equivalent fraction. Both models show the same whole.

1.

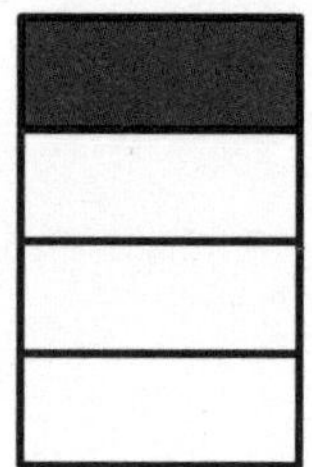

$\frac{1}{4} = \frac{\square}{\square}$

2.

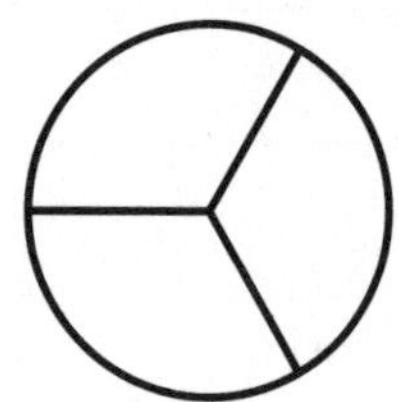

$\frac{2}{6} = \frac{\square}{\square}$

3. Shade 1 part of the model. Then divide the model into 4 equal parts. Write the equivalent fraction.

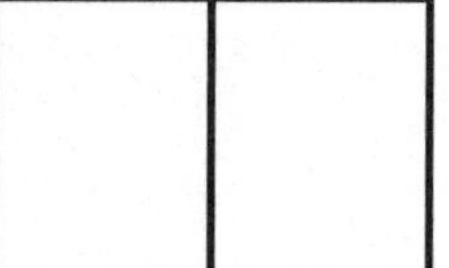

$\frac{1}{2} = \frac{\square}{\square}$

Name ______________________________

Apply and Grow: Practice

Use models to find an equivalent fraction. Both models show the same whole.

4. 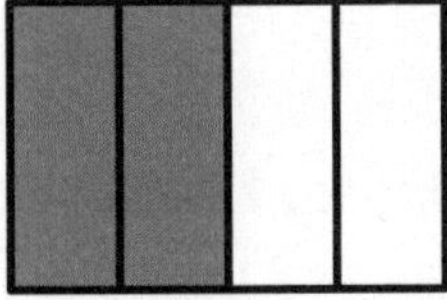

$\frac{2}{4} = \frac{\square}{\square}$

5. 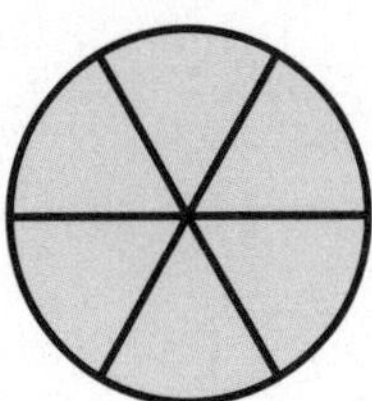

$\frac{6}{6} = \frac{\square}{\square}$

6. Shade 1 part of the model. Then divide the model into 6 equal parts. Write the equivalent fraction.

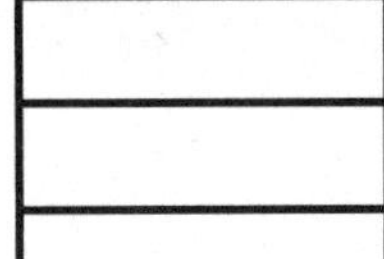

$\frac{1}{3} = \frac{\square}{\square}$

Find the equivalent fraction.

7. $\frac{1}{2} = \frac{\square}{8}$

8. $\frac{4}{4} = \frac{\square}{2}$

9. $\frac{2}{3} = \frac{\square}{6}$

10. $\frac{3}{6} = \frac{\square}{2}$

11. MP **Structure** Descartes shades $\frac{3}{4}$ of a rectangle. Divide and shade the model to show an equivalent fraction for $\frac{3}{4}$.

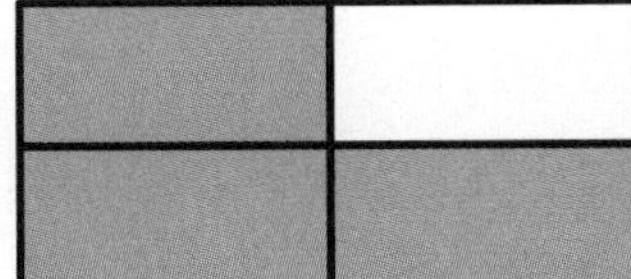

12. **Which One Doesn't Belong?** Which model does *not* belong with the other three?

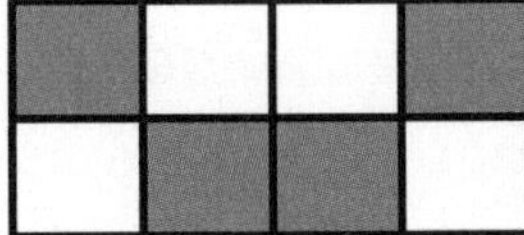

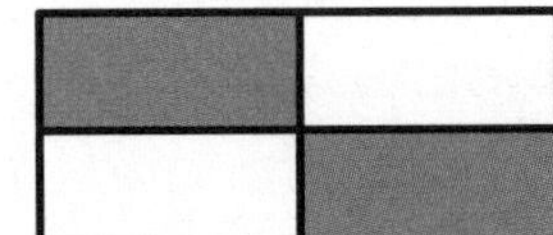

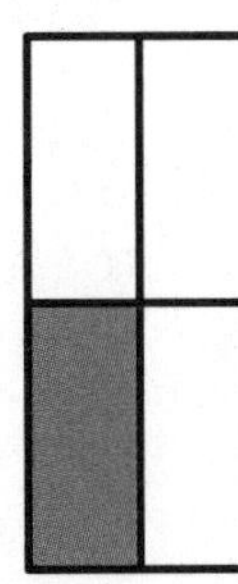

Think and Grow: Modeling Real Life

You, Newton, and Descartes divide your posters for a science fair as shown. You finish 3 parts, Newton finishes 2 parts, and Descartes finishes 4 parts. Who has finished the same amount?

Model: You Newton Descartes

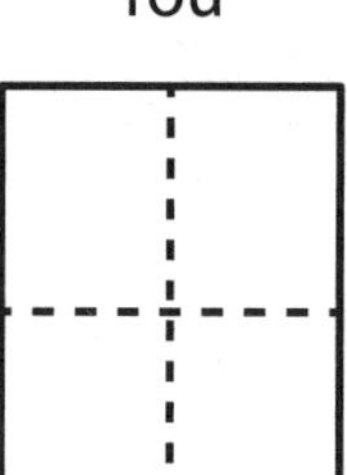

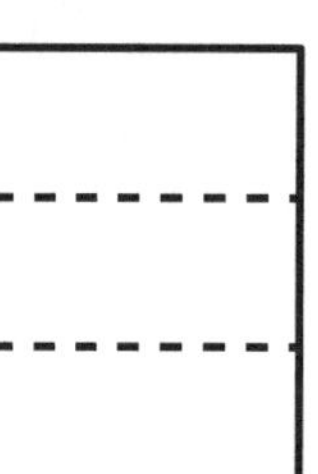

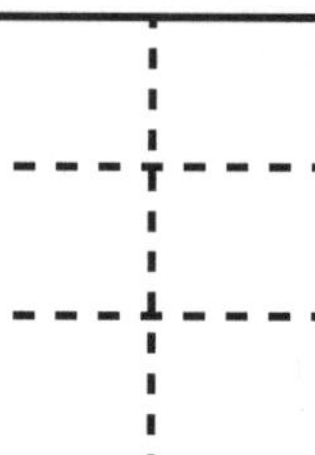

Fraction finished:

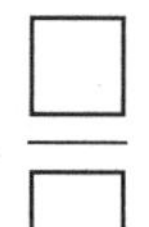

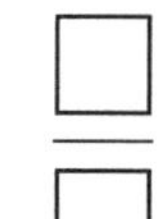

_________ and _________ finish the same amount.

Show and Grow *I can think deeper!*

13. You, Newton, and Descartes divide your submarine sandwiches as shown. You eat 1 part, Newton eats 2 parts, and Descartes eats 2 parts. Who eats the same amount?

You Newton Descartes

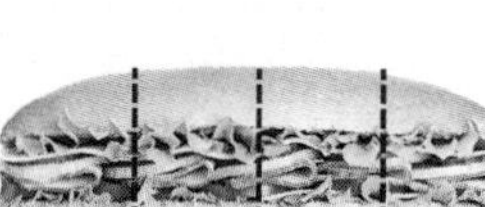

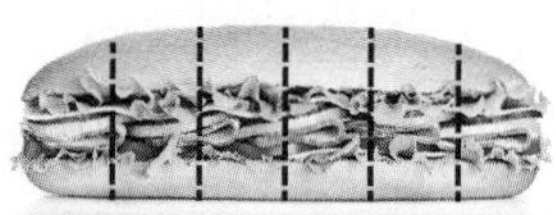

14. **DIG DEEPER!** You and your friend have small pizzas. You cut your pizza into sixths. Your friend cuts her pizza into eighths. You eat $\frac{3}{6}$ of your pizza. Your friend eats the same amount of her pizza. What fraction of her pizza does your friend eat? How many slices does your friend eat? Explain.

Name ______________________________

Homework & Practice 11.1

Learning Target: Model and write equivalent fractions.

Example Use the models to find an equivalent fraction for $\frac{3}{4}$.

Both models show the same whole.

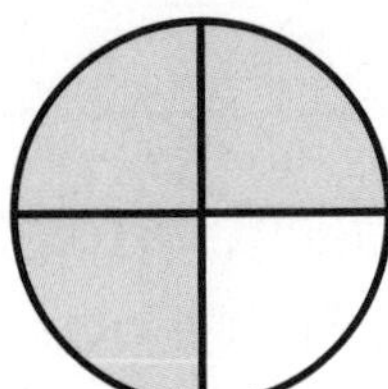

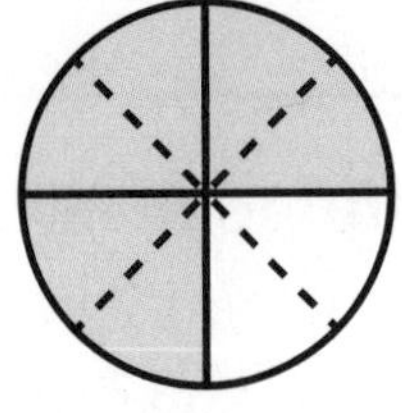

$\frac{3}{4}$ $\frac{\boxed{6}}{8}$

$\frac{3}{4}$ and $\frac{\boxed{6}}{8}$ are equivalent fractions. So, $\frac{3}{4} = \frac{\boxed{6}}{8}$.

Use models to find an equivalent fraction. Both models show the same whole.

1.

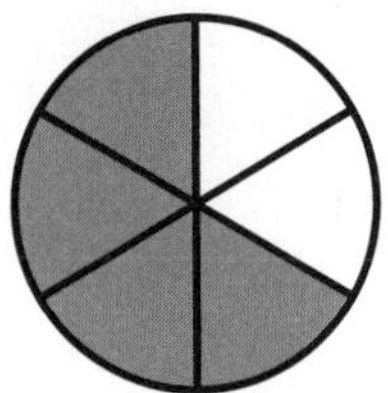

$\frac{4}{6} = \frac{\square}{\square}$

2.

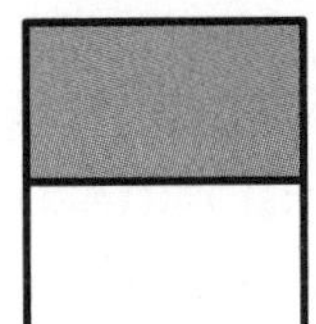

$\frac{1}{2} = \frac{\square}{\square}$

3. Shade 1 part of the model. Then divide the model into 8 equal parts. Write the equivalent fraction.

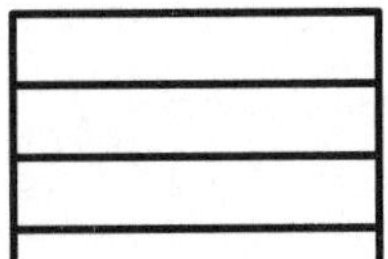

$\frac{1}{4} = \frac{\square}{\square}$

Find the equivalent fraction.

4. $\frac{2}{2} = \frac{\square}{8}$

5. $\frac{6}{8} = \frac{\square}{4}$

6. $\frac{1}{3} = \frac{\square}{6}$

7. $\frac{2}{4} = \frac{\square}{2}$

8. **Open-Ended** Divide one model into an odd number of equal parts and the other model into an even number of equal parts. Then model and write two equivalent fractions.

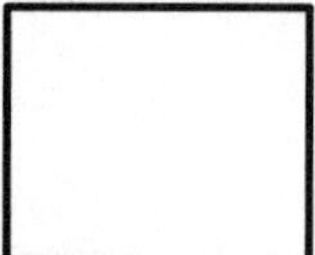

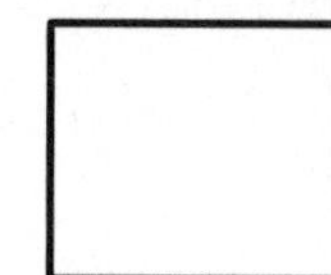

$\frac{\square}{\square} = \frac{\square}{\square}$

---

9. **MP Modeling Real Life** You, Newton, and Descartes divide your portrait canvases as shown. You paint 2 parts, Newton paints 2 parts, and Descartes paints 8 parts. Who paints the same amount of the portrait canvas?

You

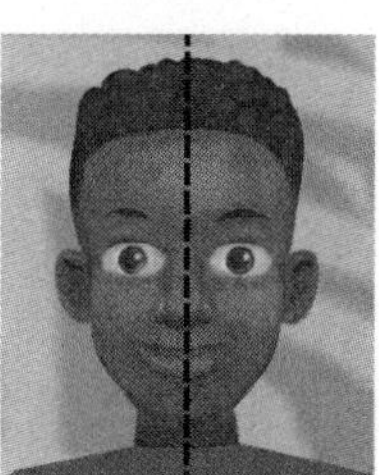

Newton

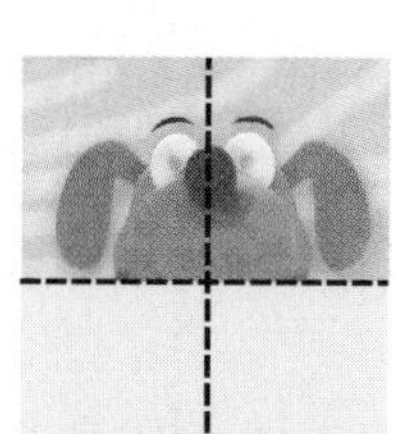

Descartes

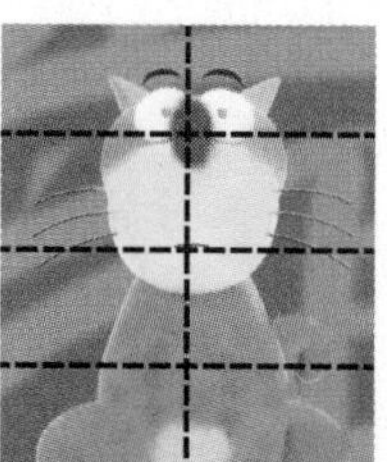

---

10. **DIG DEEPER!** You and your friend paint 2 roundabouts for a park. You divide your roundabout into thirds. Your friend divides his roundabout into sixths. You paint $\frac{1}{3}$ of your roundabout. Your friend paints the same amount of his roundabout. What fraction does your friend paint? Explain.

Review & Refresh

11. Round to the nearest ten to estimate the sum.

$$\begin{array}{r} 431 \\ +\ 109 \\ \hline \end{array}$$

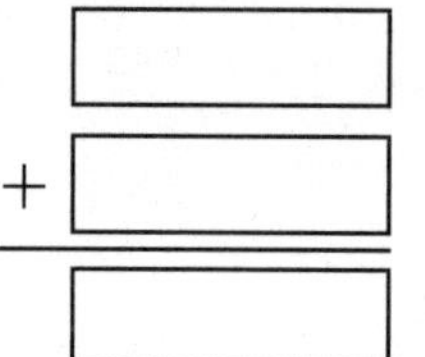

12. Round to the nearest hundred to estimate the sum.

$$\begin{array}{r} 551 \\ +\ 268 \\ \hline \end{array}$$

$$\begin{array}{r} \square \\ +\ \square \\ \hline \square \end{array}$$

Name ________________________________

Equivalent Fractions on a Number Line

11.2

Learning Target: Use a number line to find equivalent fractions.

Success Criteria:

- I can plot fractions on a number line.
- I can find equivalent fractions on a number line.
- I can explain how to use a number line to find equivalent fractions.

Explore and Grow

Use Fraction Strips to label thirds on the number line.

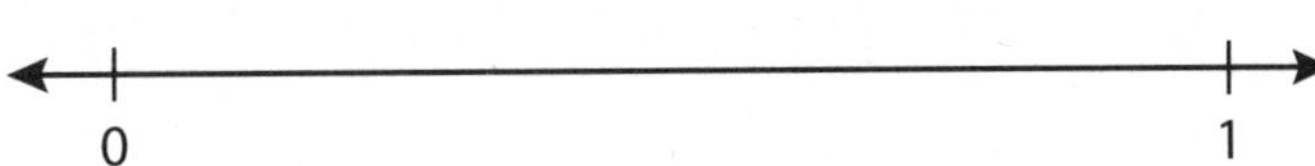

Use Fraction Strips to label sixths on the number line.

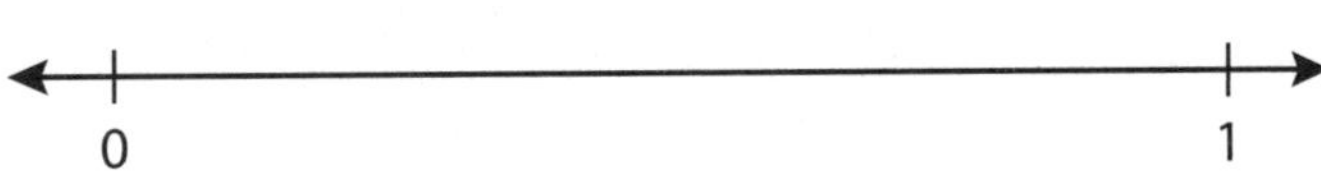

Use the number lines to complete the equivalent fraction.

$$\frac{1}{3} = \frac{\square}{6}$$

Structure How can you tell whether fractions are equivalent using a number line?

Think and Grow: Equivalent Fractions on a Number Line

You can use a number line to find equivalent fractions. Equivalent fractions represent the same point on a number line.

Example Use a number line to find an equivalent fraction for $\frac{3}{4}$.

Step 1: Plot $\frac{3}{4}$ on a number line.

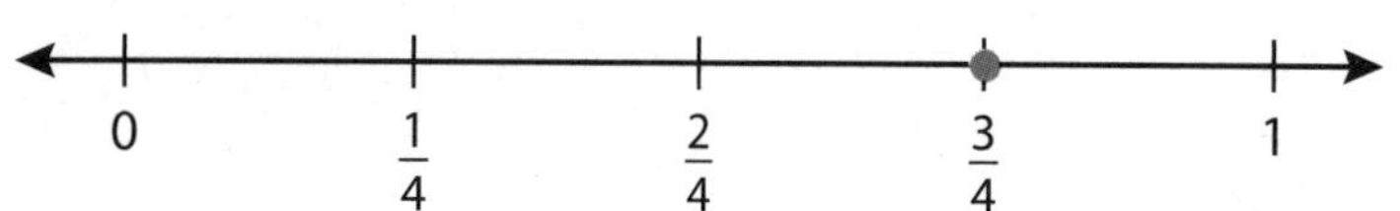

Step 2: Divide the number line into eighths. Label each tick mark to show eighths.

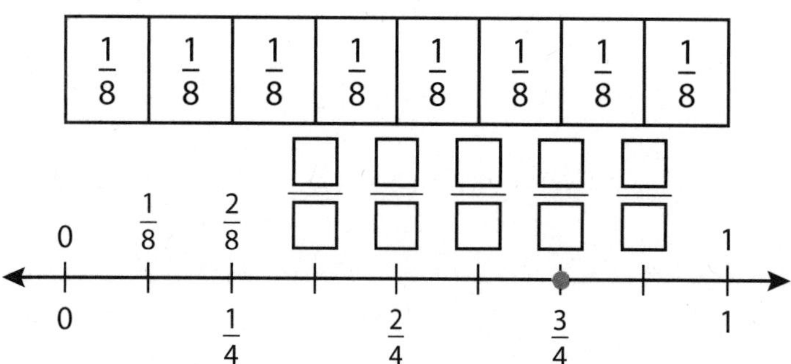

The fractions that name the same point are $\frac{3}{4}$ and $\frac{\square}{\square}$. So, $\frac{3}{4} = \frac{\square}{\square}$.

Show and Grow *I can do it!*

1. Use the number line to find an equivalent fraction.

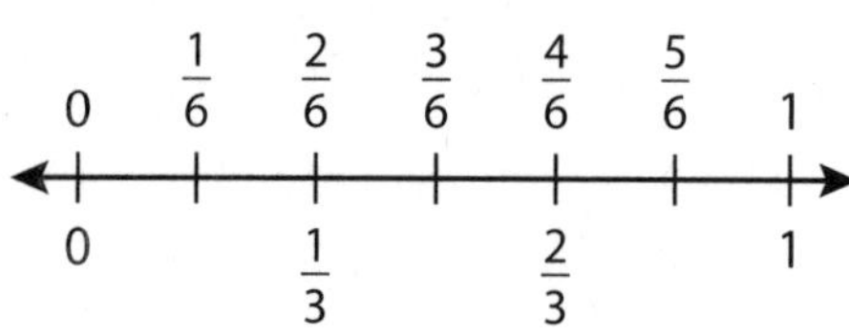

$\frac{2}{3} = \frac{\square}{\square}$

2. Write two fractions that name the point shown.

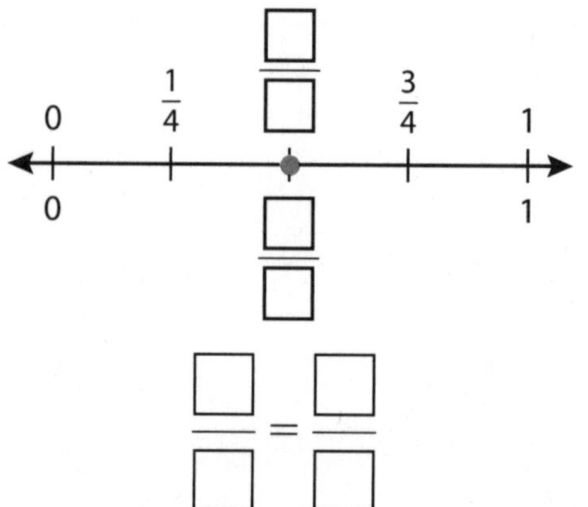

$\frac{\square}{\square} = \frac{\square}{\square}$

Name ______________________________

Apply and Grow: Practice

Write two fractions that name the point shown.

3.

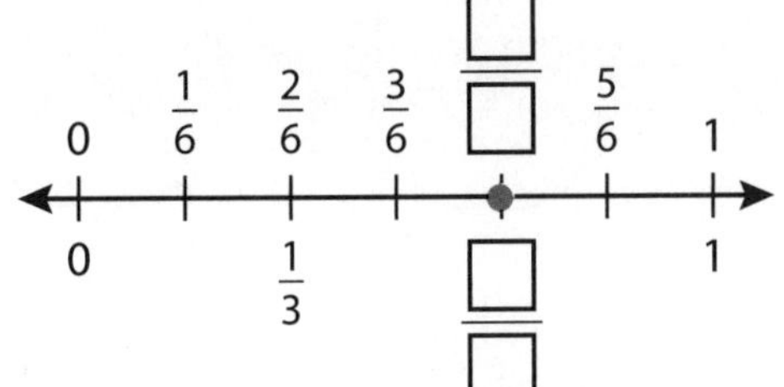

$\frac{\square}{\square} = \frac{\square}{\square}$

4.

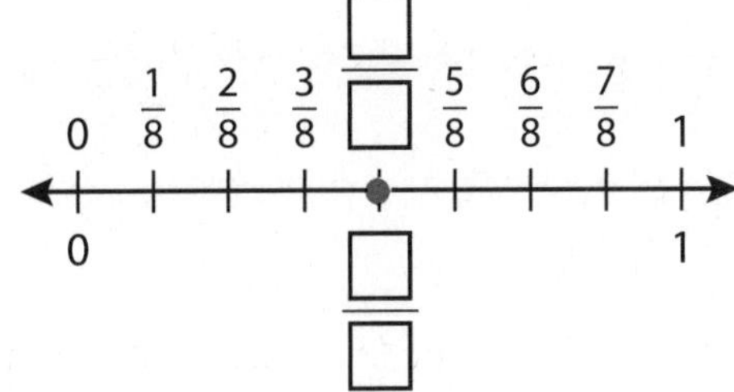

$\frac{\square}{\square} = \frac{\square}{\square}$

5.

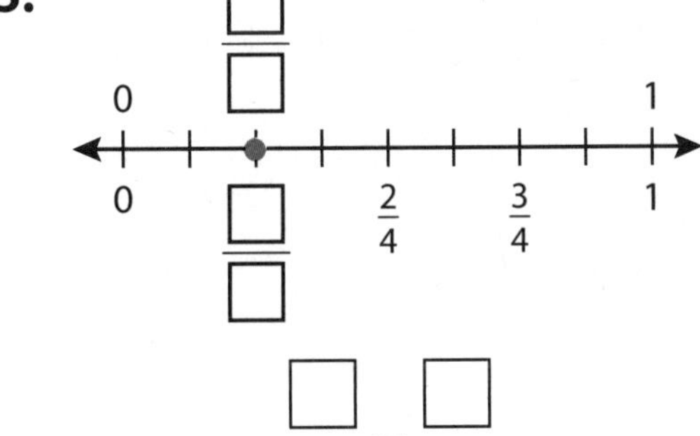

$\frac{\square}{\square} = \frac{\square}{\square}$

6.

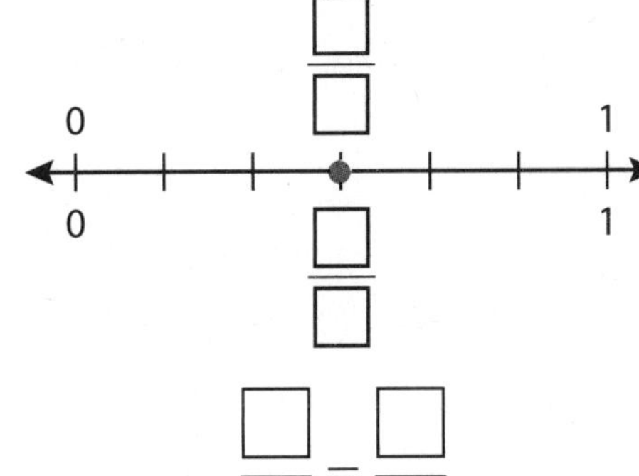

$\frac{\square}{\square} = \frac{\square}{\square}$

7. **MP YOU BE THE TEACHER** Your friend says $\frac{3}{4}$ and $\frac{6}{8}$ are *not* equivalent because they are not the same distance from 0. Is your friend correct? Explain.

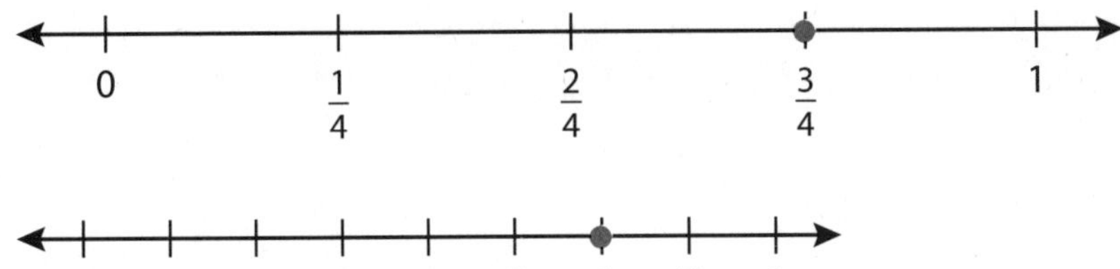

8. **MP Communicate Clearly** Explain why $\frac{1}{3}$ is equal to two $\frac{1}{6}$s.

Think and Grow: Modeling Real Life

Newton rests after biking $\frac{2}{3}$ of a race. Descartes rests after biking $\frac{2}{6}$ of the same race. Do they rest at the same point along the race path?

Model:

They ________ rest at the same point.

Explain:

Show and Grow *I can think deeper!*

9. Newton hikes $\frac{7}{8}$ of a trail. Descartes hikes $\frac{3}{4}$ of the same trail. Do they hike the same distance along the trail?

10. Newton chases Descartes for $\frac{3}{6}$ mile. Descartes turns around and chases Newton an equal distance. Write two equivalent fractions that can describe how far Descartes chases Newton.

11. **DIG DEEPER!** You cut a quiche into 8 equal slices. Your family eats $\frac{1}{2}$ of the quiche. How many slices does your family eat? Explain.

Name ____________________

Homework & Practice 11.2

Learning Target: Use a number line to find equivalent fractions.

Example Use a number line to find an equivalent fraction for $\frac{1}{3}$.

Step 1: Plot $\frac{1}{3}$ on the number line.

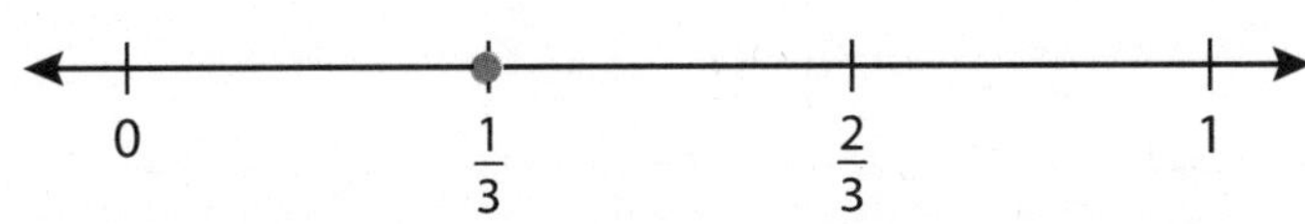

Step 2: Divide the number line into sixths. Label each tick mark to show sixths.

$\frac{1}{6}$	$\frac{1}{6}$	$\frac{1}{6}$	$\frac{1}{6}$	$\frac{1}{6}$	$\frac{1}{6}$

Top labels: 0, $\frac{1}{6}$, $\frac{2}{6}$, $\frac{3}{6}$, $\frac{4}{6}$, $\frac{5}{6}$, 1

Bottom labels: 0, $\frac{1}{3}$, $\frac{2}{3}$, 1

The fractions that name the same points are $\frac{1}{3}$ and $\frac{2}{6}$. So, $\frac{1}{3} = \frac{2}{6}$.

1. Use the number line to find an equivalent fraction.

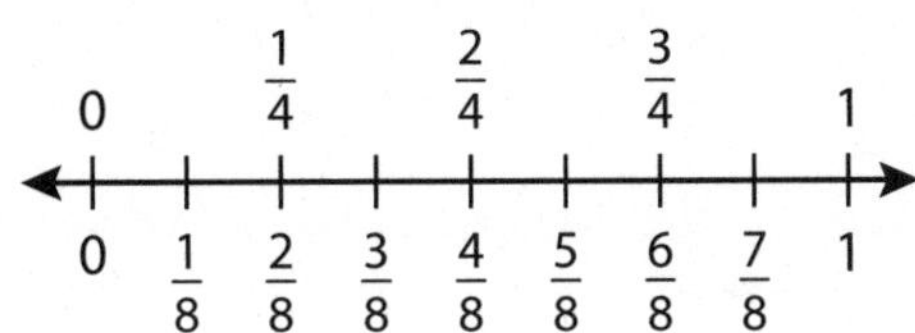

$\frac{2}{8} = \frac{\square}{\square}$

2. Write two fractions that name the point shown.

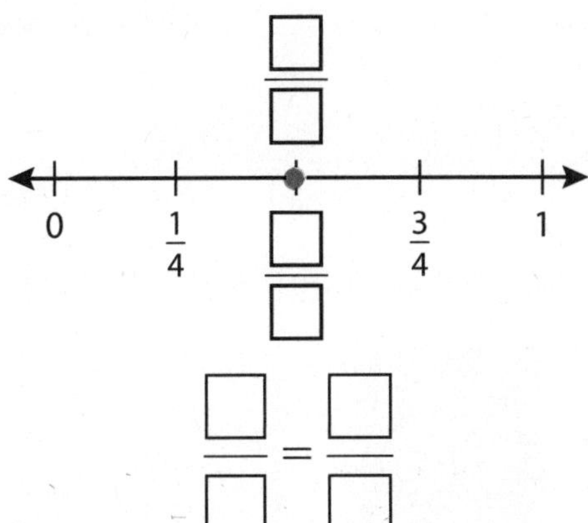

$\frac{\square}{\square} = \frac{\square}{\square}$

Write two fractions that name the same point shown.

3.

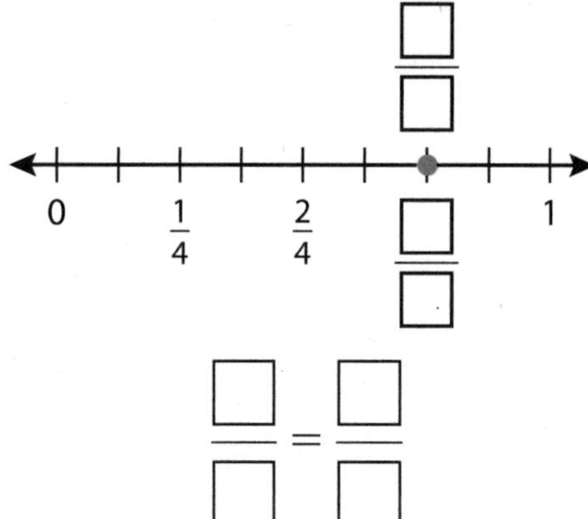

$\frac{\square}{\square} = \frac{\square}{\square}$

4.

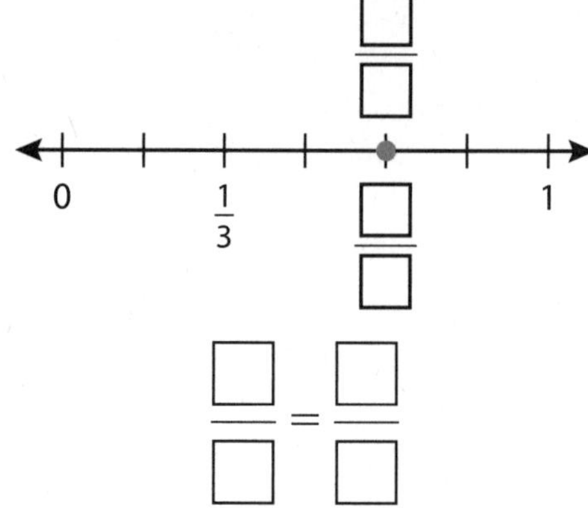

$\frac{\square}{\square} = \frac{\square}{\square}$

5. **Which One Doesn't Belong?** Which fraction does *not* belong with the other three? Explain.

$\frac{2}{4}$ $\frac{3}{6}$ $\frac{2}{3}$ $\frac{4}{8}$

6. MP **Justify a Result** How do you know that $\frac{3}{8}$ and $\frac{3}{4}$ are *not* equivalent when plotting the fractions on a number line?

7. MP **Modeling Real Life** You run $\frac{6}{8}$ of a race. Your friend runs $\frac{3}{4}$ of the same race. Do you and your friend run the same distance?

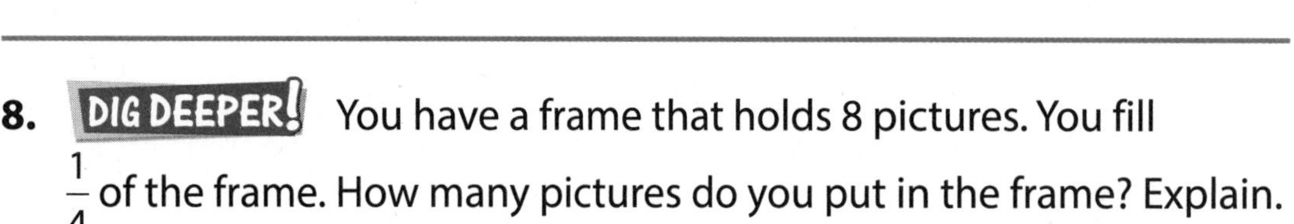

8. DIG DEEPER! You have a frame that holds 8 pictures. You fill $\frac{1}{4}$ of the frame. How many pictures do you put in the frame? Explain.

Review & Refresh

What fraction of the whole is shaded?

9.

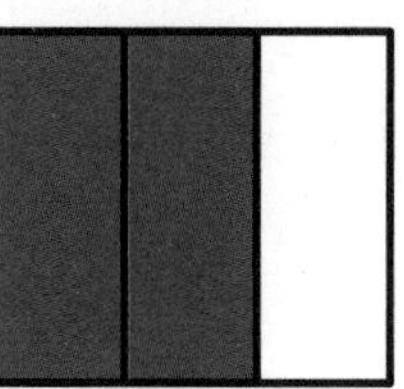

$\frac{\square}{\square}$ is shaded.

10.

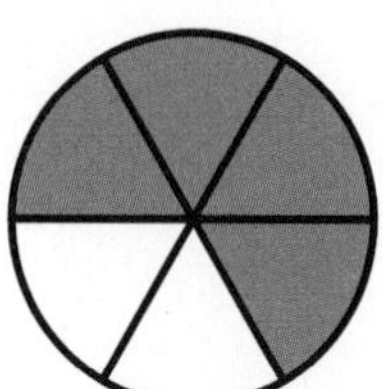

$\frac{\square}{\square}$ is shaded.

Name ______________________________

Relate Fractions and Whole Numbers 11.3

Learning Target: Relate fractions and whole numbers.

Success Criteria:

- I can label fractions on a number line.
- I can write whole numbers as fractions.
- I can use a number line to relate fractions and whole numbers.

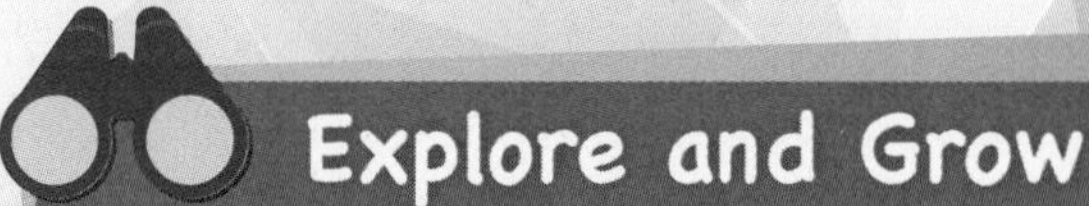

Use Fraction Strips to complete the fractions. Draw to show your models.

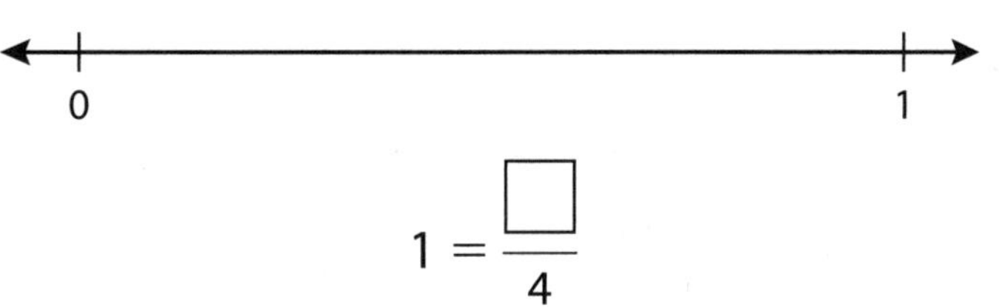

$1 = \frac{\square}{4}$

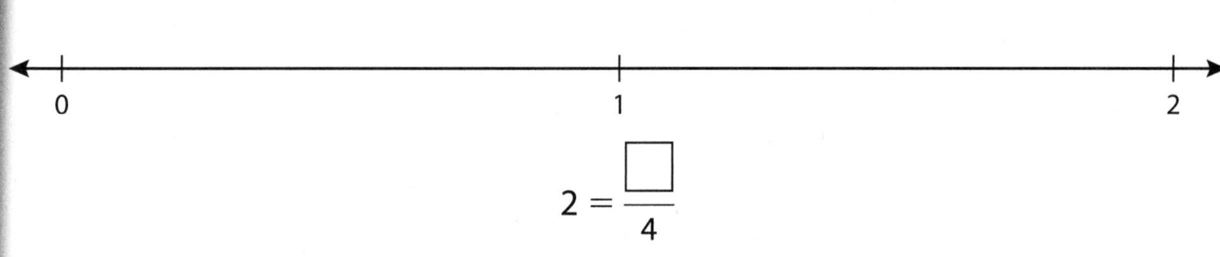

$2 = \frac{\square}{4}$

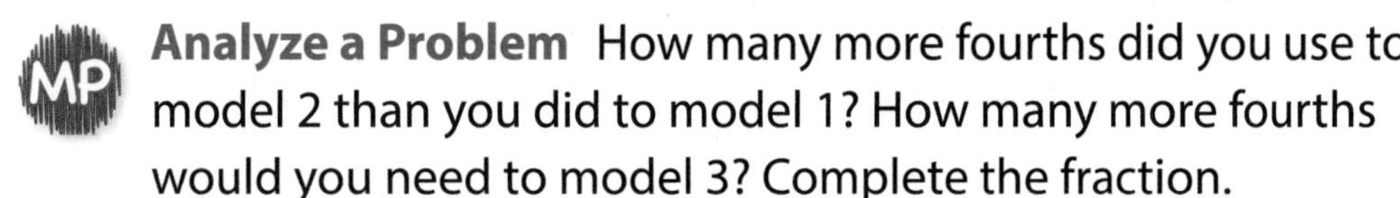

Analyze a Problem How many more fourths did you use to model 2 than you did to model 1? How many more fourths would you need to model 3? Complete the fraction.

$3 = \frac{\square}{4}$

Think and Grow: Equivalent Fractions and Whole Numbers

Example Write the numbers 1 and 2 as fractions.

The number line shows 2 wholes. Each whole is divided into 1 equal part.

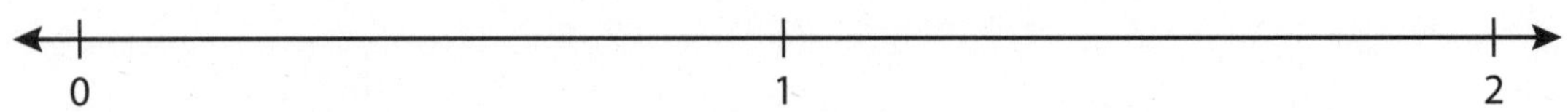

1 whole divided into 1 equal part can be written as $\frac{\square}{1}$.

2 wholes each divided into 1 equal part can be written as $\frac{\square}{1}$.

So, $1 = \frac{\square}{1}$ and $2 = \frac{\square}{1}$.

Example Write equivalent fractions for the numbers 1 and 2.

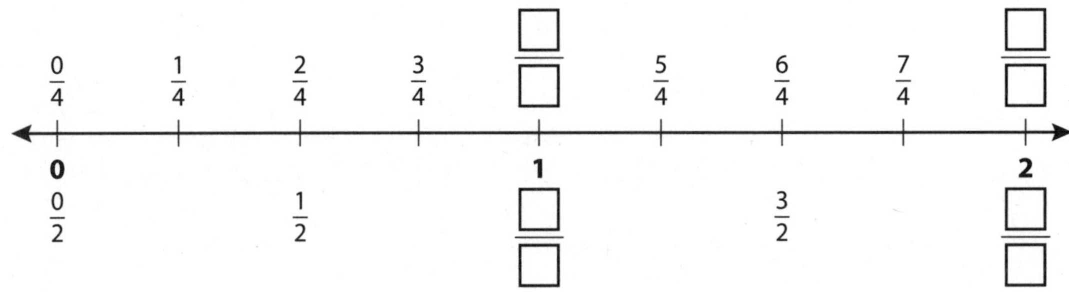

$1 = \frac{\square}{1} = \frac{\square}{2} = \frac{\square}{4}$ $2 = \frac{\square}{1} = \frac{\square}{2} = \frac{\square}{4}$

Show and Grow *I can do it!*

1. Complete the number line. Then complete the statements.

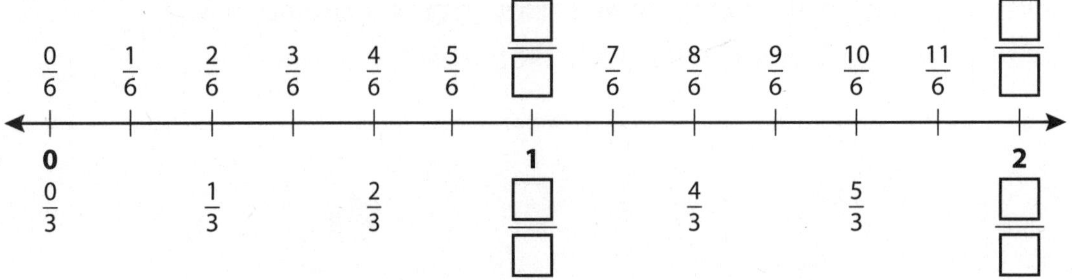

$1 = \frac{\square}{1} = \frac{\square}{3} = \frac{\square}{6}$ $2 = \frac{\square}{1} = \frac{\square}{3} = \frac{\square}{6}$

Name ______________________________

Apply and Grow: Practice

2. Complete the number line. Then write equivalent fractions for the numbers 3 and 4.

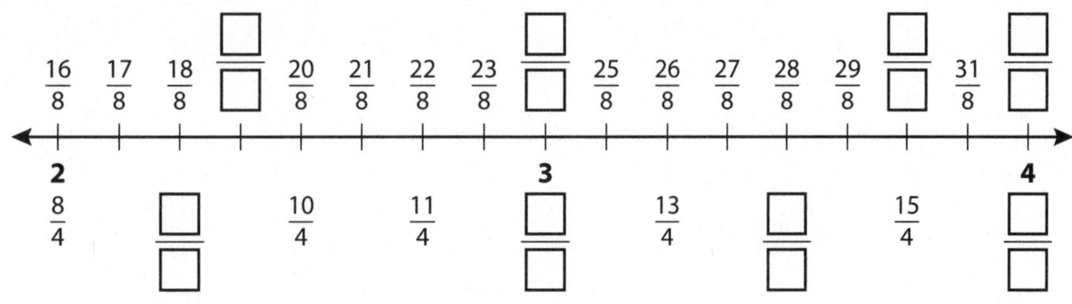

$3 = \frac{\square}{1} = \frac{\square}{4} = \frac{\square}{8}$ $4 = \frac{\square}{1} = \frac{\square}{4} = \frac{\square}{8}$

Write two equivalent fractions for the whole number.

3. $2 = \frac{\square}{3} = \frac{\square}{6}$

4. $1 = \frac{\square}{2} = \frac{\square}{3}$

5. $3 = \frac{\square}{1} = \frac{\square}{2}$

Write the equivalent whole number.

6. $\frac{16}{2} = \frac{8}{1} = \square$

7. $\frac{4}{4} = \frac{6}{6} = \square$

8. $\frac{16}{4} = \frac{12}{3} = \square$

9. You cut a sandwich into 4 pieces. You eat the whole sandwich. What fraction of the sandwich do you eat?

10. MP **Repeated Reasoning** Write three fractions that are equivalent to 6 using the denominators 1, 2, and 6.

11. MP **Structure** Use a number line to show $\frac{5}{5} = 1$.

Think and Grow: Modeling Real Life

You run around a track 12 times. Each lap is $\frac{1}{4}$ mile. How many miles do you run? Write your answer as a whole number and as a fraction.

Model:

You run _____ or _____ miles.

Show and Grow I can think deeper!

12. You ride your bike around a city block 24 times. Each time around is $\frac{1}{6}$ mile. How many miles do you ride? Write your answer as a whole number and as a fraction.

13. There are 5 Great Lakes: Lake Erie, Lake Huron, Lake Michigan, Lake Ontario, and Lake Superior. You complete a project and use 1 whole poster for each lake. Write a fraction that gives the number of posters you use in all.

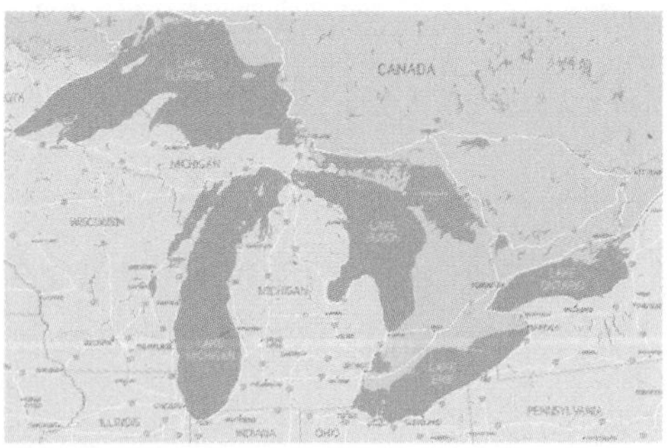

14. DIG DEEPER! You and your friends order 3 pizzas. Each pizza is cut into 8 slices. You and your friends eat $\frac{16}{8}$ of the pizzas. Write a fraction that shows the number of eighths that are left.

Name ______________________

Homework & Practice 11.3

Learning Target: Relate fractions and whole numbers.

Example Write equivalent fractions for the numbers 1 and 2.

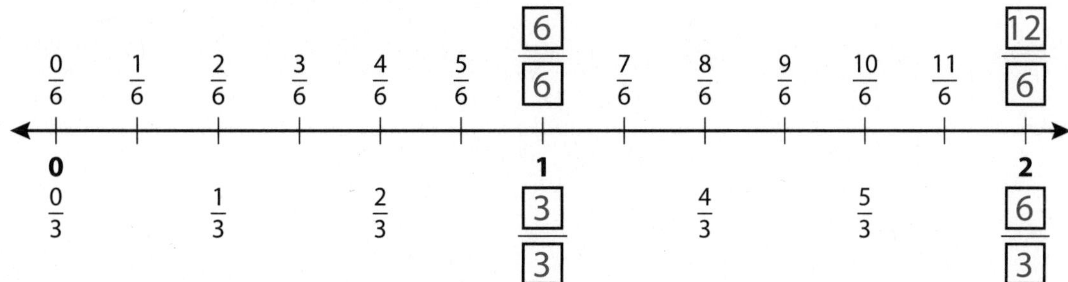

$1 = \frac{1}{1} = \frac{3}{3} = \frac{6}{6}$ $2 = \frac{2}{1} = \frac{6}{3} = \frac{12}{6}$

1. Complete the number line. Then write equivalent fractions for the numbers 3 and 4.

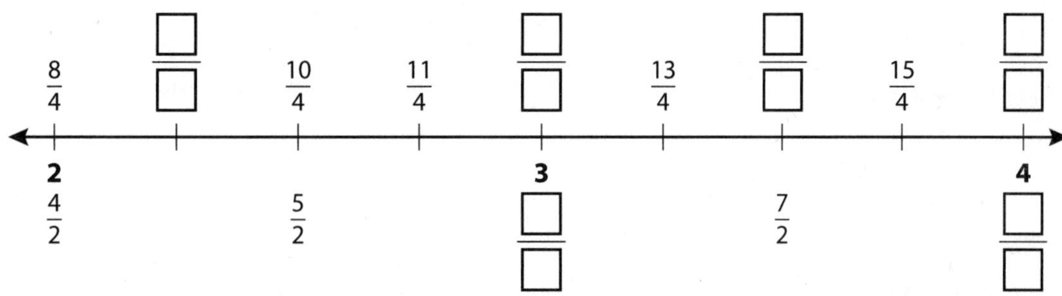

$3 = \frac{\square}{1} = \frac{\square}{2} = \frac{\square}{4}$ $4 = \frac{\square}{1} = \frac{\square}{2} = \frac{\square}{4}$

Write two equivalent fractions for the whole number.

2. $1 = \frac{\square}{3} = \frac{\square}{8}$

3. $4 = \frac{\square}{1} = \frac{\square}{2}$

4. $3 = \frac{\square}{4} = \frac{\square}{6}$

Write the equivalent whole number.

5. $\frac{4}{2} = \frac{2}{1} = \square$

6. $\frac{3}{3} = \frac{8}{8} = \square$

7. $\frac{18}{3} = \frac{12}{2} = \square$

8. MP **Maintain Accuracy** Match each whole number to its equivalent fractions.

4	$\frac{8}{2}$ and $\frac{4}{1}$
1	$\frac{9}{3}$ and $\frac{6}{2}$
3	$\frac{6}{6}$ and $\frac{3}{3}$

9. MP **YOU BE THE TEACHER** Descartes says a fraction equivalent to 3 has a 3 in the denominator and a 1 in the numerator. Is Descartes correct? Explain.

10. MP **Patterns** Describe and complete the pattern.

$\frac{8}{8}, \frac{16}{8}, \frac{24}{8}, \frac{\square}{8}, \frac{\square}{8}$

11. MP **Modeling Real Life** You run around a park 18 times. Each lap is $\frac{1}{6}$ mile. How many miles do you run? Write your answer as a whole number and as a fraction.

12. MP **Modeling Real Life** Christopher Columbus had 3 ships on his first voyage: the *Niña*, the *Pinta*, and the *Santa Maria*. You complete a project and use 1 whole poster for each ship. Write a fraction that gives the number of posters you use in all.

13. **DIG DEEPER!** A teacher has 4 tables. Each table is divided into 4 sections. $\frac{12}{4}$ of the tables have supplies on them. Write a fraction that shows the number of fourths that do *not* have supplies on them.

Review & Refresh

Estimate. Then find the sum. Check whether your answer is reasonable.

14. Estimate: ______

$$\begin{array}{r} 837 \\ +\ \ 46 \\ \hline \end{array}$$

15. Estimate: ______

$$\begin{array}{r} 396 \\ +\ 108 \\ \hline \end{array}$$

16. Estimate: ______

$$\begin{array}{r} 551 \\ +\ 279 \\ \hline \end{array}$$

Name ____________________

Compare Fractions with the Same Denominator

11.4

Learning Target: Compare fractions that have the same denominator.

Success Criteria:

- I can model fractions that have the same denominator.
- I can use the numerators to compare fractions.
- I can explain how to compare fractions that have the same denominator.

Explore and Grow

Color to show each fraction. Circle the greater fraction.

$\frac{1}{4}$

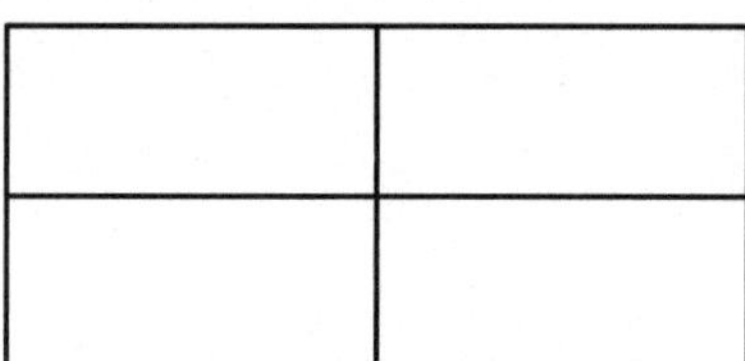

$\frac{3}{4}$

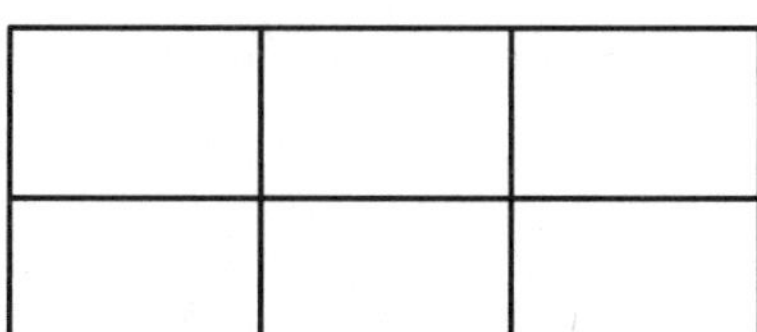

$\frac{5}{6}$

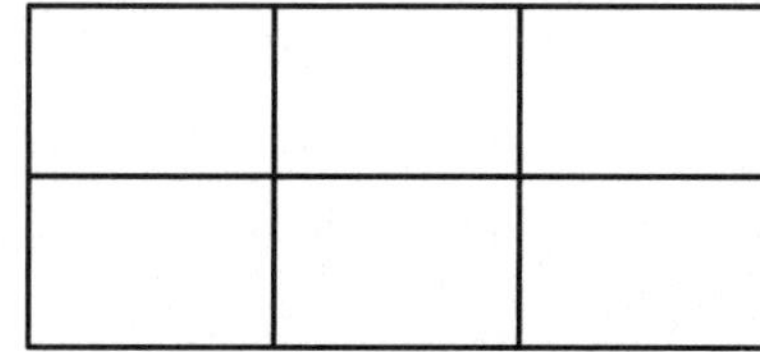

$\frac{2}{6}$

Communicate Clearly Explain to your partner how you can compare fractions with the same denominator.

Think and Grow: Compare Fractions That Have the Same Denominator

Example Compare $\frac{3}{8}$ and $\frac{7}{8}$.

One Way: Use Fraction Strips.

The fractions have the same denominator, 8.

Three $\frac{1}{8}$s is $\frac{3}{8}$. Seven $\frac{1}{8}$s is $\frac{7}{8}$. Shade the Fraction Strips.

	1							
$\frac{3}{8}$	$\frac{1}{8}$	$\frac{1}{8}$	$\frac{1}{8}$	$\frac{1}{8}$	$\frac{1}{8}$	$\frac{1}{8}$	$\frac{1}{8}$	$\frac{1}{8}$
$\frac{7}{8}$	$\frac{1}{8}$	$\frac{1}{8}$	$\frac{1}{8}$	$\frac{1}{8}$	$\frac{1}{8}$	$\frac{1}{8}$	$\frac{1}{8}$	$\frac{1}{8}$

More $\frac{1}{8}$s are shaded to show $\frac{7}{8}$.

So, $\frac{3}{8}$ is ______________ $\frac{7}{8}$, and $\frac{3}{8}$ ◯ $\frac{7}{8}$.

Another Way: When the denominators are the same, the whole is divided into the same number of equal parts. So, look at the numerators 3 and 7 to compare. The fraction with the greater numerator is the greater fraction.

Because 3 ◯ 7, $\frac{3}{8}$ ◯ $\frac{7}{8}$.

Show and Grow *I can do it!*

Shade to compare the fractions.

1.

1					
$\frac{1}{6}$	$\frac{1}{6}$	$\frac{1}{6}$	$\frac{1}{6}$	$\frac{1}{6}$	$\frac{1}{6}$
$\frac{1}{6}$	$\frac{1}{6}$	$\frac{1}{6}$	$\frac{1}{6}$	$\frac{1}{6}$	$\frac{1}{6}$

$\frac{5}{6}$ ◯ $\frac{2}{6}$

2.

1		
$\frac{1}{3}$	$\frac{1}{3}$	$\frac{1}{3}$
$\frac{1}{3}$	$\frac{1}{3}$	$\frac{1}{3}$

$\frac{1}{3}$ ◯ $\frac{3}{3}$

Name ____________________

Apply and Grow: Practice

Shade to compare the fractions.

3.

1							
$\frac{1}{8}$	$\frac{1}{8}$	$\frac{1}{8}$	$\frac{1}{8}$	$\frac{1}{8}$	$\frac{1}{8}$	$\frac{1}{8}$	$\frac{1}{8}$
$\frac{1}{8}$	$\frac{1}{8}$	$\frac{1}{8}$	$\frac{1}{8}$	$\frac{1}{8}$	$\frac{1}{8}$	$\frac{1}{8}$	$\frac{1}{8}$

$\frac{5}{8} \bigcirc \frac{3}{8}$

4.

1			
$\frac{1}{4}$	$\frac{1}{4}$	$\frac{1}{4}$	$\frac{1}{4}$
$\frac{1}{4}$	$\frac{1}{4}$	$\frac{1}{4}$	$\frac{1}{4}$

$\frac{2}{4} \bigcirc \frac{2}{4}$

Compare.

5. $\frac{2}{3} \bigcirc \frac{3}{3}$

6. $\frac{1}{2} \bigcirc \frac{1}{2}$

7. $\frac{3}{8} \bigcirc \frac{1}{8}$

8. $\frac{4}{6} \bigcirc \frac{2}{6}$

9. $\frac{5}{8} \bigcirc \frac{6}{8}$

10. $\frac{0}{4} \bigcirc \frac{1}{4}$

11. **MP Maintain Accuracy** Which statements are true?

$\frac{2}{3} \overset{?}{<} \frac{3}{3}$ $\frac{5}{6} \overset{?}{>} \frac{1}{6}$

$\frac{3}{4} \overset{?}{>} \frac{2}{4}$ $\frac{2}{2} \overset{?}{<} \frac{1}{2}$

12. **MP Justify a Result** How can you show that $\frac{3}{8}$ is less than $\frac{6}{8}$?

13. **MP Structure** Which statement correctly compares the fraction of circles shaded in Group A to the fraction of circles shaded in Group B?

Group A     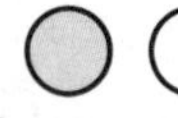 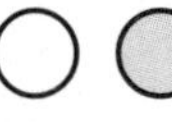  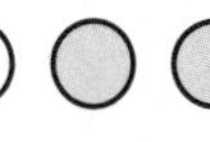

Group B 

$\frac{3}{10} > \frac{6}{10}$ $\frac{6}{10} > \frac{3}{10}$ $\frac{5}{10} > \frac{8}{10}$ $\frac{5}{10} < \frac{3}{10}$

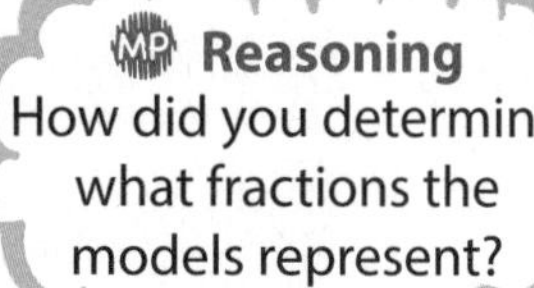

Think and Grow: Modeling Real Life

Newton and Descartes have the same number of chores. Newton finishes $\frac{2}{3}$ of his chores. Descartes finishes $\frac{1}{3}$ of his chores. Who finishes more of his chores?

Model:

_____________ finishes more of his chores.

Explain:

Show and Grow I can think deeper!

14. At the pet store, a green lizard is $\frac{5}{6}$ foot long. A brown lizard is $\frac{6}{6}$ foot long. You pick up the longer lizard. Which lizard do you pick up?

15. You and a friend each have a burrito. The burritos are the same size. You eat $\frac{3}{4}$ of your burrito. Your friend eats $\frac{1}{4}$ of his burrito. Who has less burrito left to eat? Explain.

16. DIG DEEPER! You walk $\frac{5}{8}$ of the distance to the library from your home. Your friend walks $\frac{5}{8}$ of the distance to school from his home. You walk a greater distance than your friend. Explain how this is possible.

Name ______________________________

Homework & Practice 11.4

Learning Target: Compare fractions that have the same denominator.

Example Compare $\frac{4}{6}$ and $\frac{1}{6}$.

One Way: Use Fractions Strips.

	1					
$\frac{4}{6}$	$\frac{1}{6}$	$\frac{1}{6}$	$\frac{1}{6}$	$\frac{1}{6}$	$\frac{1}{6}$	$\frac{1}{6}$
$\frac{1}{6}$	$\frac{1}{6}$	$\frac{1}{6}$	$\frac{1}{6}$	$\frac{1}{6}$	$\frac{1}{6}$	$\frac{1}{6}$

More $\frac{1}{6}$s are shaded to show $\frac{4}{6}$.

So, $\frac{4}{6}$ is greater than $\frac{1}{6}$ and $\frac{4}{6} > \frac{1}{6}$.

Another Way:

When the denominators are the same, the whole is divided into the same number of equal parts. So, look at the numerators to compare. The fraction with the greater numerator is the greater fraction.

Because $4 > 1$, $\frac{4}{6} > \frac{1}{6}$.

Shade to compare the fractions.

1.

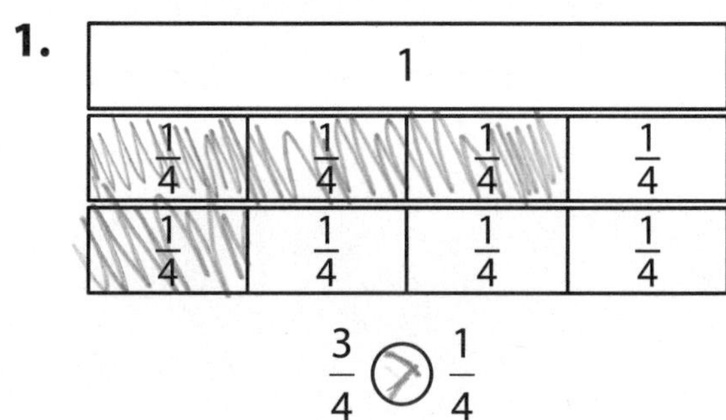

$\frac{3}{4}$ $\bigcirc$ $\frac{1}{4}$

2.

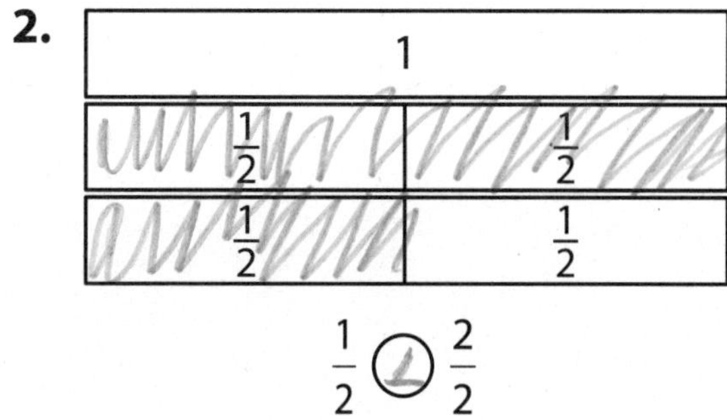

$\frac{1}{2}$ $\bigcirc$ $\frac{2}{2}$

Compare.

3. $\frac{5}{8}$ $\bigcirc$ $\frac{7}{8}$

4. $\frac{6}{6}$ $\bigcirc$ $\frac{5}{6}$

5. $\frac{1}{3}$ $\bigcirc$ $\frac{2}{3}$

6. $\frac{2}{4}$ $\bigcirc$ $\frac{4}{4}$

7. $\frac{0}{3}$ $\bigcirc$ $\frac{1}{3}$

8. $\frac{3}{6}$ $\bigcirc$ $\frac{4}{6}$

9. **YOU BE THE TEACHER** Your friend says $\frac{3}{4} > \frac{2}{4}$. Is your friend correct? Explain.

10. **Logic** Two fractions are equivalent and have the same denominator. What must be true about the numerators of the fractions?

Open-Ended Write a number to make the statement true.

11. $\frac{★}{8} < \frac{6}{8}$

★ = ______

12. $\frac{▲}{4} > \frac{2}{4}$

▲ = ______

13. $\frac{●}{6} < \frac{4}{6}$

● = ______

14. **Modeling Real Life** You and your friend had the same number of baby teeth. You have lost $\frac{3}{4}$ of your baby teeth. Your friend has lost $\frac{2}{4}$ of her baby teeth. Who has lost more teeth?

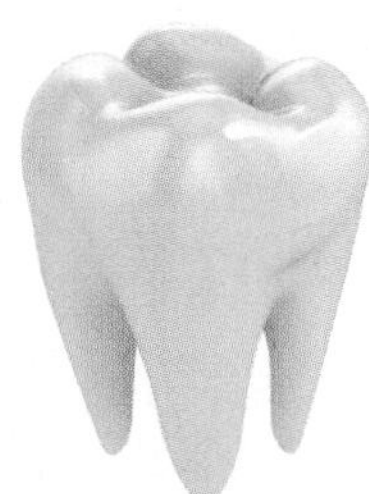

15. **Construct an Argument** Your class paints $\frac{7}{8}$ of a mural. Your friend's class paints $\frac{5}{8}$ of a different mural. Your friend says his class has painted a greater area than your class. Is it possible that your friend is correct? Explain.

Review & Refresh

Find the product.

16. $9 \times 80 =$ ______

17. $5 \times 30 =$ ______

18. $6 \times 40 =$ ______

Name ______________________________

Compare Fractions with the Same Numerator 11.5

Learning Target: Compare fractions that have the same numerator.

Success Criteria:

- I can model fractions that have the same numerator.
- I can use the denominators to compare fractions.
- I can explain how to compare fractions that have the same numerator.

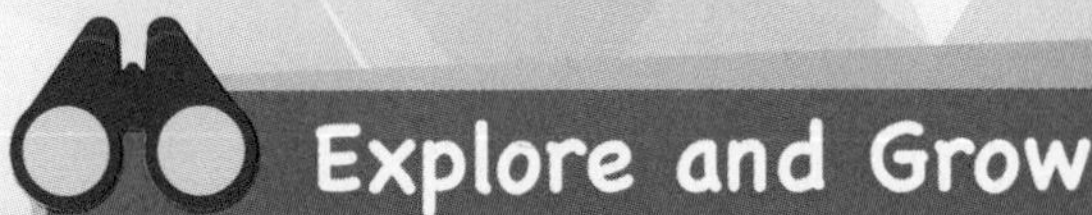

Explore and Grow

Color to show each fraction. Circle the greater fraction.

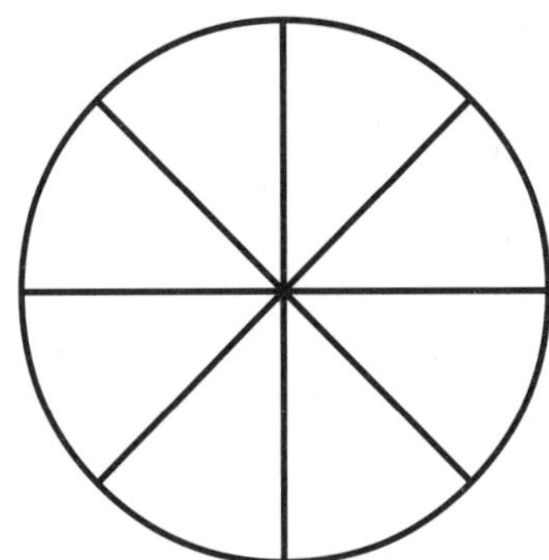

$\frac{1}{8}$

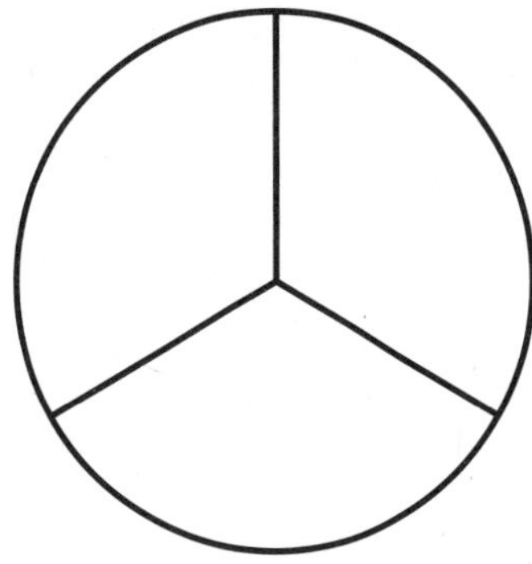

$\frac{1}{3}$

Check Your Work How can you use Fraction Strips to check your answer? Draw to show.

Think and Grow: Compare Fractions That Have the Same Numerator

Example Compare $\frac{2}{4}$ and $\frac{2}{6}$.

One Way: Use Fraction Strips.

Both fractions have the same numerator, 2. Two $\frac{1}{4}$s is $\frac{2}{4}$. Two $\frac{1}{6}$s is $\frac{2}{6}$.

Shade the Fraction Strips. Compare the parts.

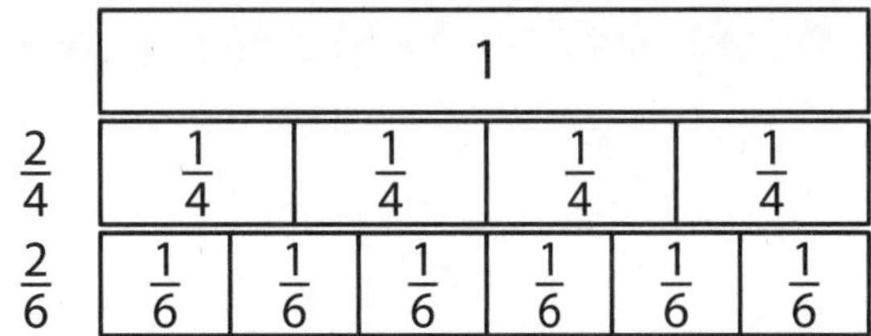

Think: $\frac{1}{6}$ is not as long as $\frac{1}{4}$.

So, $\frac{2}{4}$ is ________________ $\frac{2}{6}$, and $\frac{2}{4}$ ◯ $\frac{2}{6}$.

Another Way: When the numerators are the same, look at the denominators 4 and 6 to compare the sizes of the parts.

- The more parts the whole is divided into, the smaller the parts are.
- The fewer parts the whole is divided into, the larger the parts are.

The fraction with the greater denominator is the lesser fraction.

So, $\frac{1}{4}$ is ________________ $\frac{1}{6}$, and $\frac{2}{4}$ ◯ $\frac{2}{6}$.

Show and Grow *I can do it!*

Shade to compare the fractions.

1.

1							
$\frac{1}{6}$	$\frac{1}{6}$	$\frac{1}{6}$	$\frac{1}{6}$	$\frac{1}{6}$	$\frac{1}{6}$		
$\frac{1}{8}$	$\frac{1}{8}$	$\frac{1}{8}$	$\frac{1}{8}$	$\frac{1}{8}$	$\frac{1}{8}$	$\frac{1}{8}$	$\frac{1}{8}$

$\frac{3}{6}$ ◯ $\frac{3}{8}$

2.

1			
$\frac{1}{4}$	$\frac{1}{4}$	$\frac{1}{4}$	$\frac{1}{4}$
$\frac{1}{3}$	$\frac{1}{3}$	$\frac{1}{3}$	

$\frac{2}{4}$ ◯ $\frac{2}{3}$

Name ________________________________

Apply and Grow: Practice

Shade to compare the fractions.

3.

1		
$\frac{1}{2}$	$\frac{1}{2}$	
$\frac{1}{3}$	$\frac{1}{3}$	$\frac{1}{3}$

$\frac{2}{2} \bigcirc \frac{2}{3}$

4.

1					
$\frac{1}{6}$	$\frac{1}{6}$	$\frac{1}{6}$	$\frac{1}{6}$	$\frac{1}{6}$	$\frac{1}{6}$
$\frac{1}{3}$	$\frac{1}{3}$	$\frac{1}{3}$			

$\frac{1}{6} \bigcirc \frac{1}{3}$

Compare.

5. $\frac{2}{6} \bigcirc \frac{2}{4}$

6. $\frac{1}{1} \bigcirc \frac{1}{6}$

7. $\frac{6}{8} \bigcirc \frac{6}{8}$

8. $\frac{2}{3} \bigcirc \frac{2}{4}$

9. $\frac{8}{8} \bigcirc \frac{8}{8}$

10. $\frac{3}{4} \bigcirc \frac{3}{3}$

11. **Open-Ended** Use the models to compare two fractions that have the same numerators.

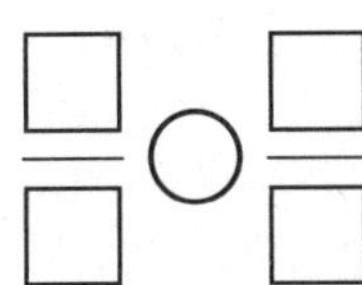

1							
$\frac{1}{8}$	$\frac{1}{8}$	$\frac{1}{8}$	$\frac{1}{8}$	$\frac{1}{8}$	$\frac{1}{8}$	$\frac{1}{8}$	$\frac{1}{8}$
$\frac{1}{4}$	$\frac{1}{4}$	$\frac{1}{4}$	$\frac{1}{4}$				

12. You spend $\frac{2}{3}$ of an hour playing soccer on Wednesday. You spend $\frac{2}{6}$ of an hour playing soccer on Friday. On which day do you spend more time playing soccer? Explain.

13. MP **YOU BE THE TEACHER** Your friend says $\frac{1}{4} > \frac{1}{2}$ because $\frac{1}{4}$ of one circle is bigger than $\frac{1}{2}$ of the other circle. Is your friend correct? Explain.

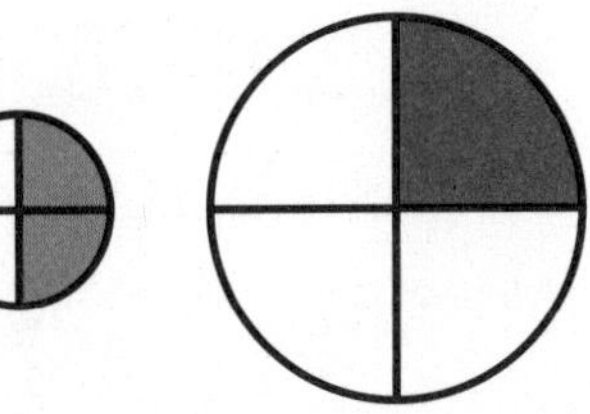

Think and Grow: Modeling Real Life

Newton and Descartes have piggy banks that are the same size. Newton fills $\frac{3}{4}$ of his bank with pennies. Descartes fills $\frac{3}{6}$ of his bank with pennies. Whose bank is filled more? Explain.

Model:

Explain: ______________ bank is filled more.

Show and Grow I can think deeper!

14. You use $\frac{1}{3}$ of a bottle of glitter for an art project. Your friend uses $\frac{1}{4}$ of a bottle for his art project. The bottles are the same size. Who uses more glitter?

15. A train and a plane are traveling the same distance from New York to Pittsburgh. The train completes $\frac{5}{8}$ of its journey. The plane completes $\frac{5}{6}$ of its journey. Which is farther away from Pittsburgh? Explain.

16. **DIG DEEPER!** You cut a piece of lasagna that is $\frac{1}{8}$ of a tray. Your friend cuts a piece of lasagna that is $\frac{1}{6}$ of a tray. Your piece is larger than your friend's piece. Explain how this is possible.

Name ______________________________

Homework & Practice 11.5

Learning Target: Compare fractions that have the same numerator.

Example Compare $\frac{3}{8}$ and $\frac{3}{3}$.

One Way: Use Fraction Strips.

Shade the Fraction Strips. Compare the parts.

1							
$\frac{1}{8}$	$\frac{1}{8}$	$\frac{1}{8}$	$\frac{1}{8}$	$\frac{1}{8}$	$\frac{1}{8}$	$\frac{1}{8}$	$\frac{1}{8}$
$\frac{1}{3}$			$\frac{1}{3}$			$\frac{1}{3}$	

So, $\frac{3}{8}$ is less than $\frac{3}{3}$,

and $\frac{3}{8}$ $<$ $\frac{3}{3}$.

Another Way: When the numerators are the same, look at the denominators 8 and 3 to compare the sizes of the parts.

- The more parts the whole is divided into, the smaller the parts are.
- The fewer parts the whole is divided into, the larger the parts are.

So, $\frac{1}{8}$ is less than $\frac{1}{3}$, and $\frac{3}{8}$ $<$ $\frac{3}{3}$.

Shade to compare the fractions.

1.

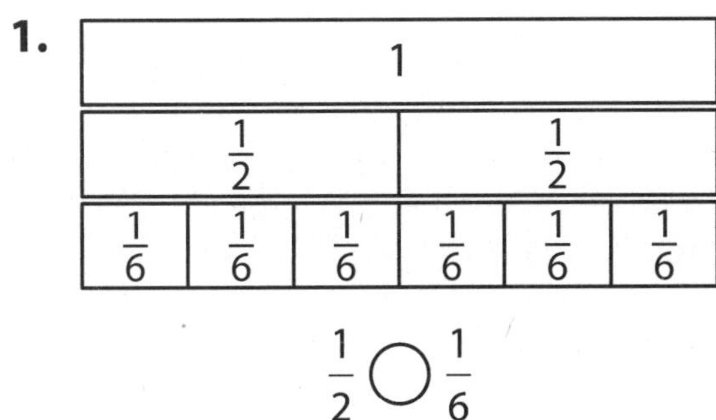

$\frac{1}{2}$ ◯ $\frac{1}{6}$

2.

1							
$\frac{1}{4}$		$\frac{1}{4}$		$\frac{1}{4}$		$\frac{1}{4}$	
$\frac{1}{8}$	$\frac{1}{8}$	$\frac{1}{8}$	$\frac{1}{8}$	$\frac{1}{8}$	$\frac{1}{8}$	$\frac{1}{8}$	$\frac{1}{8}$

$\frac{2}{4}$ ◯ $\frac{2}{8}$

Compare.

3. $\frac{1}{8}$ ◯ $\frac{1}{4}$

4. $\frac{6}{6}$ ◯ $\frac{6}{8}$

5. $\frac{2}{6}$ ◯ $\frac{2}{3}$

6. $\frac{4}{8}$ ◯ $\frac{4}{6}$

7. $\frac{2}{3}$ ◯ $\frac{2}{4}$

8. $\frac{3}{8}$ ◯ $\frac{3}{6}$

9. Open-Ended Use the models to compare two fractions that have the same numerators.

1							
$\frac{1}{2}$				$\frac{1}{2}$			
$\frac{1}{8}$	$\frac{1}{8}$	$\frac{1}{8}$	$\frac{1}{8}$	$\frac{1}{8}$	$\frac{1}{8}$	$\frac{1}{8}$	$\frac{1}{8}$

$\frac{\square}{\square} \bigcirc \frac{\square}{\square}$

10. MP YOU BE THE TEACHER Newton says that if two fractions have the same numerator, then the fraction with the greater denominator is the greater fraction. Is Newton correct? Explain.

11. MP Communicate Clearly How is comparing fractions with the same numerator similar to comparing fractions with the same denominator? How is it different?

12. MP Modeling Real Life You play a video game for $\frac{1}{2}$ of an hour. Your friend plays the video game for $\frac{1}{6}$ of an hour. Who plays the video game longer? Explain.

13. DIG DEEPER! A car's gasoline tank is $\frac{4}{6}$ full. A truck's gasoline tank is $\frac{4}{8}$ full. The truck's tank has more gasoline. Explain how this is possible.

Review & Refresh

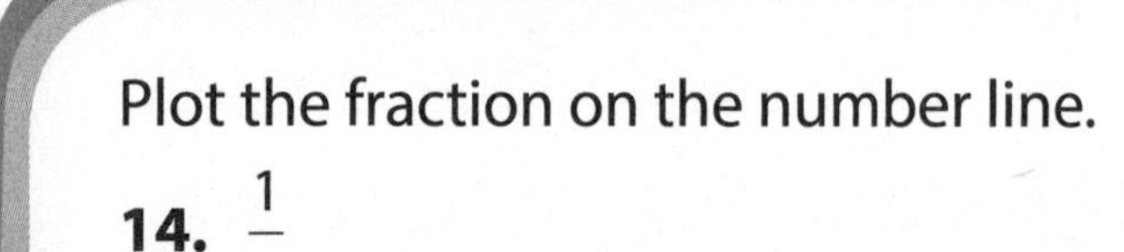

Plot the fraction on the number line.

14. $\frac{1}{4}$

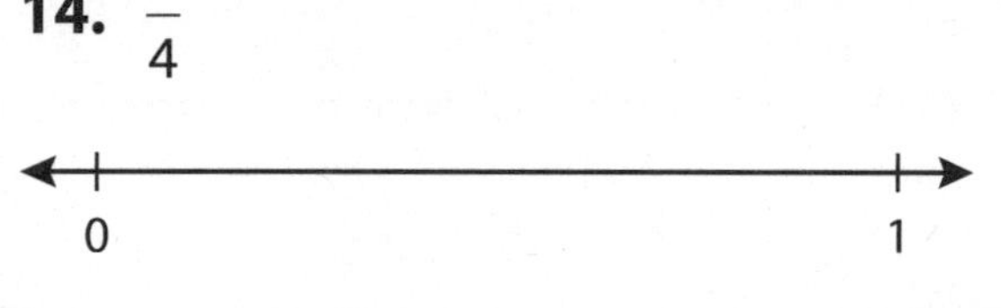

15. $\frac{2}{3}$

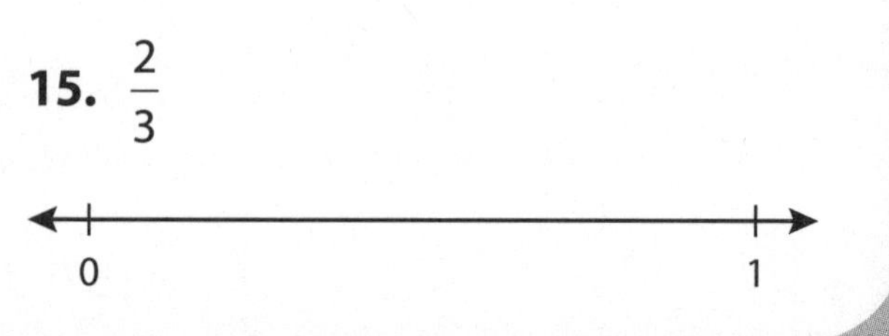

Name ______________________________

Compare Fractions on a Number Line 11.6

Learning Target: Use a number line to compare fractions.

Success Criteria:

- I can plot fractions on a number line.
- I can tell which fraction is closer to 0.
- I can compare fractions on a number line.

Explore and Grow

Use Fraction Strips to plot each fraction on the number line. Circle the greater fraction.

$\frac{2}{8}$ $\frac{7}{8}$

Communicate Clearly Tell your partner how to use a number line to compare the fractions.

$\frac{1}{7}$ ○ $\frac{3}{7}$

Reasoning How is using a number line to compare two fractions similar to using a ruler to compare two lengths?

Think and Grow: Compare Fractions on a Number Line

On a number line, fractions to the left are less than fractions to the right. Fractions to the right are greater than fractions to the left.

Example Use a number line to compare $\frac{3}{4}$ and $\frac{1}{4}$.

Plot the fractions on a number line. Both have the same denominator.

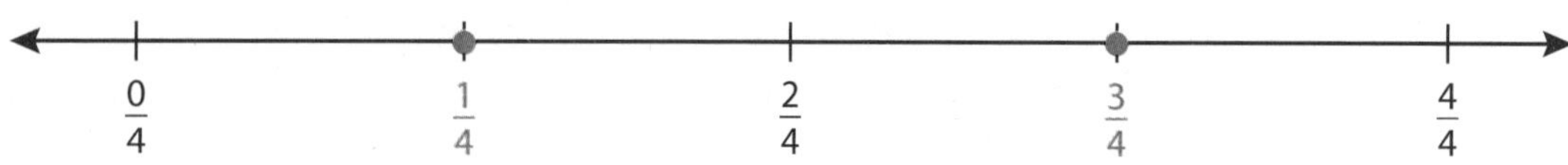

$\frac{3}{4}$ is to the ______________ of $\frac{1}{4}$. So, $\frac{3}{4}$ ◯ $\frac{1}{4}$.

Looking at the number line, $\frac{1}{4}$ is closer to $\frac{0}{4}$, or 0, and $\frac{3}{4}$ is closer to $\frac{4}{4}$, or 1.

Example Use number lines to compare $\frac{2}{8}$ and $\frac{2}{3}$.

Plot each fraction on a number line. Both fractions have the same numerator.

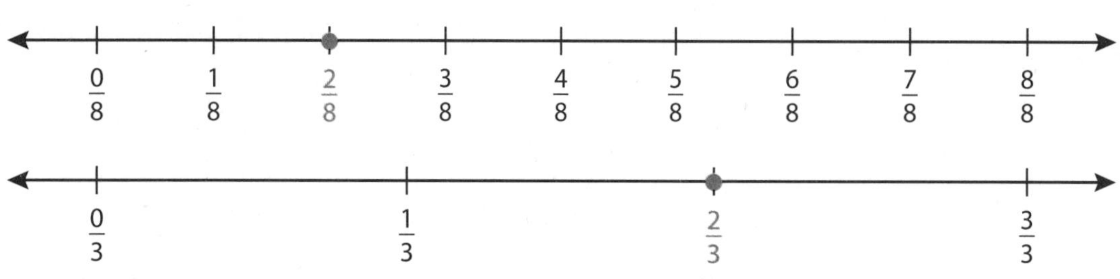

$\frac{2}{8}$ is to the ______________ of $\frac{2}{3}$. So, $\frac{2}{8}$ ◯ $\frac{2}{3}$.

Show and Grow I can do it!

Use the number line to compare the fractions.

1. 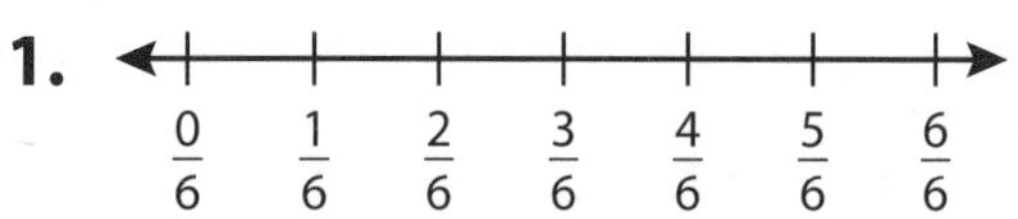

$\frac{5}{6}$ ◯ $\frac{4}{6}$

2. 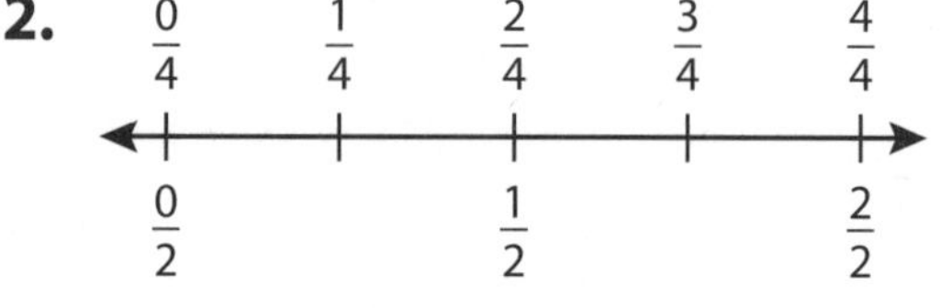

$\frac{1}{2}$ ◯ $\frac{2}{4}$

Name ______________________________

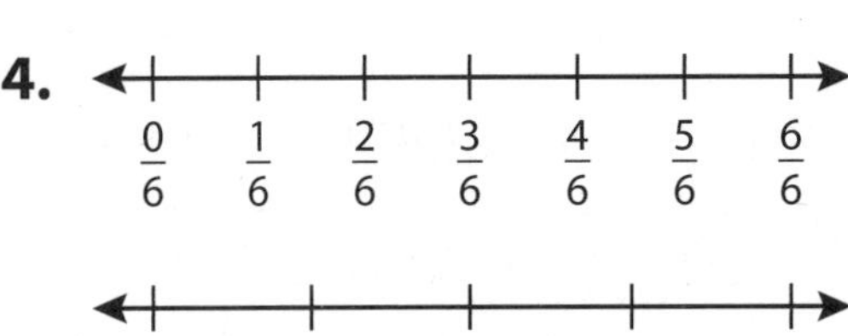

Apply and Grow: Practice

Compare.

3. $\frac{0}{8}$ $\frac{1}{8}$ $\frac{2}{8}$ $\frac{3}{8}$ $\frac{4}{8}$ $\frac{5}{8}$ $\frac{6}{8}$ $\frac{7}{8}$ $\frac{8}{8}$

$\frac{0}{4}$ $\frac{1}{4}$ $\frac{2}{4}$ $\frac{3}{4}$ $\frac{4}{4}$

$\frac{3}{4} \bigcirc \frac{6}{8}$

4. $\frac{0}{6}$ $\frac{1}{6}$ $\frac{2}{6}$ $\frac{3}{6}$ $\frac{4}{6}$ $\frac{5}{6}$ $\frac{6}{6}$

$\frac{0}{4}$ $\frac{1}{4}$ $\frac{2}{4}$ $\frac{3}{4}$ $\frac{4}{4}$

$\frac{4}{6} \bigcirc \frac{4}{4}$

5. $\frac{1}{2} \bigcirc \frac{1}{3}$

6. $\frac{2}{8} \bigcirc \frac{2}{6}$

7. $\frac{4}{8} \bigcirc \frac{1}{2}$

8. $\frac{4}{4} \bigcirc \frac{4}{6}$

9. $\frac{5}{8} \bigcirc \frac{7}{8}$

10. $\frac{1}{6} \bigcirc \frac{2}{6}$

11. Write a fraction that is greater than $\frac{5}{6}$.

12. Write a fraction that is less than $\frac{3}{4}$.

13. Newton buys $\frac{1}{4}$ pound of cheese. Descartes buys $\frac{3}{4}$ pound of cheese. Who buys more cheese?

14. MP **Number Sense** Which fractions are greater than $\frac{2}{4}$?

$\frac{1}{4}$ $\frac{1}{2}$ $\frac{3}{4}$ $\frac{4}{4}$ $\frac{2}{3}$ $\frac{2}{6}$

Think and Grow: Modeling Real Life

Does the recipe call for more salt or more pepper?

Models:

The recipe calls for more ______________.

Explain:

Vegetable Soup

2 cups chicken broth
$\frac{3}{2}$ cups tomato juice
$\frac{1}{2}$ cup chopped celery
$\frac{1}{2}$ cup chopped onion
1 cup diced tomatoes
1 cup water
1 cup diced potatoes
$\frac{1}{4}$ cup corn kernels
$\frac{2}{3}$ cup chopped green beans
$\frac{3}{4}$ cup diced carrots
$\frac{3}{8}$ teaspoon Creole seasoning
$\frac{3}{4}$ teaspoon lemon juice
$\frac{1}{2}$ teaspoon salt
$\frac{1}{4}$ teaspoon pepper

Show and Grow *I can think deeper!*

15. Does the recipe above call for more Creole seasoning or more lemon juice? Explain.

16. You and your friend each catch a fish. Your fish is $\frac{5}{3}$ feet long, and your friend's fish is $\frac{2}{3}$ foot long. Whose fish is shorter? Explain.

17. **DIG DEEPER!** You eat $\frac{4}{8}$ of a quesadilla. Your friend eats $\frac{2}{8}$ of a different quesadilla. Can you tell who ate more quesadilla? Explain.

Name ____________________

Homework & Practice 11.6

Learning Target: Use a number line to compare fractions.

Example Use a number line to compare $\frac{1}{2}$ and $\frac{1}{6}$.

Plot the fractions on a number line. Both fractions have the same numerator.

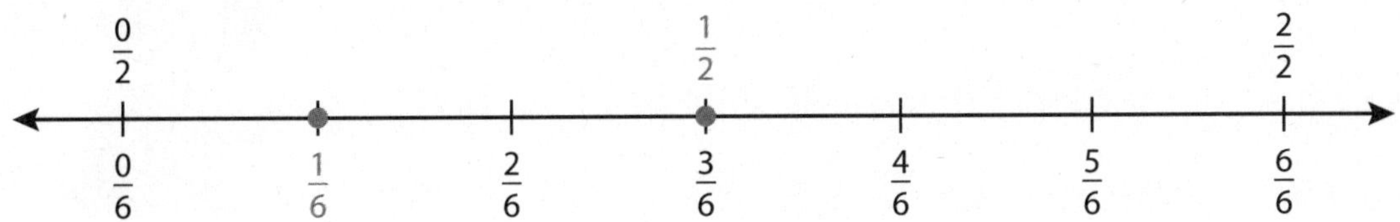

$\frac{1}{2}$ is to the right of $\frac{1}{6}$. So, $\frac{1}{2} > \frac{1}{6}$.

Use the number line to compare the fractions.

1. Number line: $\frac{0}{8}$, $\frac{1}{8}$, $\frac{2}{8}$, $\frac{3}{8}$, $\frac{4}{8}$, $\frac{5}{8}$, $\frac{6}{8}$, $\frac{7}{8}$, $\frac{8}{8}$

$\frac{2}{8} \bigcirc \frac{5}{8}$

2. Number line: $\frac{0}{3}$, $\frac{1}{3}$, $\frac{2}{3}$, $\frac{3}{3}$ (top); $\frac{0}{6}$, $\frac{1}{6}$, $\frac{2}{6}$, $\frac{3}{6}$, $\frac{4}{6}$, $\frac{5}{6}$, $\frac{6}{6}$ (bottom)

$\frac{2}{6} \bigcirc \frac{1}{3}$

Compare.

3. $\frac{1}{3} \bigcirc \frac{1}{4}$

4. $\frac{3}{6} \bigcirc \frac{4}{6}$

5. $\frac{1}{3} \bigcirc \frac{2}{3}$

6. $\frac{1}{3} \bigcirc \frac{2}{6}$

7. $\frac{2}{4} \bigcirc \frac{2}{6}$

8. $\frac{1}{6} \bigcirc \frac{3}{6}$

9. $\frac{4}{8} \bigcirc \frac{4}{4}$

10. $\frac{1}{6} \bigcirc \frac{1}{3}$

11. $\frac{3}{4} \bigcirc \frac{1}{4}$

12. Write a fraction that is greater than $\frac{1}{3}$.

13. Write a fraction that is less than $\frac{1}{2}$.

14. MP **Communicate Clearly** Explain how to compare $\frac{2}{3}$ and $\frac{4}{3}$ on a number line.

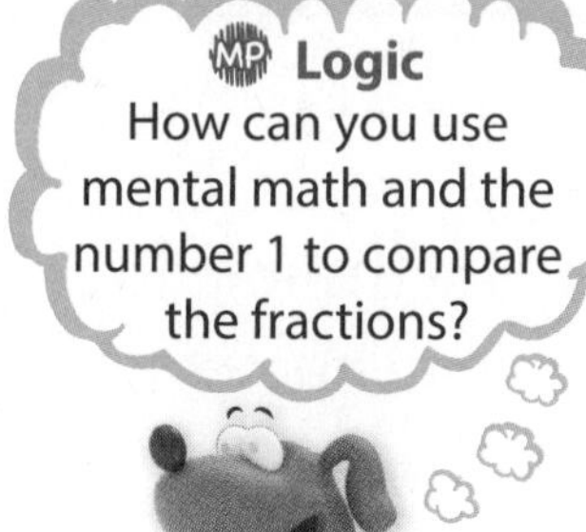

15. MP **Number Sense** Which fractions are less than $\frac{4}{6}$?

$\frac{2}{3}$ $\frac{2}{6}$ $\frac{1}{6}$ $\frac{4}{4}$ $\frac{4}{8}$

MP **Modeling Real Life** Use the recipe shown.

16. Does the recipe call for more butter or more sugar? Explain.

17. **DIG DEEPER!** Your friend makes 2 batches of banana bread. Does she use more flour or more nuts? How much more? Explain.

Banana Bread

3 bananas
$\frac{1}{3}$ cup melted butter
$\frac{2}{3}$ cup sugar
1 egg
$\frac{3}{4}$ teaspoon vanilla
$\frac{1}{2}$ teaspoon baking soda
$\frac{3}{2}$ cups flour
$\frac{3}{4}$ cup nuts

Review & Refresh

Find the missing number.

18. 98 + _____ = 98

19. 52 + (_____ + 16) = (52 + 28) + 16

20. 33 + _____ + 46 = 33 + 46

21. 14 + 67 = 67 + _____

Name ____

Compare Fractions 11.7

Learning Target: Compare fractions.

Success Criteria:

- I can choose a strategy to compare two fractions.
- I can compare two fractions.

Use a strategy to find the greater fraction.

$\frac{2}{3}$ $\frac{2}{8}$

Use a different strategy to check your answer.

Construct an Argument Tell your partner which strategy you prefer. Explain.

Think and Grow: Compare Fractions

Example Compare $\frac{5}{6}$ and $\frac{2}{3}$.

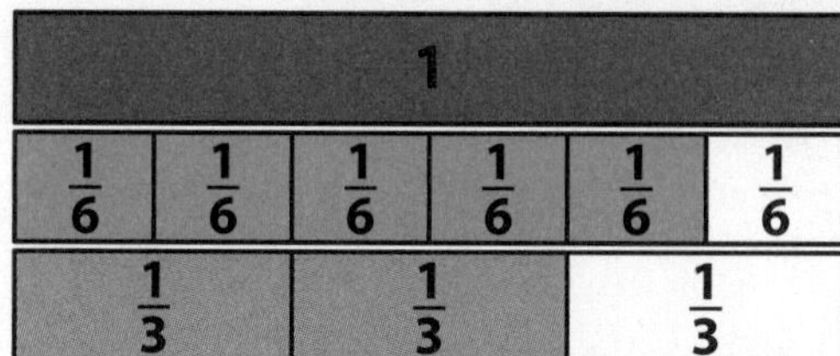

Use Fraction Strips.

In some cases, it is easier to compare the parts that are missing. Notice that each fraction is 1 part away from being equivalent to 1. Compare the missing pieces.

Because $\frac{1}{6}$ ◯ $\frac{1}{3}$, a larger piece is missing from $\frac{2}{3}$.

So, $\frac{5}{6}$ ◯ $\frac{2}{3}$.

Example Compare $\frac{3}{8}$ and $\frac{5}{8}$.

The denominators are the same. Compare the numerators, 3 and 5.

Because 3 ◯ 5, $\frac{3}{8}$ ◯ $\frac{5}{8}$.

Example Compare $\frac{4}{6}$ and $\frac{4}{8}$.

The numerators are the same. Look at the denominators 6 and 8 to compare the sizes of the parts. The fraction with the greater denominator is the lesser fraction.

So, $\frac{4}{6}$ ◯ $\frac{4}{8}$.

Show and Grow I can do it!

Compare.

1. $\frac{1}{2}$ ◯ $\frac{1}{8}$

2. $\frac{3}{4}$ ◯ $\frac{5}{6}$

3. $\frac{0}{6}$ ◯ $\frac{0}{2}$

4. $\frac{8}{8}$ ◯ $\frac{7}{8}$

Name ________________

Apply and Grow: Practice

Compare.

5. $\frac{1}{4} \bigcirc \frac{2}{4}$	**6.** $\frac{3}{4} \bigcirc \frac{3}{6}$	**7.** $\frac{7}{8} \bigcirc \frac{3}{4}$
8. $\frac{1}{6} \bigcirc \frac{3}{6}$	**9.** $\frac{1}{4} \bigcirc \frac{2}{8}$	**10.** $\frac{2}{4} \bigcirc \frac{2}{8}$
11. $\frac{1}{2} \bigcirc \frac{4}{8}$	**12.** $\frac{2}{3} \bigcirc \frac{5}{6}$	**13.** $\frac{1}{3} \bigcirc \frac{2}{3}$

Complete the statement.

14. $\frac{3}{6} < \frac{\square}{\square}$

15. $\frac{2}{8} > \frac{\square}{\square}$

16. $\frac{1}{4} < \frac{\square}{\square}$

17. Newton and Descartes have the same-sized lunch. Newton eats $\frac{2}{3}$ of his lunch. Descartes eats $\frac{1}{2}$ of his lunch. Who eats more of his lunch?

18. DIG DEEPER! Use the fractions and symbols to make two true statements.

$\frac{3}{4}$ $\frac{1}{2}$ $\frac{5}{6}$ $\frac{1}{3}$ $>$ $<$

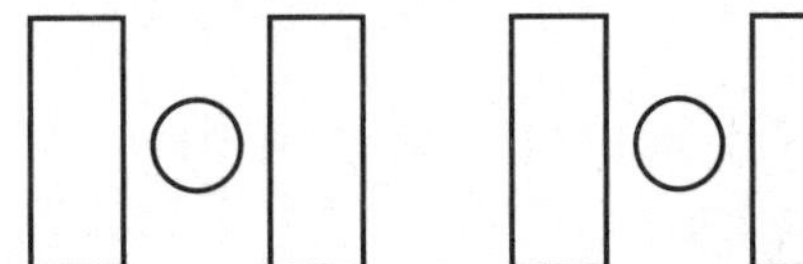

Think and Grow: Modeling Real Life

Newton walks $\frac{3}{8}$ mile to school. Descartes walks $\frac{5}{6}$ mile to school. Who walks farther to school?

Understand the problem:

Make a plan:

Solve:

______________ walks farther to school.

Show and Grow *I can think deeper!*

19. Two apartment buildings have the same number of floors. New carpeting is installed on $\frac{2}{3}$ of the floors in Building A and $\frac{3}{6}$ of the floors in Building B. Which building has more floors with new carpeting?

20. Newton buys $\frac{5}{8}$ pound of peanuts and $\frac{1}{2}$ pound of cashews. Which weighs less? Explain.

21. **DIG DEEPER!** You are painting a backdrop for a school play. You paint $\frac{1}{3}$ of the backdrop blue. You paint more of the backdrop yellow than blue. What fraction can represent the part of the backdrop that is yellow? Explain.

Name ___________________________

Homework & Practice 11.7

Learning Target: Compare fractions.

Example Compare $\frac{7}{8}$ and $\frac{1}{2}$.

Use Fraction Strips.

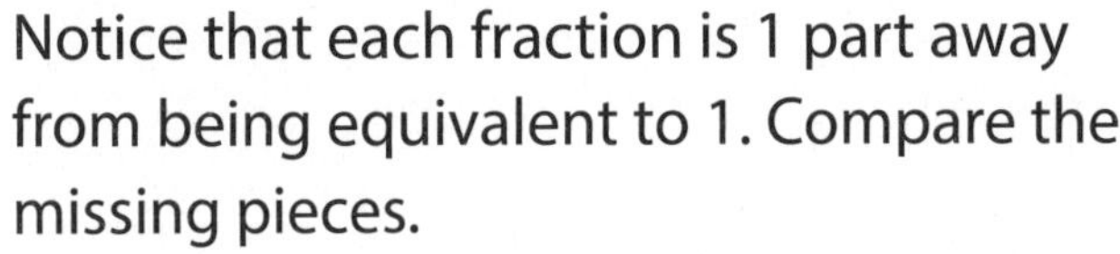

Notice that each fraction is 1 part away from being equivalent to 1. Compare the missing pieces.

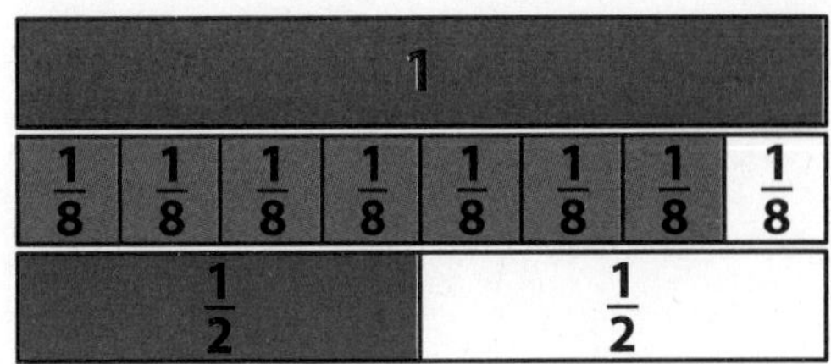

Because $\frac{1}{8}$ (<) $\frac{1}{2}$, a larger piece is missing from $\frac{1}{2}$.

So, $\frac{7}{8}$ (>) $\frac{1}{2}$.

Compare.

1. $\frac{2}{4} \bigcirc \frac{2}{6}$

2. $\frac{1}{2} \bigcirc \frac{3}{6}$

3. $\frac{1}{4} \bigcirc \frac{3}{4}$

4. $\frac{4}{6} \bigcirc \frac{6}{6}$

5. $\frac{3}{4} \bigcirc \frac{6}{8}$

6. $\frac{1}{2} \bigcirc \frac{7}{8}$

7. $\frac{3}{6} \bigcirc \frac{3}{8}$

8. $\frac{2}{3} \bigcirc \frac{3}{4}$

Complete the statement.

9. $\frac{5}{6} < \frac{\square}{\square}$

10. $\frac{7}{8} > \frac{\square}{\square}$

11. $\frac{2}{4} < \frac{\square}{\square}$

12. **Number Sense** Which statements are true?

$\frac{3}{8} \overset{?}{<} \frac{3}{4}$ $\frac{2}{3} \overset{?}{>} \frac{7}{8}$ $\frac{3}{4} \overset{?}{<} \frac{1}{4}$ $\frac{1}{2} \overset{?}{>} \frac{1}{4}$

13. **Communicate Clearly** Explain how to compare $\frac{2}{3}$ and $\frac{7}{8}$ using missing pieces.

14. **Modeling Real Life** Newton and Descartes each have a phone with the same amount of storage. Newton's storage is $\frac{3}{4}$ full. Descartes's storage is $\frac{2}{8}$ full. Whose phone has more storage left?

15. **DIG DEEPER!** A restaurant wants to serve three different-sized hamburgers. The largest hamburger will be $\frac{1}{2}$ pound. The smallest hamburger will be $\frac{1}{4}$ pound. Name a fraction that could represent the other hamburger's size.

Review & Refresh

16. There are 37 students on a bus. The bus stops 5 times. Seven students get off at each stop. How many students are left on the bus?

Name ______________________________

Compare and Order Fractions 11.8

Learning Target: Compare and order fractions.

Success Criteria:

- I can choose a strategy to compare three fractions.
- I can order three fractions from least to greatest.
- I can order three fractions from greatest to least.

Explore and Grow

Plot the fractions on the number line. Order the fractions from least to greatest.

$\frac{3}{6}$ $\frac{1}{6}$ $\frac{5}{6}$

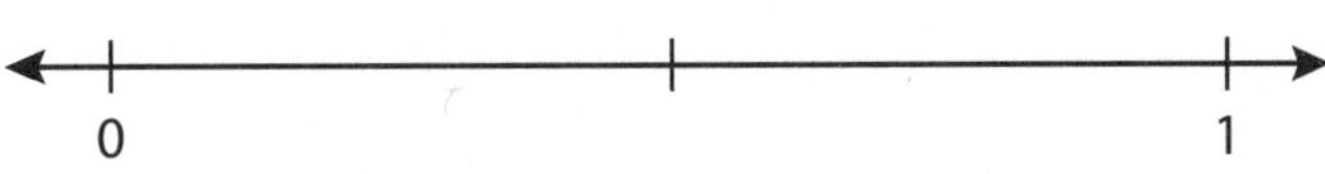

$\frac{\square}{\square}$, $\frac{\square}{\square}$, $\frac{\square}{\square}$

Least Greatest

Reasoning How can you use the fraction $\frac{1}{2}$ to compare and order fractions?

Think and Grow: Compare and Order Fractions

Example Order the fractions $\frac{7}{8}$, $\frac{1}{8}$, and $\frac{5}{8}$ from least to greatest.

Plot the fractions on the number line. All 3 fractions have the same denominator, 8.

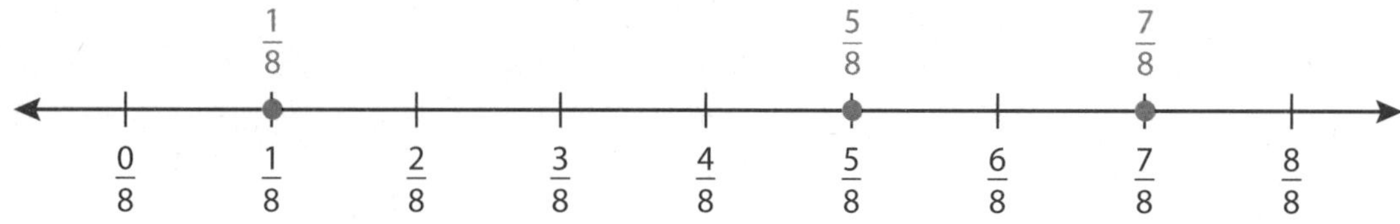

$\frac{\square}{8}$ is farthest to the left. $\frac{\square}{8}$ is farthest to the right.

$\frac{\square}{8}$ is between the other two fractions.

Think: $\frac{7}{8}$ is close to 1. $\frac{1}{8}$ is close to 0. $\frac{5}{8}$ is close to $\frac{4}{8}$, or $\frac{1}{2}$.

So, the order from least to greatest is $\frac{\square}{\square}$, $\frac{\square}{\square}$, $\frac{\square}{\square}$.

Example Order the fractions $\frac{2}{4}$, $\frac{2}{3}$, and $\frac{2}{6}$ from least to greatest.

Use Fraction Strips. All three fractions have the same numerator, 2.

1					
$\frac{1}{4}$	$\frac{1}{4}$	$\frac{1}{4}$	$\frac{1}{4}$		
$\frac{1}{3}$	$\frac{1}{3}$	$\frac{1}{3}$			
$\frac{1}{6}$	$\frac{1}{6}$	$\frac{1}{6}$	$\frac{1}{6}$	$\frac{1}{6}$	$\frac{1}{6}$

Shade the Fraction Strips. Compare the parts.

$\frac{2}{\square}$ is the shortest. $\frac{2}{\square}$ is the longest.

$\frac{2}{\square}$ is between the other two fractions.

So, the order from least to greatest is $\frac{\square}{\square}$, $\frac{\square}{\square}$, $\frac{\square}{\square}$.

Show and Grow *I can do it!*

1. Order the fractions $\frac{3}{3}$, $\frac{3}{4}$, and $\frac{3}{8}$ from least to greatest.

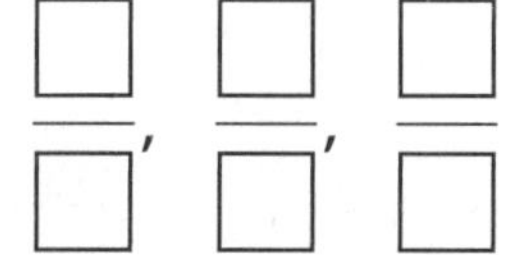

Name ____

Apply and Grow: Practice

Order the fractions from least to greatest.

2. $\frac{1}{6}, \frac{6}{6}, \frac{5}{6}$ $\quad \frac{\square}{\square}, \frac{\square}{\square}, \frac{\square}{\square}$

3. $\frac{3}{3}, \frac{3}{1}, \frac{3}{2}$

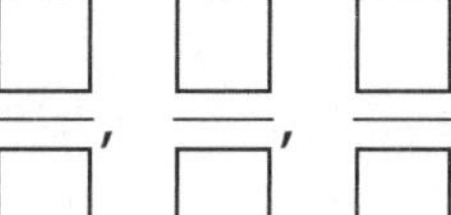

4. $\frac{4}{4}, \frac{0}{4}, \frac{3}{4}$ $\quad \frac{\square}{\square}, \frac{\square}{\square}, \frac{\square}{\square}$

5. $\frac{6}{1}, \frac{6}{6}, \frac{6}{8}$

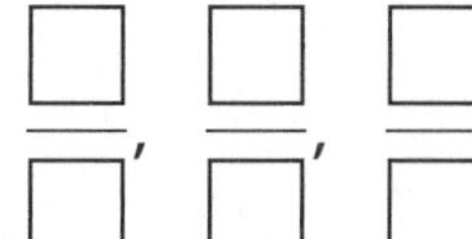

Order the fractions from greatest to least.

6. $\frac{4}{8}, \frac{3}{8}, \frac{6}{8}$

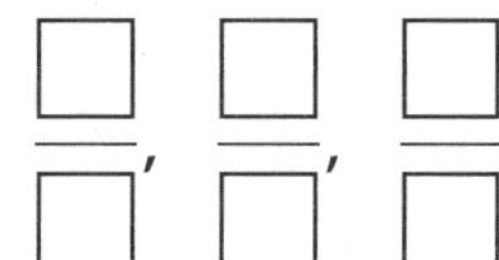

7. $\frac{2}{4}, \frac{2}{1}, \frac{2}{6}$

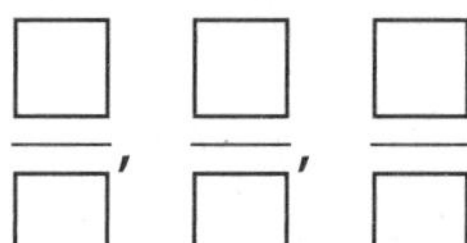

8. MP **Communicate Clearly** Three fractions have the same denominator. How do you know which fraction is the greatest?

9. **Open-Ended** Write a fraction that is between $\frac{2}{8}$ and $\frac{2}{3}$.

10. MP **Patterns** The fractions below are in order from least to greatest. Describe and complete the pattern.

$\frac{2}{8}, \frac{2}{7}, \frac{2}{6}, \frac{2}{5}, \frac{2}{\square}, \frac{2}{\square}, \frac{2}{\square}, \frac{2}{\square}$

Think and Grow: Modeling Real Life

A construction crew replaces $\frac{1}{8}$ mile of a road on Monday, $\frac{1}{4}$ mile of the road on Tuesday, and $\frac{1}{6}$ mile of the road on Wednesday. On which day does the crew replace the longest piece of the road? On which day does the crew replace the shortest piece? Explain.

Model:

The crew replaces the longest piece of the road on ______________

and the shortest piece on ______________.

Explain:

Show and Grow *I can think deeper!*

11. You place three plants in order from shortest to tallest. A cactus is $\frac{4}{6}$ foot tall, a fern is $\frac{4}{4}$ foot tall, and an aloe vera plant is $\frac{4}{8}$ foot tall. Which plant is first? Which plant is last? Explain.

12. You measure the lengths of three spiders. The longest one is $\frac{3}{4}$ inch long. The shortest one is $\frac{1}{4}$ inch long. What is a possible length for the third spider? Explain.

13. DIG DEEPER! You are ordering three fractions. You know which fraction is the greatest and which fraction is the least. What do you know about the third fraction?

Name ________________________________

Homework & Practice 11.8

Learning Target: Compare and order fractions.

Example Order the fractions $\frac{4}{4}$, $\frac{4}{8}$, and $\frac{4}{6}$ from least to greatest.

Use Fraction Strips. All three fractions have the same numerator, 4. Shade the fraction strips. Compare the parts.

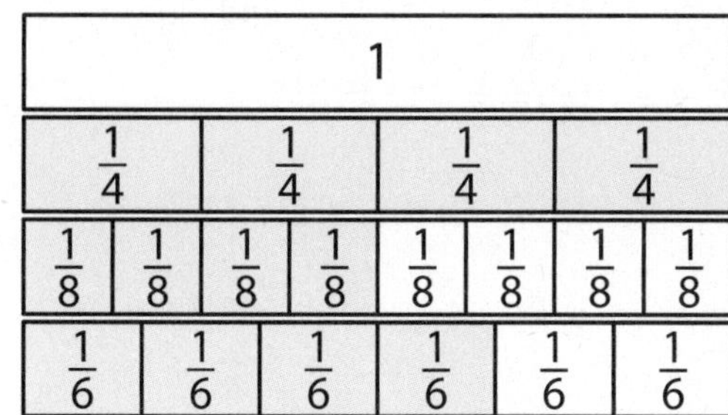

$\frac{4}{\boxed{8}}$ is the shortest. $\frac{4}{\boxed{4}}$ is the longest.

$\frac{4}{\boxed{6}}$ is between the other two fractions.

So, the order from least to greatest is $\frac{\boxed{4}}{\boxed{8}}, \frac{\boxed{4}}{\boxed{6}}, \frac{\boxed{4}}{\boxed{4}}$.

Order the fractions from least to greatest.

1. $\frac{8}{4}, \frac{8}{1}, \frac{8}{3}$ $\frac{\square}{\square}, \frac{\square}{\square}, \frac{\square}{\square}$

2. $\frac{2}{4}, \frac{1}{4}, \frac{3}{4}$ $\frac{\square}{\square}, \frac{\square}{\square}, \frac{\square}{\square}$

3. $\frac{16}{8}, \frac{3}{8}, \frac{5}{8}$ $\frac{\square}{\square}, \frac{\square}{\square}, \frac{\square}{\square}$

4. $\frac{4}{2}, \frac{4}{8}, \frac{4}{6}$ $\frac{\square}{\square}, \frac{\square}{\square}, \frac{\square}{\square}$

Order the fractions from greatest to least.

5. $\frac{1}{6}, \frac{1}{4}, \frac{1}{8}$ $\frac{\square}{\square}, \frac{\square}{\square}, \frac{\square}{\square}$

6. $\frac{0}{2}, \frac{2}{2}, \frac{1}{2}$ $\frac{\square}{\square}, \frac{\square}{\square}, \frac{\square}{\square}$

7. $\frac{3}{3}, \frac{1}{3}, \frac{2}{3}$ $\frac{\square}{\square}, \frac{\square}{\square}, \frac{\square}{\square}$

8. $\frac{6}{3}, \frac{6}{8}, \frac{6}{2}$ $\frac{\square}{\square}, \frac{\square}{\square}, \frac{\square}{\square}$

9. **MP Communicate Clearly** Three fractions have the same numerator. How do you know which fraction is the greatest?

10. **MP Precision** Which set of fractions is ordered from least to greatest?

$\frac{2}{1}, \frac{2}{6}, \frac{2}{10}$ $\frac{1}{4}, \frac{3}{4}, \frac{2}{4}$

$\frac{5}{6}, \frac{4}{6}, \frac{0}{6}$ $\frac{5}{6}, \frac{5}{5}, \frac{5}{3}$

11. **DIG DEEPER!** Use the number line to order $\frac{3}{6}$, $\frac{2}{3}$, and $\frac{5}{12}$ from least to greatest.

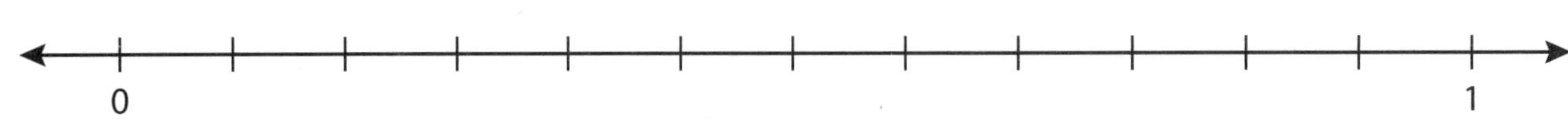

12. **MP Modeling Real Life** You survey your classmates about their favorite subject. $\frac{5}{8}$ of the students choose math, $\frac{1}{8}$ choose reading, and $\frac{2}{8}$ choose science. Which subject receives the most votes? Which subject receives the least votes? Explain.

13. **MP Modeling Real Life** A carpenter has three drill bits. The thickest one is $\frac{3}{4}$ inch. The thinnest one is $\frac{3}{8}$ inch. What is a possible width for the third drill bit? Explain.

Review & Refresh

14. You clean lunch tables. There are 6 rows of tables with 7 tables in each row. How many tables do you clean?

Name ____

Performance Task 11

1. You invite five friends to dinner. You start making chili using the recipe shown at 4:00.

   a. What time should you tell your friends the chili will be ready?

   b. Which ingredient do you use the same amount of as crushed garlic?

   c. Do you use more chopped green pepper or onion? Explain.

   d. How many ounces of beans do you use in all?

Vegetarian Chili

Number of Servings: 16

2 cups water

$\frac{1}{8}$ cup olive oil

$\frac{2}{8}$ cup crushed garlic

2 cups carrots

cups diced tomatoes

$\frac{1}{2}$ cup onion

$\frac{3}{4}$ cup chopped green pepper

$\frac{1}{4}$ cup chili powder

2 8-ounce cans pinto beans

2 8-ounce cans black beans

Salt and pepper to taste

Prep time: 20 minutes

Cook time: 40 minutes

   e. You know there is $\frac{1}{4}$ cup of diced tomatoes in each serving. How many cups of diced tomatoes do you need?

Analyze a Problem What additional information do you need to solve?

   f. You and your friends each eat 2 servings of chili. How many servings are left? Write an equation to solve. Use letters to represent unknown numbers.

Fraction Spin and Compare

Directions:

1. Players take turns.
2. On your turn, spin both spinners. Cover a box that makes the statement true.
3. If there are no fractions left that make the statement true, then you lose your turn.
4. Play until all boxes are covered.
5. The player with the most boxes covered wins!

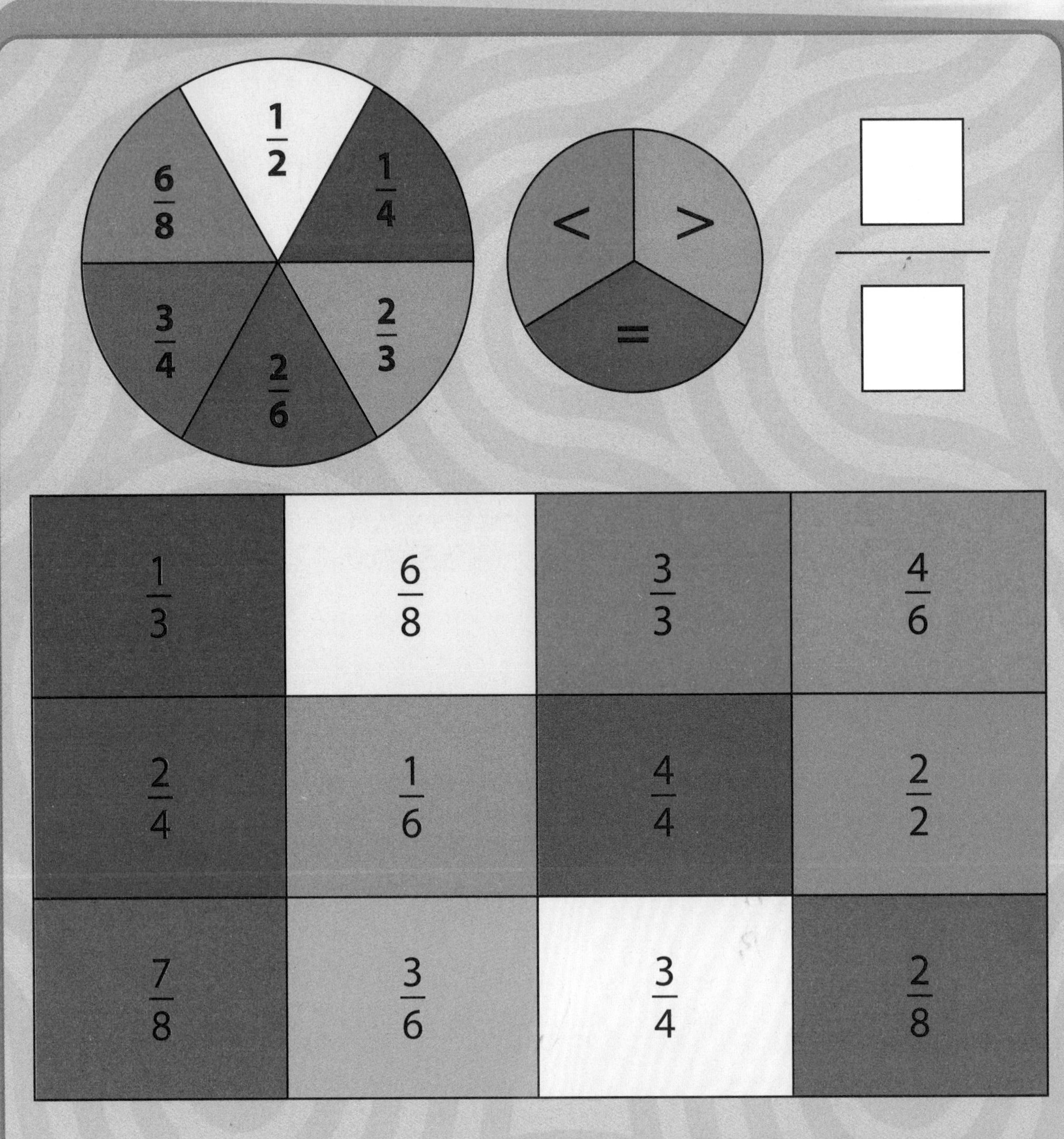

$\frac{1}{3}$	$\frac{6}{8}$	$\frac{3}{3}$	$\frac{4}{6}$
$\frac{2}{4}$	$\frac{1}{6}$	$\frac{4}{4}$	$\frac{2}{2}$
$\frac{7}{8}$	$\frac{3}{6}$	$\frac{3}{4}$	$\frac{2}{8}$

Name ______________________________

Chapter Practice 11

11.1 Equivalent Fractions

Use the models to find an equivalent fraction. Both models show the same whole.

1.

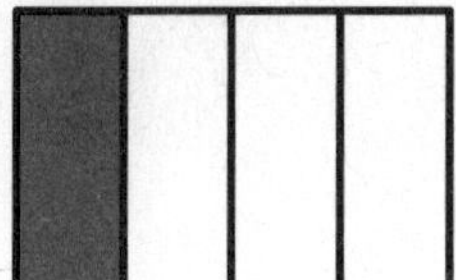

$\frac{1}{4} = \frac{\square}{8}$

2.

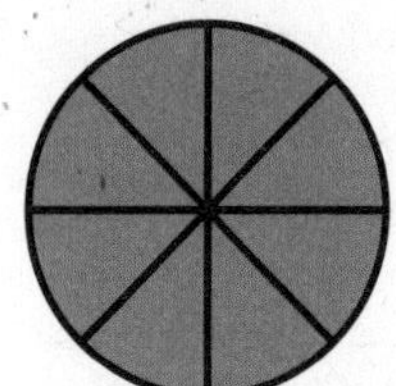

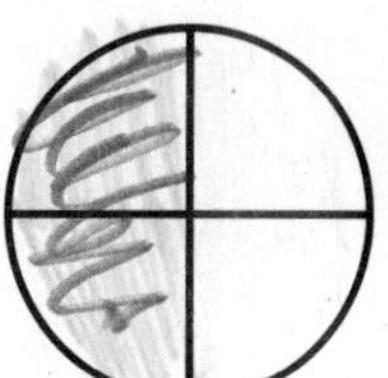

$\frac{8}{8} = \frac{\square}{4}$

3. **Which One Doesn't Belong?** Which one does *not* belong with the other three?

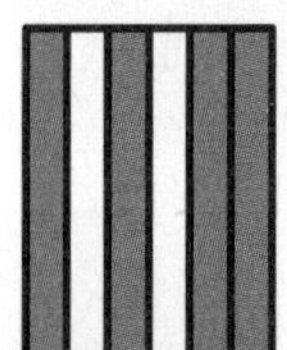

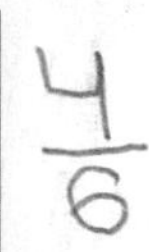

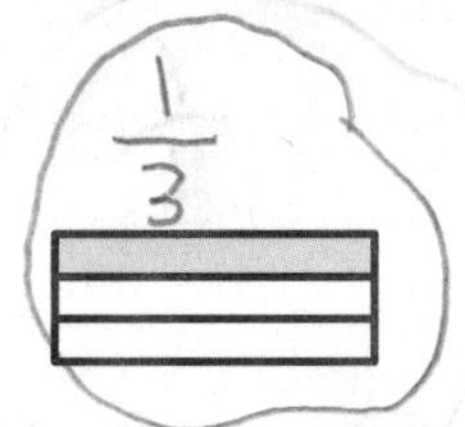

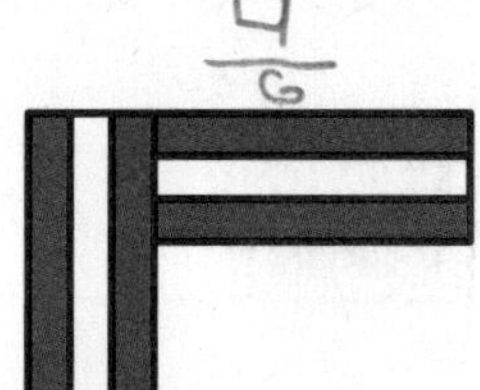

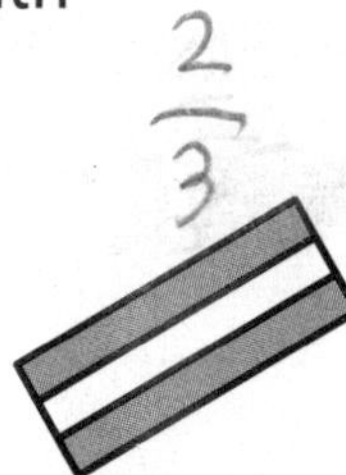

11.2 Equivalent Fractions on a Number Line

Write two fractions that name the point shown.

4.

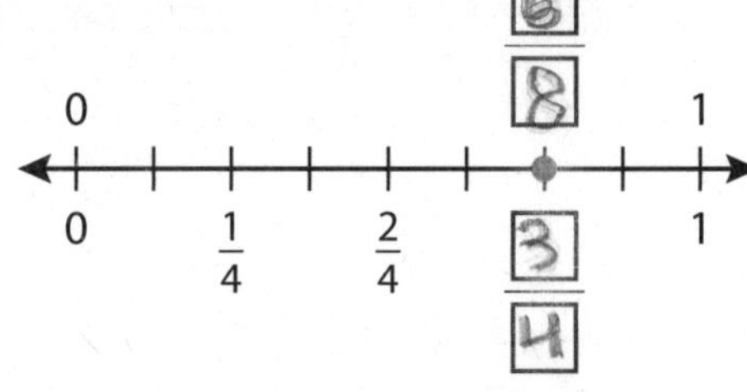

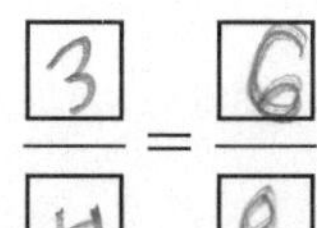

$\frac{\square}{\square} = \frac{\square}{\square}$

5.

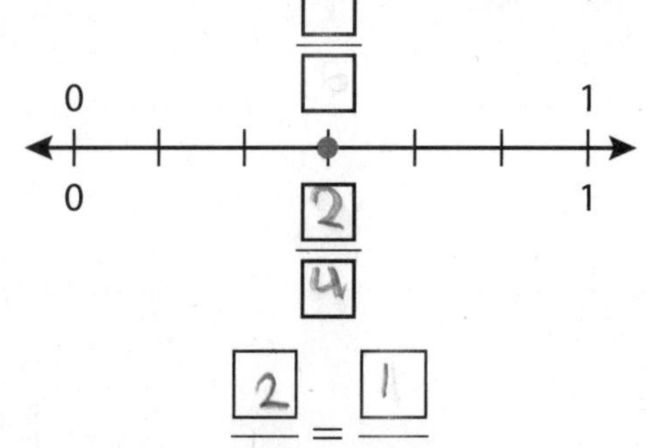

$\frac{\square}{\square} = \frac{\square}{\square}$

11.3 Relate Fractions and Whole Numbers

6. Complete the number line. Then write equivalent fractions for the numbers 1 and 2.

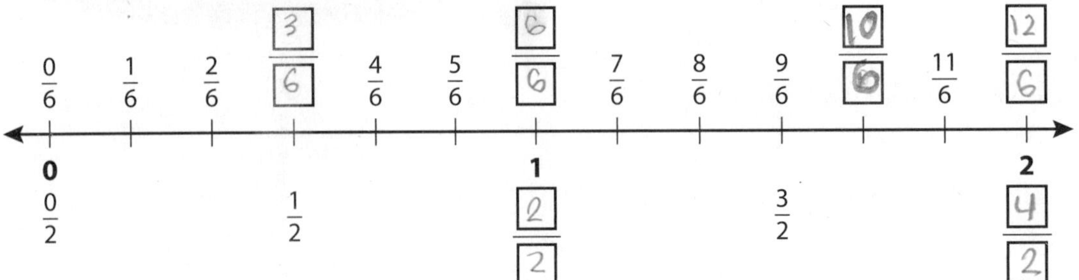

$1 = \frac{1}{1} = \frac{2}{2} = \frac{6}{6}$ $2 = \frac{2}{1} = \frac{4}{2} = \frac{12}{6}$

Write two equivalent fractions for the whole number.

7. $2 = \frac{8}{4} = \frac{12}{6}$

8. $6 = \frac{18}{3} = \frac{24}{4}$

9. $4 = \frac{8}{2} = \frac{32}{8}$

Write the equivalent whole number.

10. $\frac{4}{4} = \frac{1}{1} = 1$

11. $\frac{24}{8} = \frac{12}{4} = 3$

12. $\frac{24}{6} = \frac{16}{4} = 4$

11.4 Compare Fractions with the Same Denominator

Shade to compare the fractions.

13.

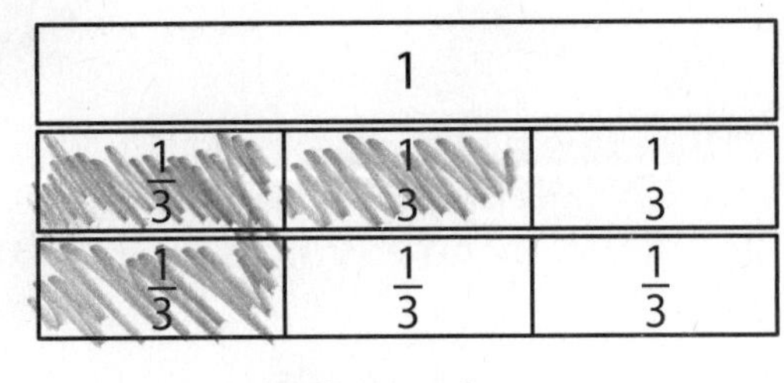

$\frac{2}{3} > \frac{1}{3}$

14.

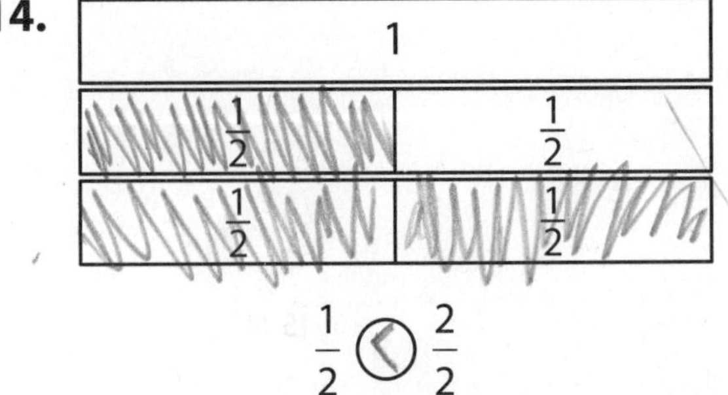

$\frac{1}{2} < \frac{2}{2}$

Compare.

15. $\frac{2}{4} < \frac{3}{4}$

16. $\frac{1}{3} = \frac{1}{3}$

17. $\frac{1}{6} < \frac{5}{6}$

11.5 Compare Fractions with the Same Numerator

Compare.

18. $\frac{1}{8} \bigcirc \frac{1}{6}$

19. $\frac{4}{6} \bigcirc \frac{4}{4}$

20. $\frac{2}{3} \bigcirc \frac{2}{4}$

21. $\frac{3}{6} \bigcirc \frac{3}{8}$

22. $\frac{6}{8} \bigcirc \frac{6}{6}$

23. $\frac{3}{8} \bigcirc \frac{3}{4}$

24. MP **Modeling Real Life** Your glass of orange juice is $\frac{1}{2}$ full. Your friend's glass of orange juice is $\frac{1}{3}$ full. Your friend has more orange juice. Explain how this is possible.

11.6 Compare Fractions on a Number Line

Compare.

25. Number line: $\frac{0}{3}$, $\frac{1}{3}$, $\frac{2}{3}$, $\frac{3}{3}$

$\frac{2}{3} \bigcirc \frac{1}{3}$

26.

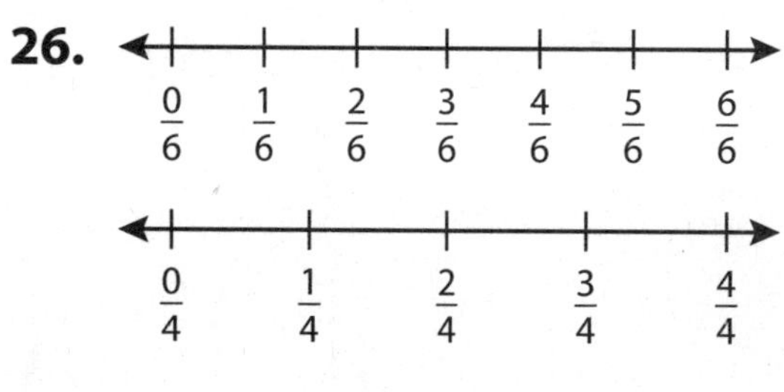

$\frac{2}{6} \bigcirc \frac{2}{4}$

27. $\frac{4}{8} \bigcirc \frac{4}{6}$

28. $\frac{5}{8} \bigcirc \frac{3}{8}$

29. $\frac{5}{6} \bigcirc \frac{2}{6}$

30. Write a fraction that is greater than $\frac{1}{8}$.

31. Write a fraction that is less than $\frac{2}{3}$.

11.7 Compare Fractions

Compare.

32. $\frac{1}{1} \bigcirc \frac{1}{2}$	**33.** $\frac{3}{6} \bigcirc \frac{5}{6}$	**34.** $\frac{4}{6} \bigcirc \frac{4}{8}$
35. $\frac{1}{3} \bigcirc \frac{2}{3}$	**36.** $\frac{2}{2} \bigcirc \frac{2}{8}$	**37.** $\frac{3}{4} \bigcirc \frac{7}{8}$

38. MP **Number Sense** Which statements are true?

$\frac{2}{3} \stackrel{?}{<} \frac{7}{8}$ $\qquad$ $\frac{1}{8} \stackrel{?}{<} \frac{1}{4}$ $\qquad$ $\frac{5}{6} \stackrel{?}{>} \frac{3}{4}$ $\qquad$ $\frac{1}{2} \stackrel{?}{>} \frac{0}{2}$

11.8 Compare and Order Fractions

Order the fractions from least to greatest.

39. $\frac{4}{4}, \frac{4}{8}, \frac{4}{6}$ $\qquad \frac{\square}{\square}, \frac{\square}{\square}, \frac{\square}{\square}$

40. $\frac{3}{6}, \frac{5}{6}, \frac{1}{6}$ $\qquad \frac{\square}{\square}, \frac{\square}{\square}, \frac{\square}{\square}$

Order the fractions from greatest to least.

41. $\frac{1}{3}, \frac{0}{3}, \frac{2}{3}$ $\qquad \frac{\square}{\square}, \frac{\square}{\square}, \frac{\square}{\square}$

42. $\frac{2}{6}, \frac{2}{1}, \frac{2}{4}$ $\qquad \frac{\square}{\square}, \frac{\square}{\square}, \frac{\square}{\square}$

43. MP **Modeling Real Life** You, your friend, and your cousin have the same-sized aquarium. You fill your aquarium $\frac{2}{3}$ full, your friend fills hers $\frac{2}{6}$ full, and your cousin fills his $\frac{2}{4}$ full. Which aquarium is the least full? Which aquarium is the most full? Explain.

12 Understand Time, Liquid Volume, and Mass

Chapter Learning Target:
Understand time and measurement.

Chapter Success Criteria:

- I can explain how to tell time to the nearest minute.
- I can find the appropriate way to measure an object.
- I can solve time interval problems.
- I can compare one measurement to another.

- What is the weather today? What do you think the weather will be at 5 o'clock?
- The sun rises at 6:32. How do you know whether the time is A.M. or P.M.? How can knowing how much time has passed help you in your daily life?

Name ______________________________

12 Vocabulary

Review Words

A.M.

P.M.

Organize It

Use the review words to complete the graphic organizer.

Morning	Night
  Eat breakfast. 7:00 ☐	  Read a book. 7:00 ☐

Define It

Use your vocabulary cards to identify the word. Find the word in the word search.

1. The standard metric unit used to measure mass
2. The standard metric unit used to measure liquid volume
3. The amount of matter in an object

M	T	U	E	K	L	U	G
S	A	E	R	T	I	V	R
O	N	S	E	Q	U	I	A
M	A	L	S	S	A	T	M
V	C	R	P	F	L	D	E
F	S	Y	D	O	K	H	G
K	I	L	I	T	E	R	M

Chapter 12 Vocabulary Cards

elapsed time

gram (g)

kilogram (kg)

liquid volume

liter (L)

mass

milliliter (mL)

time interval

The standard metric unit used to measure mass

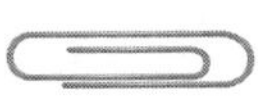

The mass of a paper clip is about 1 **gram**.

The amount of time that passes from a starting time to an ending time

The elapsed time is 38 minutes.

The amount of liquid in a container

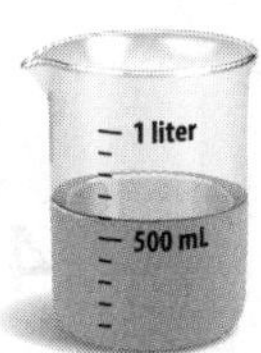

A metric unit used to measure mass

The mass of a baseball bat is about 1 **kilogram**.

The amount of matter in an object

The standard metric unit used to measure liquid volume

There is about 1 **liter** of liquid in the water bottle.

An amount of time

15 minutes

30 minutes

57 minutes

42 minutes

A metric unit used to measure liquid volume

20 drops of liquid from an eyedropper is about 1 **milliliter**.

Name ___________________________________

Time to the Nearest Minute 12.1

Learning Target: Tell time to the nearest minute.

Success Criteria:

- I can write the time to the nearest minute.
- I can write the time in multiple ways.
- I can explain how to tell time to the nearest minute.

Explore and Grow

Write each time.

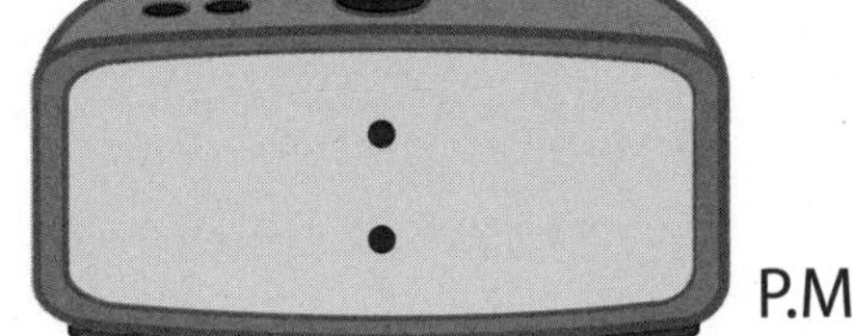

P.M.

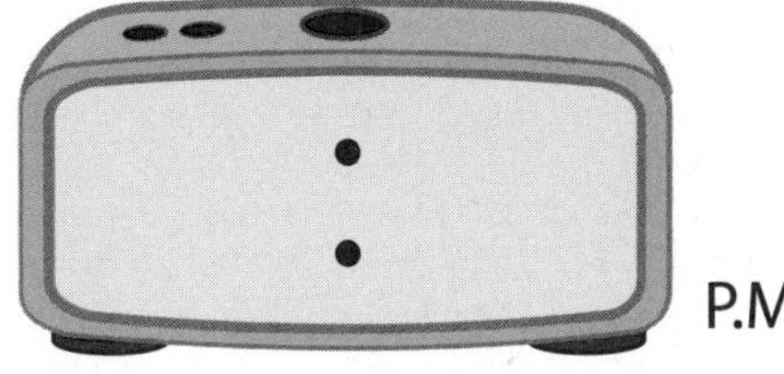

P.M.

Communicate Clearly How did you find each time?

Think and Grow: Tell Time to the Nearest Minute

Example What time does the clock show? What are some other ways to say the time?

1 minute

It takes 1 minute for the minute hand to move from one mark to the next.

Step 1: Look at the hour hand.

- The hour hand is between the 4 and the 5.
- So, it is after 4:00 and before 5:00.

Step 2: Look at the minute hand.

- Count by 5s from the 12 to the 7.
- Count on by 1s from the 7 to the mark where the minute hand is pointing.

So, the time is _____ : _____.

Count the minutes after the hour. Say, "_____ minutes after 4."

Count the minutes before the next hour. Say, "_____ minutes before 5."

Show and Grow *I can do it!*

Write the time. Write another way to say the time.

1.

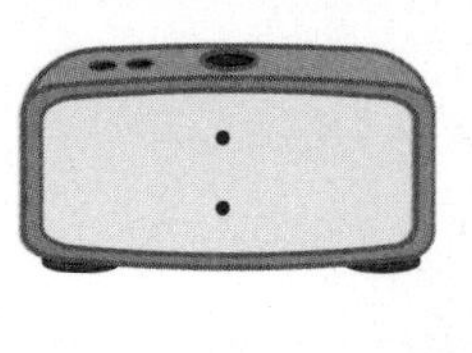

2.

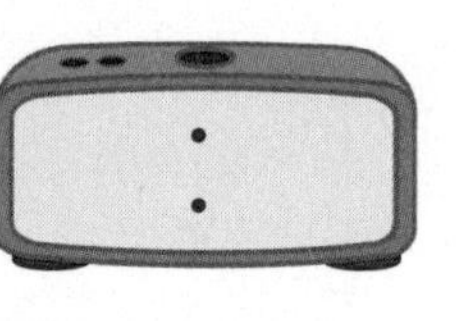

Name ______________________________

Apply and Grow: Practice

Write the time. Write another way to say the time.

3.

4.

5.

Write the time. Write two other ways to say the time.

6.

7.

8.

Write the time.

9. 24 minutes after 3

10. 13 minutes before 9

11. 7 minutes before 1

12. Which One Doesn't Belong? Which time does *not* belong with the other three?

27 minutes after 4

33 minutes before 5

Think and Grow: Modeling Real Life

A train leaves a station at 12 minutes before 8. Show and write the time the train leaves the station.

Show and Grow I can think deeper!

13. You go for a walk at 26 minutes after 2. Show and write the time you go for a walk.

14. DIG DEEPER! Newton and Descartes start playing a game at 3:11. They play for 47 minutes. Show and write the time they stop playing the game.

15. You eat breakfast at 34 minutes before 9. You eat dinner at 42 minutes after 6. Show and write the times. Circle *A.M.* or *P.M.*

Breakfast

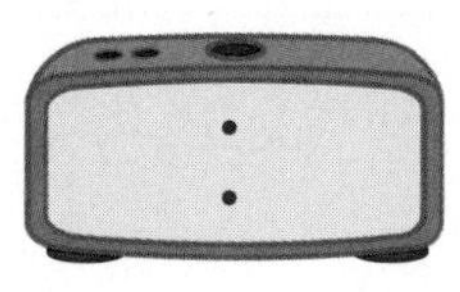

A.M. P.M.

Dinner

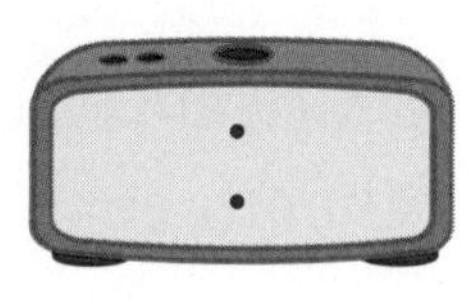

A.M. P.M.

Which time is earlier? Explain.

Name ________________________________

Homework & Practice 12.1

Learning Target: Tell time to the nearest minute.

Example What time does the clock show? What are some other ways to say the time?

Step 1: Look at the hour hand.

- The hour hand is between the 9 and the 10.
- So, it is after 9:00 and before 10:00.

Step 2: Look at the minute hand.

- Count by 5s from the 12 to the 4.
- Count on by 1s from the 4 to the mark where the minute hand is pointing.

The time is <u>23</u> minutes after 9, or <u>37</u> minutes before 10.

Write the time. Write another way to say the time.

1.

2.

Write the time. Write two other ways to say the time.

3.

4.

5.

Write the time.

6. 32 minutes after 10

7. 8 minutes before 6

8. 16 minutes before 8

9. **Writing** Explain when you would stop counting by 5s and start counting by 1s when telling time to the nearest minute.

10. **MP Communicate Clearly** Explain where the hands of an analog clock point at 1:27.

11. **MP Modeling Real Life** You start practicing taekwondo 19 minutes before 7. Show and write the time you start practicing.

12. **DIG DEEPER!** Some friends start jumping rope at 12:22. They jump rope for 24 minutes. Show and write the time they stop jumping rope.

Review & Refresh

Find the difference. Check whether your answer is reasonable.

13. Estimate: _____

$$\begin{array}{r} 526 \\ -\ 203 \\ \hline \end{array}$$

14. Estimate: _____

$$\begin{array}{r} 945 \\ -\ 362 \\ \hline \end{array}$$

15. Estimate: _____

$$\begin{array}{r} 412 \\ -\ 145 \\ \hline \end{array}$$

Name ______________________________

Measure Elapsed Time within the Hour 12.2

Learning Target: Measure elapsed time, in minutes, within the same hour.

Success Criteria:

- I can identify start and end times.
- I can find the amount of time that passes between two times.
- I can explain how to find elapsed time within the same hour.

Explore and Grow

Write each time. How much time has passed?

Start

End

___ : ___ A.M.

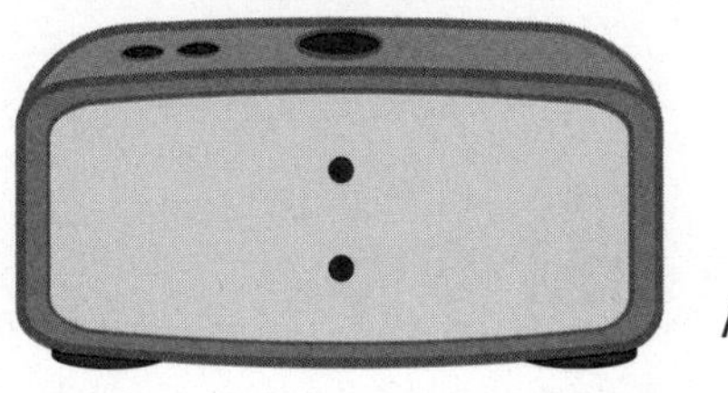

___ : ___ A.M.

_____ minutes have passed.

Reasoning How many more minutes until a half hour has passed? Explain.

Think and Grow: Measure Elapsed Time

Elapsed time is the amount of time that passes from a starting time to an ending time.

Example Find the elapsed time between 2:05 P.M. and 2:43 P.M.

One Way: Use an analog clock.

Step 1: Draw the starting time.

Step 2: Mark the ending time.

Step 3: Count the minutes by 5s and 1s until you reach the ending time.

So, the elapsed time is _____ minutes.

Another Way: Use a number line.

Step 1: Plot the starting time on a number line.

Step 2: Count on until you reach the ending time.

Step 3: Add the jumps to find the elapsed time.

+10 min +10 min +10 min +5 min +3 min = _____ minutes

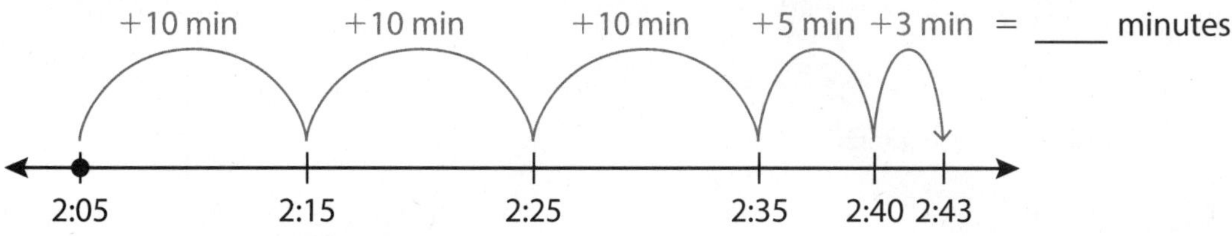

So, the elapsed time is _____ minutes.

Show and Grow *I can do it!*

Find the elapsed time.

1. Start: 11:10 A.M. End: 11:34 A.M.

_____ minutes

2. Start: 1:25 P.M. End: 1:56 P.M.

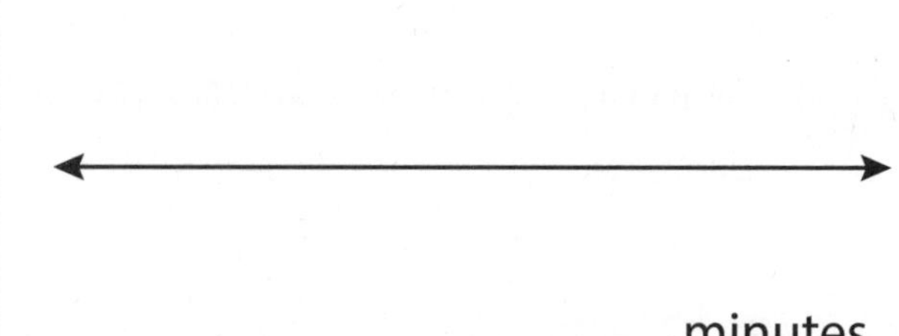

_____ minutes

Name ______________________________

Apply and Grow: Practice

Find the elapsed time.

3. Start: 7:30 A.M. End: 7:53 A.M.

_____ minutes

4. Start: 5:15 P.M. End: 5:41 P.M.

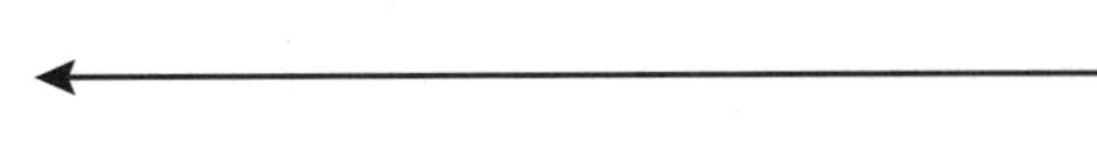

_____ minutes

5. Start: 10:50 A.M. End: 10:59 A.M.

_____ minutes

6. Start: 8:05 P.M. End: 8:37 P.M.

_____ minutes

7. MP **Structure** Find the elapsed time and the end time.

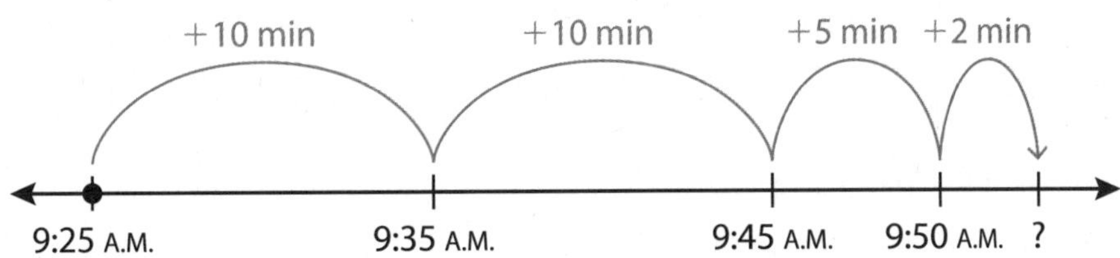

Elapsed time: _____ minutes End time: _____ A.M.

8. MP **Communicate Clearly** Explain how to use an analog clock to find the elapsed time from 6:20 P.M. to 6:38 P.M.

Think and Grow: Modeling Real Life

A magic show starts at 3:15 P.M. It ends at 3:57 P.M. How long is the show?

Model:

The show is _____ minutes long.

Show and Grow I can think deeper!

9. A nature walk starts at 10:30 A.M. It ends at 10:46 A.M. How long is the walk?

10. An Internet video is 13 minutes long. You start the video at 1:23 P.M. At what time does the video end?

11. DIG DEEPER! You play hopscotch for 27 minutes. You stop at 4:40 P.M. At what time did you start playing hopscotch?

12. You practice the guitar from 12:06 P.M. to 12:35 P.M. on Saturday and from 9:25 A.M. to 9:47 A.M. on Sunday. How long did you spend practicing the guitar in all?

Name ______________________

Homework & Practice 12.2

Learning Target: Measure elapsed time, in minutes, within the same hour.

Example Find the elapsed time from 8:45 A.M. to 8:57 A.M.

One Way: Use an analog clock.

Step 1: Draw the starting time.

Step 2: Mark the ending time.

Step 3: Count the minutes by 5s and 1s until you reach the ending time.

So, the elapsed time is 12 minutes.

Another Way: Use a number line.

Step 1: Plot the starting time on a number line.

Step 2: Count on until you reach the ending time.

Step 3: Add the jumps to find the elapsed time.

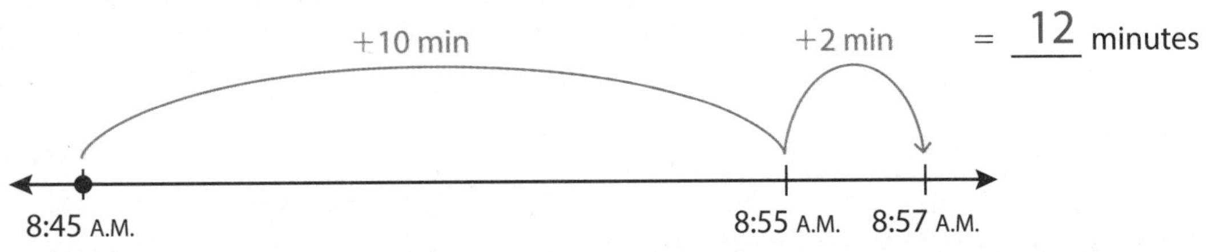

= 12 minutes

So, the elapsed time is 12 minutes.

Find the elapsed time.

1. Start: 6:05 A.M. End: 6:44 A.M.

_____ minutes

2. Start: 3:30 P.M. End: 3:51 P.M.

_____ minutes

Find the elapsed time.

3. Start: 4:10 P.M. End: 4:56 P.M.

_____ minutes

4. Start: 9:25 A.M. End: 9:33 A.M.

_____ minutes

5. **MP YOU BE THE TEACHER** Is Newton correct? Explain.

6. **MP Communicate Clearly** Explain how to use a number line to find the elapsed time from 10:15 A.M. to 10:49 A.M.

7. **MP Modeling Real Life** Your teacher places a beaker of water over a burner at 2:15 P.M. The water boils at 2:26 P.M. How long does it take for the water to boil?

8. **DIG DEEPER!** Descartes plays outside from 1:32 P.M. to 1:45 P.M. He stops to eat lunch. Then he plays outside from 2:20 P.M. to 2:47 P.M. Does he play outside longer than one hour? Explain.

Review & Refresh

9. There are 134 third graders and 106 fourth graders at a state park. There are 220 fewer teachers than students at the park. How many teachers are at the park?

Name ______________________________

Measure Elapsed Time Across the Hour 12.3

Learning Target: Measure elapsed time, in minutes, from one hour to the next.

Success Criteria:

- I can identify start and end times.
- I can find the amount of time that passes between two times.
- I can explain how to find elapsed time from one hour to the next.

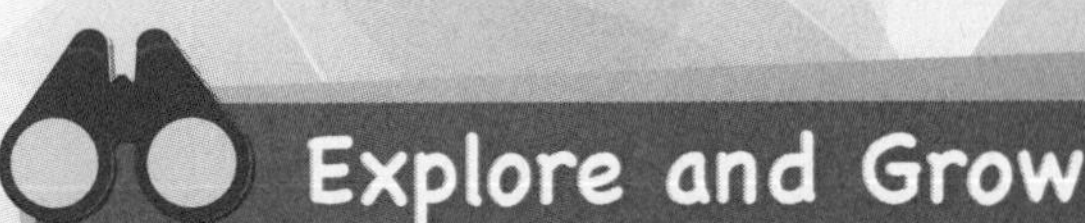

Write each time. How much time has passed?

Start

End

: P.M. : P.M.

_____ minutes have passed.

YOU BE THE TEACHER Newton says one hour has passed because the digit for the hour increased by 1. Why is Newton incorrect?

Think and Grow: Measure Elapsed Time Across an Hour

Example Find the elapsed time between 7:45 A.M. and 8:12 A.M.

One Way: Use an analog clock.

Step 1: Draw the starting time.

Step 2: Mark the ending time.

Step 3: Count the minutes by 5s and 1s until you reach the ending time.

So, the elapsed time is _____ minutes.

Another Way: Use a number line.

Step 1: Plot the starting time on a number line.

Step 2: Count the minutes from the starting time to the next hour. Then count the minutes from the hour to the ending time.

Step 3: Add the jumps to find the elapsed time.

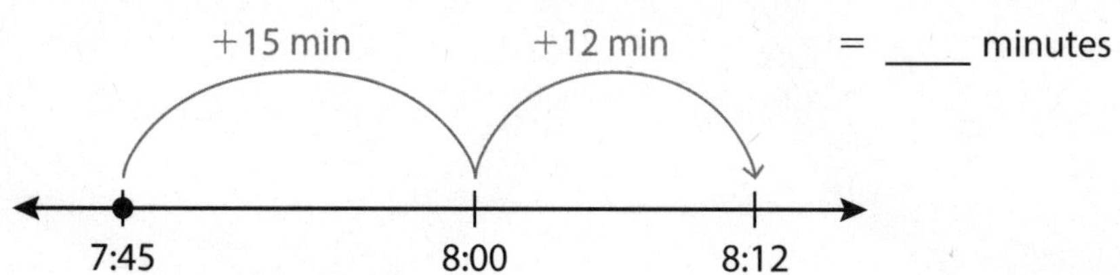

= _____ minutes

So, the elapsed time is _____ minutes.

Show and Grow I can do it!

Find the elapsed time.

1. Start: 3:55 P.M. End: 4:41 P.M.

_____ minutes

2. Start: 10:40 A.M. End: 11:19 A.M.

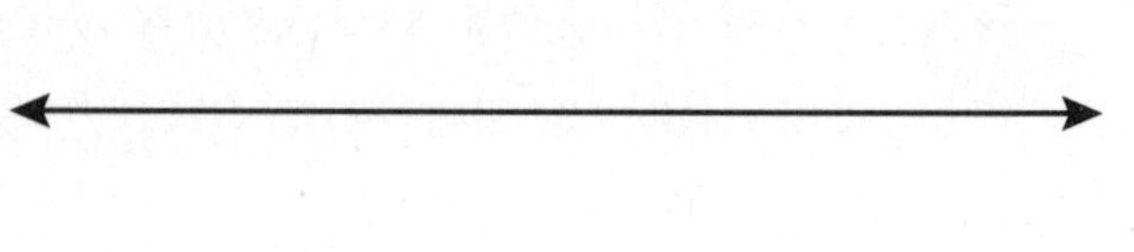

_____ minutes

Name ________________

Apply and Grow: Practice

Find the elapsed time.

3. Start: 1:35 P.M. End: 2:11 P.M.

_____ minutes

4. Start: 8:50 A.M. End: 9:34 A.M.

_____ minutes

5. Start: 5:25 P.M. End: 6:07 P.M.

_____ minutes

6. Start: 11:30 A.M. End: 12:26 P.M.

_____ minutes

7. **MP Maintain Accuracy** Find the end time.

Start: 4:42 P.M.

Elapsed time: 38 minutes

End: _____ P.M.

8. **Writing** Explain two different ways to find the elapsed time from 6:55 A.M. to 7:29 A.M.

Think and Grow: Modeling Real Life

A volleyball game begins at 5:45 P.M. It ends at 6:17 P.M. How long is the game?

Model:

The game is ____ minutes long.

Show and Grow *I can think deeper!*

9. You start playing a virtual reality game at 1:50 P.M. You stop playing at 2:09 P.M. How long do you play the game?

10. You listen to an audiobook that is 47 minutes long. The book ends at 10:25 A.M. At what time did you start the book?

11. Newton roller-skates from 11:35 A.M. to 12:12 P.M. Descartes roller-skates from 3:40 P.M. to 4:26 P.M. Who skates longer?

12. **DIG DEEPER!** You practice juggling from 10:40 A.M. to 11:04 A.M. Your friend practices juggling for the same amount of time as you. She stops at 11:21 A.M. At what time did your friend start juggling?

Name ___________________________

Homework & Practice 12.3

Learning Target: Measure elapsed time, in minutes, from one hour to the next.

Example Find the elapsed time from 5:40 P.M. to 6:14 P.M.

One Way: Use an analog clock.

Step 1: Draw the starting time.

Step 2: Mark the ending time.

Step 3: Count the minutes by 5s and 1s until you reach the ending time.

So, the elapsed time is 34 minutes.

Another Way: Use a number line.

Step 1: Plot the starting time on a number line.

Step 2: Count the minutes from the starting time to the next hour. Then count the minutes from the hour to the ending time.

Step 3: Add the jumps to find the elapsed time.

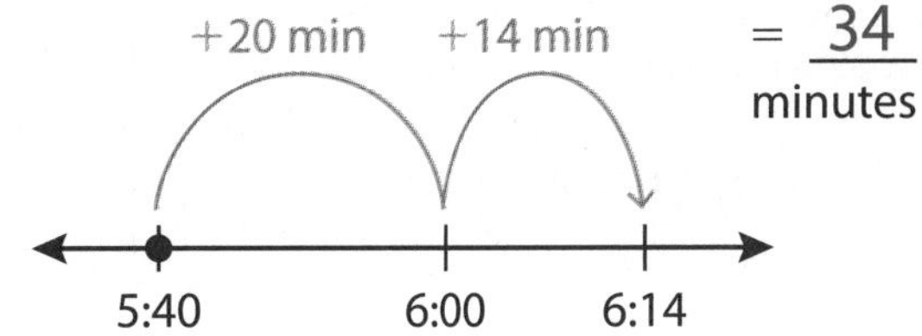

= 34 minutes

So, the elapsed time is 34 minutes.

Find the elapsed time.

1. Start: 3:50 P.M. End: 4:06 P.M.

_____ minutes

2. Start: 9:35 A.M. End: 10:23 A.M.

_____ minutes

Find the elapsed time.

3. Start: 2:20 P.M. End: 3:03 P.M.

_____ minutes

4. Start: 11:15 P.M. End: 12:12 A.M.

_____ minutes

5. MP **YOU BE THE TEACHER** Is Descartes correct? Explain.

6. **Writing** Write a word problem that requires finding an elapsed time.

7. MP **Modeling Real Life** You start looking for animal tracks at 10:25 A.M. You find some at 11:06 A.M. How long does it take you to find the tracks?

8. **DIG DEEPER!** You create pictographs from 4:40 P.M. to 5:02 P.M. Your friend creates pictographs for the same amount of time as you. He stops at 6:16 P.M. What time did your friend start creating pictographs?

Review & Refresh

9. Plot $\frac{11}{6}$ on the number line.

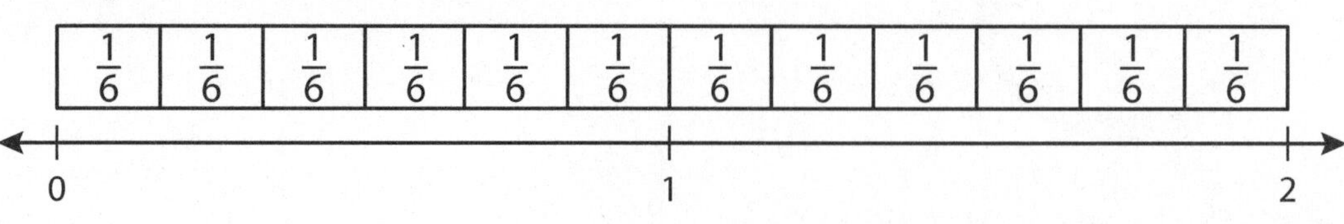

Name ______________________________

Problem Solving: Time Interval Problems 12.4

Learning Target: Use the problem-solving plan to solve time interval problems.

Success Criteria:
- I can understand a problem.
- I can make a plan to solve.
- I can solve a problem.

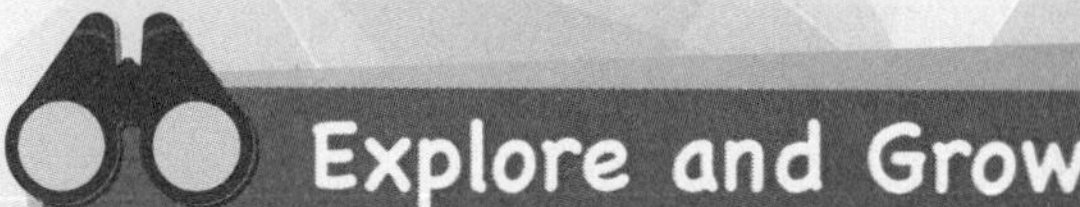

You wait in line for 16 minutes to ride a roller coaster. Then you wait in line for 15 minutes to ride a Ferris wheel. How much time do you spend waiting in the lines altogether?

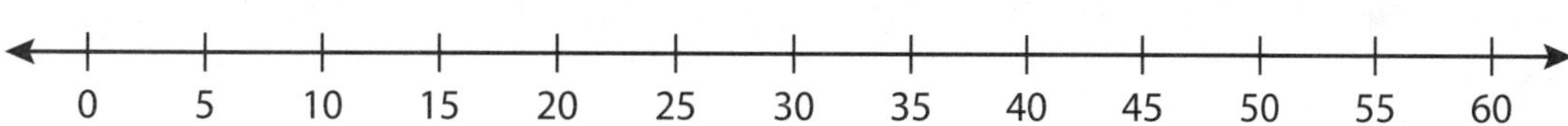

MP **Analyze a Problem** Write an equation for the problem. What operation did you use? Why?

Think and Grow: Solve Time Interval Problems

A **time interval** is an amount of time.

Example Some friends have 60 minutes to solve a mystery. They have been working for 44 minutes. How much time do they have left to solve the mystery?

Understand the Problem

What do you know?	What do you need to find?
• Some friends have _____ minutes to solve a mystery. • They have been working for _____ minutes.	• You need to find how much _____ they have left to solve the mystery.

Make a Plan

How will you solve?

- Subtract _____ from _____ to find how much _____ they have left.

Solve

Use a number line to represent the problem and show the time intervals.

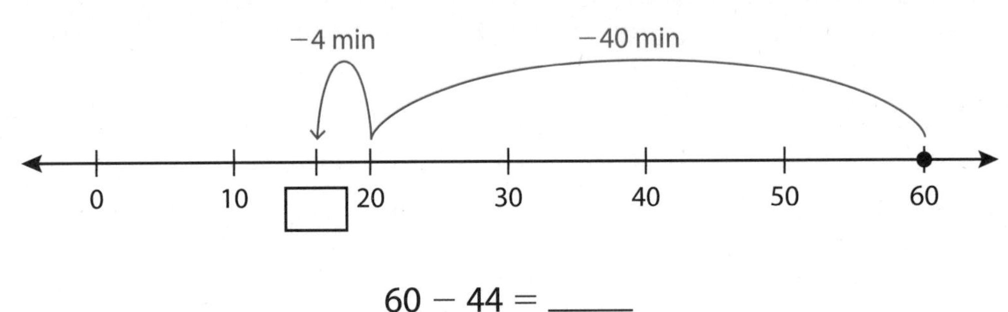

60 − 44 = _____

So, the friends have _____ minutes left to solve the mystery.

Show and Grow I can do it!

1. You spend 26 minutes playing games on a tablet and 17 minutes listening to music on a tablet. How much time do you spend using the tablet?

Name ______________________________

Apply and Grow: Practice

2. You have 30 minutes to play outside before dinner. You already played for 19 minutes. How much time do you have left to play?

3. Library class is 43 minutes long. During class, you spend 15 minutes searching for books and the rest of the time reading. How much time do you spend reading?

4. You spend 13 fewer minutes planning a constellation picture than creating it. You spend 12 minutes planning the picture. How much time do you spend creating it?

5. **DIG DEEPER!** You spend 3 hours at an adventure park. Which equations show how many minutes you spend at the park?

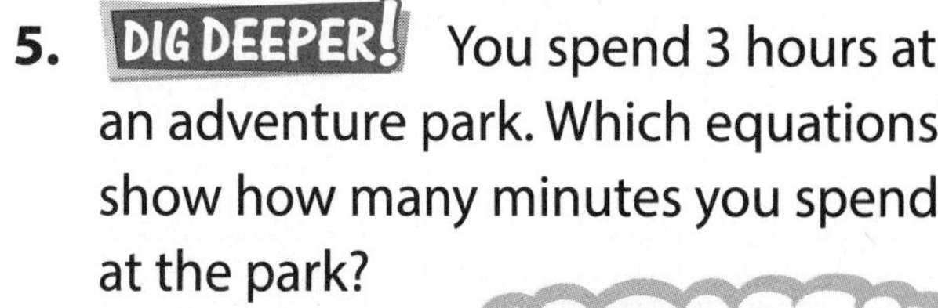

Remember: 1 hour is equal to 60 minutes!

$3 + 60 = 63$

$3 \times 60 = 180$

$3 \times 1 + 60 = 63$

$60 + 60 + 60 = 180$

Think and Grow: Modeling Real Life

You write and illustrate a short story. You spend 36 minutes writing the story, 15 minutes drawing the pictures, and 13 minutes coloring the pictures. How many more minutes do you spend writing than illustrating?

Understand the problem:

Make a plan:

Solve:

You spend _____ more minutes writing the story.

Show and Grow *I can think deeper!*

6. A play with three acts is 57 minutes long. The first act is 24 minutes long, and the second act is 19 minutes long. How long is the third act?

7. **DIG DEEPER!** How many more minutes do you spend playing sports after school than doing homework? How much time do you spend on all of your after-school activities?

After-School Activities

Activity	Time Interval
Soccer drills	35 min
Kickball game	52 min
Math homework	23 min
Science homework	18 min

You start your math homework at 3:35 P.M. You start your science homework immediately after you finish your math homework. At what time do you finish your science homework? Explain.

Name ________________________________

Homework & Practice 12.4

Learning Target: Use the problem-solving plan to solve time interval problems.

Example You spend 38 more minutes swimming than playing in the sand. You play in the sand for 20 minutes. How much time do you spend swimming?

Think: What do you know? What do you need to find? How will you solve?

Use a number line to represent the problem and show the time intervals.

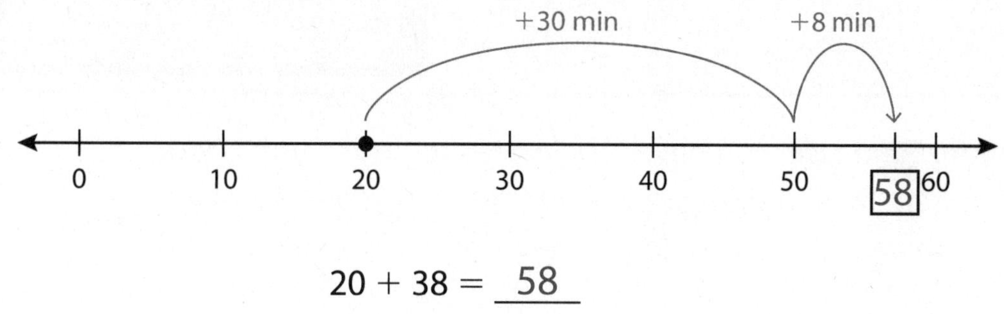

$20 + 38 =$ 58

So, you spend 58 minutes swimming.

1. You spend 28 fewer minutes stretching than practicing. You practice for 40 minutes. How much time do you spend stretching?

2. You spend 11 more minutes playing a board game than you do creating it. You spend 49 minutes playing the board game. How much time do you spend creating the board game?

3. Open-Ended A dog groomer has 60 minutes to give 3 dogs a bath. Each bath takes at least 15 minutes, and the first bath takes the longest. What is one way the 60 minutes can be divided among the three baths?

Bath 1: _____ minutes

Bath 2: _____ minutes

Bath 3: _____ minutes

4. MP Analyze a Problem Which two events can be done back-to-back in less than a half hour? Explain.

5. MP Modeling Real Life You have 55 minutes to find 3 items. You find the first item in 26 minutes, and you find the second item in 9 minutes. How many minutes do you have left to find the third item?

6. DIG DEEPER! How many more minutes do you spend dancing than playing musical instruments? How much time do you spend on all of your activities?

After-School Activities	
Activity	**Time Interval**
Step dance	25 min
Hip-hop dance	34 min
Play drums	22 min
Play piano	19 min

You start playing the drums at 5:25 P.M. You start playing the piano immediately after you finish playing the drums. At what time do you finish playing musical instruments? Explain.

Review & Refresh

Find the equivalent fraction.

7. $\frac{5}{5} = \frac{\square}{7}$

8. $\frac{1}{2} = \frac{\square}{4}$

9. $\frac{2}{4} = \frac{\square}{8}$

10. $\frac{2}{6} = \frac{\square}{3}$

Name ______________________________

Understand and Estimate Liquid Volume 12.5

Learning Target: Understand and estimate liquid volumes in metric units.

Success Criteria:

- I can tell the difference between a milliliter and a liter.
- I can identify which unit to use to measure a liquid volume.
- I can estimate a liquid volume.

Explore and Grow

About how many bottles of water would fill the pot?

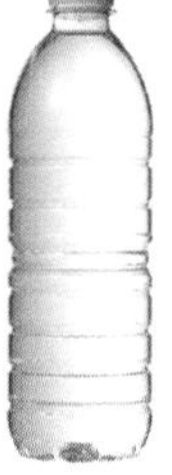

_____ bottles

Reasoning The bottle holds 1 liter of water. How can you estimate the number of liters of water the pot can hold?

Think and Grow: Understand Liquid Volume

Liquid volume is the amount of liquid in a container.

A **liter (L)** is the standard metric unit used to measure liquid volume.

A **milliliter (mL)** is another metric unit used to measure liquid volume.

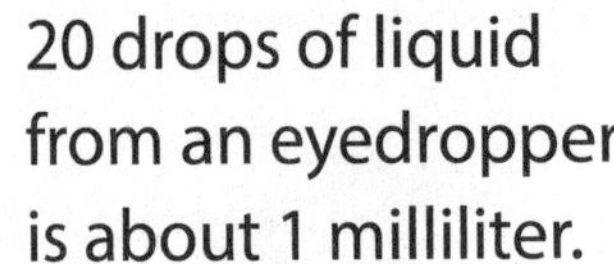

Remember *capacity* is the total amount of liquid that a container can hold.

20 drops of liquid from an eyedropper is about 1 milliliter.

There is about 1 liter of liquid in the water bottle.

1,000 milliliters = 1 liter

Example Which units should you use to measure the liquid volume, *liters* or *milliliters*? Explain.

____

A fishbowl contains ____________ liquid than a 1-liter water bottle.

____

A small glass contains ____________ liquid than a 1-liter water bottle.

Show and Grow I can do it!

Which units should you use to measure the liquid volume, *liters* or *milliliters*? Explain.

1. 

2. 

Name ___

Apply and Grow: Practice

Which units should you use to measure the liquid volume, *liters* or *milliliters*? Explain.

3. 

4. 

Choose the better estimate.

5. 

250 mL 250 L

6. 

15 mL 15 L

MP Use a Similar Problem How can you use the Example to help you solve?

7. 

30 mL 3 L

8. 

4 L 40 L

9. **MP Maintain Accuracy** Match.

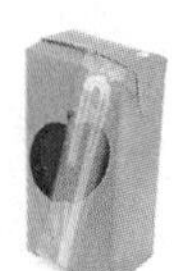

60 mL 4 L 2 L 200 mL

Think and Grow: Modeling Real Life

Use Picture A to estimate the liquid volume shown in Picture B.

Compare:

Picture A

5 L

Picture B

_____ L

The liquid volume is about _____ liters.

Show and Grow I can think deeper!

10. Use Picture C to estimate the liquid volume shown in Picture D.

Picture C

125 mL

Picture D

_____ mL

11. DIG DEEPER! Use Picture X to estimate the liquid volumes shown in Pictures Y and Z.

Picture X

25 L

Picture Y

_____ L

Picture Z

_____ L

Name ________________________________

Homework & Practice 12.5

Learning Target: Understand and estimate liquid volumes in metric units.

Example Which units should you use to measure the liquid volume, *liters* or *milliliters*? Explain.

You should use milliliters to measure the liquid volume.

A carton contains less liquid than a 1-liter water bottle.

Which units should you use to measure the liquid volume, *liters* or *milliliters*? Explain.

1. 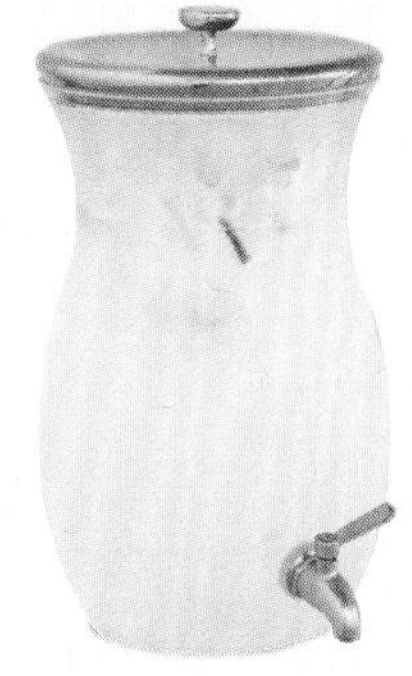

2. 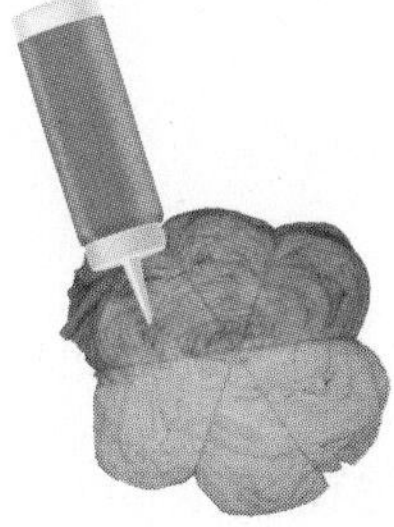

Choose the better estimate.

3. 

300 mL

300 L

4. 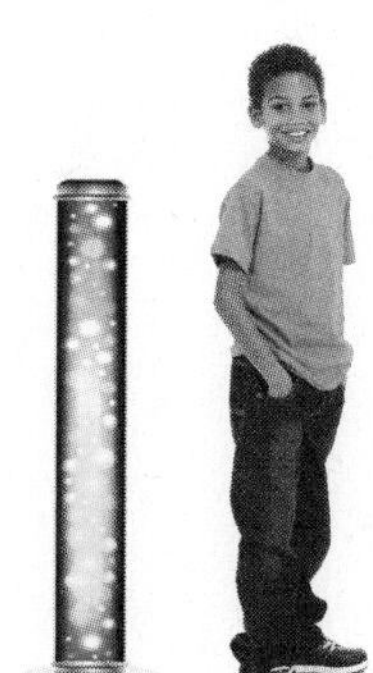

6 mL

6 L

5. 

270 mL

27 L

6. 

1 L

10 L

7. **MP Construct an Argument** Descartes wants to estimate how much water Newton used to fill his dog pool. Would 1,000 milliliters or 100 liters be a better estimate? Explain.

8. **MP YOU BE THE TEACHER** Your friend says the liquid volume in the bowl is less than 10 milliliters. Is your friend correct? Explain.

10 L

9. **MP Number Sense** Order the liquid volumes from least to greatest.

50 mL 5 L 2,000 mL 1 mL

10. **MP Reasoning** An elephant can hold up to 10 liters of water in its trunk. Which of the following is *not* an amount of water an elephant can hold? Explain.

1 L 1,000 mL 100 L 100 mL

11. **MP Modeling Real Life** Use Picture A to estimate the liquid volume shown in Picture B.

Picture A

350 mL

Picture B

_____ mL

Review & Refresh

12. Your friend saves \$5 each week for 6 weeks. He spends all of the money on 3 toys that each cost the same amount. How much does each toy cost?

Name ______________________________

Measure Liquid Volume 12.6

Learning Target: Measure liquid volumes in liters and milliliters.

Success Criteria:
- I can measure a liquid volume in liters.
- I can measure a liquid volume in milliliters.
- I can measure a liquid volume in liters and milliliters.

Estimate the capacities of four different containers. Then use a 1-liter beaker to fill each container with liquid. What is the actual liquid volume in each container?

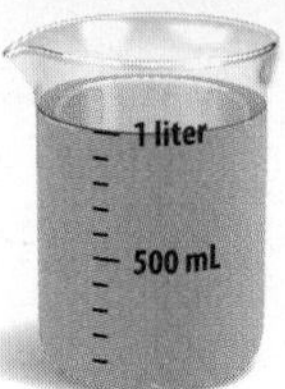

Container	Estimate	Actual Liquid Volume

Precision How can you use your results to get a better estimate for a fifth container?

Think and Grow: Measure Liquid Volume

Example What is the liquid volume in each container?

The liquid volume in the soup can is _____ milliliters.

The liquid volume in the coffeepot is _____ liters _____ milliliters.

Show and Grow I can do it!

What is the liquid volume in the container?

1.

2.

Write the total liquid volume shown.

3.

4.

Name ______________________________

Apply and Grow: Practice

Write the total liquid volume shown.

5.

6.

7.

8.

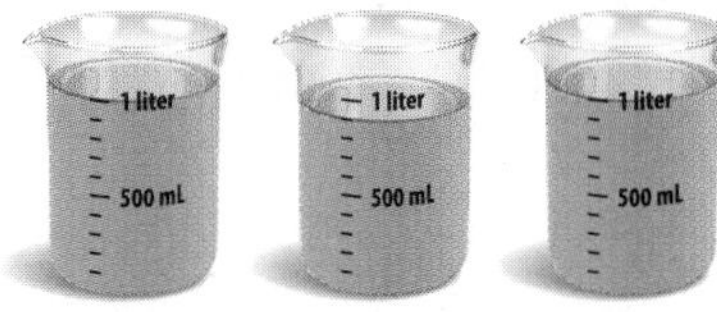

9. **Which One Doesn't Belong?** Which group of beakers does *not* have the same liquid volume as the other two?

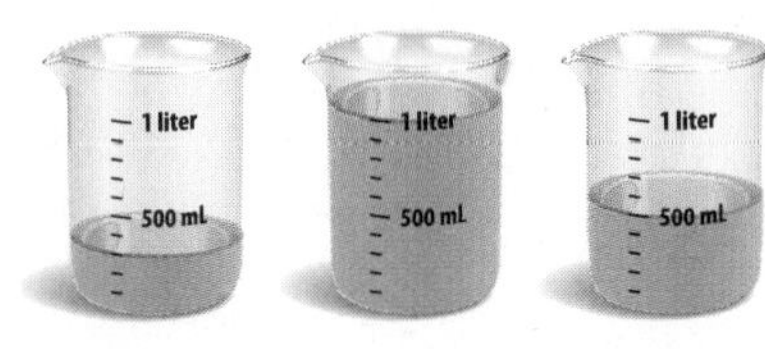

10. MP **Analyze a Problem** How much water did the basketball team drink during practice? Explain.

Before Practice After Practice

Think and Grow: Modeling Real Life

You drink two of the cartons of milk shown. How many milliliters of milk do you drink?

Equation:

You drink ______ milliliters of milk.

Show and Grow I can think deeper!

11. You pour 250 milliliters of the juice shown into a cup. How many milliliters of juice are left in the jug?

12. A school custodian repaints 5 classrooms. He needs 9 liters of paint for each classroom. How many liters of paint does he need in all?

13. A baby pool holds 72 liters of water. You use an 8-liter bucket to fill the pool with water. How many times do you fill the bucket?

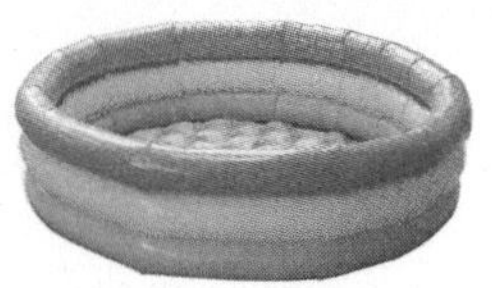

14. **DIG DEEPER!** A frozen treat tray has 6 molds. Each mold holds 90 milliliters of liquid. You mix 375 milliliters of orange juice with 175 milliliters of pineapple juice. Do you have enough juice to fill the tray? Explain.

Name ______________________________

Homework & Practice 12.6

Learning Target: Measure liquid volumes in liters and milliliters.

Example What is the liquid volume in each container?

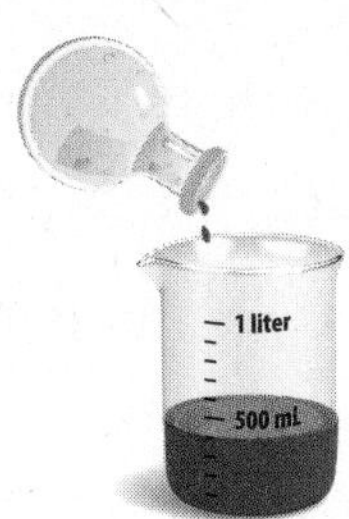

The liquid volume in the jar is 400 milliliters.

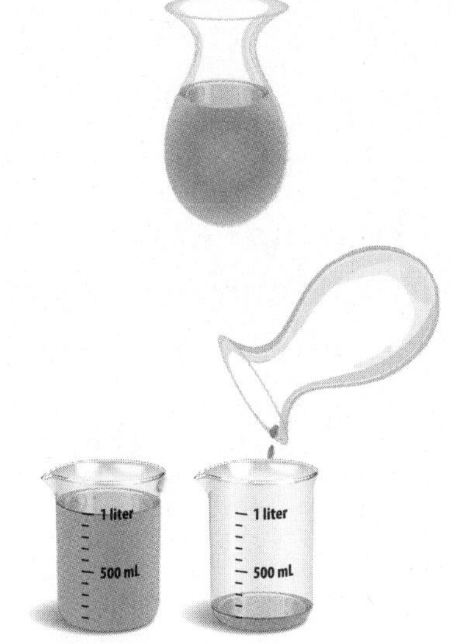

The liquid volume in the vase is 1 liter 100 milliliters.

Write the total liquid volume shown.

1.

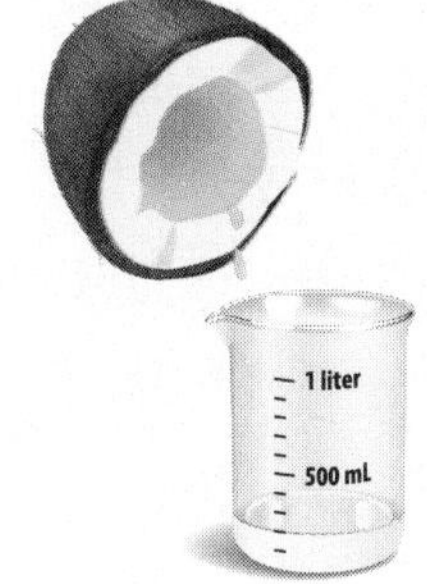

2.

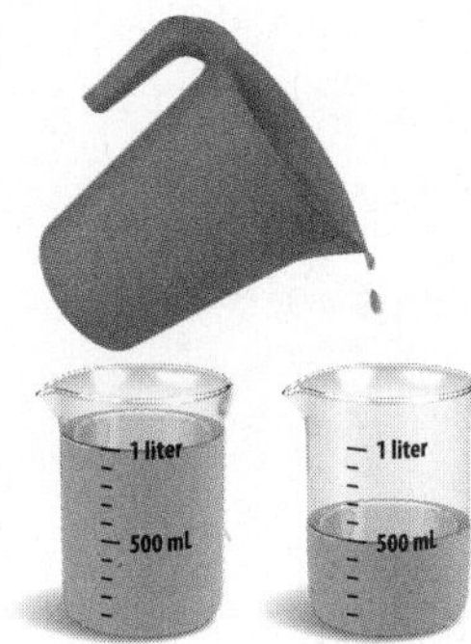

3.

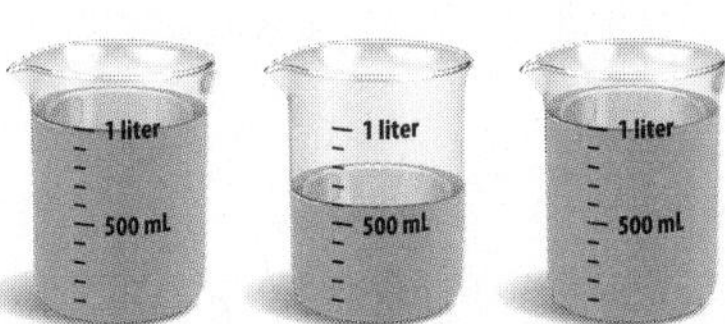

4.

5. **MP Precision** You mix the two juices shown. How much juice do you have in all?

Blue Raspberry Juice

Lemonade

6. **MP YOU BE THE TEACHER** Your friend says the liquid volume of the beaker is 100 liters. Is your friend correct? Explain.

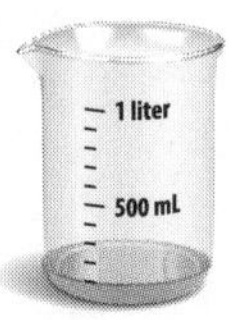

7. **MP Modeling Real Life** You and your friend each drink one of the juice bottles shown. How many milliliters of juice do you and your friend drink in all?

8. **MP Modeling Real Life** You use 120 milliliters of water from the spray bottle shown. How many milliliters of water are left in the bottle?

215 mL

9. **MP Modeling Real Life** You use 20 liters of water to water a garden. You use a 5-liter watering can to water the garden. How many times do you fill the can? Explain.

10. **DIG DEEPER!** A muffin tray has 6 molds. Each mold holds 60 milliliters of batter. You make 184 milliliters of blueberry batter and 145 milliliters of banana batter. Do you have enough batter to fill the tray? Explain.

Review & Refresh

Circle the value of the underlined digit.

11.	1<u>5</u>7	5	50	500
12.	<u>9</u>02	900	9	90

Name ______________________________

Understand and Estimate Mass

Learning Target: Understand and estimate masses of objects.

Success Criteria:

- I can tell the difference between a gram and a kilogram.
- I can identify which unit to use to measure the mass of an object.
- I can estimate the mass of an object.

 The mass of a tennis ball is 59 grams.	 The mass of an orange is 262 grams.

Which object has more mass?

Reasoning Examine a $1 bill and a $10 bill. What do you notice about the masses and the values?

Think and Grow: Understand Mass

Mass is the amount of matter in an object.

A **gram (g)** is the standard metric unit used to measure mass.

A **kilogram (kg)** is another metric unit used to measure mass.

The mass of a paper clip is about 1 gram.

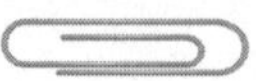

The mass of a baseball bat is about 1 kilogram.

1,000 grams = 1 kilogram

Example Which units should you use to measure the mass, *grams* or *kilograms?* Explain.

______

An apple has ______ matter than a baseball bat.

______

An watermelon has ______ matter than a baseball bat.

Show and Grow I can do it!

Which units should you use to measure the mass, *grams* or *kilograms?* Explain.

1. 

2. 

Name ________________________________

Apply and Grow: Practice

Which units should you use to measure the mass, *grams* or *kilograms*? Explain.

3. 

4. 

Choose the better estimate.

5. 

300 g   300 kg

6. 

27 g   27 kg

7. 

8 g   1 kg

8. 

15 g   150 g

9. MP **YOU BE THE TEACHER** Your friend says 50 grams is a greater unit of measurement than 50 kilograms because 50 liters is greater than 50 milliliters. Is your friend correct? Explain.

10. MP **Reasoning** A bowling ball and a beach ball are the same size. Do the objects have about the same mass? Explain.

Think and Grow: Modeling Real Life

Use the mass of the small bag of potatoes to estimate the mass of the large bag of potatoes.

Compare:

2 kg

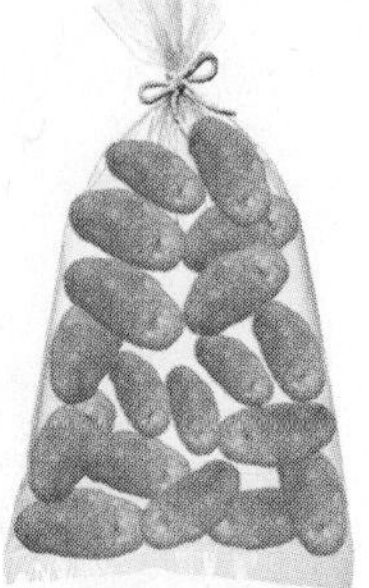

4 kg

The mass is about 4 kilograms.

Show and Grow I can think deeper!

11. Use the mass of the banana to estimate the mass of the bunch of bananas.

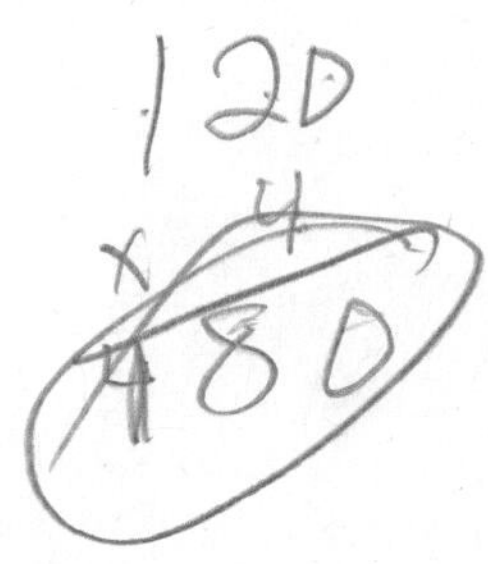

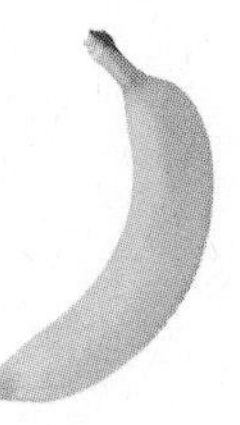

120 g

480 g

---

12. DIG DEEPER! Use the mass of the small egg carton to estimate the mass of the larger egg cartons.

290 g

580 g

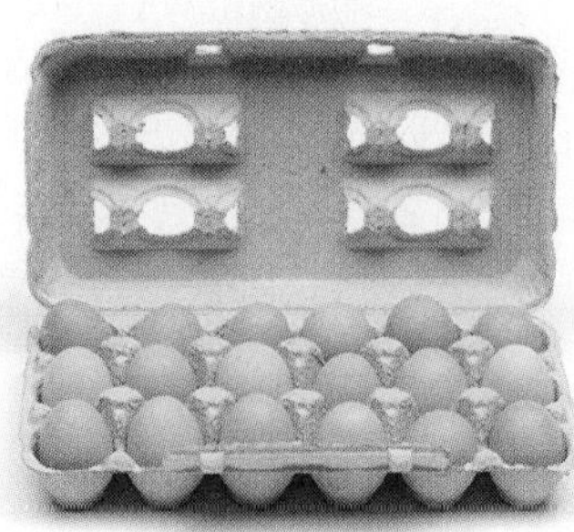

870 g

Name ____________________

Homework & Practice 12.7

Learning Target: Understand and estimate masses of objects.

Example Which units should you use to measure the mass, *grams* or *kilograms*? Explain.

You should use grams to measure the mass.

A quarter has less matter than a baseball bat.

Which units should you use to measure the mass, *grams* or *kilograms*? Explain.

1. 

grams

2. 

Kilograms

Choose the better estimate.

3. 

(30 g) 30 kg

4. 

9 g (9 kg)

5. 

(100 g) 10 kg

6. 

(2 kg) 20 kg

7. **Logic** Which objects have a mass greater than 1 kilogram?

Pencil	Computer
Desk	Scissors
Cherry	Microwave

8. **YOU BE THE TEACHER** Your friend says the mass of the kangaroo is greater than 25 grams. Is your friend correct? Explain.

25 kg

9. **Number Sense** Order the masses from least to greatest.

1 kg   3,000 g   6 g   20 kg

10. **Writing** Write a word problem that requires estimating masses.

11. **Modeling Real Life** Use the mass of the lightbulb to estimate the mass of the box of lightbulbs.

37 g

_____ g

Review & Refresh

Compare.

12. $\frac{3}{4} \bigcirc \frac{3}{6}$

13. $\frac{1}{2} \bigcirc \frac{3}{4}$

14. $\frac{6}{8} \bigcirc \frac{5}{8}$

15. $\frac{3}{3} \bigcirc \frac{1}{3}$

16. $\frac{2}{4} \bigcirc \frac{4}{8}$

17. $\frac{5}{6} \bigcirc \frac{7}{8}$

Name ___________________________________

Measure Mass 12.8

Learning Target: Measure masses in grams and kilograms.

Success Criteria:
- I can measure a mass in grams.
- I can measure a mass in kilograms.
- I can measure a mass in grams and kilograms.

Estimate the masses of four different objects. Then use a balance and weights to measure the actual mass of each object to the nearest gram or kilogram.

Object	Estimate	Actual Mass

Precision How can you use your results to get a better estimate for a fifth object?

Think and Grow: Measure Mass

Example What is the mass of each object?

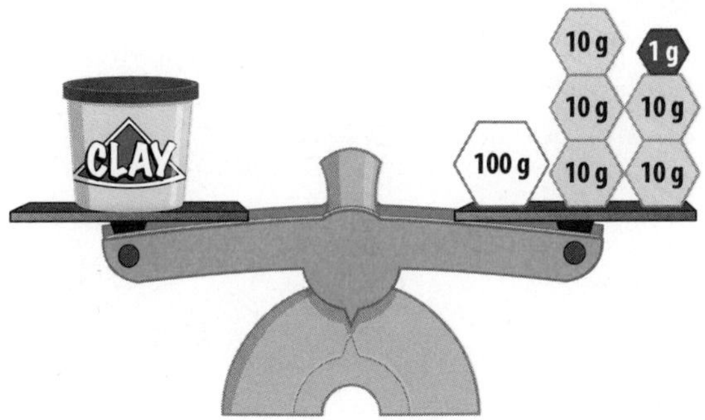

The mass of the tub of clay is _____ grams.

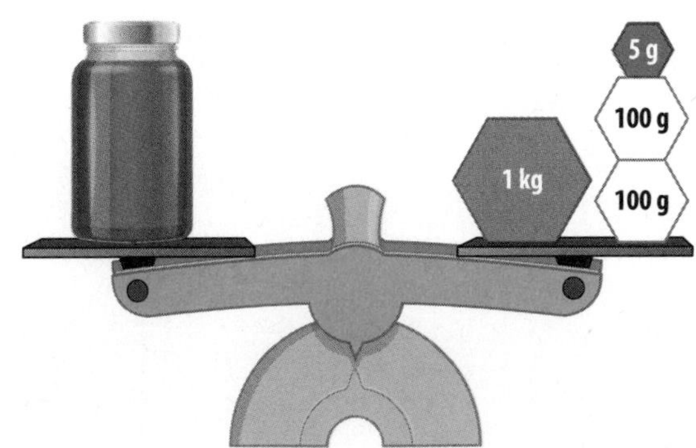

The mass of the candle is _____ kilogram _____ grams.

Show and Grow *I can do it!*

Write the total mass shown.

1. 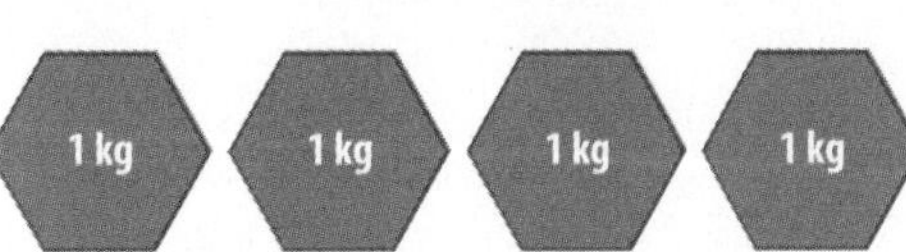

2. 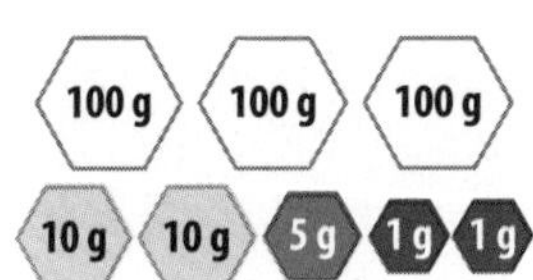

3. 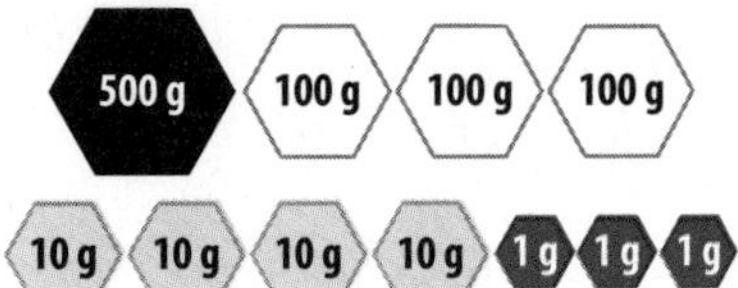

4. 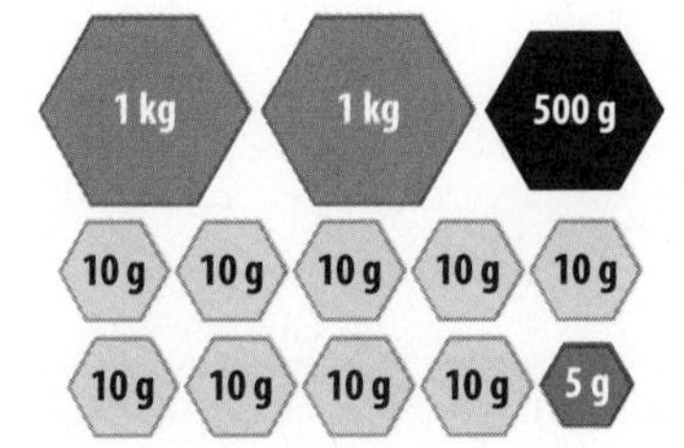

Name ______________________________

Apply and Grow: Practice

Write the total mass shown.

5.

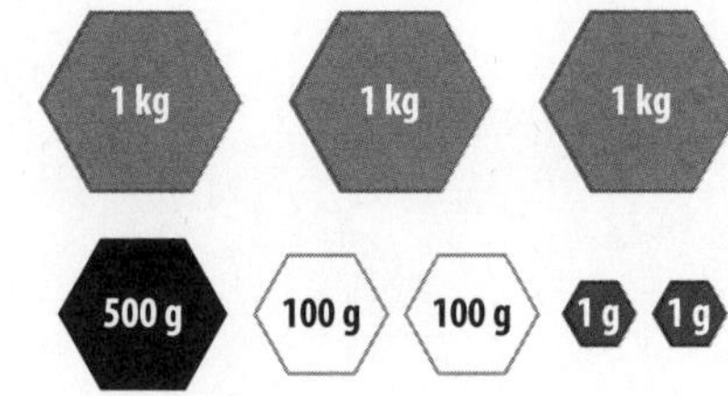

6.

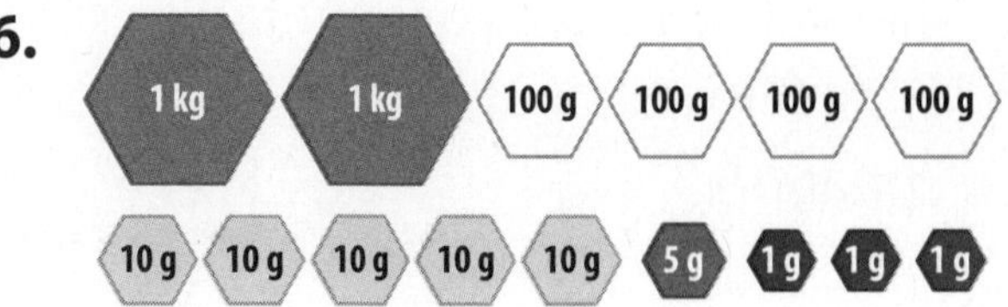

7.

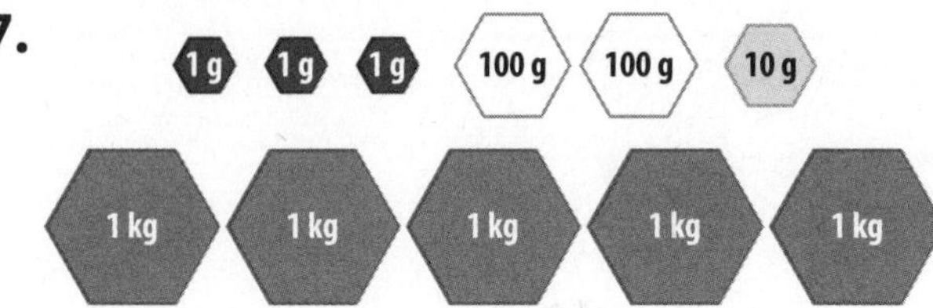

8.

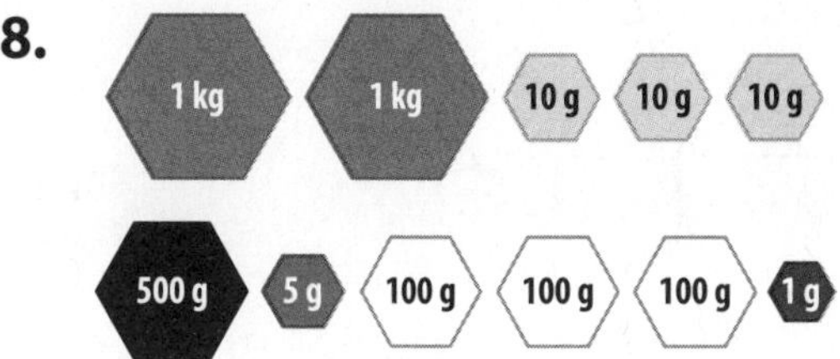

9. MP **YOU BE THE TEACHER** Your friend says the stuffed animal has a mass that is less than 25 grams. Is your friend correct? Explain.

10. MP **Choose Tools** Choose the best tool to measure each item.

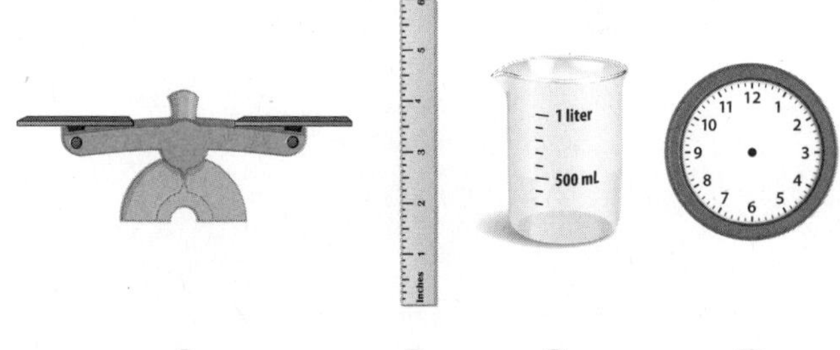

A B C D

The liquid volume of a bowl: ______

The length of a spoon: ______

The mass of an orange: ______

The number of minutes you jog: ______

Think and Grow: Modeling Real Life

Third graders should eat 454 grams of vegetables each day. You eat the vegetables shown on the balance. How many more grams of vegetables should you eat today?

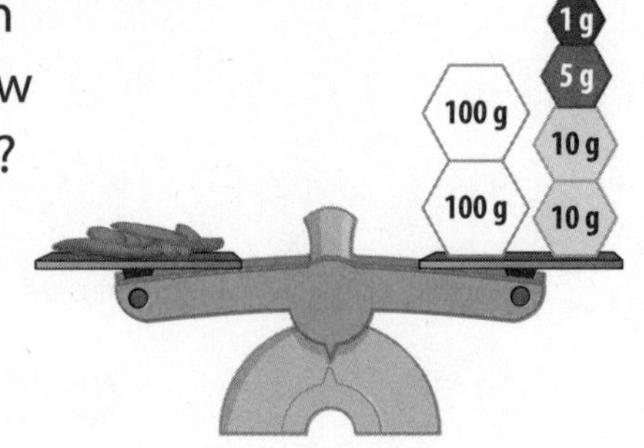

Equation:

You should eat _____ more grams of vegetables.

Show and Grow *I can think deeper!*

11. A tablet's mass is 324 grams more than the cell phone's mass. What is the mass of the tablet?

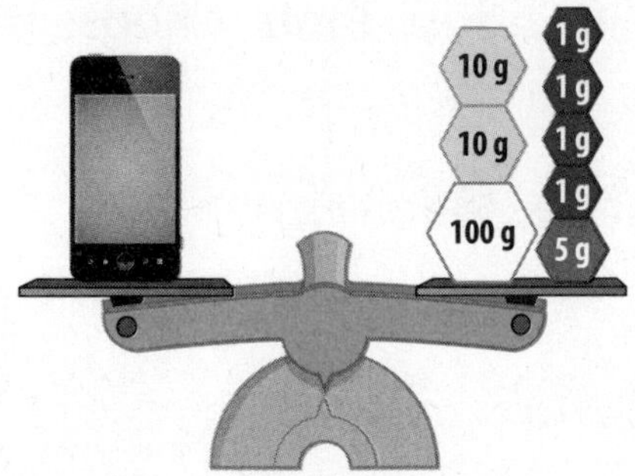

12. The mass of a nickel is 5 grams. There are 40 nickels in a standard roll. What is the mass of a standard roll of nickels?

13. Newton eats 6 kilograms of dog food each week. He buys a 24-kilogram bag of dog food. For how many weeks will Newton eat from the bag of dog food?

14. **DIG DEEPER!** You make fruit smoothies using 369 grams of strawberries, 227 grams of raspberries, and 283 grams of blueberries. Do you use more than 1 kilogram of fruit? Explain.

Name ______________________________

Homework & Practice 12.8

Learning Target: Measure masses in grams and kilograms.

Example What is the mass of the lamp?

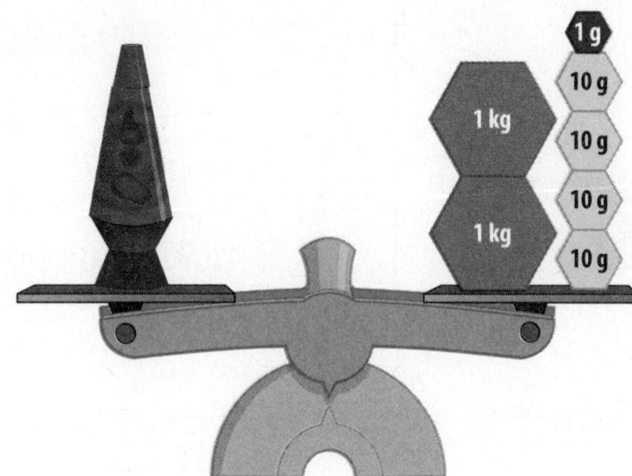

The mass of the lamp is 2 kilograms 41 grams.

Write the total mass shown.

1.

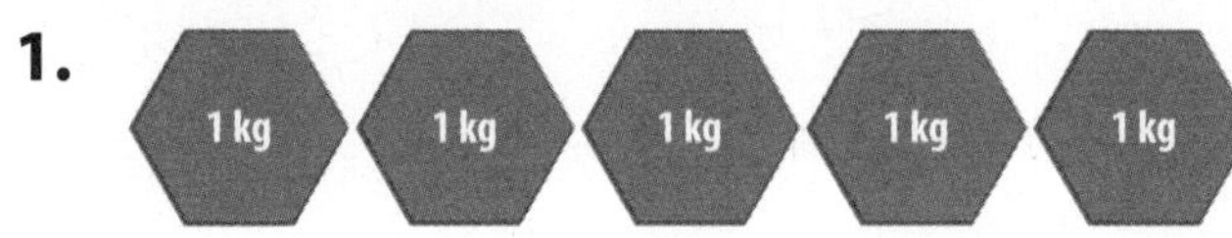

2.

500 g 100 g 100 g 100 g 100 g

10 g 10 g 1 g 1 g 1 g

3.

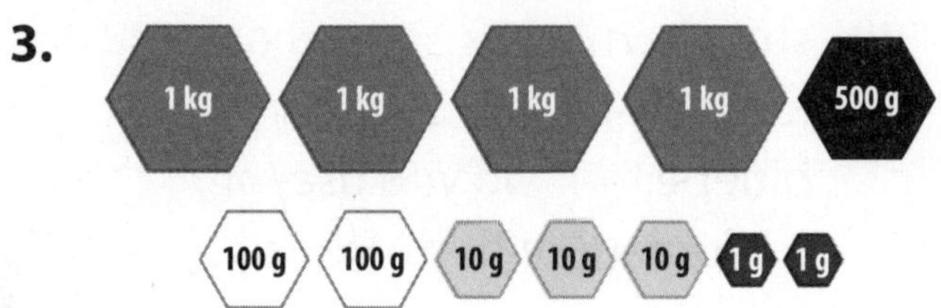

4.

1 kg 5 g 100 g 100 g 100 g 100 g

1 g 1 g 1 g 1 g 10 g 10 g 10 g 10 g

5. Open-Ended Choose two objects that have different masses. Draw the objects on the balance with one object on each side.

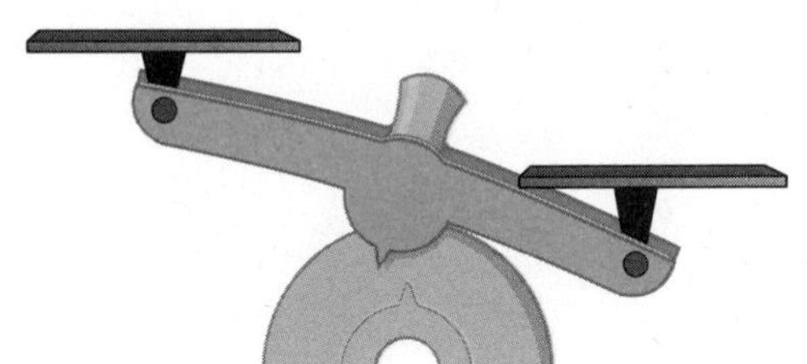

6. Precision Use each measurement once to complete the list.

4 L　　2 kg　　125 in.

Shopping List

_______ of flour

_______ of waxed paper

_______ of milk

7. Modeling Real Life 216 grams of strawberries count as a daily serving of fruit for children. You eat the berries shown. How many more grams of berries should you eat today?

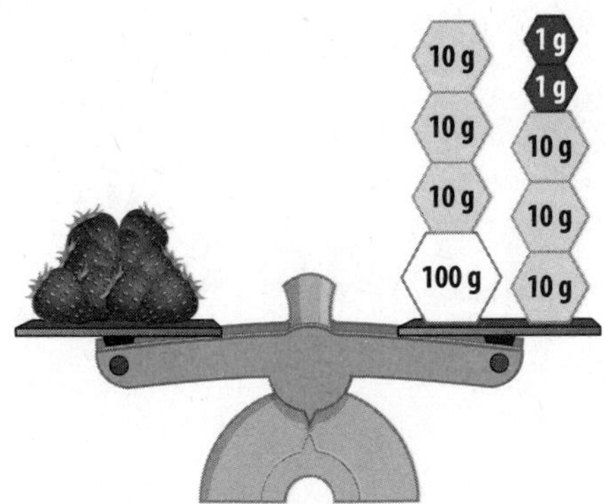

8. DIG DEEPER! A Japanese one-yen coin weighs 1 gram. Newton and Descartes each have 70 one-yen coins. How many more coins do they need to have a total mass of 200 grams? Explain.

Review & Refresh

What fraction of the whole is shaded?

9. 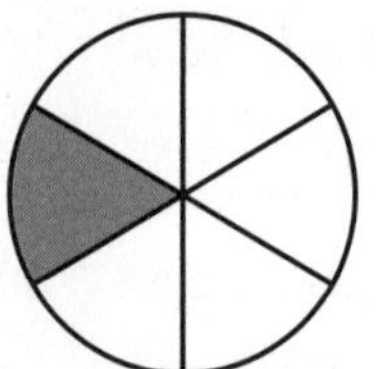 $\frac{\square}{\square}$ is shaded.

10. 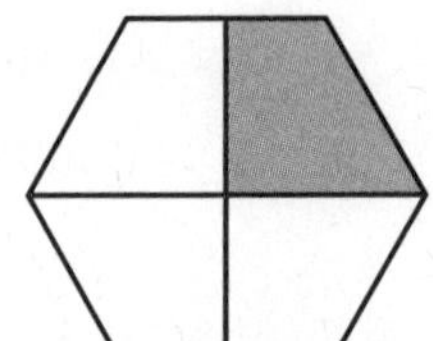 $\frac{\square}{\square}$ is shaded.

Name ______________________________

Performance Task 12

1. You decide to keep track of the weather today.

a. The rain begins 14 minutes before 1. The rain stops at 2:45. How many minutes does the rain last?

b. MP **Communicate Clearly** Write another way to say the time the rain stops.

c. The rain starts again 48 minutes after it stopped the first time. Show the time.

---

2. This morning, you set a beaker outside before it started to rain.

a. You check the beaker after the first time the rain stops. Write the amount.

b. You check the beaker after the last time the rain stops. The beaker has 200 more milliliters of water. What is the total amount of water in the beaker today?

c. Did you collect more or less than half of a liter of water today? Explain.

---

3. You color the model to show the number of days it rained last week. What fraction of the week did it *not* rain?

Sun	Mon	Tues	Wed	Thurs	Fri	Sat

$\frac{\square}{\square}$

Roll to Cover: Elapsed Time

Directions:

1. Take turns rolling a die. Find a problem on the board with the number you rolled .
2. Find the elapsed time. Tell whether the time is greater than or less than a half hour.
3. Cover the answer and the problem. The player with the most answers covered wins!

1 **Start: 7:04 A.M.** **End: 7:44 A.M.**	2 **Start: 8:11 A.M.** **End: 8:30 A.M.**	3 **Start: 9:45 A.M.** **End: 10:03 A.M.**	4 **Start: 11:54 A.M.** **End: 12:20 P.M.**
5 **Start: 1:02 P.M.** **End: 1:33 P.M.**	6 **Start: 4:13 P.M.** **End: 4:47 P.M.**	1 **Start: 6:55 A.M.** **End: 7:05 A.M.**	2 **Start: 5:27 P.M.** **End: 5:53 P.M.**
3 **Start: 2:01 P.M.** **End: 2:12 P.M.**	4 **Start: 12:57 A.M.** **End: 1:12 A.M.**	5 **Start: 8:43 P.M.** **End: 9:30 P.M.**	6 **Start: 5:04 A.M.** **End: 5:38 A.M.**
more than a half hour	**less than a half hour**	**less than a half hour**	**more than a half hour**
more than a half hour	**less than a half hour**	**more than a half hour**	**less than a half hour**
less than a half hour	**more than a half hour**	**less than a half hour**	**less than a half hour**

Name ___________________________________

Chapter Practice 12

12.1 Time to the Nearest Minute

Write the time. Write two other ways to say the time.

1. 

2. 

3. 

Write the time.

4. 8 minutes after 9

5. 14 minutes before 5

6. 3 minutes before 1

12.2 Measure Elapsed Time within the Hour

7. Find the elapsed time.

Start: 6:20 A.M. End: 6:42 A.M.

_____ minutes

8. **Modeling Real Life** A model rocket takes 23 minutes to build. You start building the rocket at 11:36 A.M. At what time do you finish it?

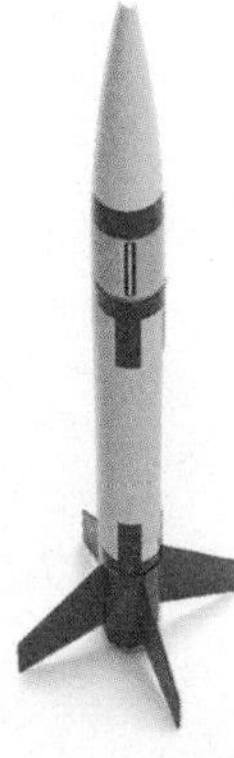

12.3 Measure Elapsed Time Across the Hour

9. Find the elapsed time.

Start: 8:45 A.M. End: 9:24 A.M.

_____ minutes

10. MP **Modeling Real Life** Newton naps from 2:50 P.M. to 3:17 P.M. Descartes naps from 3:55 P.M. to 4:23 P.M. Who naps longer?

12.4 Problem Solving: Time Interval Problems

11. You spend 24 more minutes creating a sculpture than you do painting it. You spend 18 minutes painting the sculpture. How much time do you spend creating the sculpture?

12. You spend 43 minutes on a puppet show. You spend 28 minutes writing the story and the rest performing the show. How many minutes do you spend performing the show?

12.5 Understand and Estimate Liquid Volume

Choose the better estimate.

13.

3 mL 3 L

14.

55 mL 55 L

15.

10 mL 1 L

16.

4 L 40 L

12.6 Measure Liquid Volume

Write the total liquid volume shown.

17.

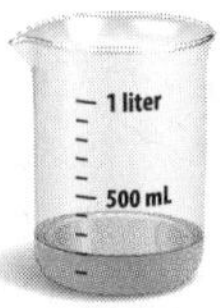

18.

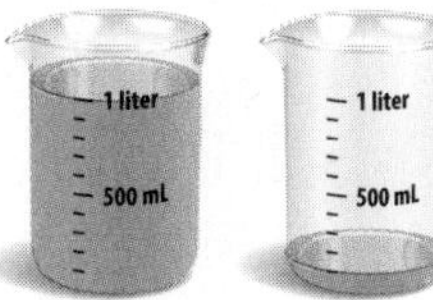

19.

20.

21.

22.

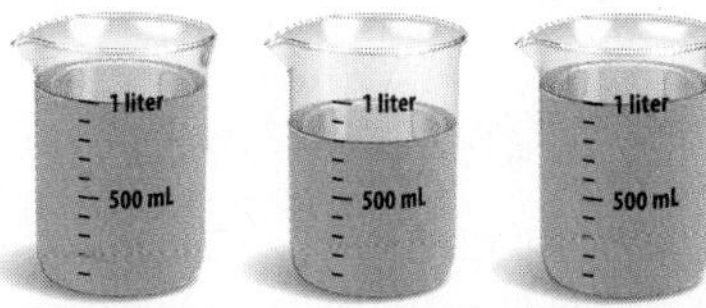

12.7 Understand and Estimate Mass

Choose the better estimate.

23.

50 g   50 kg

24.

6 g   6 kg

25.

285 g   28 kg

26.

3 kg   30 kg

12.8 Measure Mass

Write the total mass shown.

27.

28.

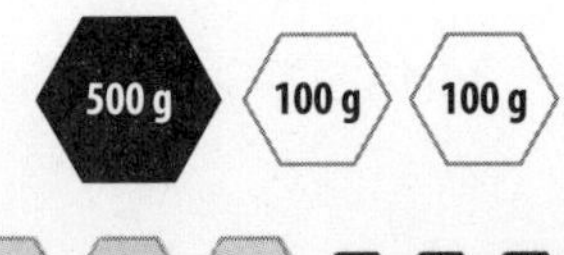

29.

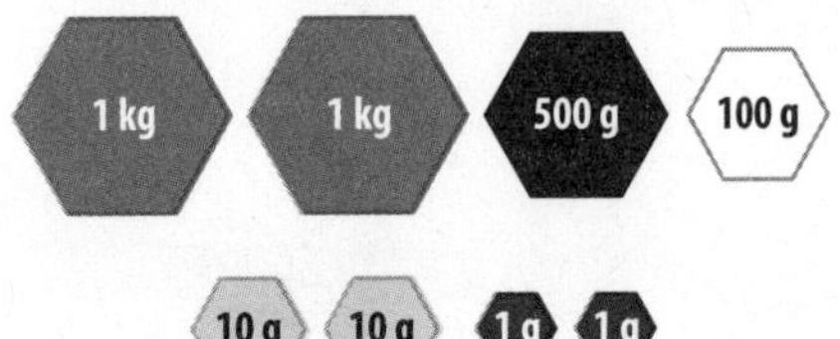

30.

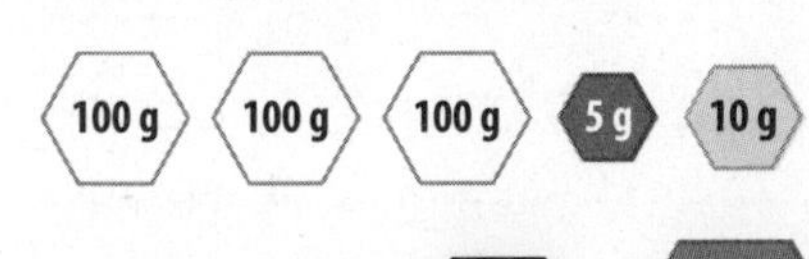

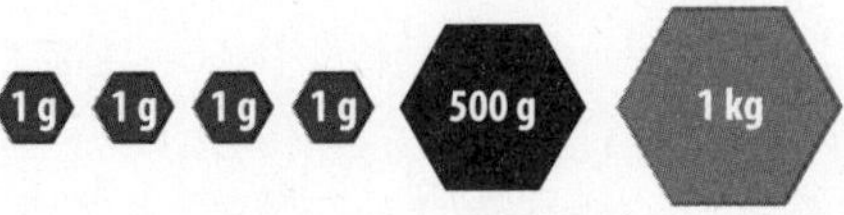

Name ___________________________________

Cumulative Practice 1–12

1. Which array matches the equation $3 \times 4 = 12$?

Ⓐ 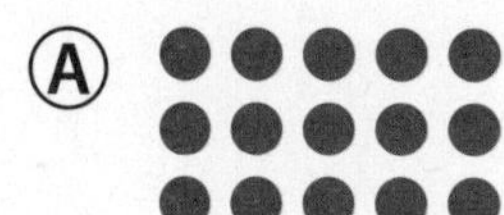

Ⓑ 

Ⓒ 

Ⓓ 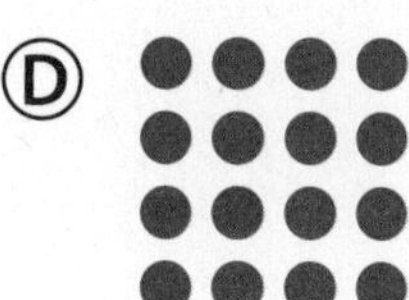

2. Which fractions name the point plotted on the number line?

☐ $\frac{4}{3}$ ☐ $\frac{4}{8}$ ☐ $\frac{1}{2}$

☐ $\frac{2}{4}$ ☐ $\frac{4}{4}$ ☐ $\frac{4}{6}$

3. What time does the clock show?

Ⓐ 9:28 Ⓑ 5:47

Ⓒ 6:47 Ⓓ 5:13

4. A package of batteries has 5 rows of 6 batteries. You use 8 batteries. How many batteries are *not* used?

Ⓐ 38 Ⓑ 22

Ⓒ 3 Ⓓ 28

5. Which statement is true?

Ⓐ $\frac{3}{4} \overset{?}{<} \frac{5}{8}$

Ⓑ $\frac{3}{4} \overset{?}{=} \frac{5}{8}$

Ⓒ $\frac{3}{4} \overset{?}{>} \frac{5}{8}$

Ⓓ $\frac{5}{8} \overset{?}{>} \frac{3}{4}$

6. The mass of a horse is 582 kilograms. The mass of a pig is 355 kilograms less than the mass of the horse. What is the mass of the pig?

7. Which number makes the equation true?

$$6 \div \square = 1$$

Ⓐ 6

Ⓑ 1

Ⓒ 0

Ⓓ 5

8. A parade starts at the time shown on the clock. It ends at 1:18 P.M. How long is the parade?

A.M.

P.M.

Ⓐ 58 minutes

Ⓑ 22 minutes

Ⓒ 33 minutes

Ⓓ 38 minutes

9. Which fraction is *not* equivalent to the number 2?

Ⓐ $\frac{2}{2}$

Ⓑ $\frac{8}{4}$

Ⓒ $\frac{6}{3}$

Ⓓ $\frac{16}{8}$

10. Which models show $\frac{1}{6}$ shaded?

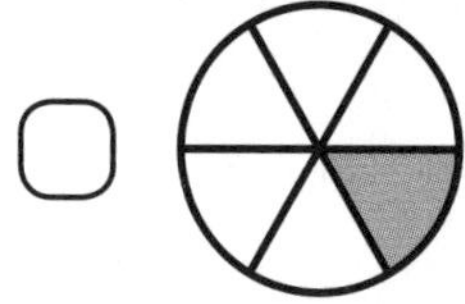

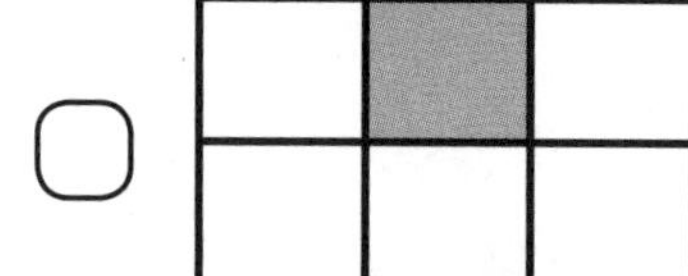

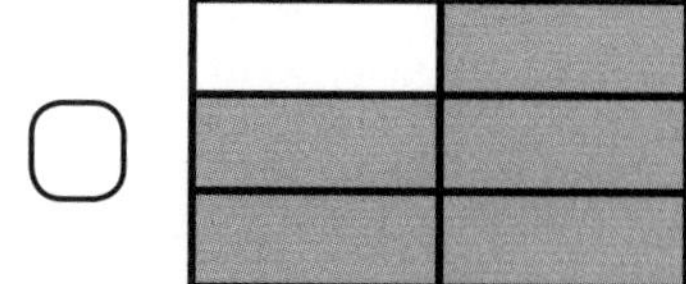

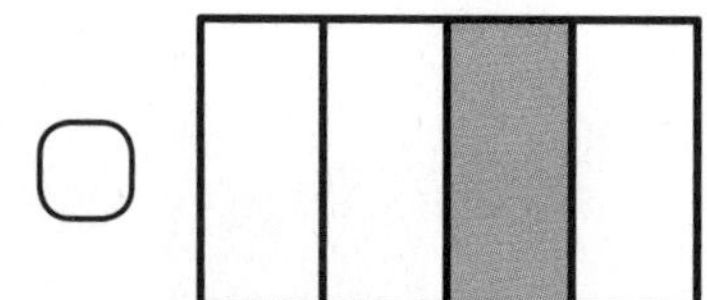

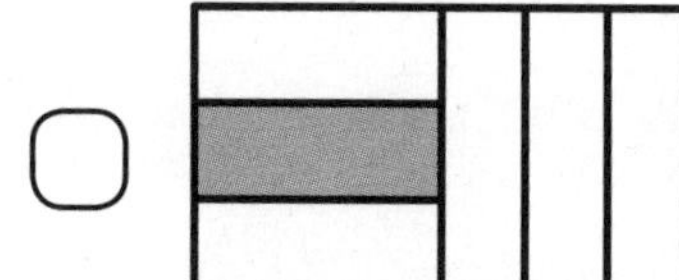

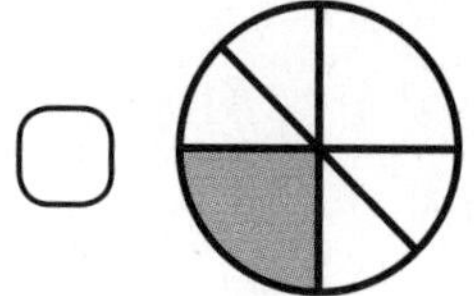

---

11. Which set of fractions is in order from least to greatest?

Ⓐ $\frac{2}{4}, \frac{2}{6}, \frac{2}{8}$

Ⓑ $\frac{5}{6}, \frac{3}{6}, \frac{1}{6}$

Ⓒ $\frac{1}{3}, \frac{4}{3}, \frac{3}{3}$

Ⓓ $\frac{7}{8}, \frac{7}{4}, \frac{7}{3}$

---

12. A customer buys a game console that costs $229 and 3 video games that cost $60 each. How much money does the customer spend?

Part A Write an equation to represent the problem. Use a letter to represent the unknown number.

Part B Solve the problem. Explain how you solved.

Part C Check whether your answer is reasonable. Explain.

13. Which equation does *not* show the Distributive Property?

Ⓐ $9 \times (10 + 10) = (9 \times 10) + (9 \times 10)$

Ⓑ $8 \times (7 \times 10) = (8 \times 7) \times 10$

Ⓒ $(4 \times 10) + (4 \times 10) + (4 \times 10) = 4 \times 30$

Ⓓ $6 \times 20 = (6 \times 10) + (6 \times 10)$

---

14. A photographer has 478 photos of people and 326 photos of nature. About how many photos does the photographer have in all?

Ⓐ 700

Ⓑ 200

Ⓒ 800

Ⓓ 900

---

15. Which liquid volumes should be measured in liters?

☐ swimming pool ☐ soup can ☐ mug

☐ bathtub ☐ watering can ☐ cooking pot

---

16. Which number line shows the fractions $\frac{3}{3}$, $\frac{1}{3}$, $\frac{3}{1}$, and $\frac{4}{3}$ plotted correctly?

Ⓐ
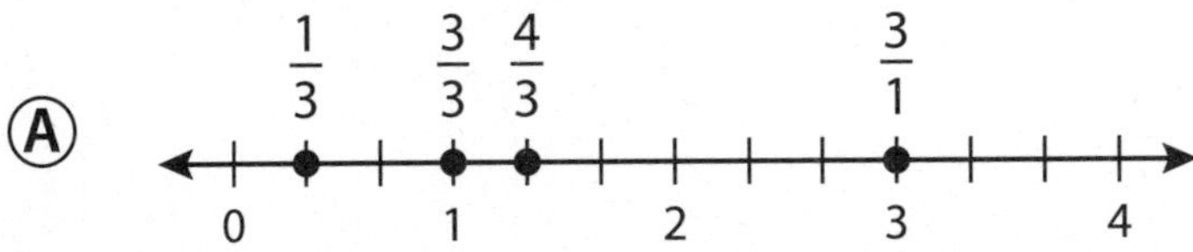

Ⓑ $\frac{1}{3}$, $\frac{3}{1}$, $\frac{4}{3}$, $\frac{3}{3}$; 0, 1, 2, 3, 4

Ⓒ $\frac{3}{1}$, $\frac{1}{3}$, $\frac{3}{3}$, $\frac{4}{3}$; 0, 1, 2, 3, 4

Ⓓ $\frac{1}{3}$, $\frac{3}{3}$, $\frac{4}{3}$, $\frac{3}{1}$; 0, 1, 2, 3, 4

Name ______________________________

STEAM Performance Task 1–12

1. Newton and Descartes are warming up for a baseball game.

a. Which units should be used to measure the mass of the baseball bat, *grams* or *kilograms*? Explain.

b. Which units should be used to measure the liquid volume of the team water jug, *milliliters* or *liters*? Explain.

c. Who practices baseball longer, Newton or Descartes? Explain.

Baseball Practice		
Activity	**Newton's Time Interval**	**Descartes's Time Interval**
Hitting	29 min	24 min
Fielding	8 min	9 min
Throwing	20 min	27 min

2. Your doctor recommends that you exercise about an hour each day, get plenty of sleep, and drink about 1,500 milliliters of water daily.

a. What are some ways you like to exercise?

b. You drink 3 cups of water. Each cup holds 300 milliliters. Did you drink enough water to meet your doctor's recommendation?

3. Your heart rate is the number of times your heart beats in 1 minute. Your heart rate is lower when you are at rest and higher when you are active. One way doctors measure your health is finding your resting heart rate.

a. You count the number of times your heart beats in 6 seconds. How can you use this number to find the number of times your heart beats in 1 minute?

b. Your heart beats 8 times in 6 seconds while you are at rest. What is your resting heart rate?

c. After playing outside, your heart beats 13 times in 6 seconds. How much greater, in beats per minute, is your heart rate now than when you were at rest?

d. MP **YOU BE THE TEACHER** Your friend says that another way to find the number of beats per minute is to multiply the number of times your heart beats in 10 seconds by 6. Is your friend correct? Explain.

---

4. You can use your pulse to find your heart rate.

a. How many times does your heart beat in 6 seconds? Use this number to find your resting heart rate.

b. Count the number of times your heart beats in one minute. How does this number compare to your answer above? Explain.

c. MP **Repeated Reasoning** About how many times does your heart beat in one hour? one day? Explain.

13 Classify Two-Dimensional Shapes

- What is a fossil? What types of fossils are there?
- How can archaeologists use math when they dig for fossils? Why do you think archaeologists lay grids over fossil dig sites?

B 12

B 13

Chapter Learning Target:
Understand two-dimensional shapes.

Chapter Success Criteria:
- I can define two-dimensional shapes.
- I can explain different shapes and their features.
- I can compare one shape to another.
- I can draw a shape.

Name ______________________

13 Vocabulary

Review Words
hexagon
octagon
pentagon

Organize It

Use the review words to complete the graphic organizer.

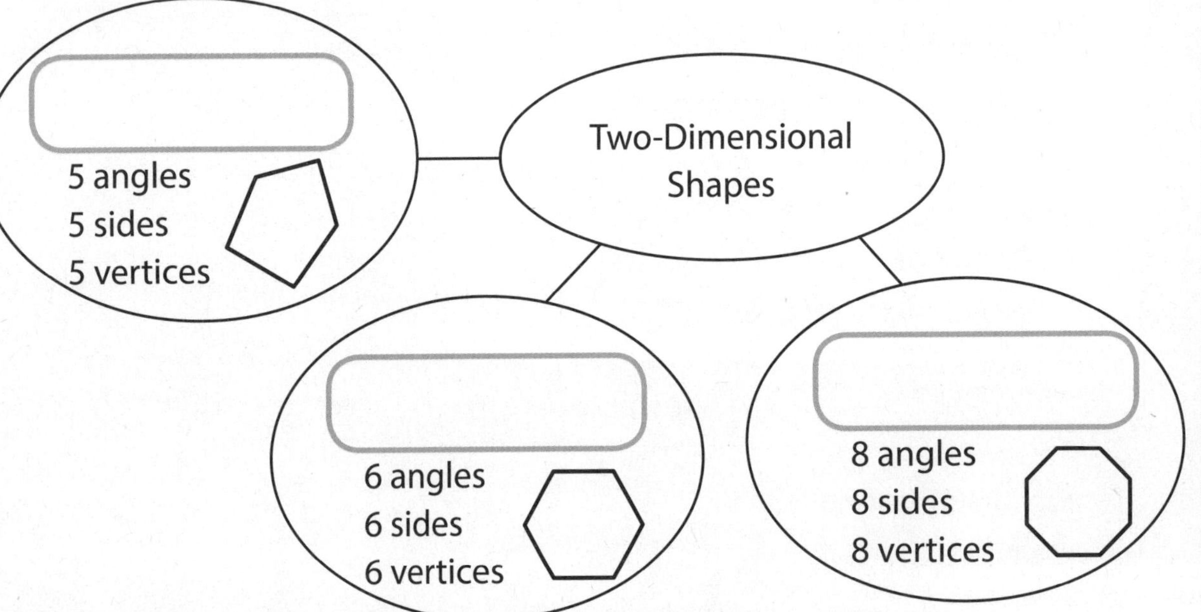

Define It

Use your vocabulary cards to complete the puzzle.

Across

1. A parallelogram with four equal sides

Down

2. A closed, two-dimensional shape with three or more sides
3. A parallelogram with four right angles and four equal sides

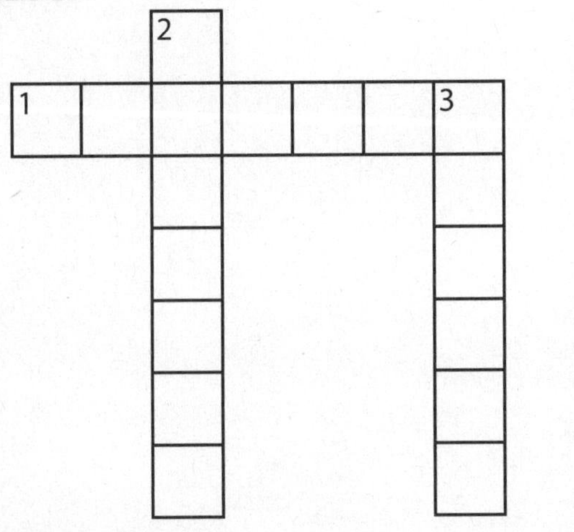

Chapter 13 Vocabulary Cards

angle

parallel sides

parallelogram

polygon

quadrilateral

rectangle

rhombus

right angle

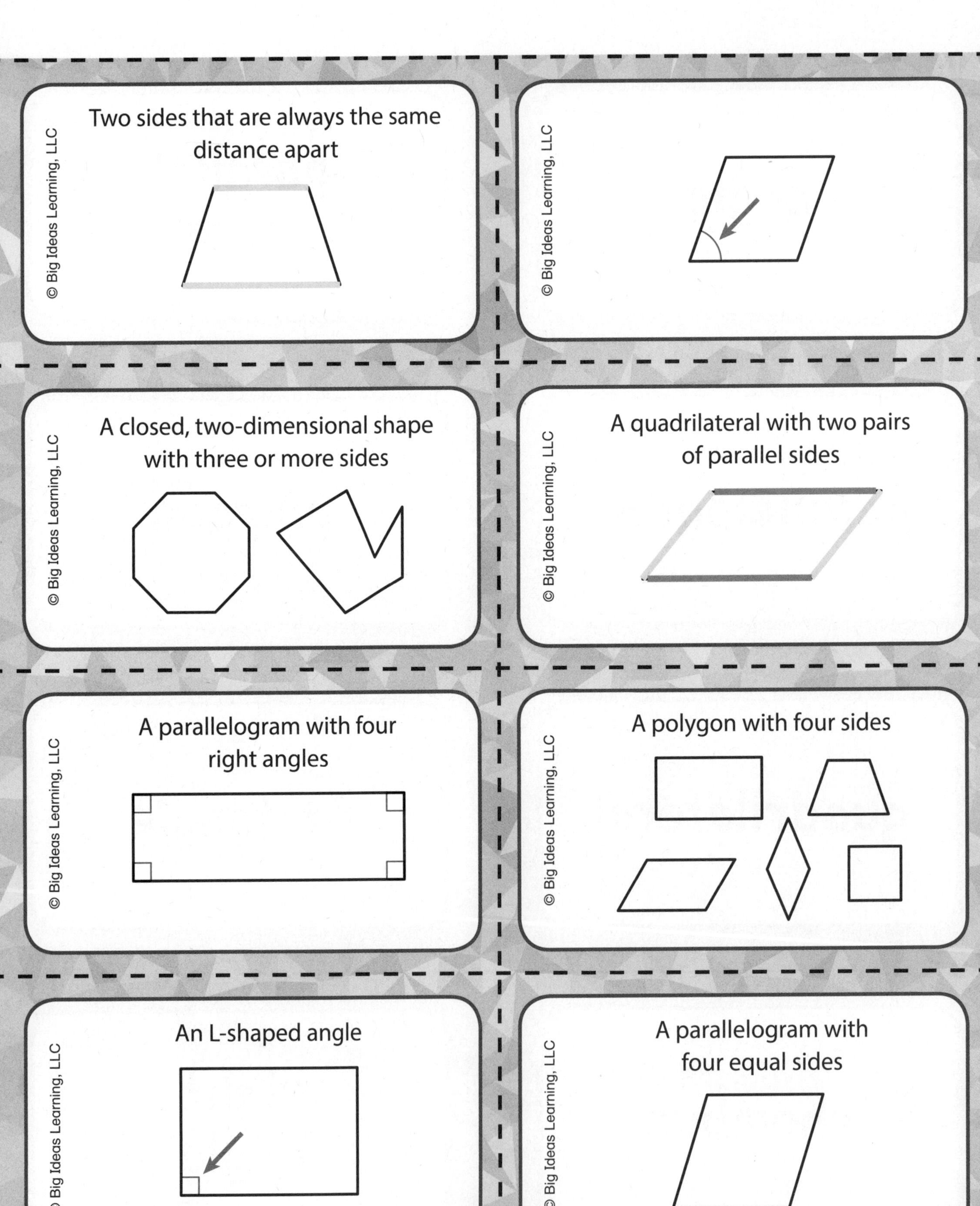

Two sides that are always the same distance apart
© Big Ideas Learning, LLC
© Big Ideas Learning, LLC
A closed, two-dimensional shape with three or more sides
© Big Ideas Learning, LLC
A quadrilateral with two pairs of parallel sides
© Big Ideas Learning, LLC
A parallelogram with four right angles
© Big Ideas Learning, LLC
A polygon with four sides
© Big Ideas Learning, LLC
An L-shaped angle
© Big Ideas Learning, LLC
A parallelogram with four equal sides
© Big Ideas Learning, LLC

Chapter 13 Vocabulary Cards

side

square

trapezoid

vertex

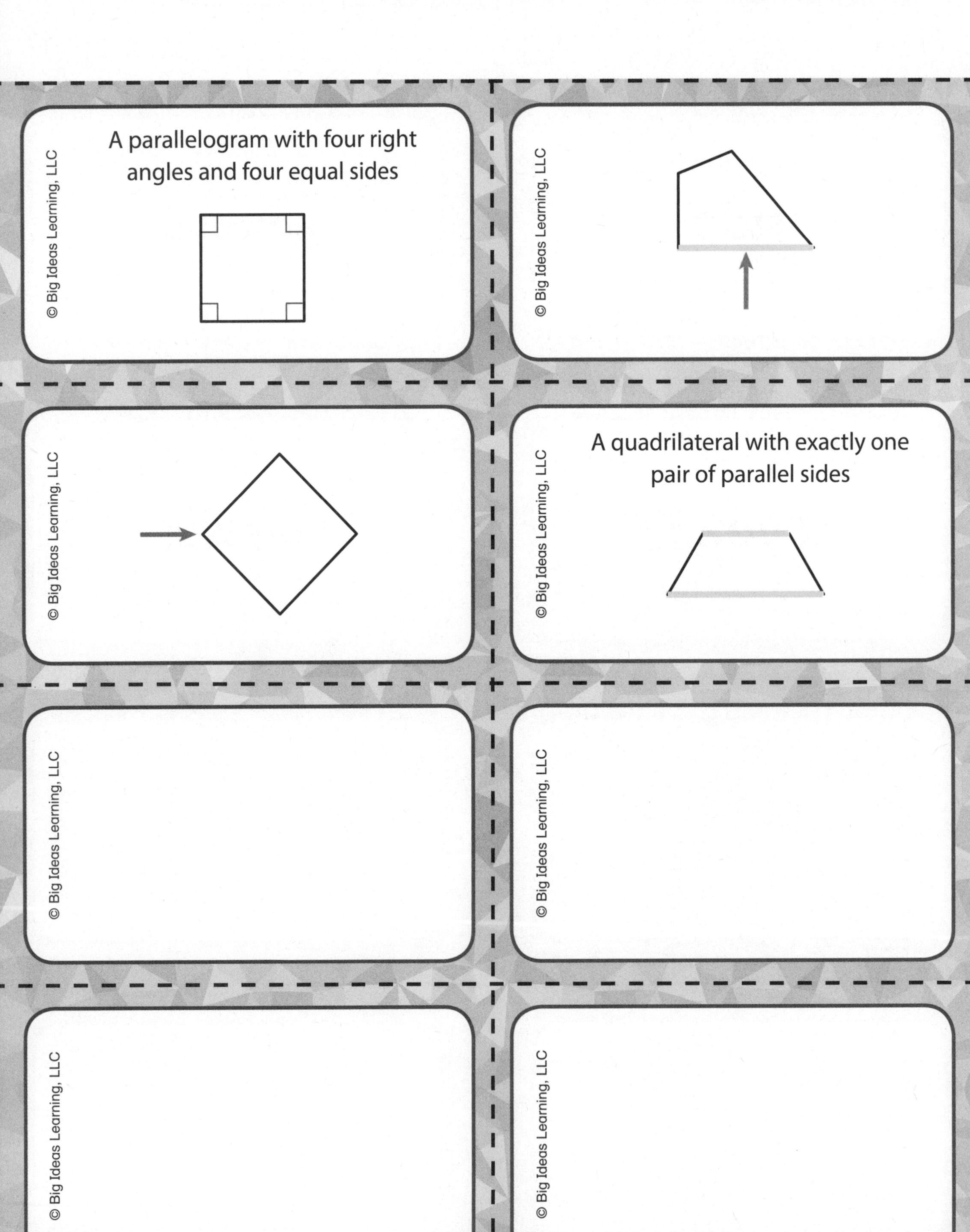
A parallelogram with four right angles and four equal sides
A quadrilateral with exactly one pair of parallel sides

Name ________________________________

Identify Sides and Angles of Quadrilaterals

Learning Target: Identify parallel sides and right angles of quadrilaterals.

Success Criteria:

- I can identify when two sides of a quadrilateral are parallel.
- I can identify right angles of a quadrilateral.

Explore and Grow

Sort the Polygon Cards.

Fewer Than 4 Sides	4 Sides	More Than 4 Sides

Structure Does the sort change if you sort by the number of vertices? Explain.

Think and Grow: Sides and Angles of Quadrilaterals

A **polygon** is a closed, two-dimensional shape with three or more sides.

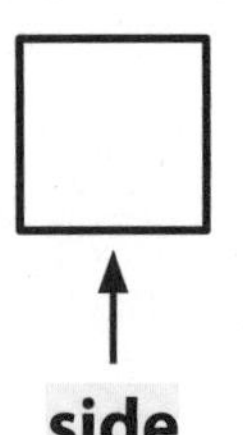

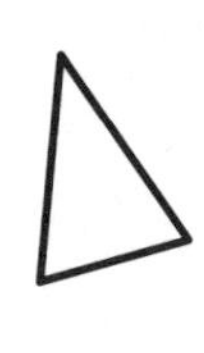

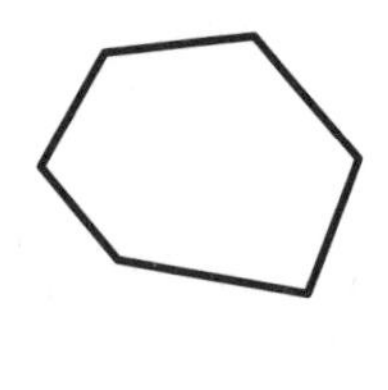

A **quadrilateral** is a polygon with four sides. Quadrilaterals have four vertices and four angles.

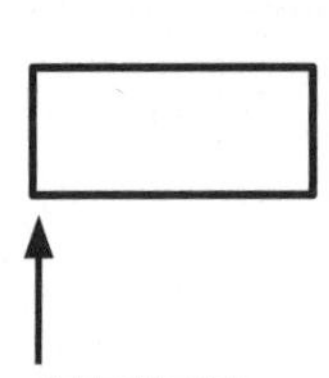

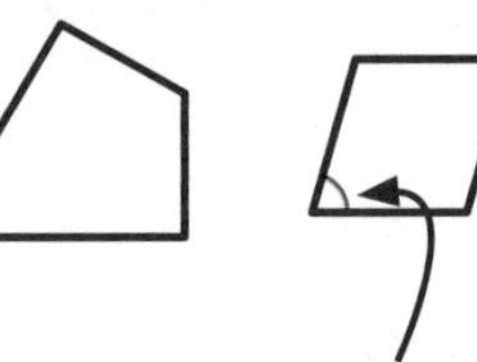

Quadrilaterals can have parallel sides and right angles. **Parallel sides** are two sides that are always the same distance apart. A **right angle** is an L-shaped angle.

The symbol ∟ shows a right angle.

1 right angle

1 pair of parallel sides

4 right angles

2 pairs of parallel sides

Example Identify the number of right angles and pairs of parallel sides.

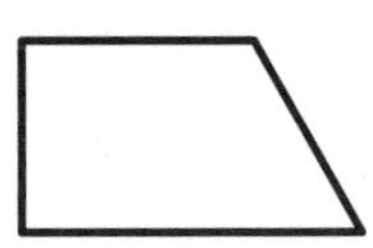

Right angles: ______

Pairs of parallel sides: ______

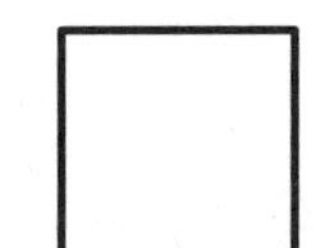

Right angles: ______

Pairs of parallel sides: ______

Show and Grow *I can do it!*

Identify the number of right angles and pairs of parallel sides.

1. 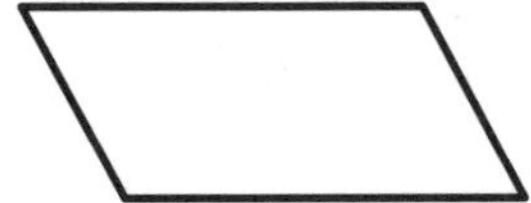

Right angles: ______

Pairs of parallel sides: ______

2. 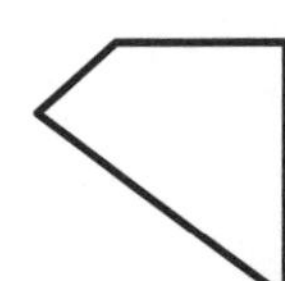

Right angles: ______

Pairs of parallel sides: ______

Name ____________________

Apply and Grow: Practice

Identify the number of right angles and pairs of parallel sides.

3. 

Right angles: _____

Pairs of parallel sides: _____

4. 

Right angles: _____

Pairs of parallel sides: _____

5. 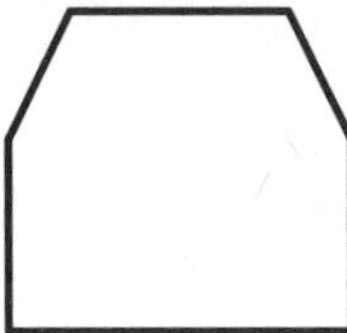

Right angles: _____

Pairs of parallel sides: _____

6. 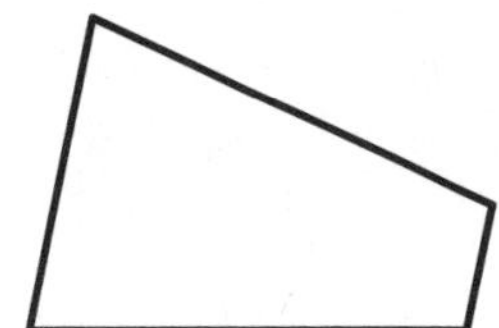

Right angles: _____

Pairs of parallel sides: _____

7. 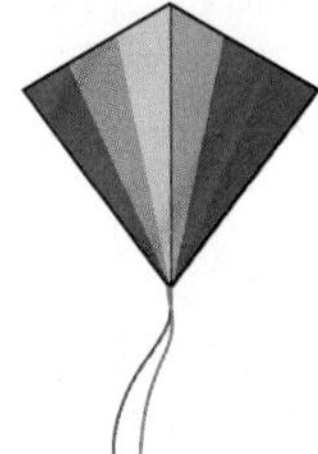

Right angles: _____

Pairs of parallel sides: _____

8. 

Right angles: _____

Pairs of parallel sides: _____

Use Math Tools How can you use different colors to help you count each pair of parallel sides?

9. **YOU BE THE TEACHER** Your friend says the yellow sides are parallel. Is your friend correct? Explain.

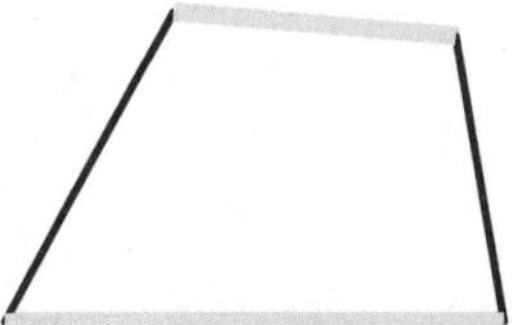

Think and Grow: Modeling Real Life

Use quadrilateral pattern blocks to complete the puzzle.

Number of Blocks	Description of Block
3	• 0 right angles • 1 pair of parallel sides
2	• 0 right angles • 2 pairs of parallel sides
2	• 4 right angles • 2 pairs of parallel sides

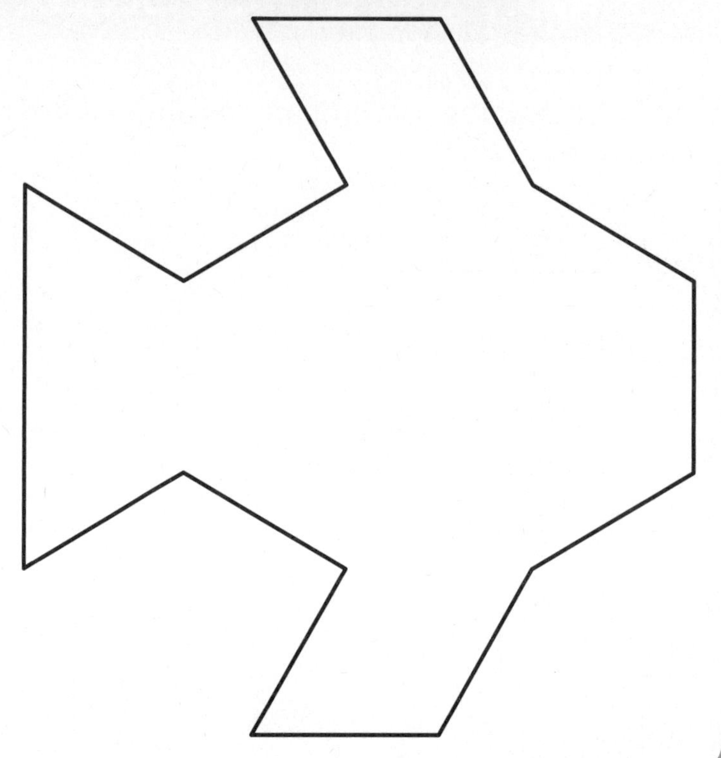

Show and Grow I can think deeper!

10. Use quadrilateral pattern blocks to complete the puzzle.

Number of Blocks	Description of Block
4	• 0 right angles • 1 pair of parallel sides
3	• 0 right angles • 2 pairs of parallel sides
3	• 4 right angles • 2 pairs of parallel sides

Use Math Tools Can you complete the puzzle using the same blocks but in different positions? Explain.

Name ______________________________

Learning Target: Identify parallel sides and right angles of quadrilaterals.

Example Identify the number of right angles and pairs of parallel sides.

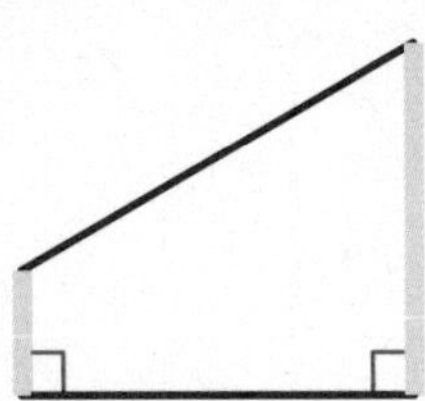

Right angles: 2

Pairs of parallel sides: 1

Identify the number of right angles and pairs of parallel sides.

1.

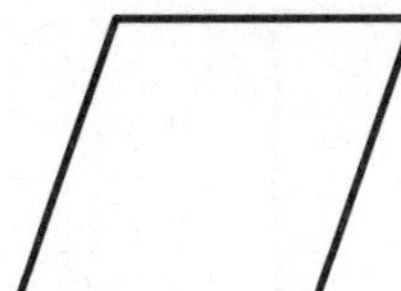

Right angles: ______

Pairs of parallel sides: ______

2.

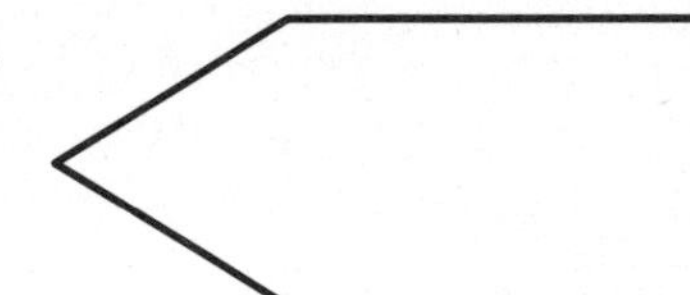

Right angles: ______

Pairs of parallel sides: ______

3.

Right angles: ______

Pairs of parallel sides: ______

4.

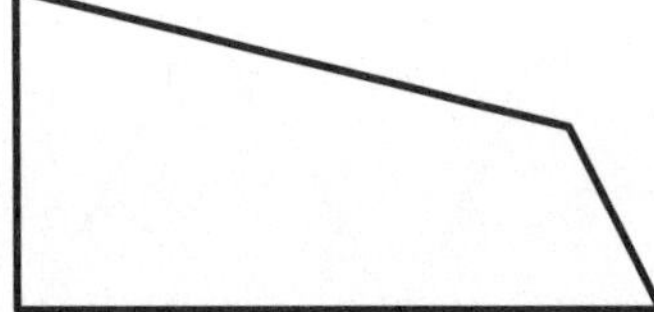

Right angles: ______

Pairs of parallel sides: ______

5.

Right angles: ______

Pairs of parallel sides: ______

6.

Right angles: ______

Pairs of parallel sides: ______

7. **MP Construct an Argument** Can a quadrilateral have exactly three right angles? Explain.

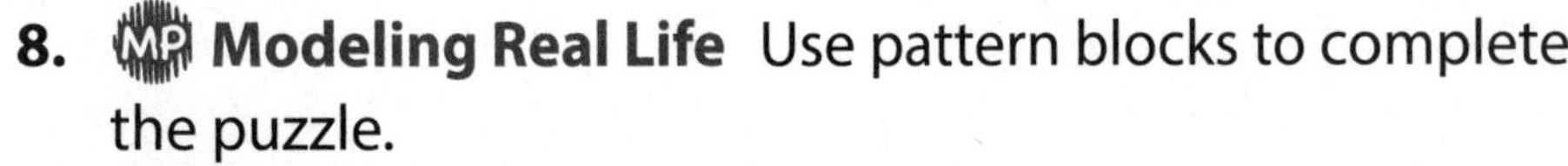

8. **MP Modeling Real Life** Use pattern blocks to complete the puzzle.

Number of Blocks	Description of Block
4	• 0 right angles • 2 pairs of parallel sides
5	• 4 right angles • 2 pairs of parallel sides
4	• 0 right angles • 1 pair of parallel sides

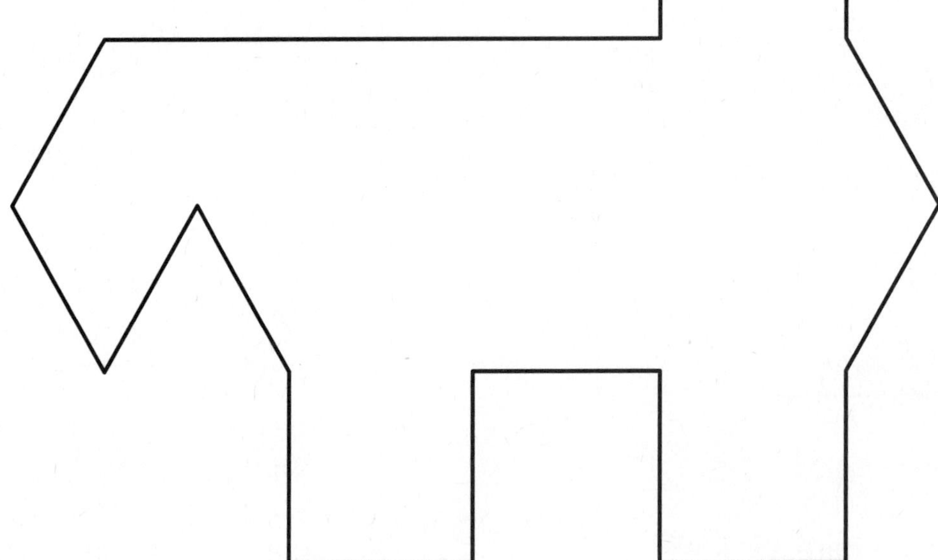

Review & Refresh

9. Newton has 28 cards. Descartes has 24 cards. Newton divides his cards into 4 equal stacks and gives Descartes one stack. How many cards does Descartes have now?

Name ________________________________

Describe Quadrilaterals 13.2

Learning Target: Describe quadrilaterals using sides and angles.

Success Criteria:

- I can use sides and angles to identify a quadrilateral.
- I can explain why a quadrilateral can have more than one name.

Explore and Grow

Sort the Quadrilateral Cards.

No Parallel Sides	Parallel Sides

Structure What is another way you can sort the quadrilaterals?

Think and Grow: Identify Quadrilaterals

You can identify a quadrilateral using its sides and angles. A quadrilateral can have more than one name.

Quadrilateral

4 sides
4 angles

Trapezoid

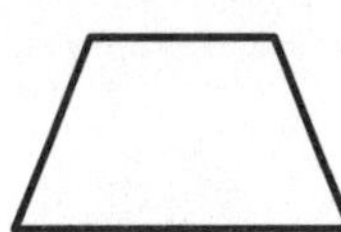

exactly 1 pair of parallel sides

Parallelogram

2 pairs of parallel sides

Rectangle

2 pairs of parallel sides
4 right angles

Rhombus

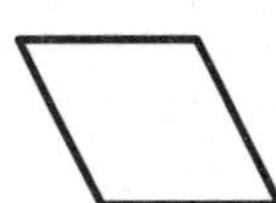

2 pairs of parallel sides
4 equal sides

Square

2 pairs of parallel sides
4 equal sides
4 right angles

Example Circle all of the names for the quadrilateral.

Pairs of parallel sides: _____

Equal sides: _____

Right angles: _____

Rhombus Square

Rectangle Parallelogram

Show and Grow *I can do it!*

Circle all of the names for the quadrilateral.

1. 

Trapezoid Rectangle

Rhombus Parallelogram

2. 

Square Parallelogram

Rectangle Trapezoid

Name ______________________________

Apply and Grow: Practice

Write all of the names for the quadrilateral.

3.

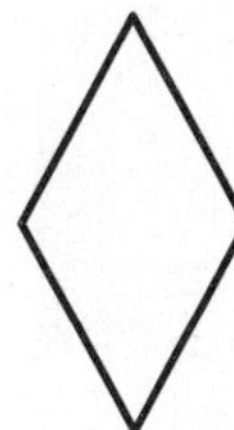

4.

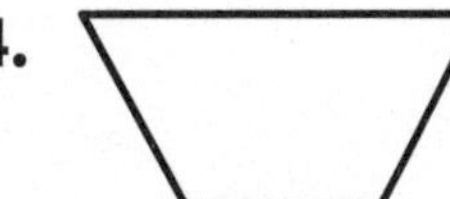

Name all of the quadrilaterals that can have the given attribute.

5. 2 pairs of parallel sides

6. 4 right angles

MP Repeated Reasoning Which quadrilaterals did you write for both Exercises 5 and 6? Why?

7. **MP Precision** Is the shape a rhombus? Explain.

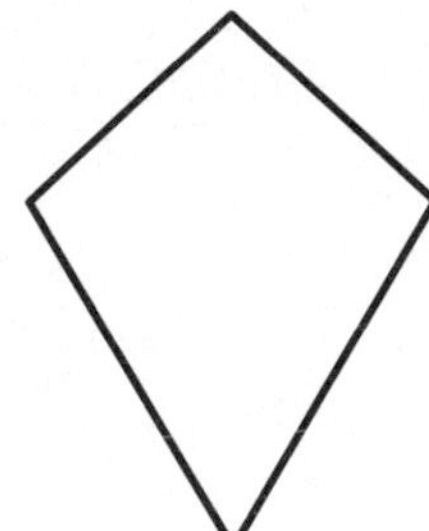

8. **MP YOU BE THE TEACHER** Your friend says the shape is *not* a rhombus. Is your friend correct? Explain.

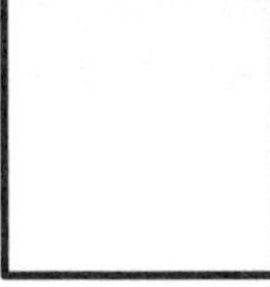

Think and Grow: Modeling Real Life

Write all of the names for the red quadrilateral in the painting.

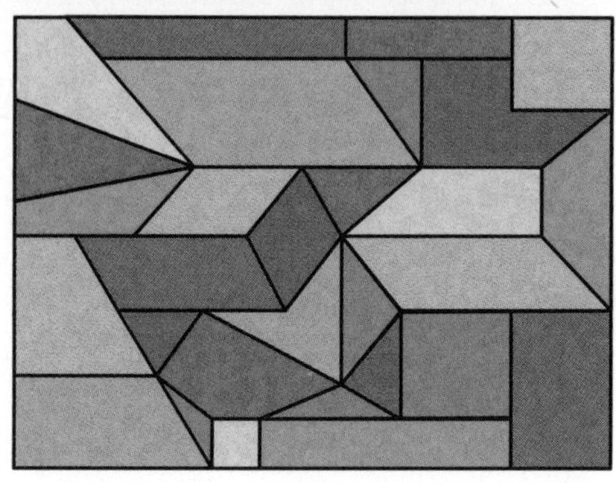

Show and Grow I can think deeper!

Use the painting above.

9. Write all of the names for the blue quadrilateral.

10. What color is the rhombus that is *not* a square?

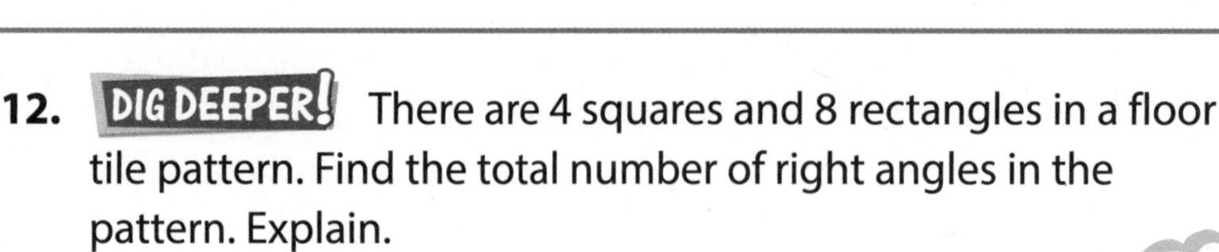

11. How many trapezoids are in the painting? Circle them.

12. DIG DEEPER! There are 4 squares and 8 rectangles in a floor tile pattern. Find the total number of right angles in the pattern. Explain.

Check Your Work
How can you use a drawing to check your work?

Name ______________________________

Homework & Practice 13.2

Learning Target: Describe quadrilaterals using sides and angles.

Example Circle all of the names for the quadrilateral.

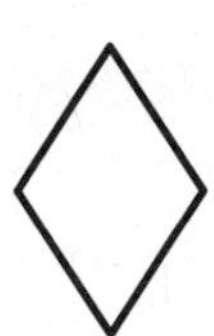

Pairs of parallel sides: 2

Equal sides: 4

Right angles: 0

Square Trapezoid (Rhombus) Rectangle

Circle all of the names for the quadrilateral.

1. 

Rhombus Rectangle

Square Parallelogram

2. 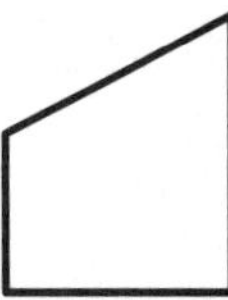

Rectangle Parallelogram

Trapezoid Rhombus

Write all of the names for the quadrilateral.

3. 

4. 

Name all of the quadrilaterals that can have the given attributes.

5. 4 sides and 4 angles

6. exactly 1 pair of parallel sides

7. **Writing** Explain how a trapezoid is different from a parallelogram.

8. **MP Reasoning** Explain why the rectangle shown is *not* a square.

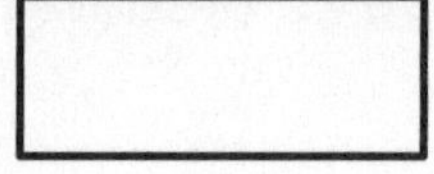

9. **DIG DEEPER!** What is Descartes's shape?

My quadrilateral has four right angles and two pairs of parallel sides. One pair of sides is greater in length than the other pair.

10. **Which One Doesn't Belong?** Which does *not* belong with the other three? Explain.

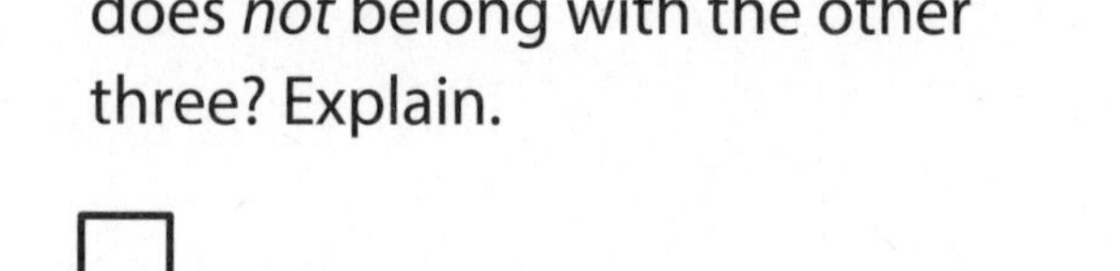

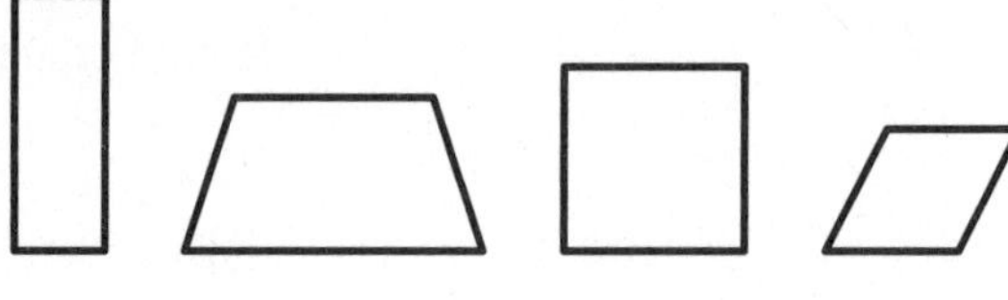

MP Modeling Real Life Use the mosaic.

11. Write all of the names for the purple quadrilateral.

____

12. How many parallelograms are in the mosaic? Circle them.

Review & Refresh

Find the area of the rectangle.

13.

_____ × _____ = _____

Area = _______________

14.

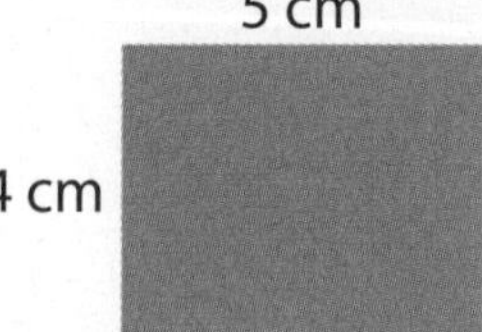

_____ × _____ = _____

Area = _______________

Name ______________________________

Classify Quadrilaterals 13.3

Learning Target: Classify quadrilaterals based on their attributes.

Success Criteria:

- I can tell what is alike between two groups of quadrilaterals.
- I can tell what is different between two groups of quadrilaterals.
- I can classify two types of quadrilaterals in one or more ways.

Explore and Grow

Use each description to model a quadrilateral on your geoboard. Draw each quadrilateral.

Two pairs of parallel sides	Exactly one pair of parallel sides
Four right angles that do *not* form a square	Two pairs of parallel sides and no right angles

Does It Make Sense? Compare your quadrilaterals to your partner's. Are your quadrilaterals the same? Are you both correct? Explain.

Think and Grow: Classify Quadrilaterals

Example How are the parallelograms and rhombuses alike? How are they different?

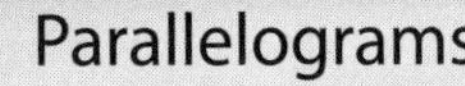
Parallelograms

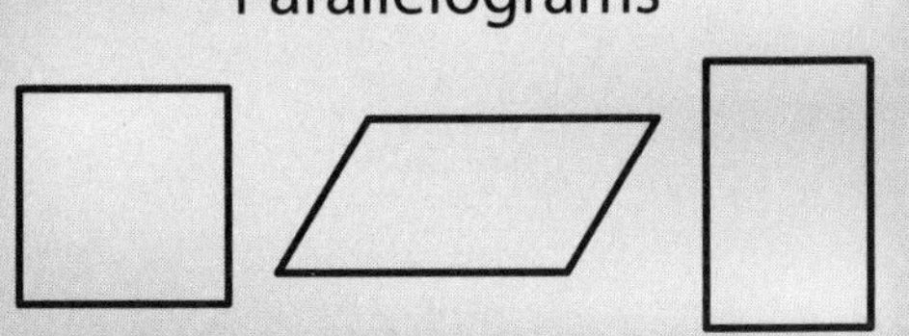

Rhombuses

Ways they are alike:

Each has ______ sides.

Each has ______ angles.

Each has ______ pairs of parallel sides.

Ways they are different:

Rhombuses always have ______ equal sides.

What names can you use to classify all parallelograms and rhombuses?

______________ and ______________

Show and Grow *I can do it!*

Squares

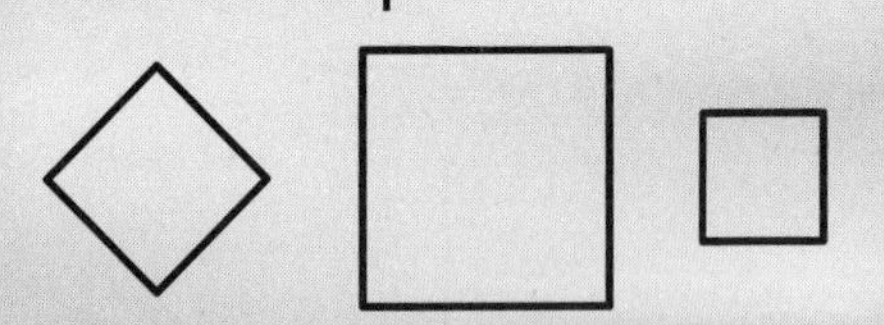

Rectangles

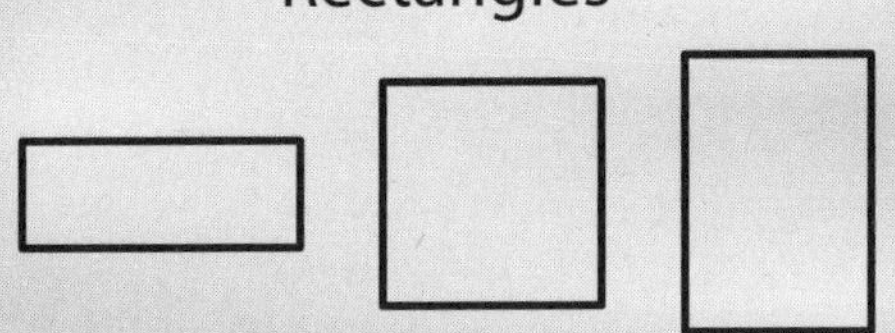

1. How are squares and rectangles alike? How are they different?

2. What names can you use to classify all squares and rectangles?

3. Draw a quadrilateral that is *not* a square or a rectangle. Explain.

Name ______________________________

Apply and Grow: Practice

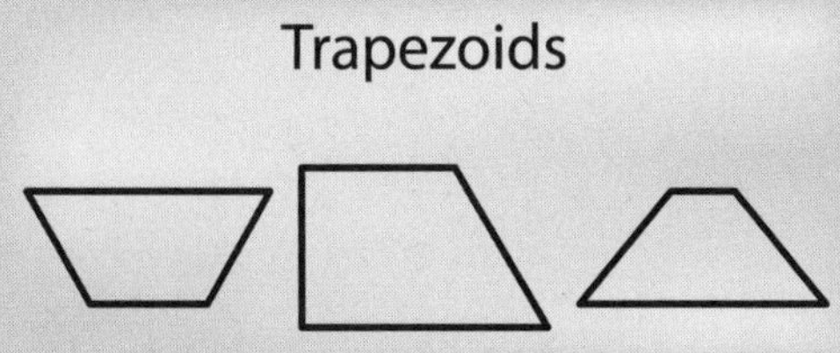

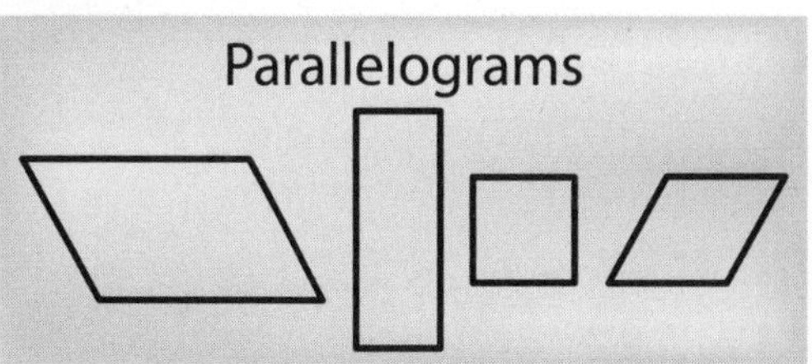

4. How are trapezoids and parallelograms alike? How are they different?

5. What name can you use to classify all trapezoids and parallelograms?

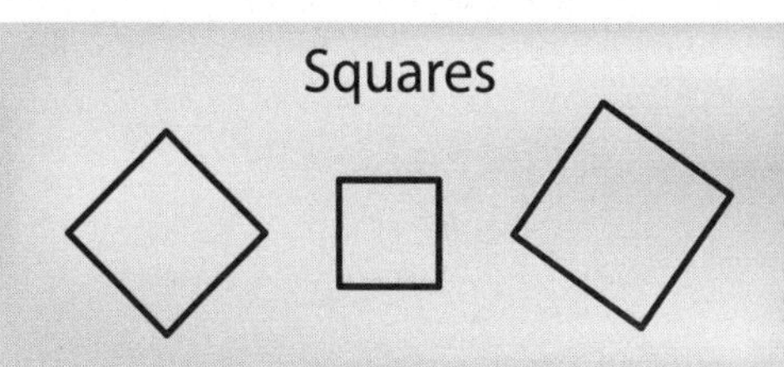

6. How are rhombuses and squares alike? How are they different?

7. What names can you use to classify all rhombuses and squares?

8. Draw a quadrilateral that is a rhombus but *not* a square.

9. Draw a quadrilateral that is *not* a rhombus or a square. Explain.

Think and Grow: Modeling Real Life

Sort the road signs into two groups by shape. What is alike and what is different between the two groups? What name can you use to classify all of the road sign shapes?

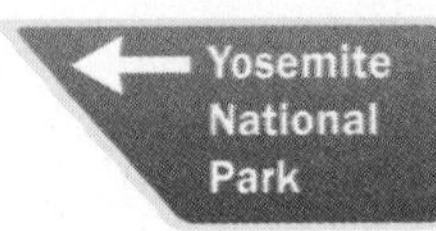

Show and Grow *I can think deeper!*

10. Sort the road signs into two groups by shape. What is alike and what is different between the two groups? What names can you use to classify all of the road sign shapes?

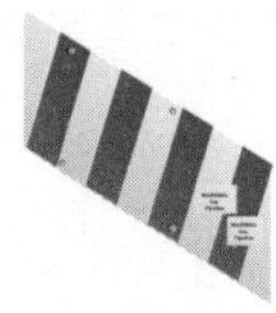

Name ________________________________

Homework & Practice 13.3

Learning Target: Classify quadrilaterals based on their attributes.

Example How are parallelograms and squares alike? How are they different?

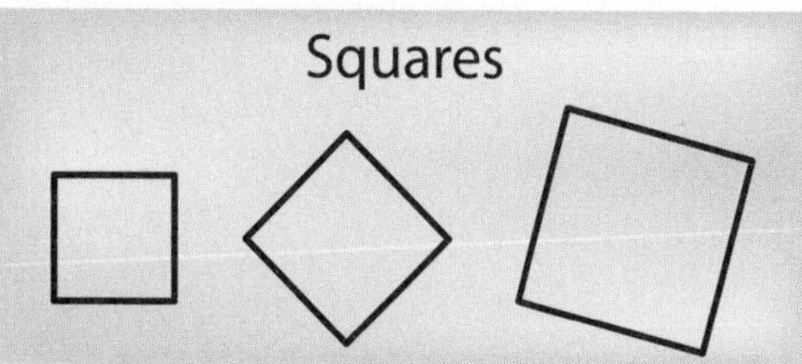

Ways they are alike:

Each has __4__ sides.

Each has __4__ angles.

Each has __2__ pairs of parallel sides.

Ways they are different:

Squares always have __4__ equal sides and __4__ right angles.

What names can you use to classify all parallelograms and squares?

__parallelograms__ and __quadrilaterals__

Rectangles

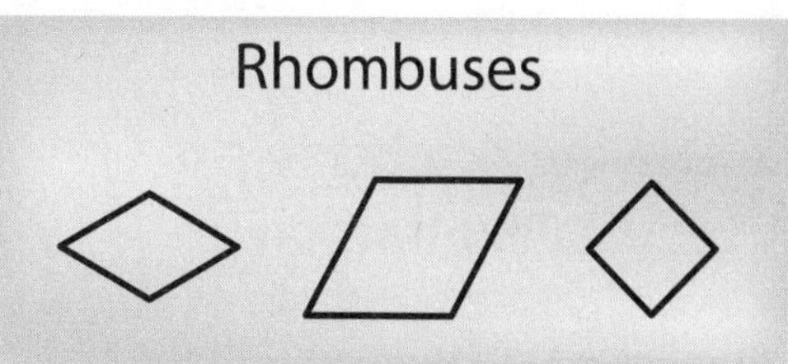

1. How are rectangles and rhombuses alike? How are they different?

2. What names can you use to classify all rectangles and rhombuses?

3. **DIG DEEPER!** Your friend says a shape is a rectangle. Newton says the same shape is a rhombus, and Descartes says it is a square. Can they all be correct? Explain.

4. **MP YOU BE THE TEACHER** Is Newton correct? Explain.

5. **MP Modeling Real Life** Sort the earrings into two groups by shape. What is alike and what is different between the two groups? What name can you use to classify all of the earring shapes?

 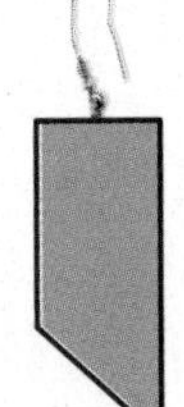    

Review & Refresh

6. Use the number line to find an equivalent fraction.

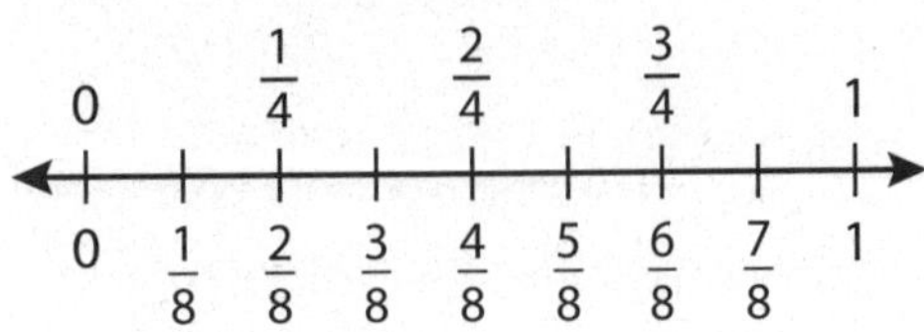

$\frac{6}{8} = \frac{\square}{\square}$

7. Write two fractions that name the point shown.

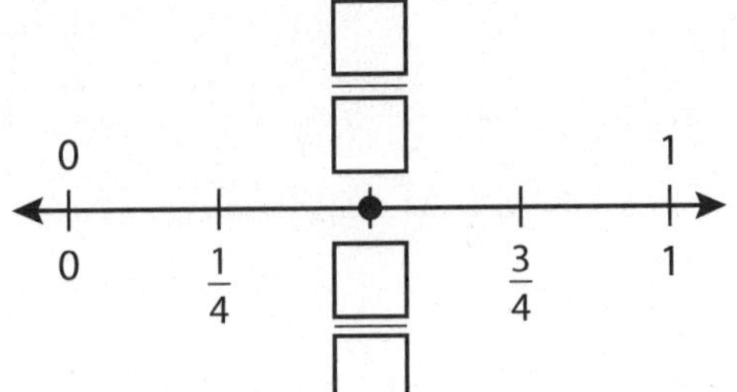

$\frac{\square}{\square} = \frac{\square}{\square}$

Name ______________________________

Draw Quadrilaterals 13.4

Learning Target: Draw quadrilaterals.

Success Criteria:

- I can draw and name a quadrilateral given a description.
- I can draw a quadrilateral that does not belong to a given group.

Model each quadrilateral on your geoboard. Move one vertex of each quadrilateral to create a new quadrilateral. Draw each new quadrilateral.

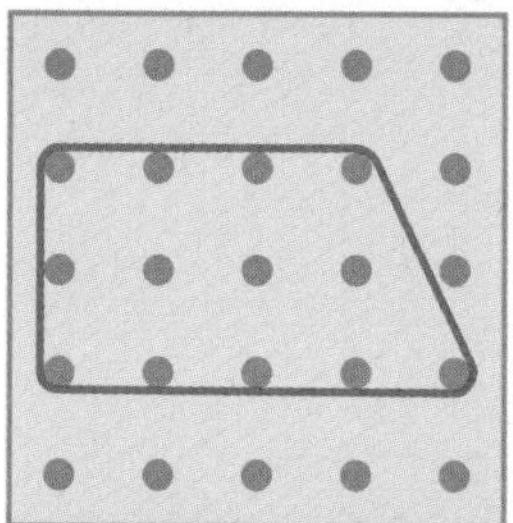

Trapezoid to Parallelogram

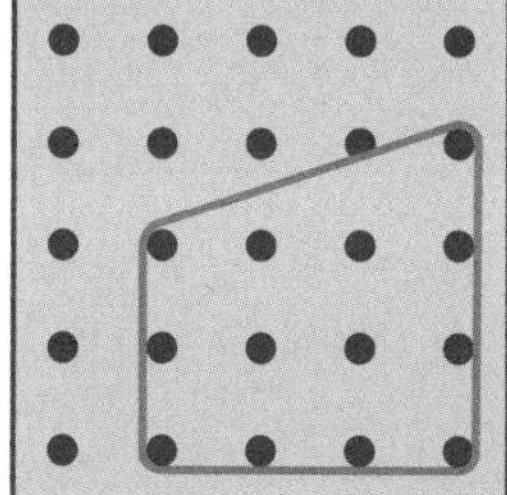

Trapezoid to Rectangle

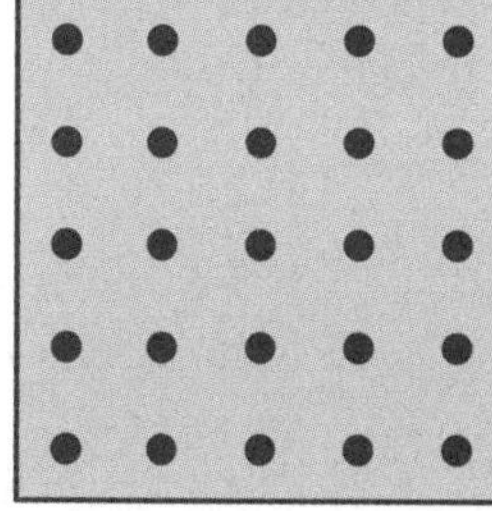

Structure Create your own quadrilateral. Move one vertex to create a new quadrilateral. Draw your quadrilaterals. Name each quadrilateral.

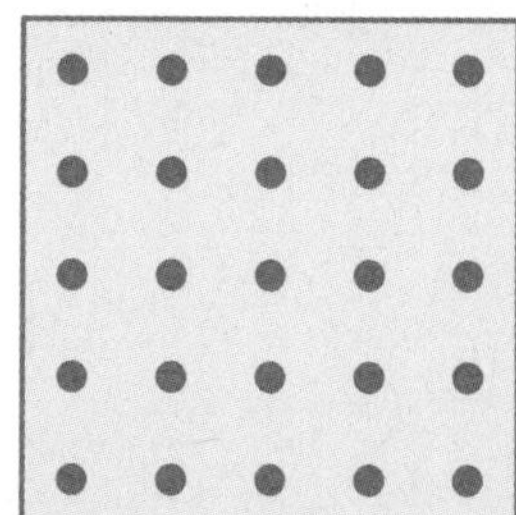

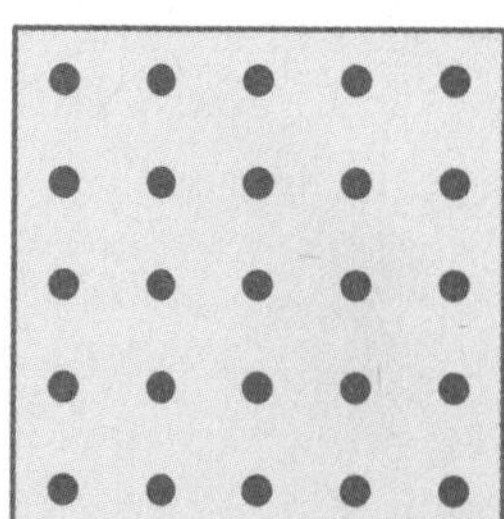

Think and Grow: Draw Quadrilaterals

Example Draw a quadrilateral that has four right angles. Name the quadrilateral.

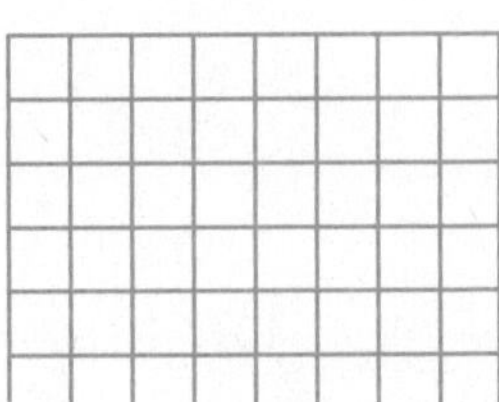

____

Example Below are three rhombuses. Draw a quadrilateral that is *not* a rhombus. Explain why it is not a rhombus.

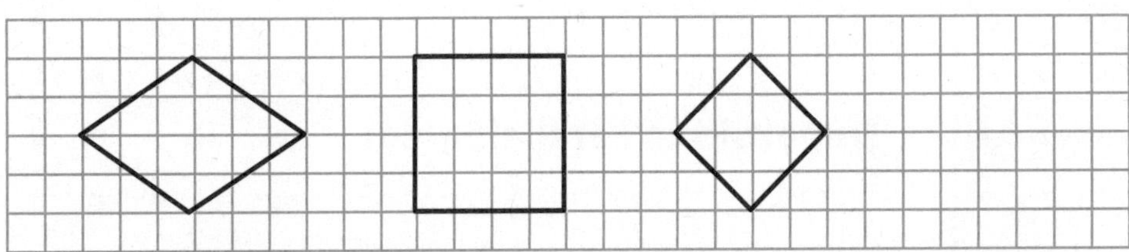

The quadrilateral is not a rhombus because _______________

_______________.

Show and Grow *I can do it!*

1. Draw a quadrilateral that has exactly one pair of parallel sides. Name the quadrilateral.

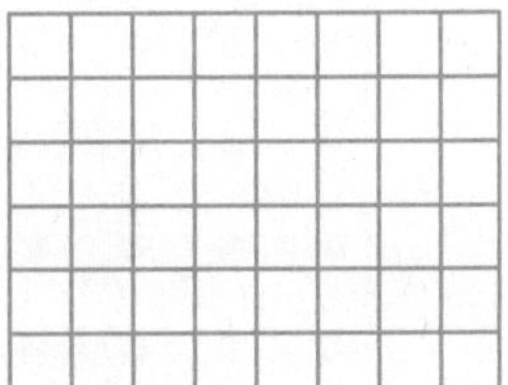

2. Draw a quadrilateral that is *not* a square. Explain why it is not a square.

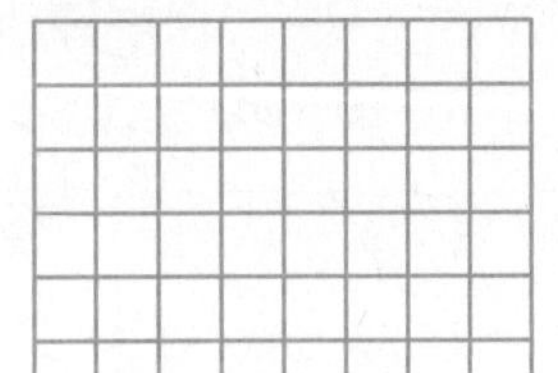

Name ______________________________

Apply and Grow: Practice

Name the group of quadrilaterals. Then draw a quadrilateral that does *not* belong in the group. Explain why it does not belong.

3. 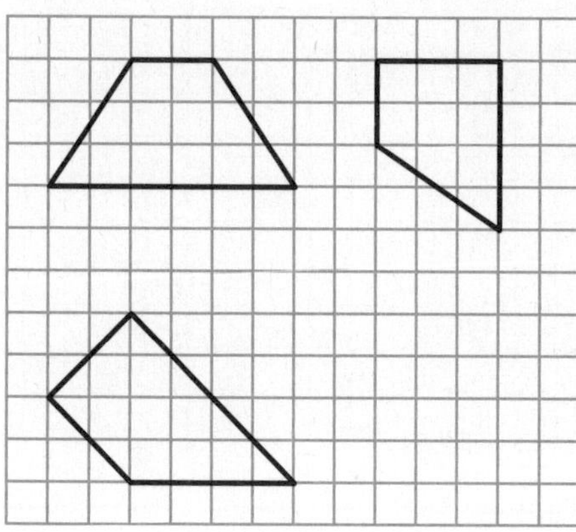

4. 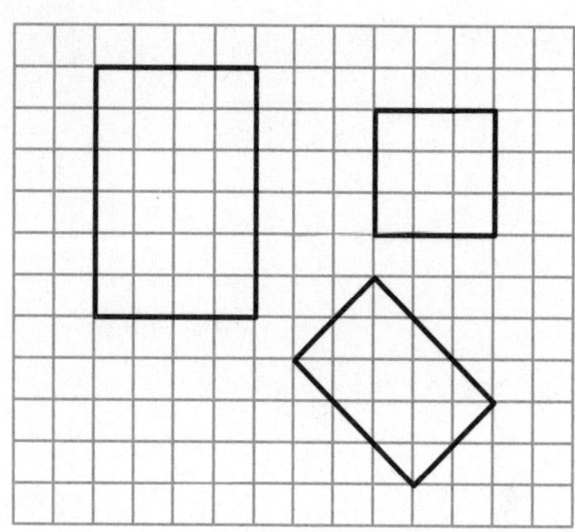

5. **Maintain Accuracy** Circle the quadrilaterals that are *not* rhombuses.

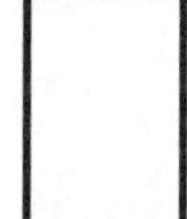      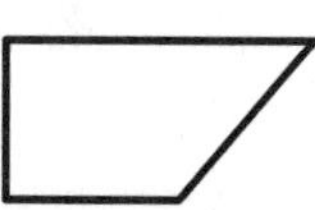

6. **YOU BE THE TEACHER** Your friend draws the shape and says it is a parallelogram because it has two pairs of parallel sides. Is your friend correct? Explain.

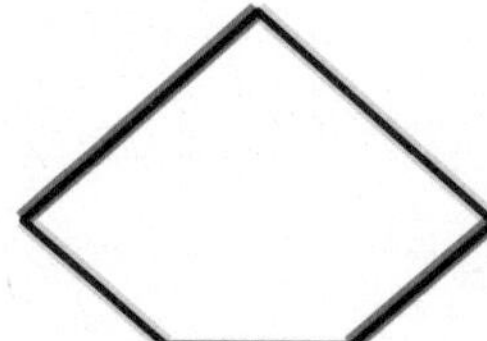

7. **DIG DEEPER!** Draw a quadrilateral with two pairs of parallel sides. One side is given.

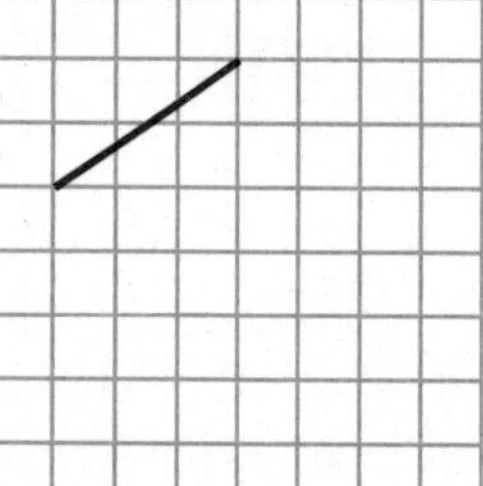

Think and Grow: Modeling Real Life

A helicopter travels to various Colorado cities. Draw to show a route that forms a parallelogram. Write the names of the cities you use.

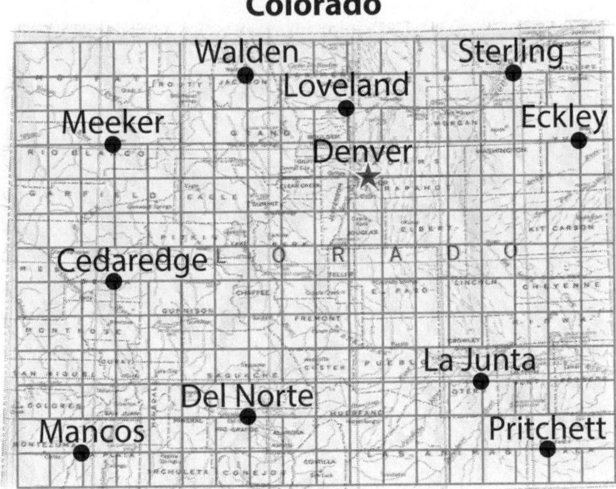

Show and Grow *I can think deeper!*

8. Use the map above. Draw to show a route that forms a trapezoid. Write the names of the cities you use.

9. You have four markers of equal length. Name all of the quadrilaterals you can make using the markers as sides.

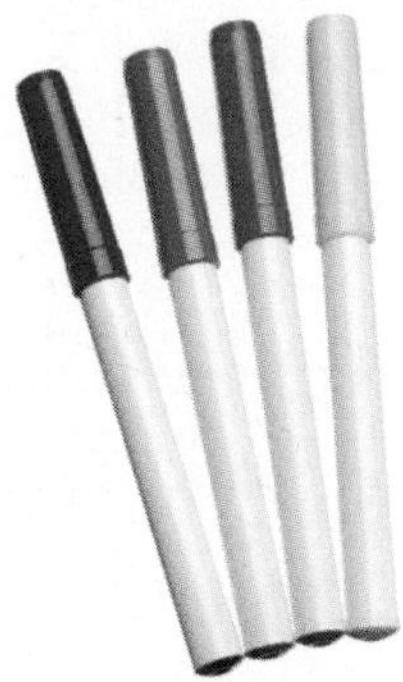

10. **DIG DEEPER!** Use a ruler to draw a trapezoid for each description.

- one side length of 1 inch
- one side length of 2 inches
- two right angles

- one side length of 1 inch
- one side length of 2 inches
- no right angles

Name ______________________

Homework & Practice 13.4

Learning Target: Draw quadrilaterals.

Example Draw a quadrilateral that has four equal sides. Name the quadrilateral.

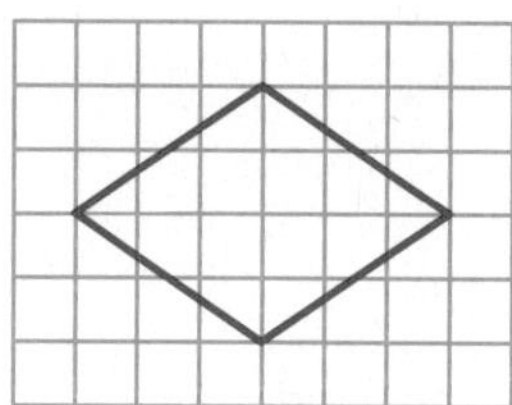

rhombus

I could have also drawn a square.

Example Below are three rectangles. Draw a quadrilateral that is *not* a rectangle. Explain why it is not a rectangle.

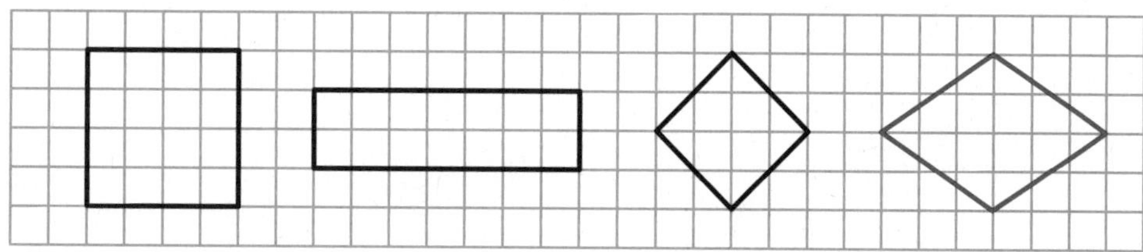

The quadrilateral is *not* a rectangle because it does not have four right angles.

1. Draw a quadrilateral that has two pairs of parallel sides. Name the quadrilateral.

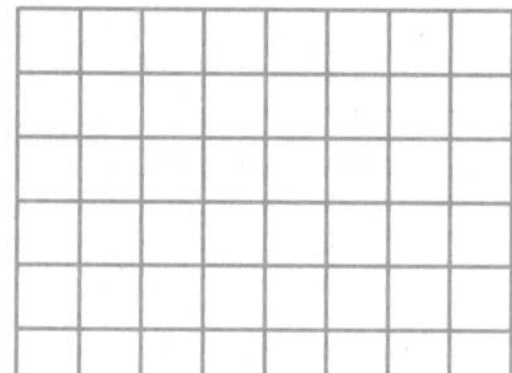

2. Draw a quadrilateral that is *not* a rhombus. Explain why it is not a rhombus.

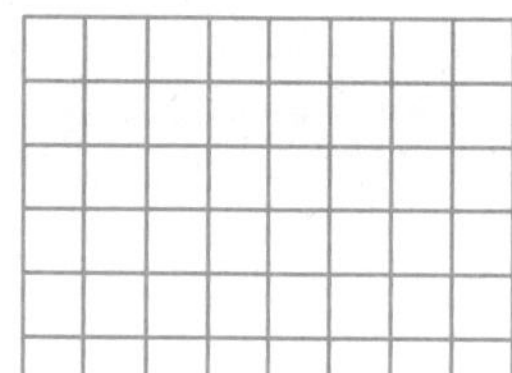

3. Name the group of quadrilaterals. Then draw a quadrilateral that does *not* belong in the group. Explain why it does not belong.

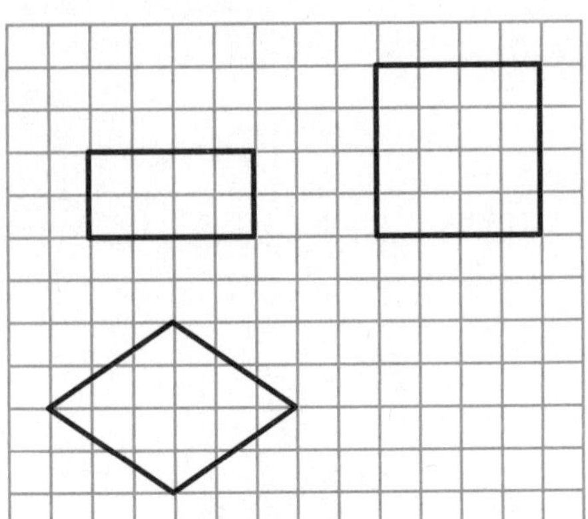

4. **Maintain Accuracy** Circle the quadrilaterals that are *not* trapezoids.

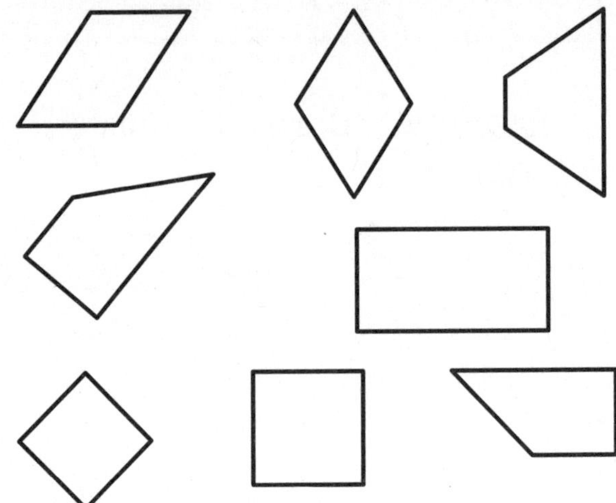

Modeling Real Life A bus tour wants to travel to various locations in New York City. Use the map.

5. Draw to show a route that forms a rectangle whose vertices are attractions on the map. Write the names of the attractions.

6. **DIG DEEPER!** Draw to show a route that forms a rectangle and passes by as many of the attractions as possible. The vertices do *not* need to be attractions on the map. How many attractions are on the route?

Review & Refresh

7. Tell whether the shape shows equal parts or unequal parts. If the shape shows equal parts, then name them.

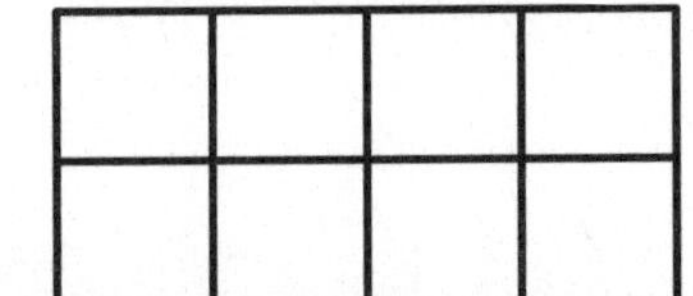

_______ parts _______________

Name ___________________________________

Performance Task 13

Your class is learning about fossils.

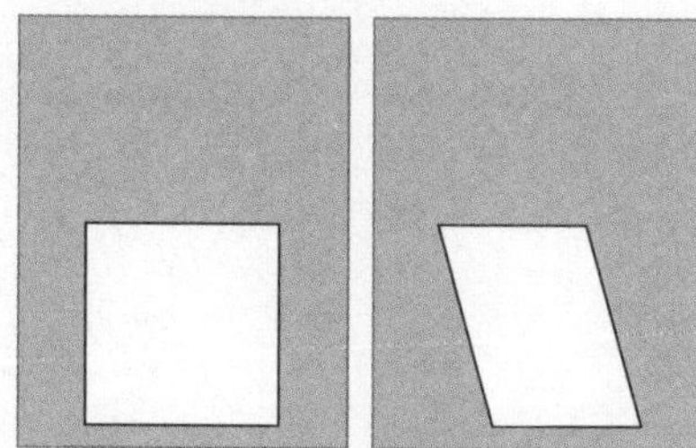

1. Your teacher wants to create cards using the fossils below. Use each polygon description to write the fossil name on the correct card.

A polygon with $4 + 1$ sides — **Dragonfly**

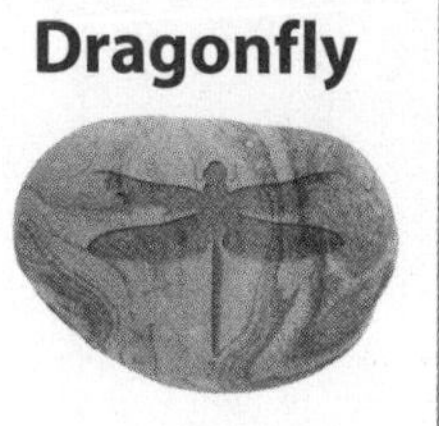

A rhombus with 4×1 right angles — **Starfish**

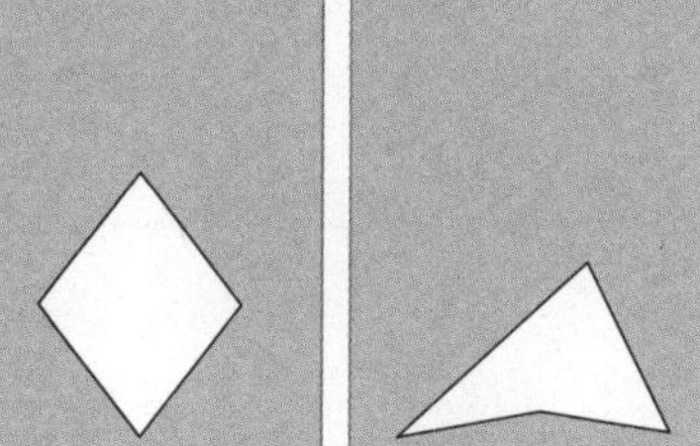

A quadrilateral with only 1 right angle — **Leaf**

A quadrilateral with $8 \div 2$ right angles and $8 \div 4$ pairs of parallel sides — **Fish**

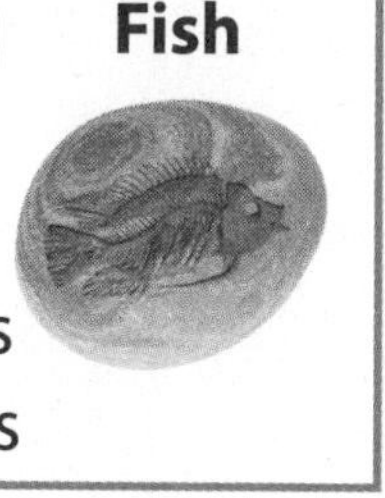

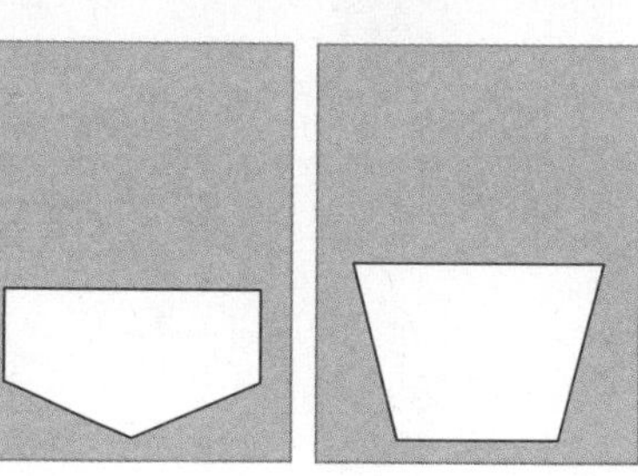

A rhombus with 4×0 right angles — **Shell**

A polygon with 2×1 pairs of parallel sides and *not* a rhombus — **Trilobite**

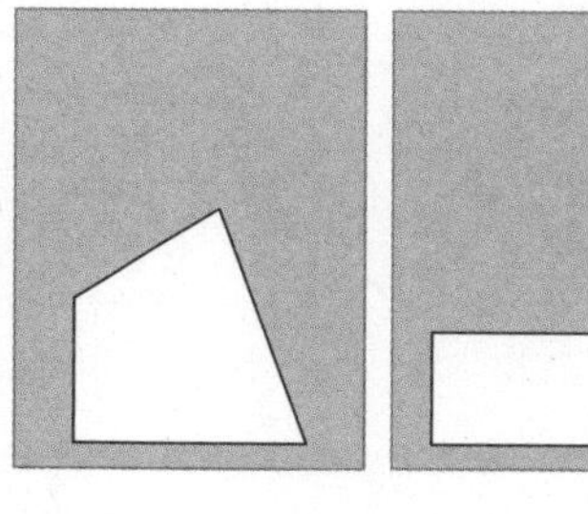

A quadrilateral with exactly 1 pair of parallel sides — **Skull**

A quadrilateral with $4 - 4$ right angles and 4×0 pairs of parallel sides — **Bone**

---

2. Your teacher uses the cards and a sandbox to create an archaeological dig site. Your teacher lays a grid with eight grid squares over the top of the sandbox. Each square has 10-inch side lengths. What is the area of the bottom of the sandbox?

Identify That Quadrilateral!

Directions:

1. Players take turns rolling a die.
2. On your turn, move your piece the number of spaces shown on the die.
3. Cover a space on the board that describes the shape where you landed.
4. If there are no spaces that match your shape, then you lose your turn.
5. The first player to cover six spaces wins!

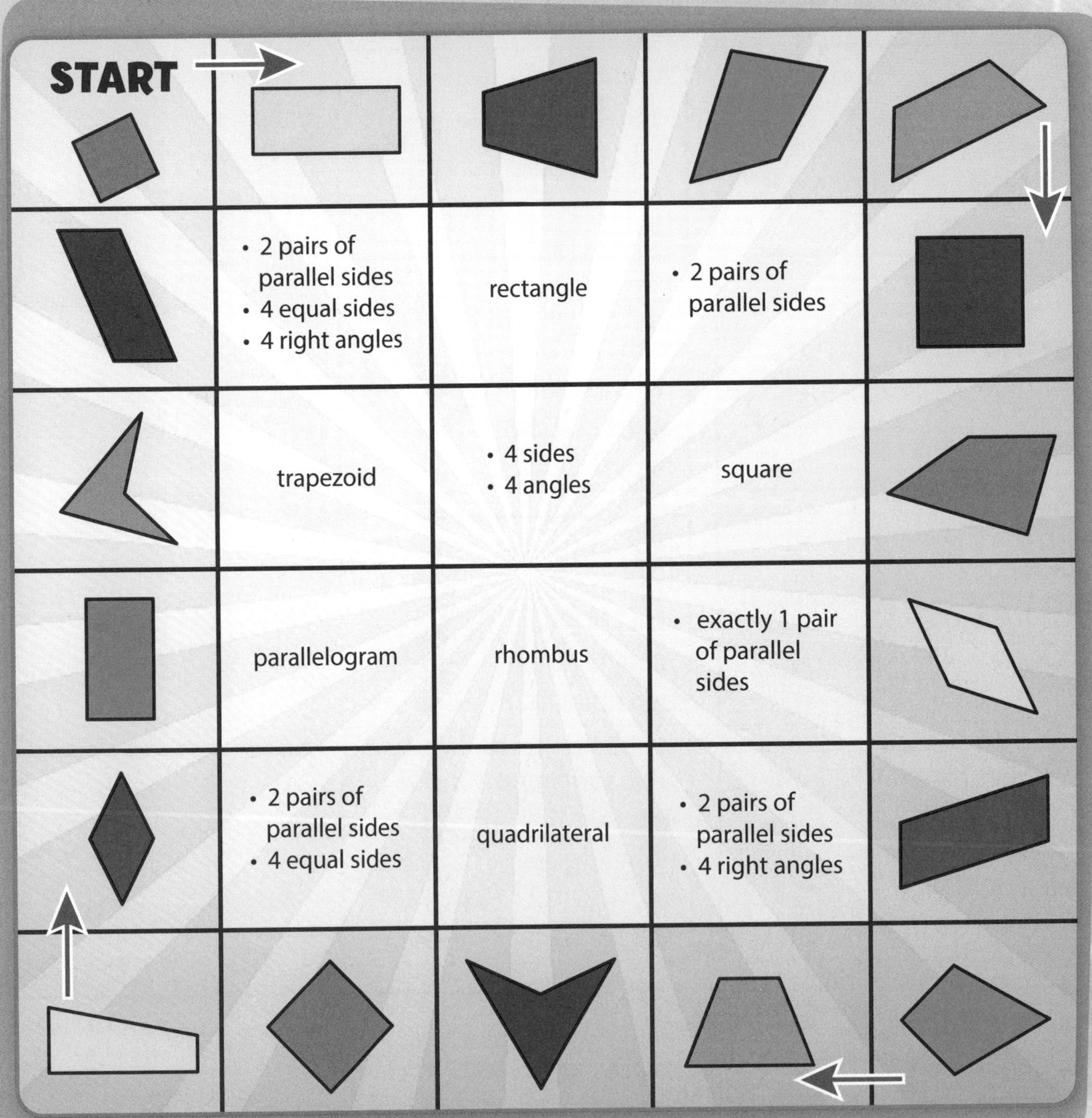

Name ___________________________________

Chapter Practice 13

13.1 Identify Sides and Angles of Quadrilaterals

Identify the number of right angles and pairs of parallel sides.

1. 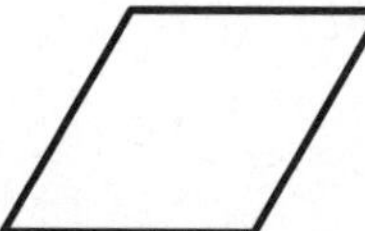

   Right angles: _____

   Pairs of parallel sides: _____

2. 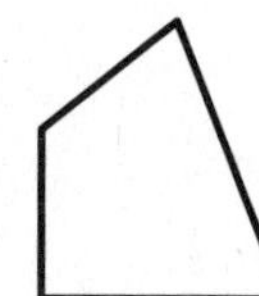

   Right angles: _____

   Pairs of parallel sides: _____

3. MP YOU BE THE TEACHER Your friend says the yellow sides are parallel. Is your friend correct? Explain.

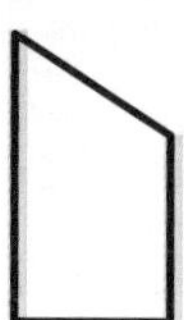

13.2 Describe Quadrilaterals

4. Write all of the names for the quadrilateral.

5. Name all of the quadrilaterals that can have no right angles.

13.3 Classify Quadrilaterals

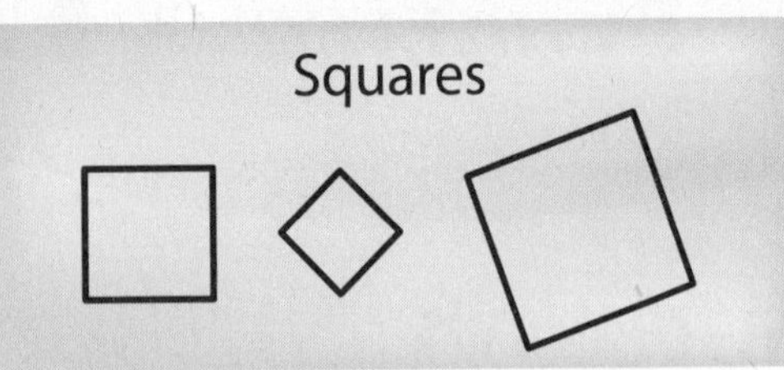

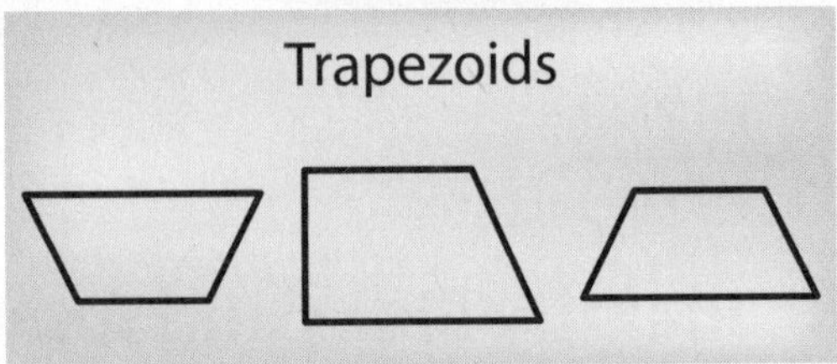

6. How are squares and trapezoids alike? How are they different?

7. What name can you use to classify all squares and trapezoids?

13.4 Draw Quadrilaterals

8. Draw a quadrilateral that has four right angles. Name the quadrilateral.

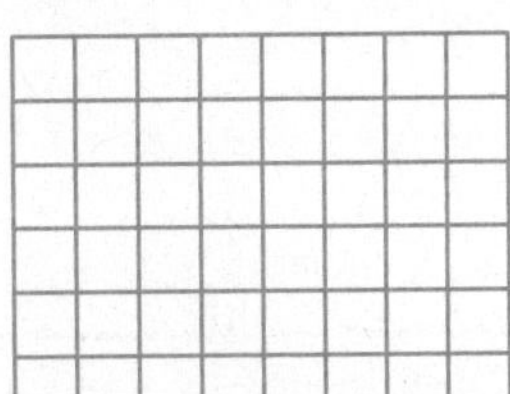

9. **MP Modeling Real Life** A helicopter travels to various locations in Wyoming. Draw to show a route that forms a square. Write the names of the locations you use.

Wyoming

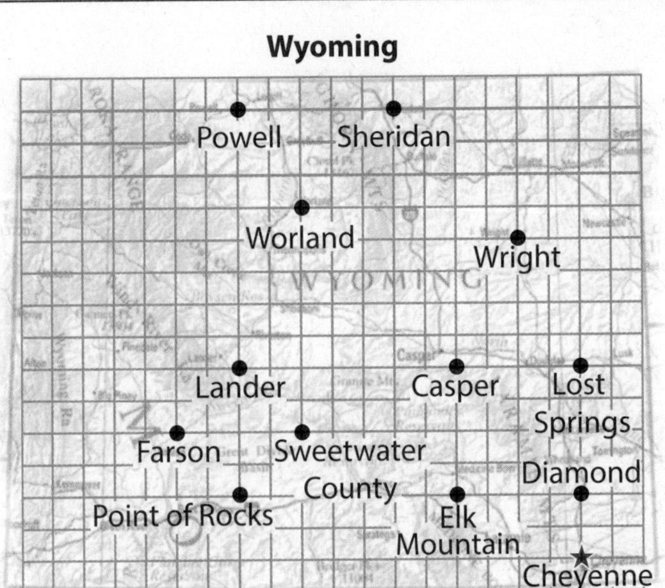

14 Represent and Interpret Data

Chapter Learning Target:
Understand data.

Chapter Success Criteria:
- I can identify a tool to collect data.
- I can create a tally chart to make a graph.
- I can represent data in different ways.
- I can interpret data in different ways.

- Bamboo is one of the fastest-growing plants in the world. What are some uses of bamboo?
- Why is it important to know how fast a plant grows? What are some ways you can represent the height of a plant?

Name ____________________

14 Vocabulary

Review Word
multiples

Organize It

Complete the graphic organizer.

Multiples Of	Examples	Non-Examples
2	4, 8, ____	3, 11, ____
3	6, 12, ____	4, 10, ____
5	10, 25, ____	9, 14, ____
10	20, 70, ____	8, 17, ____

Define It

Use your vocabulary cards to match.

1. frequency table

2. line plot

3. picture graph

Two-Color Counters	
Red	◯◯◯
Yellow	◯◯

Each ◯ = 2 flips.

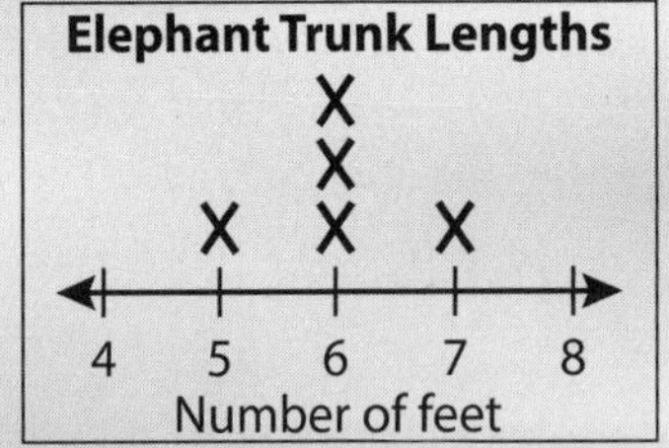

Two-Color Counters	
Red	6
Yellow	4

Chapter 14 Vocabulary Cards

bar graph

frequency table

key

line plot

picture graph

scale

A table that gives the number of times something occurs

Two-Color Counters	
Red	6
Yellow	4

A graph that shows data using bars

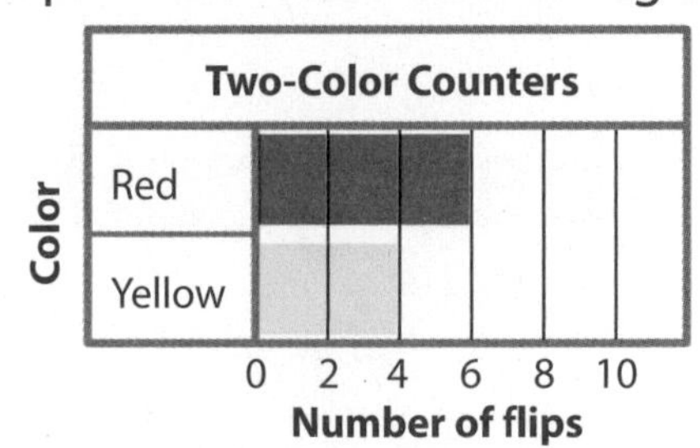

A graph that uses marks above a number line to show data values

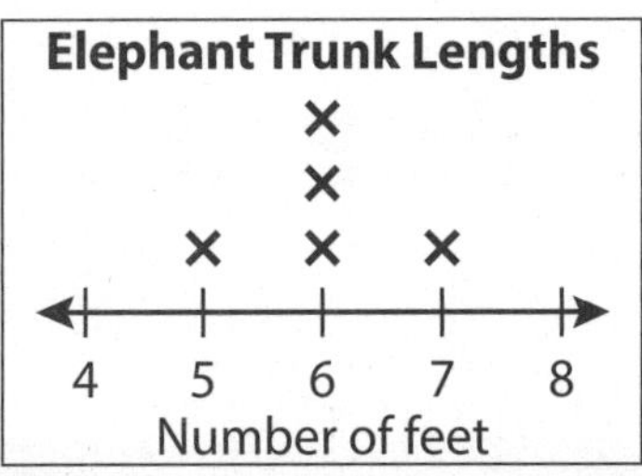

The part of a graph that gives the value of one picture or symbol

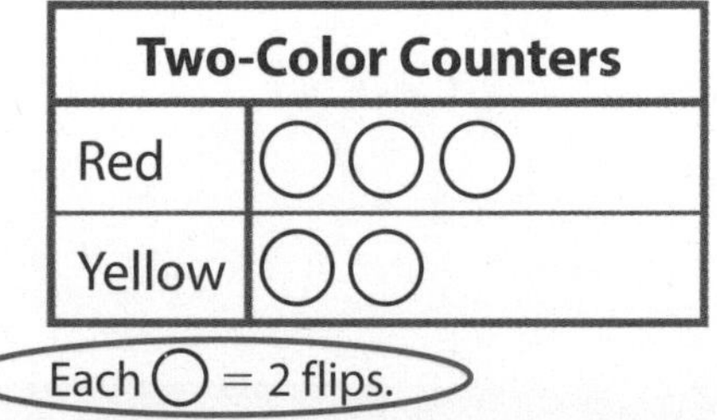

A group of labels that shows the values at equally spaced grid lines

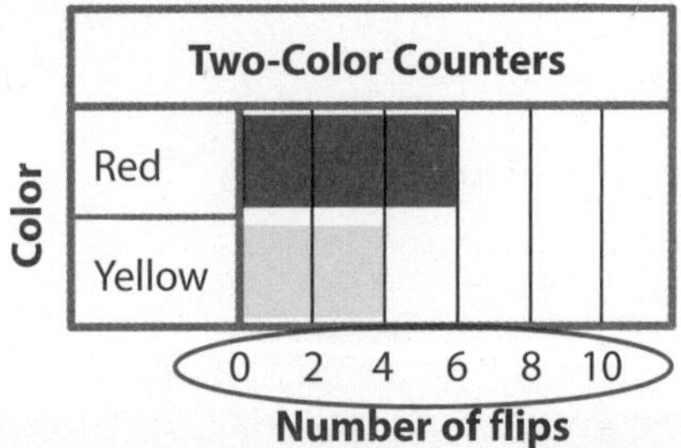

A graph that shows data using pictures or symbols

Two-Color Counters	
Red	○○○
Yellow	○○

Each ○ = 2 flips.

Name ______________________________

Read and Interpret Picture Graphs 14.1

Learning Target: Understand the data shown by a picture graph.

Success Criteria:
- I can explain how to use a key to read a picture graph.
- I can use a picture graph to answer questions.

Explore and Grow

You survey 14 students about their favorite type of party. The results are shown on the left picture graph. Use the key to represent the same data on the right picture graph.

Favorite Type of Party	
Bounce house	
Costume	
Pool	
Skating	

Each = 2 students.

Favorite Type of Party	
Bounce house	
Costume	
Pool	
Skating	

Each = 1 student.

Analyze a Problem You ask one more student to name his favorite type of party. He chooses pool party. How can you represent this on each graph? Explain.

Think and Grow: Read and Interpret Picture Graphs

A **picture graph** shows data using pictures or symbols. The **key** of a picture graph gives the value of one picture, or symbol. The value of one picture, or symbol, can be greater than 1.

Example Use the graph to answer the questions.

National Forests	
Idaho	🌲 🌲 🌲 🌲 🌲 🌲
Colorado	🌲 🌲 half 🌲
Oregon	🌲 🌲 🌲 🌲 🌲 🌲
Arizona	🌲 🌲 🌲

Each 🌲 = 2 forests. ← key

Half of a picture, or symbol, represents half the value of the whole picture. So, each half 🌲 = 1 forest.

How many national forests are in Arizona? 3 🌲s = 3 × _____ = _____

There are _____ national forests in Arizona.

How many national forests are in Colorado? 2 🌲s = 2 × _____ = _____

1 half 🌲 = _____

_____ + _____ = _____

There are _____ national forests in Colorado.

Show and Grow *I can do it!*

1. Use the graph to answer the questions.

How many students chose dog?

How many students chose fish?

Favorite Pet	
Dog	☺ ☺ ☺
Cat	☺ ☺
Fish	☺ half ☺

Each ☺ = 10 students.

Name ____

Apply and Grow: Practice

2. Use the graph to answer the questions.

What does the symbol ☺ represent?

How many more students chose skiing than ice-skating?

How many students did *not* choose sledding?

Favorite Winter Activity	
Skiing	☺ ☺ ☺ ◖
Snowboarding	☺ ☺
Sledding	☺ ☺ ☺ ☺ ◖
Ice-skating	☺ ☺ ☺

Each ☺ = 2 students.

3. Use the graph to answer the questions.

How many mangoes were eaten in June?

How many total mangoes were eaten in the months shown?

Were more mangoes eaten in July or in June and August combined?

Mangoes Eaten in Summer	
June	☼ ☼ ☼ ◖
July	☼ ☼ ☼ ☼ ☼ ☼ ☼
August	☼ ☼ ☼

Each ☼ = 6 mangoes.

4. **DIG DEEPER!** If ◯◯◖ = 25 on a picture graph, then what value does ◯ represent? Explain.

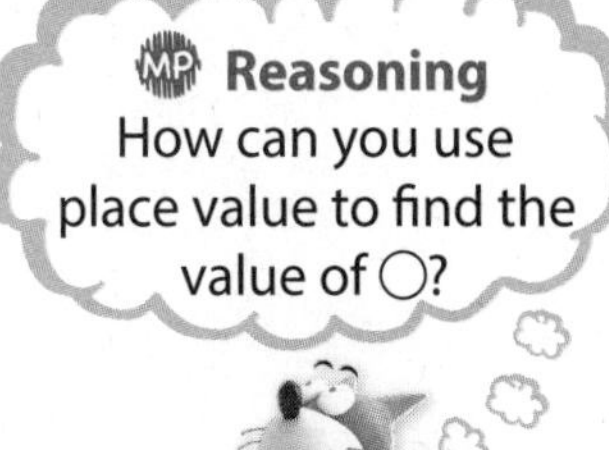

Think and Grow: Modeling Real Life

During which two weeks were a total of 52 cans recycled?

Cans Recycled	
Week 1	
Week 2	
Week 3	
Week 4	

Each = 8 cans.

During ____________ and ____________ 52 cans were recycled.

Show and Grow *I can think deeper!*

5. Which two origami animals did a total of 32 students choose?

Favorite Origami Animal	
Swan	
Butterfly	
Frog	
Penguin	

Each = 4 students.

How many more students chose frog or penguin than swan or butterfly?

Name ______________________________

Homework & Practice 14.1

Learning Target: Understand the data shown by a picture graph.

Example Use the graph to answer the questions.

Daily Sleep Totals	
Cat	★ ★ ★ ½★
Sloth	★ ★ ★ ★
Giraffe	½★
Brown bat	★ ★ ★ ★ ★
Elephant	★

Each ★ = 4 hours.

How many hours do sloths sleep each day?

4 ★s = 4 × __4__ = __16__

Sloths sleep __16__ hours each day.

How many hours do cats sleep each day?

3 ★s = 3 × __4__ = __12__

1 ½★ = __2__

__12__ + __2__ = __14__

Cats sleep __14__ hours each day.

1. Use the graph to answer the questions.

What value does the symbol ◖ represent?

How many students chose pterodactyl?

How many students chose stegosaurus or velociraptor?

How many students did *not* choose tyrannosaur?

Favorite Dinosaur	
Velociraptor	☺ ☺ ☺ ◖
Tyrannosaur	☺ ☺ ☺ ☺ ☺
Pterodactyl	☺ ☺ ☺ ☺ ◖
Stegosaurus	☺ ☺ ◖
Triceratops	☺ ☺ ☺

Each ☺ = 10 students.

2. Use the graph to answer the questions.

Favorite Dog Treat	
Dog bone	😊 😊 😊 😊
Peanut butter	😊 😊 😊 😊 😊
Cheese	😊 😊 half 😊
Biscuits	😊 😊 😊 half 😊

Each 😊 = 2 dogs.

How many dogs participated in the survey?

Which dog treat has more votes than biscuits, but fewer votes than peanut butter? How many dogs chose this treat?

DIG DEEPER! Why would it be difficult to use a key where the value of one symbol represents an odd number of dogs?

MP YOU BE THE TEACHER Newton says that one more dog likes peanut butter than dog bones. Is he correct? Explain.

---

3. **MP Modeling Real Life** Which creature has 3 more eyes than the squid?

Number of Eyes	
Spider	👁 👁 👁 👁
Praying mantis	👁 👁 half 👁
Squid	👁
Starfish	👁 👁 👁

Each 👁 = 2 eyes.

Review & Refresh

Find the area of the shape.

4.

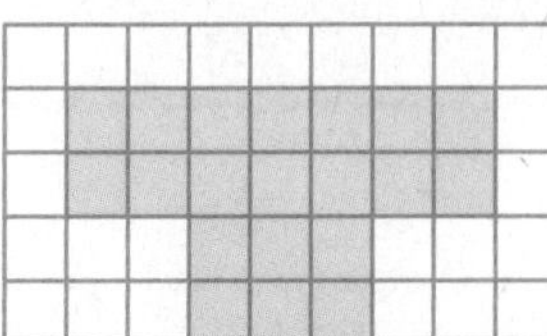

□ = 1 square centimeter

Area = ______________________

5.

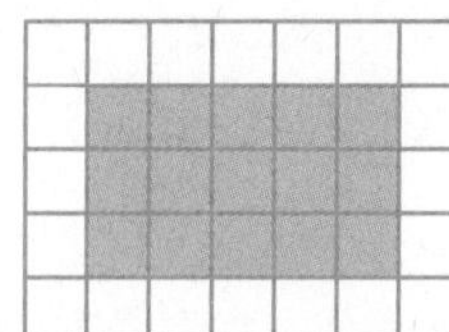

□ = 1 square meter

Area = ______________________

Name ___________________________

Make Picture Graphs 14.2

Learning Target: Use data to make picture graphs.

Success Criteria:

- I can read a frequency table.
- I can create a key for a picture graph.
- I can use a frequency table to make a picture graph.

Flip a two-color counter 10 times. Record the results. Then complete the picture graph.

Tally Chart

Color Flipped	
Red	
Yellow	

Frequency Table

Color	Total
Red	
Yellow	

Picture Graph

Two-Color Counters	
Red	
Yellow	

Each ◯ = 2 flips.

Construct an Argument Why might you change the key if you flip the counter 100 times?

Think and Grow: Make Picture Graphs

A **frequency table** is a table that gives the number of times something occurs.

Example You survey students about their favorite planet. The frequency table shows the results. Use the table to complete the picture graph.

Favorite Planet	
Earth	25
Mars	15
Saturn	30
Jupiter	20

Step 1: Write the title at the top of the picture graph. Label a row for each category.

Step 2: Look at the numbers in the table. Choose a value for the key.

Step 3: Use the key to decide how many symbols you need for each planet. Then draw the symbols.

Earth	
Mars	
Saturn	
Jupiter	

Each ☺ = _____ students.

MP Logic
How can you choose a reasonable value for the key?

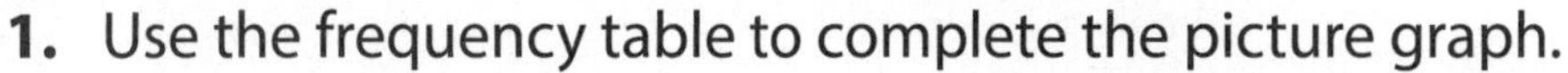

Show and Grow *I can do it!*

1. Use the frequency table to complete the picture graph.

Books You Read	
June	6
July	3
August	9

June	
July	
August	

Each ◯ = _____ books.

Name ______________________________

Apply and Grow: Practice

2. Use the frequency table to complete the picture graph.

Inches of Snowfall	
January	30
February	25
March	10

January	
February	

Each ◯ = ______ inches.

How many symbols did you draw to represent 10 inches of snowfall in March?

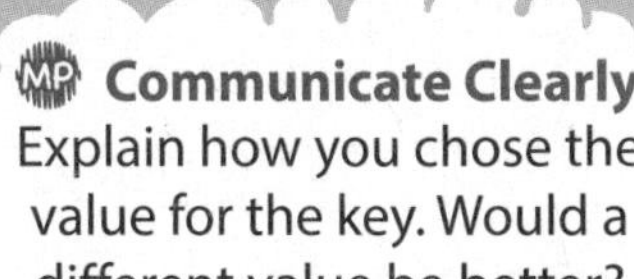

How many inches do you think April would receive?

3. Use the frequency table to complete the picture graph.

Favorite Superpower	
Flying	32
Time travel	40
Super strength	12
Invisibility	24
Super speed	28

Super strength	
Invisibility	

Each ☺ = ______ students.

Structure Choose a different value for the key. How would the picture graph change?

Think and Grow: Modeling Real Life

You survey 90 students about their favorite type of field trip. 35 students choose science center, 10 choose theater, and 20 choose zoo. The rest of the students choose museum. Complete the picture graph.

Each ☺ = _____ students.

Show and Grow I can think deeper!

4. You survey 48 students about their favorite type of movie. 8 students choose cartoon, 12 choose action, and 24 choose comedy. The rest of the students choose musical. Complete the picture graph.

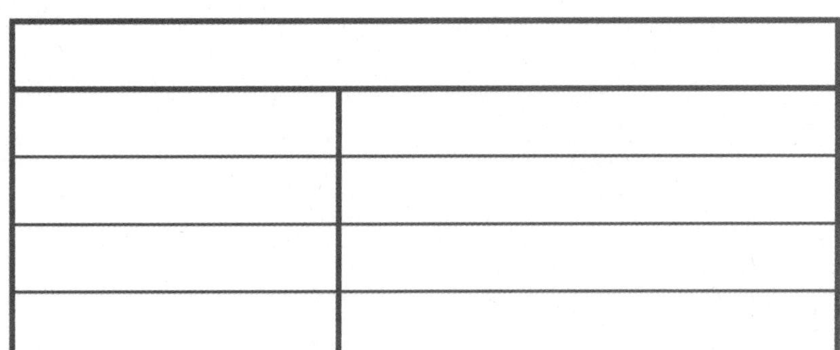

Each ☺ = _____ students.

DIG DEEPER! All of the students who chose musical go to see a movie. Each ticket costs $9. The students use two $20 bills to pay for all of the tickets. What is the change?

Name ______________________________

Homework & Practice 14.2

Learning Target: Use data to make picture graphs.

Example Use the frequency table to complete the picture graph.

Future Job	
Astronaut	70
Firefighter	55
Actor	35
Doctor	50
Scientist	65

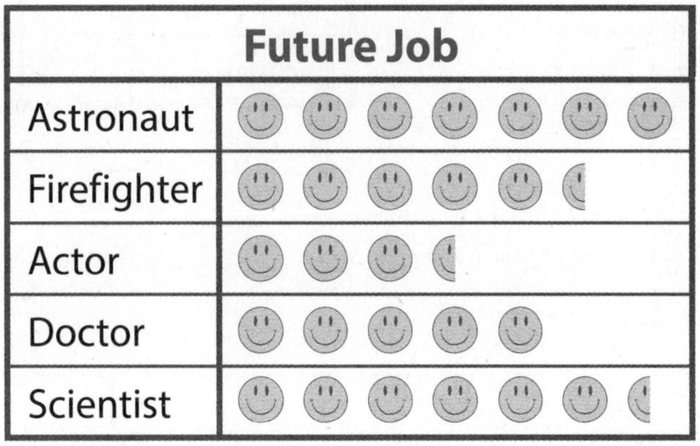

Future Job	
Astronaut	😊 😊 😊 😊 😊 😊 😊
Firefighter	😊 😊 😊 😊 😊 ◖
Actor	😊 😊 😊 ◖
Doctor	😊 😊 😊 😊 😊
Scientist	😊 😊 😊 😊 😊 😊 ◖

Each  😊 = 10 students.

1. Use the frequency table to complete the picture graph.

Favorite Type of Art	
Drawing	10
Ceramics	25
Painting	15
Crafts	30

Drawing	
Ceramics	
Painting	
Crafts	

Each 😊 = ______ students.

MP Maintain Accuracy Which type of art has more votes than painting, but fewer votes than crafts? How many students chose that type of art?

2. Use the frequency table to complete the picture graph.

Insects You See	
Ant	24
Butterfly	6
Bee	3
Ladybug	12

Butterfly	
Ladybug	

Each ◯ = _____ insects.

DIG DEEPER! You see 1 more bee and 4 more ladybugs. How might you change the key?

---

3. **MP Modeling Real Life** You survey 72 students about their favorite carnival ride. 12 choose Ferris wheel, 24 choose swings, and 6 choose bumper cars. The rest of the students choose roller coaster. Complete the picture graph.

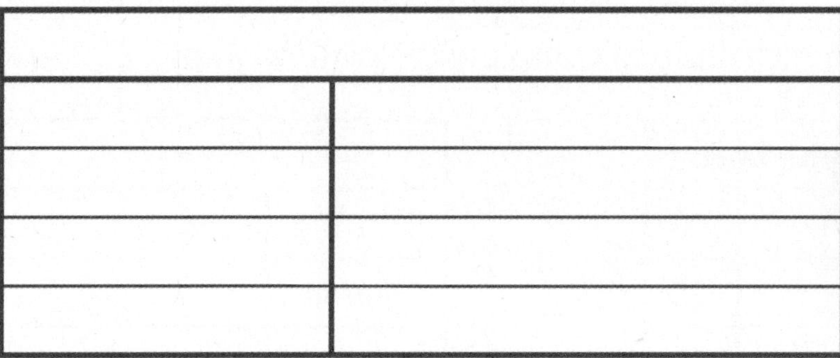

Each ☺ = _____ students.

MP Modeling Real Life All of the students who chose roller coaster want to ride together. Each ride ticket costs \$2. The students have three \$10 bills and four \$5 bills. Will they have enough to ride the roller coaster together?

Review & Refresh

Find the sum.

4. 532 + 54 = _____

5. 718 + 226 = _____

6. 81 + 647 = _____

Name ______________________________

Read and Interpret Bar Graphs 14.3

Learning Target: Understand the data shown by a bar graph.

Success Criteria:

- I can explain how to use a scale to read a bar graph.
- I can use a bar graph to answer questions.

You survey 12 students about their favorite school club. The results are shown on the picture graph. Represent the same data on the bar graph.

Favorite School Club	
Drama	☺ ☺
Math	☺
Robotics	☺ ☺ ☺

Each ☺ = 2 students.

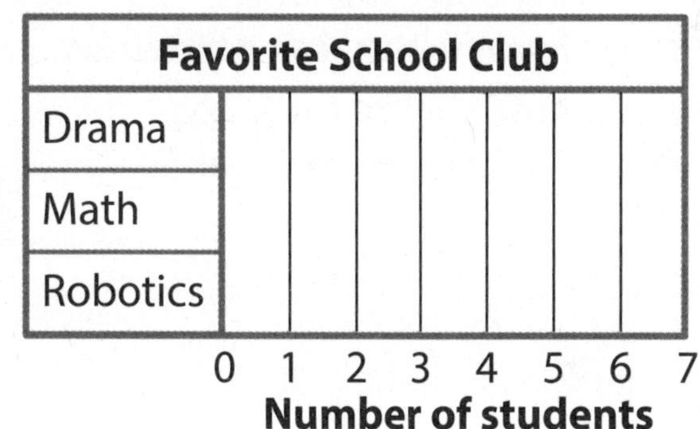

Communicate Clearly How would you change the scale of the bar graph to match the picture graph?

Think and Grow: Read and Interpret Bar Graphs

A **bar graph** shows data using bars. The **scale** of a bar graph is the group of labels that shows the values at equally spaced grid lines.

Example Use the graph to answer the questions.

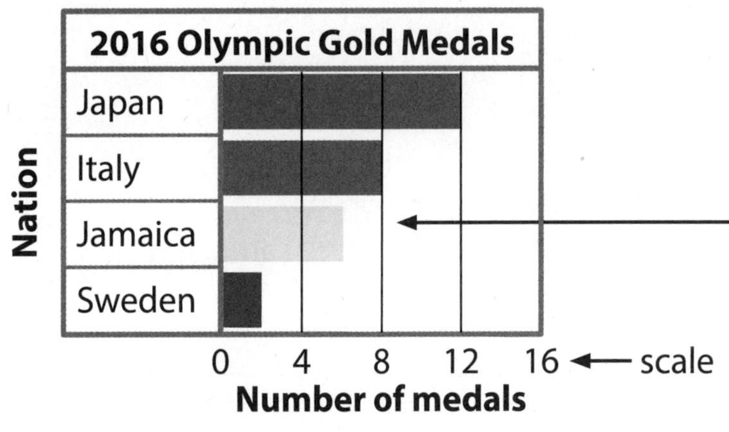

When a bar ends halfway between two grid lines, the data value for the bar is halfway between the two numbers on the scale.

How many gold medals did Japan win?

Japan won _____ gold medals.

How many gold medals did Jamaica win?

Jamaica won _____ gold medals.

Which country won the fewest gold medals?

_______________ won the fewest gold medals.

Show and Grow *I can do it!*

1. Use the graph to answer the questions.

   How many students chose grapes?

   Which fruit is the most favorite?

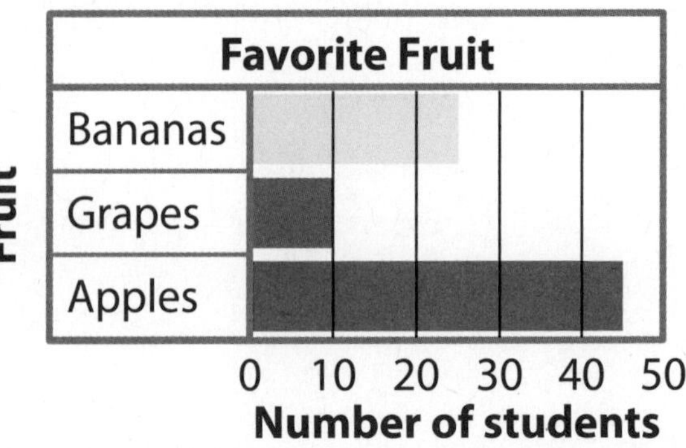

Name ______________________________

Apply and Grow: Practice

2. Use the graph to answer the questions.

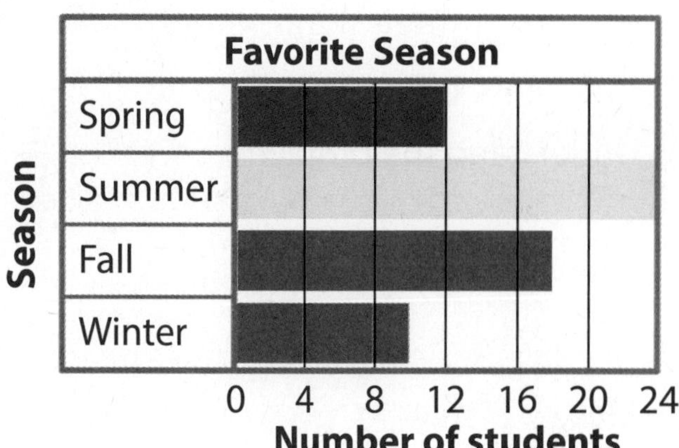

How many students does each grid line represent?

How many students chose fall?

Which season is the least favorite?

3. Use the graph to answer the questions.

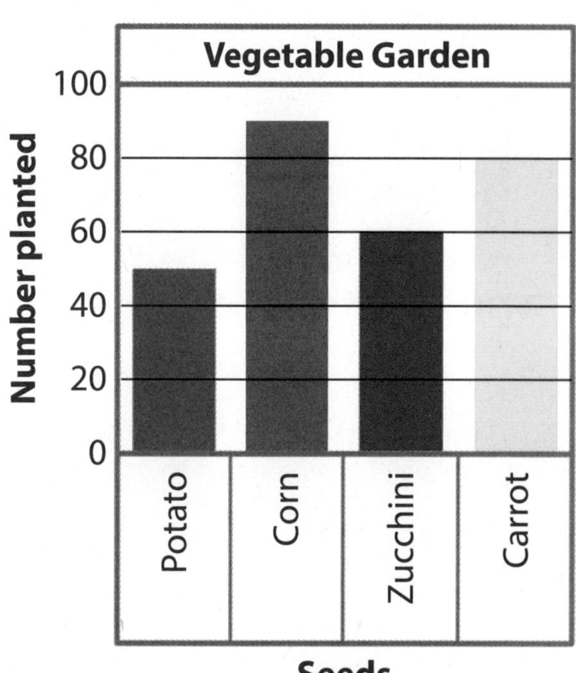

How many vegetable seeds did the farmer plant in all?

The farmer wants to plant green bean seeds. She plants more green bean seeds than zucchini seeds, but fewer than carrot seeds. How many green bean seeds could the farmer have planted?

The farmer plants 30 more potato seeds. Will the farmer have more potatoes or more corn?

4. Writing Do you think a bar graph or a picture graph is easier to read? Explain.

MP Communicate Clearly When would you use a bar graph instead of a picture graph? a picture graph instead of a bar graph?

Think and Grow: Modeling Real Life

How many more students need to choose the strategy app so that strategy is the most favorite?

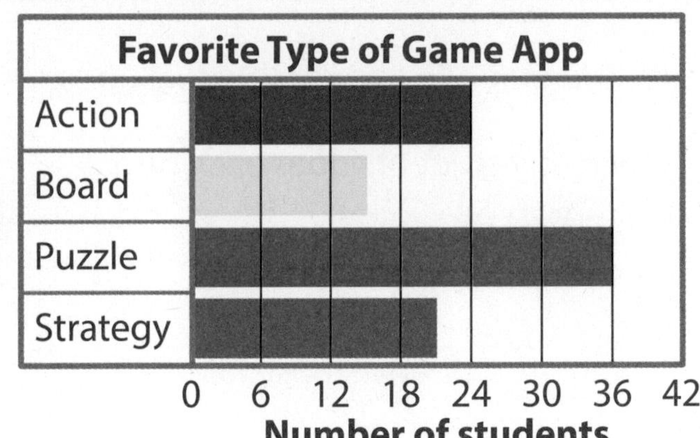

Understand the problem:

Make a plan:

Solve:

_____ more students need to choose the strategy app so it is the most favorite.

Show and Grow *I can think deeper!*

5. Each grade needs to plant 20 trees. How many more trees does second grade need to plant to complete the goal?

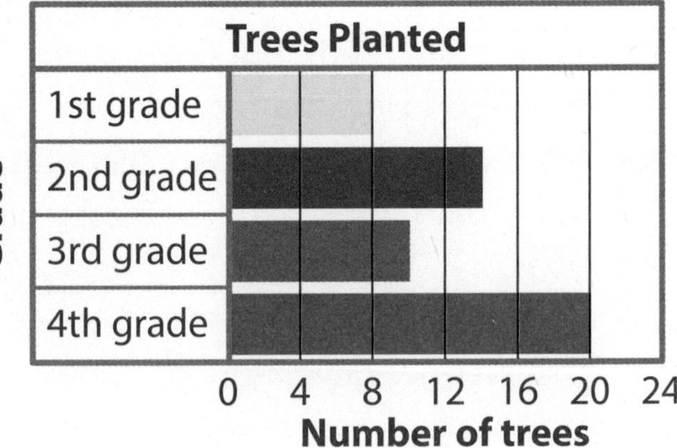

How many more trees did fourth grade plant than first grade and third grade combined?

Name ______________________________

Homework & Practice 14.3

Learning Target: Understand the data shown by a bar graph.

Example Use the graph to answer the questions.

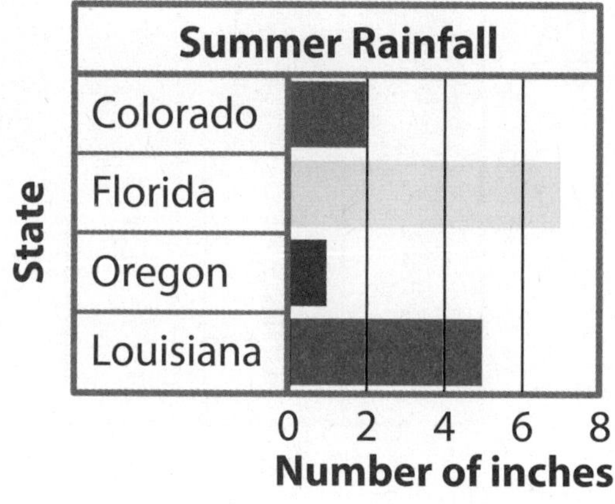

How many inches of rain did Colorado have during the summer?

Colorado had __2__ inches of rain.

How many inches of rain did Louisiana have during the summer?

Louisiana had __5__ inches of rain.

Which state had the most rainfall during the summer?

__Florida__ had the most rainfall.

1. Use the graph to answer the questions.

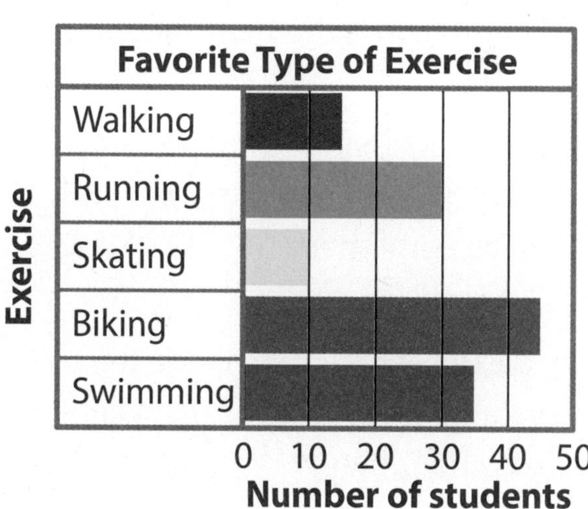

How many students does each grid line represent?

Which type of exercise is the least favorite?

How many fewer students chose running than swimming?

How many students chose walking or biking?

2. Use the graph to answer the questions.

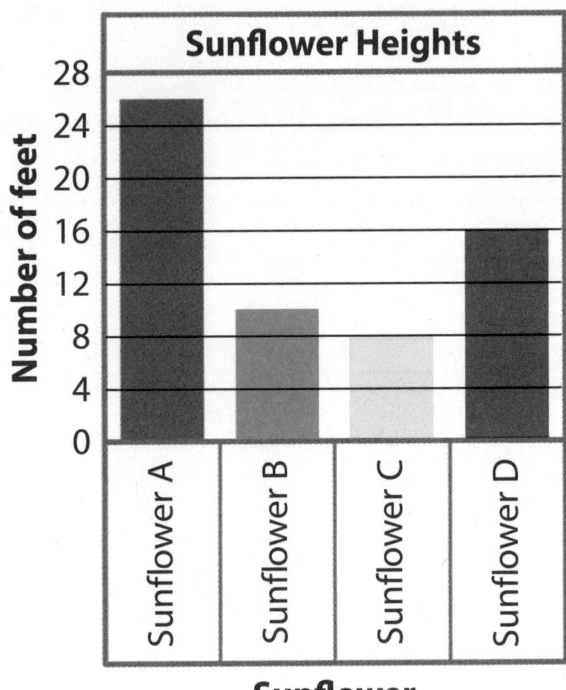

Which sunflowers are taller than 11 feet?

Sunflower E has a height of 15 feet. How much taller is Sunflower A than Sunflower E?

Writing Which sunflower is the shortest? Explain.

---

3. MP **Modeling Real Life** Use the graph to answer the questions.

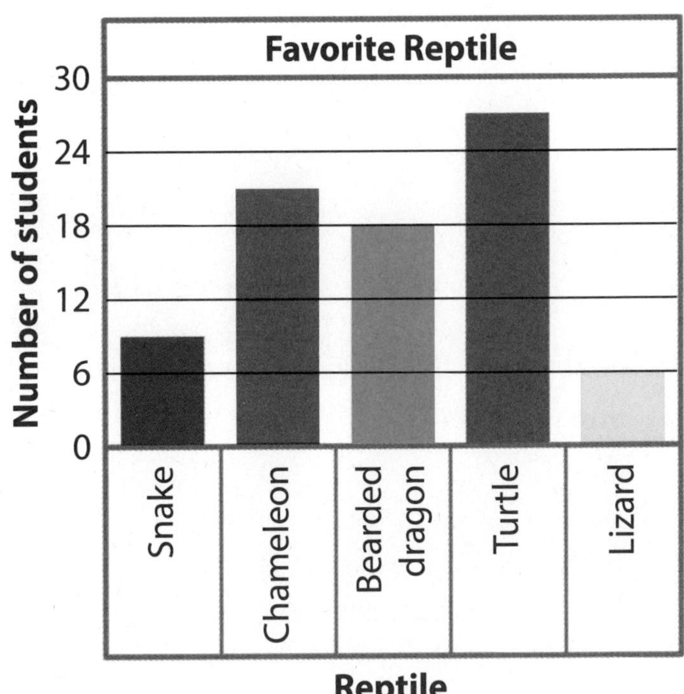

How many more students need to choose chameleon so that chameleon is the most favorite?

How many more students chose turtle than bearded dragon and lizard combined?

DIG DEEPER! You change the value of the scale to 3. Explain how this changes the bar graph.

Review & Refresh

Estimate the difference.

4. 96 − 47 ____ − ____ = ____

5. 678 − 142 ____ − ____ = ____

Name ______________________________

Make Bar Graphs 14.4

Learning Target: Use data to make bar graphs.

Success Criteria:

- I can read a frequency table.
- I can choose a scale for a bar graph.
- I can use a frequency table to make a bar graph.

Spin the Color Spinner 10 times. Record the results. Then complete the bar graph.

Tally Chart

Spin Color	
Blue	
Red	
Yellow	

Frequency Table

Spin Color	
Blue	
Red	
Yellow	

Bar Graph

Spin Color										
Blue										
Red										
Yellow										

Color (vertical axis); horizontal axis: 0 1 2 3 4 5 6 7 8 9 10

Number of spins

Repeated Reasoning Explain how you would change the scale if you spin the spinner 100 times.

Think and Grow: Make Bar Graphs

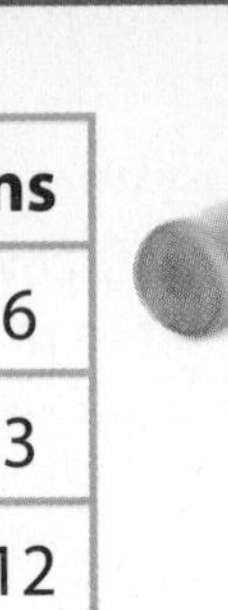

Example You record the number of times each baseball team wins. The frequency table shows the results. Use the table to complete the bar graph.

Team Wins	
Eagles	6
Tigers	3
Vipers	12
Hawks	9

Step 1: Write the title at the top of the bar graph. Label a row for each category. Label the categories.

Step 2: Look at the numbers in the table. Use a scale so that most of the bars end on a grid line. Label the scale.

Step 3: Draw and shade a bar for each team.

Team						
Eagles						
Tigers						
Vipers						
Hawks						
0	___	___	___	___	___	___

Number of wins

Show and Grow *I can do it!*

1. Use the frequency table to complete the bar graph.

Favorite Color	
Red	2
Blue	8
Pink	4
Green	5

Color				
Red				
Blue				
Pink				
Green				
0	___	___	___	___

Number of students

Name ______________________________

Apply and Grow: Practice

2. Use the frequency table to complete the bar graph.

Type of Fingerprint	
Arch	100
Loop	110
Whorl	80

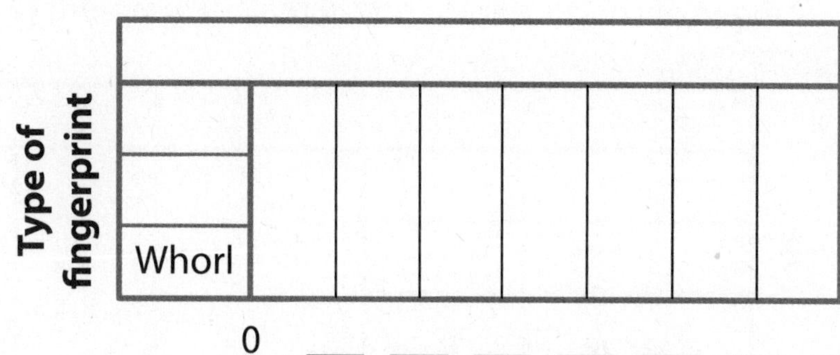

How would you use the graph to decide which type of fingerprint is the most common?

3. Use the frequency table to complete the bar graph.

Favorite Type of Food	
Italian	16
Mexican	18
Barbecue	12
Asian	6
Vegetarian	4

How many fewer students chose the least favorite type of food than the most favorite type of food?

Number of students

Barbecue

Vegetarian

Type of food

Think and Grow: Modeling Real Life

You survey 27 students about their favorite subject. Nine students choose science. Six fewer students choose English than science. The rest of the students choose math. Complete the bar graph.

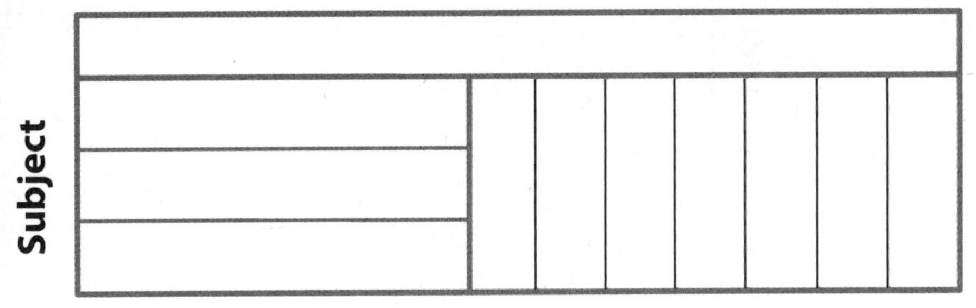

Number of students

Choose Tools
Survey the students in your class about their favorite subject. Which subject is the most favorite? the least favorite?

Show and Grow *I can think deeper!*

4. You survey 22 students about their favorite camp activity. Eight students choose archery. Four more students choose swimming than archery. The rest of the students choose hiking. Complete the bar graph.

Activity

Number of students

How many fewer students chose archery than swimming and hiking combined?

Communicate Clearly
How can you decide what title and labels to use?

Name ______________________________

Learning Target: Use data to make bar graphs.

Example Use the frequency table to complete the bar graph.

Transportation to School	
Walk	24
Car	15
Bus	36
Bike	30

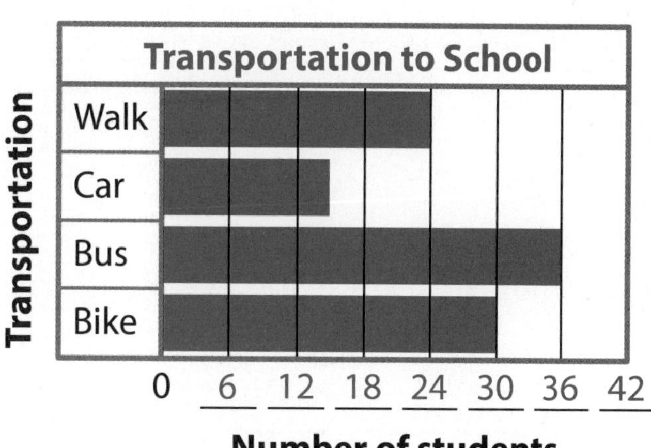

1. Use the frequency table to complete the bar graph.

Favorite Type of Music	
Rock	5
Country	10
Hip-Hop	10
Pop	30

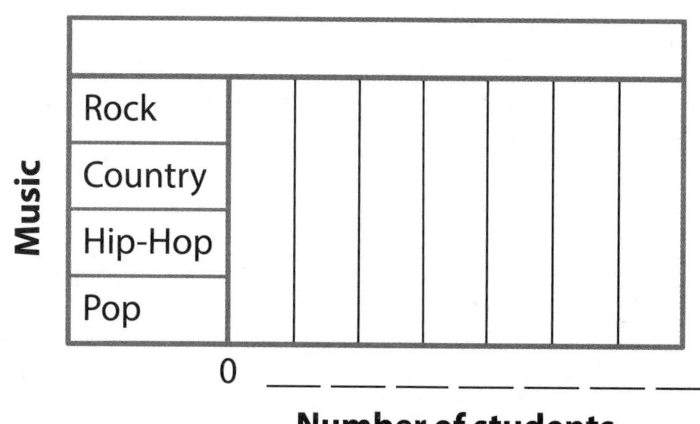

How many students does each grid line represent?

How would you use the graph to find the most favorite type of music?

2. Use the frequency table to complete the bar graph.

Weight of Backpack (pounds)	
Student A	12
Student B	10
Student C	16
Student D	4
Student E	6

Number of pounds

A			D	

Student

Structure On the last day of school, each backpack weighs less than 5 pounds. How could the scale of the bar graph change?

---

3. **Modeling Real Life** You survey 26 teachers about their favorite vacation spot. Six teachers choose amusement park. Two more teachers choose camping than amusement park. The rest of the teachers choose beach. Complete the bar graph.

How many fewer teachers chose camping than amusement park and beach combined?

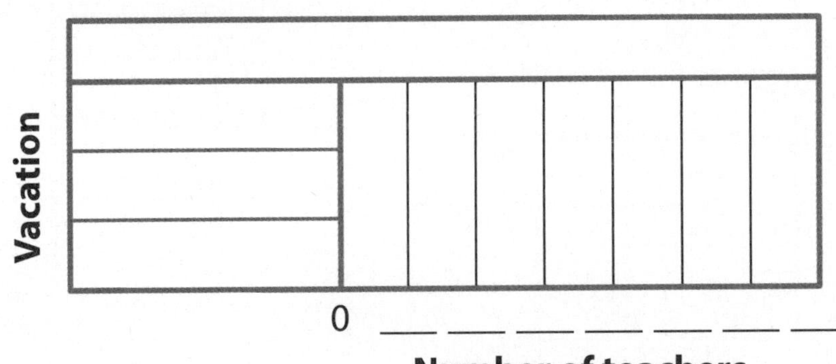

DIG DEEPER! One more person is surveyed and chooses camping. How might you change the scale? Explain.

Review & Refresh

Find the difference.

4. 474 − 19 = ____

5. 615 − 204 = ____

6. 232 − 53 = ____

Name ____________________

Learning Target: Use data to make line plots.

Success Criteria:

- I can read the data shown in a table.
- I can label the scale for a line plot.
- I can make a line plot.

Explore and Grow

A teacher asks students to line up according to the number of siblings they have. The results are shown. Create a Line Plot for the number of siblings the students in your class have.

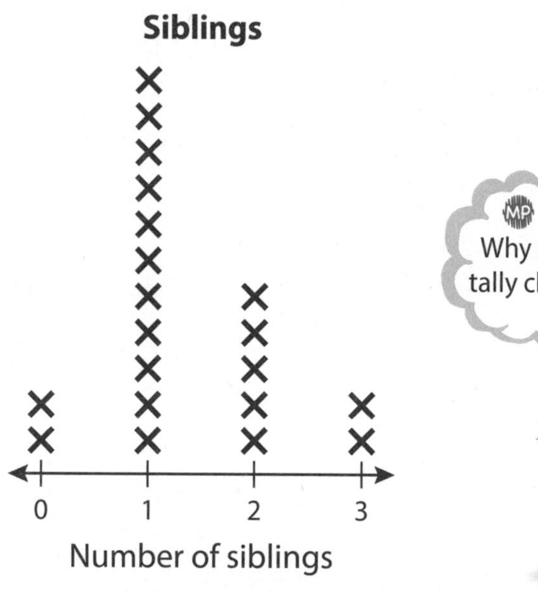

Use Math Tools Why should you make a tally chart before creating a line plot?

Communicate Clearly Compare the two line plots. How are the line plots the same? How are they different?

Think and Grow: Make Line Plots

A **line plot** uses marks above a number line to show data values.

Example The table shows the weights of 15 bald eagles. Use the table to complete the line plot.

Bald Eagle Weights (kilograms)		
3	5	4
4	5	5
5	6	4
4	3	3
4	6	4

Step 1: Write the title at the top of the line plot.

Step 2: Look at the numbers in the table. Use a scale that shows all of the data values. Draw a number line using the scale. Label the scale.

Step 3: Mark an X for each data value.

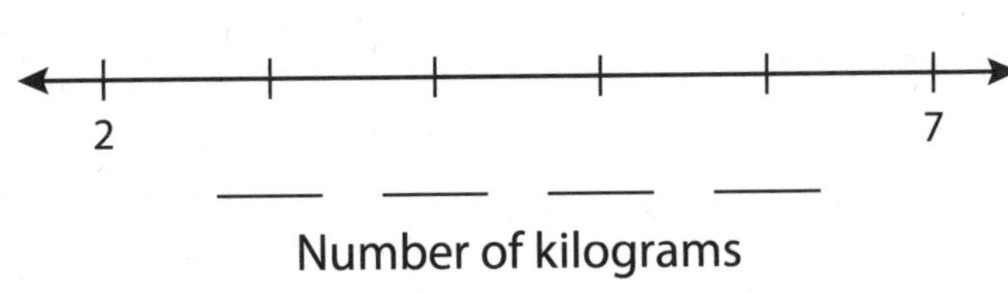

Show and Grow *I can do it!*

1. Use the table to complete the line plot.

Flower Heights (inches)		
8	10	9
6	9	8
7	10	8
7	8	10
8	8	7

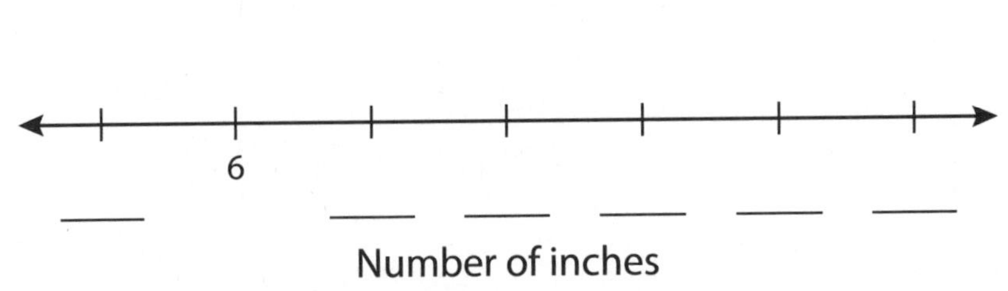

Name ___________________________

Apply and Grow: Practice

2. Use the table to complete the line plot.

Wave Heights (feet)	
29	30
25	29
28	27
30	25
29	30
27	29
28	25

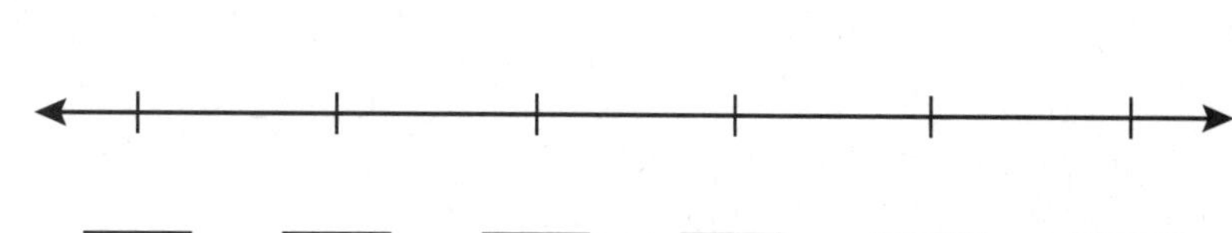

Number of feet

How many waves were 26 feet tall or taller?

3. Use the table to complete the line plot.

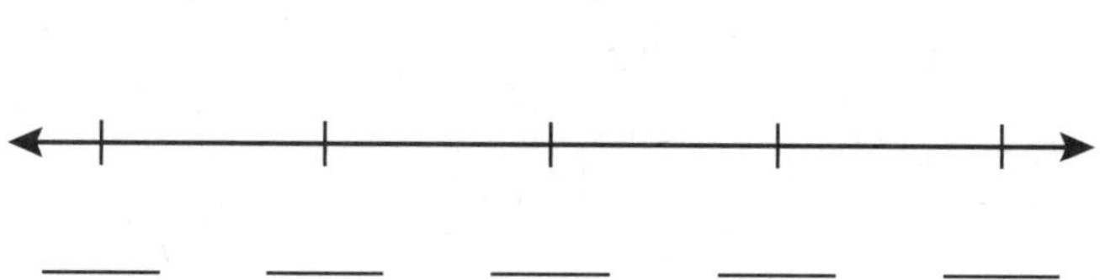

Number of inches

Which giraffe tongue length is the most common?

Giraffe Tongue Lengths (inches)	
19	20
17	19
21	20
19	21
20	17
18	20
20	17

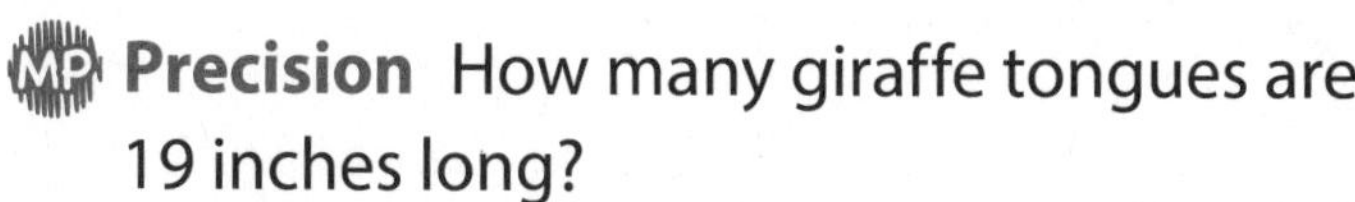

MP **Precision** How many giraffe tongues are 19 inches long?

Think and Grow: Modeling Real Life

What is the difference in height of the tallest student and the shortest student?

Subtraction equation:

Create a line plot for the heights of students in your class. Which height is the most common?

Heights of Students in Third Grade

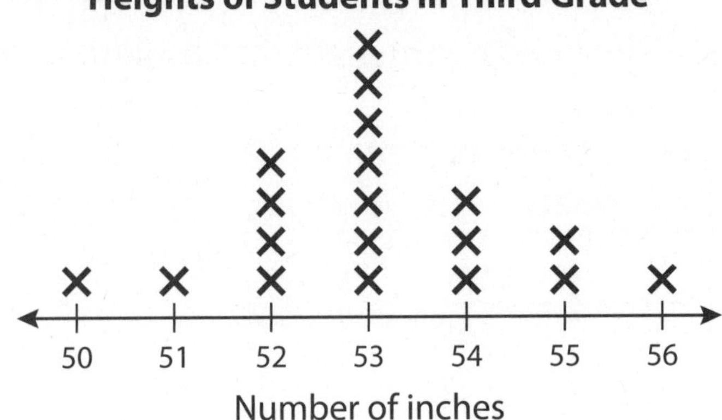

The difference in height is _____ inches.

Show and Grow *I can think deeper!*

4. What is the difference between the greatest number of floors and the least number of floors?

Floors in Skyscrapers

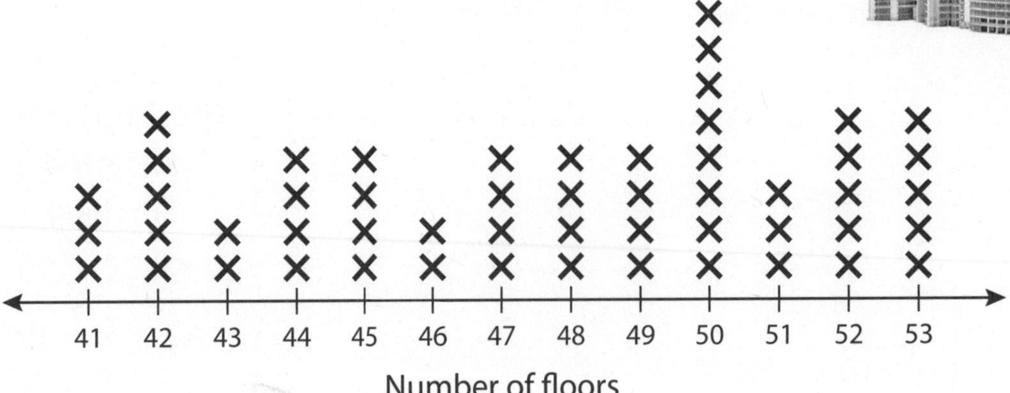

How many fewer skyscrapers are there with over 50 floors than skyscrapers with under 50 floors?

Name ________________________________

Homework & Practice 14.5

Learning Target: Use data to make line plots.

Example Use the table to complete the line plot.

Cornstalk Heights (feet)	
16	15
14	14
12	15
15	15
14	12
16	16
15	14

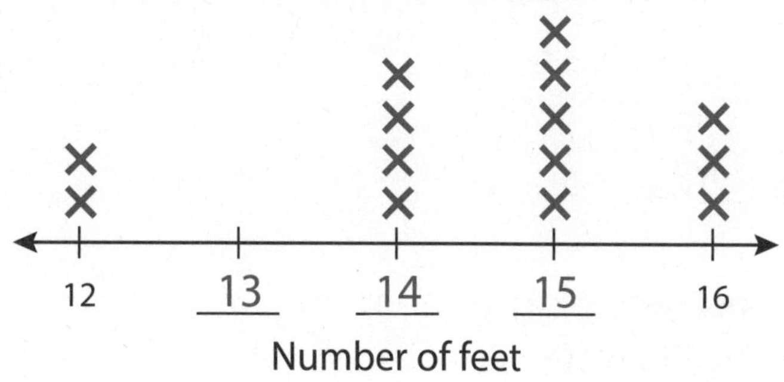

How many cornstalks are 15 feet tall?

__5__ cornstalks are 15 feet tall.

1. Use the table to complete the line plot.

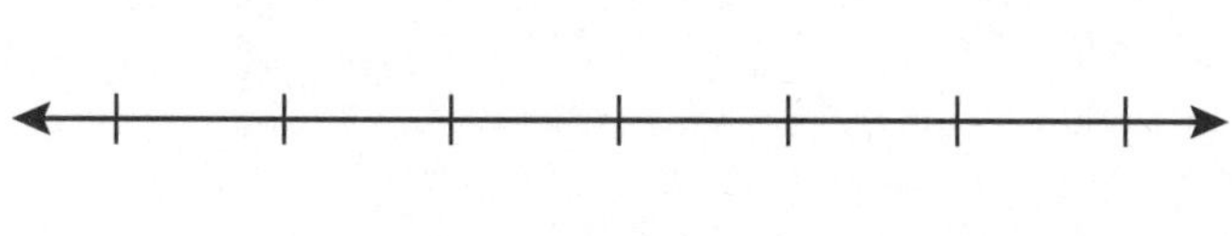

Number of feet

How many snakes are longer than 10 feet?

Snake Lengths (feet)	
10	11
7	7
6	10
9	5
10	6
7	10
6	9

Which snake length is the most common?

2. Use the table to complete the line plot.

Sit-Ups	
30	27
27	32
32	29
28	27
27	29
29	27
27	32

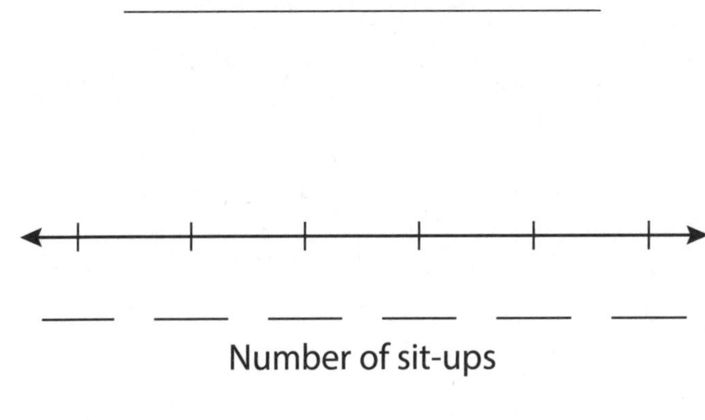

Construct an Argument Are most of the students able to complete 30 sit-ups? Explain.

DIG DEEPER! A student is selected at random from the class. How many sit-ups do you think the student is able to complete? Explain.

---

3. **Modeling Real Life** What is the difference of the most number of miles biked and the least number of miles biked?

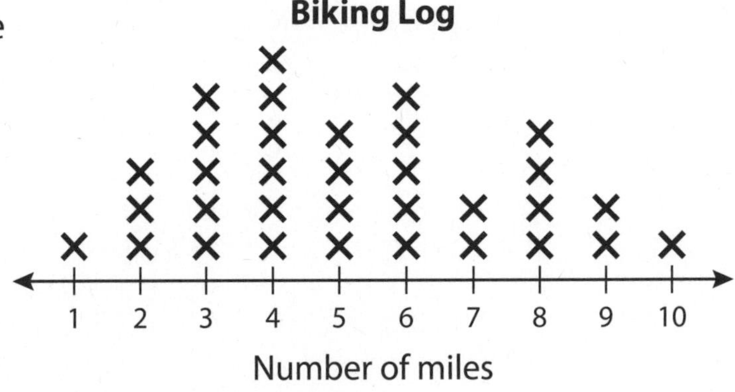

Review & Refresh

Find the sum or difference. Use the inverse operation to check.

4. $\begin{array}{r} 523 \\ +\ 237 \\ \hline \end{array}$

5. $\begin{array}{r} 403 \\ -\ 252 \\ \hline \end{array}$

6. $\begin{array}{r} 612 \\ +\ 387 \\ \hline \end{array}$

Name ____________________

Measure Lengths: Half Inch 14.6

Learning Target: Measure objects to the nearest half inch and make line plots.

Success Criteria:

- I can measure the lengths of objects to the nearest half inch.
- I can record lengths on a line plot.

Explore and Grow

How much longer is the green ribbon than the yellow ribbon? How do you know?

How much longer is the purple ribbon than the orange ribbon? How do you know?

Use Math Tools How can you use a ruler to measure an object to the nearest half inch?

Think and Grow: Measure Lengths: Half Inch

Not all objects are whole numbers of inches long. You can use a ruler to measure length to the nearest half inch. Remember to line up the end of the object with 0.

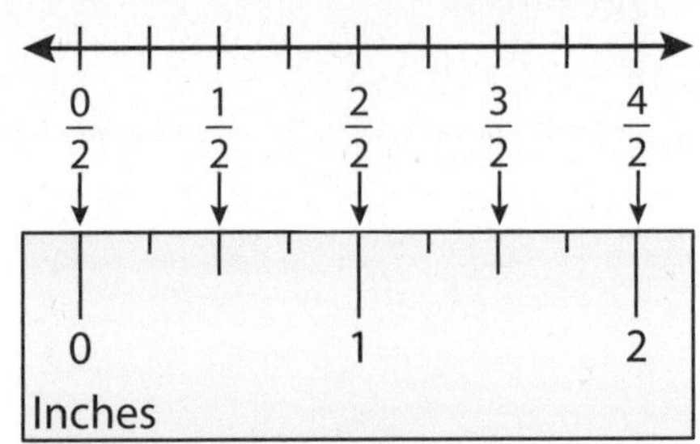

Example Measure the length of each string to the nearest half inch.

The string is $\frac{3}{2}$ inches long. You can also represent the length as 1 whole inch and one $\frac{1}{2}$ inch, or $1\frac{1}{2}$ inches.

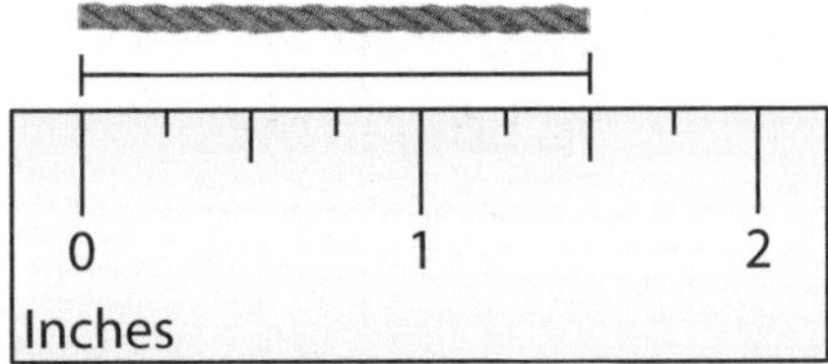

The string is between $\frac{1}{2}$ inch and 1 inch long. The half-inch marking that is closest to the end of the string is $\frac{1}{2}$. So, the string is about $\frac{1}{2}$ inch long.

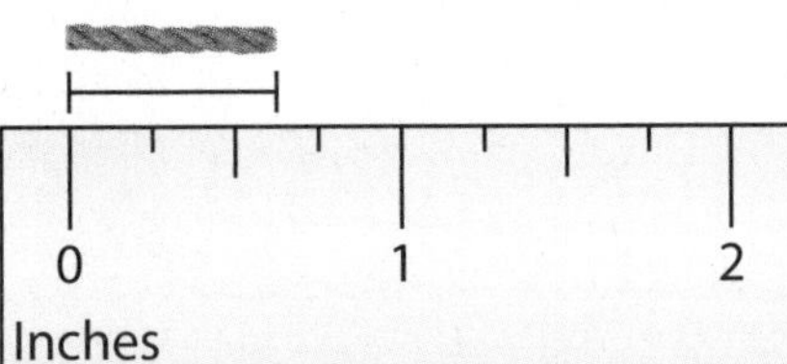

Example Measure the length of each line to the nearest half inch. Then record each length on the line plot.

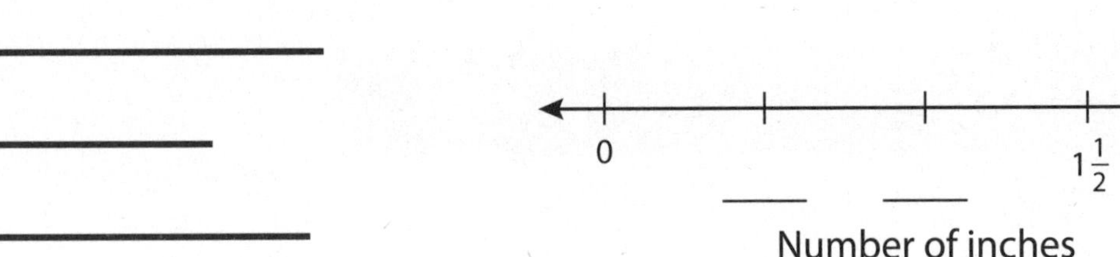

Show and Grow *I can do it!*

1. Measure the length of each line to the nearest half inch. Then record each length on the line plot above.

Name ______________________________

Apply and Grow: Practice

2. Measure the length of each line to the nearest half inch. Record each length on the line plot.

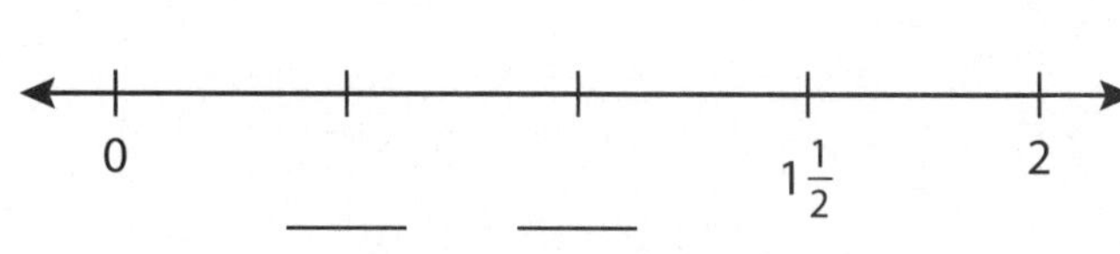

How might the scale change if the length of the line below is recorded on the line plot?

3. Measure the length of each toy to the nearest half inch. Then record each length on the line plot.

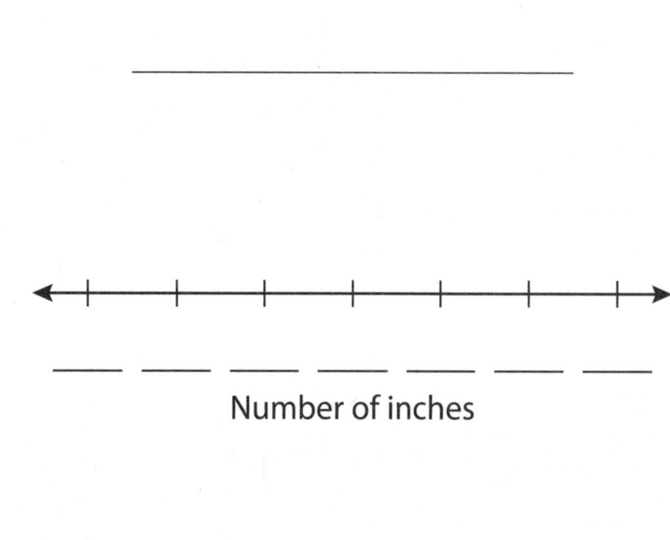

Think and Grow: Modeling Real Life

Measure the lengths of 10 crayons to the nearest half inch. Record each length on the line plot.

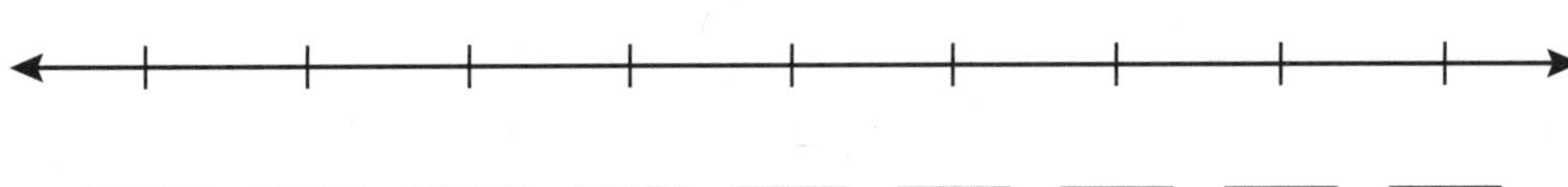

Number of inches

Show and Grow I can think deeper!

4. Measure the lengths of 10 shoes to the nearest half inch. Record each length on the line plot.

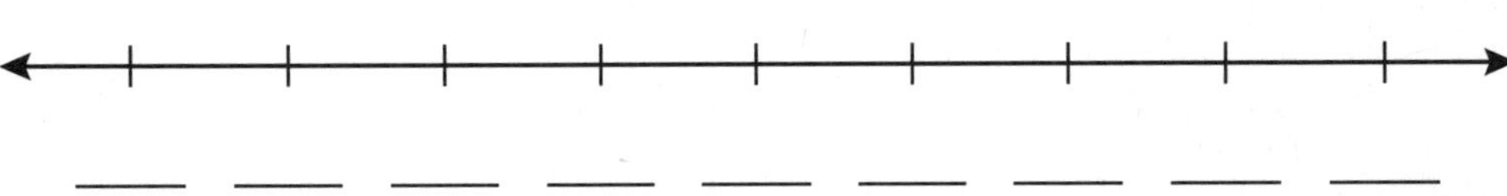

Number of inches

What is the length of the longest shoe? What is the length of the shortest shoe?

What length of shoe is the most common?

Name ______________________________

Homework & Practice 14.6

Learning Target: Measure objects to the nearest half inch and make line plots.

Example Measure the length of each ribbon to the nearest half inch. Then record each length on the line plot.

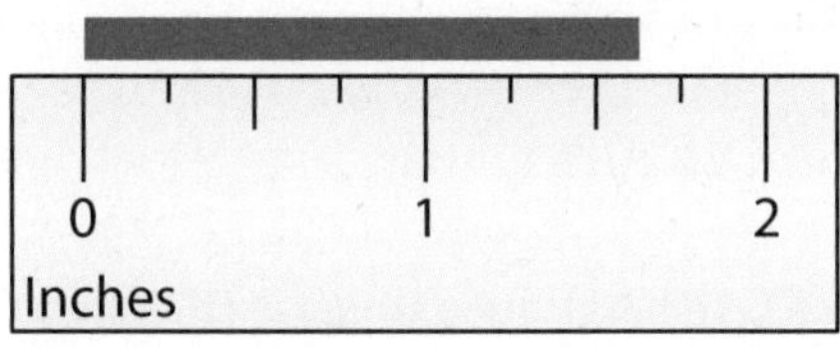

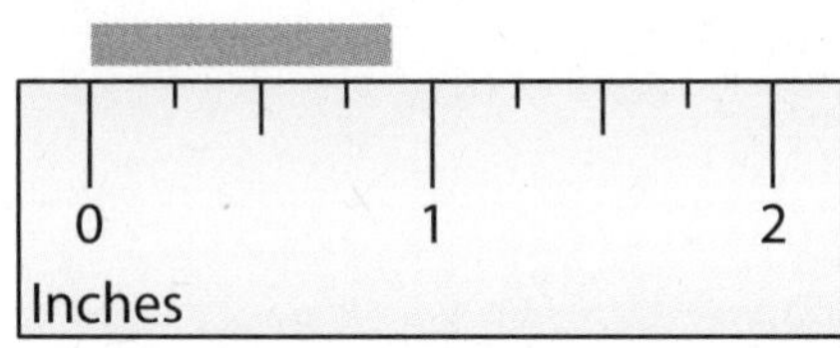

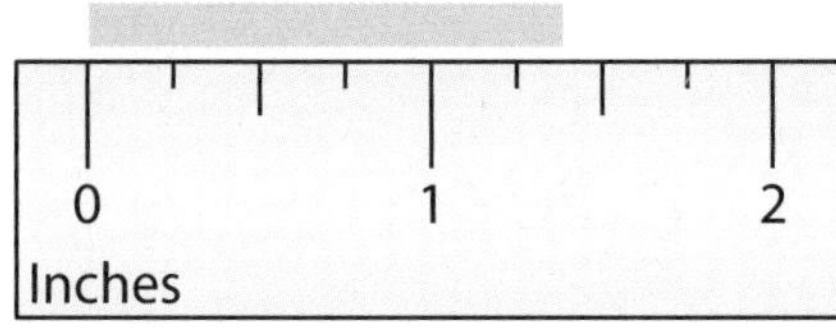

Ribbon Lengths

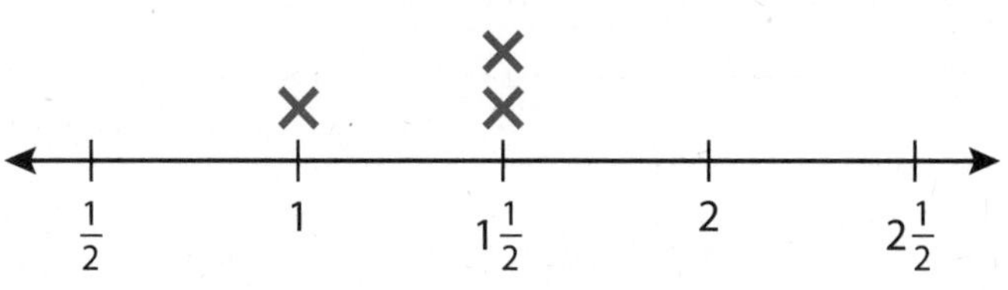

Number of inches

1. Measure the length of each pretzel stick to the nearest half inch. Record each length on the line plot.

____

$\frac{1}{2}$ ____ $1\frac{1}{2}$ ____ ____ 3

Number of inches

How many pretzel sticks are 1 inch?

2. **YOU BE THE TEACHER** Descartes says the pencil is $3\frac{1}{2}$ inches long. Is he correct? Explain.

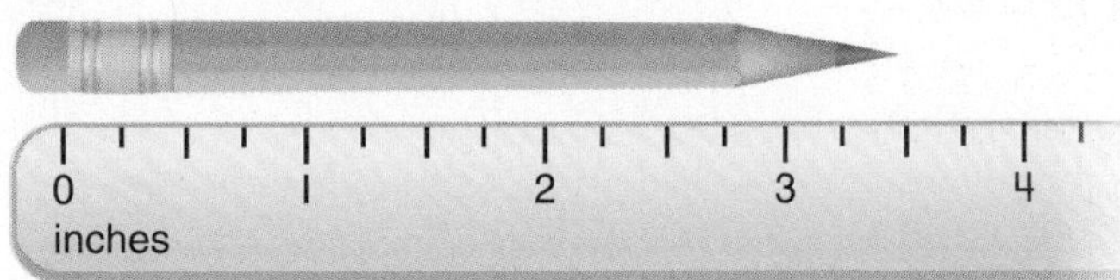

3. **Reasoning** Your friend's wrist measures $\frac{13}{2}$ inches around. His friendship bracelet is $6\frac{1}{2}$ inches. Will the bracelet fit around his wrist? Explain.

4. **Modeling Real Life** Measure the lengths of 10 plant leaves to the nearest half inch. Record each length on the line plot.

____

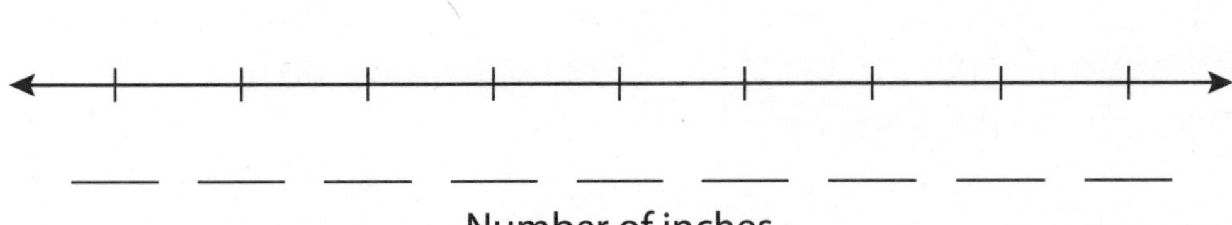

Number of inches

What is the length of the longest leaf?
What is the length of the shortest leaf?

DIG DEEPER! Choose one value to describe the lengths of the leaves. Explain your reasoning.

Review & Refresh

Find the product.

5. $5 \times 30 =$ _____

6. $9 \times 50 =$ _____

7. $6 \times 70 =$ _____

Name ______________________________

Measure Lengths: Quarter Inch 14.7

Learning Target: Measure objects to the nearest quarter inch and make line plots.

Success Criteria:

- I can measure the lengths of objects to the nearest quarter inch.
- I can record lengths on a line plot.

Explore and Grow

How much longer is the green ribbon than the yellow ribbon? How do you know?

How much longer is the purple ribbon than the orange ribbon? How do you know?

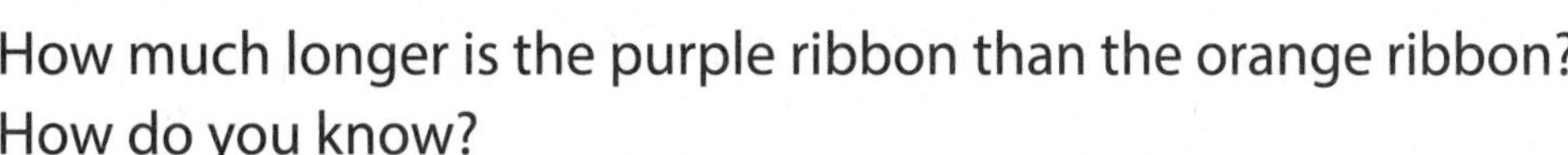

Construct an Argument Measure the line to the nearest half inch and the nearest quarter inch. Which measurement is better? Why?

Think and Grow: Measure Lengths: Quarter Inch

You know how to use a ruler to measure lengths to the nearest half inch. You can also use a ruler to measure lengths to the nearest quarter-inch.

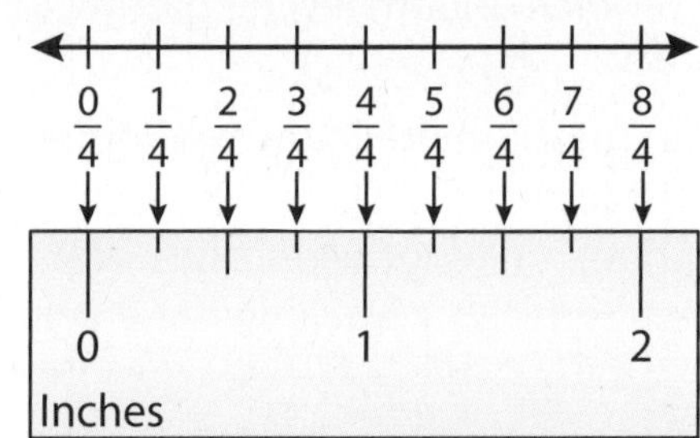

Example Measure the length of each string to the nearest quarter inch.

The string is $\frac{7}{4}$ inches long. You can also represent the length as 1 whole inch and three $\frac{1}{4}$ inches, or $1\frac{3}{4}$ inches.

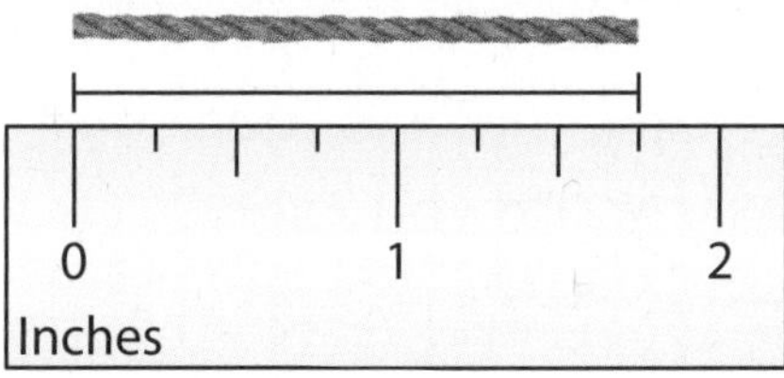

The string is between 1 inch and $1\frac{1}{4}$ inches long. The quarter-inch marking that is closest to the end of the string is $1\frac{1}{4}$. So, the string is about $1\frac{1}{4}$ inches long.

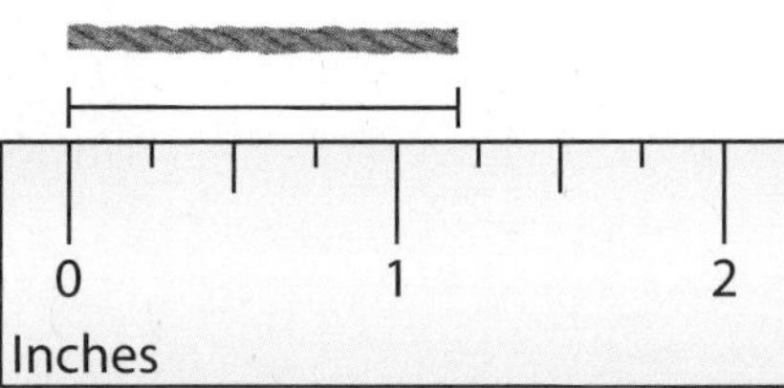

Example Measure the length of each line to the nearest quarter inch. Then record each length on the line plot.

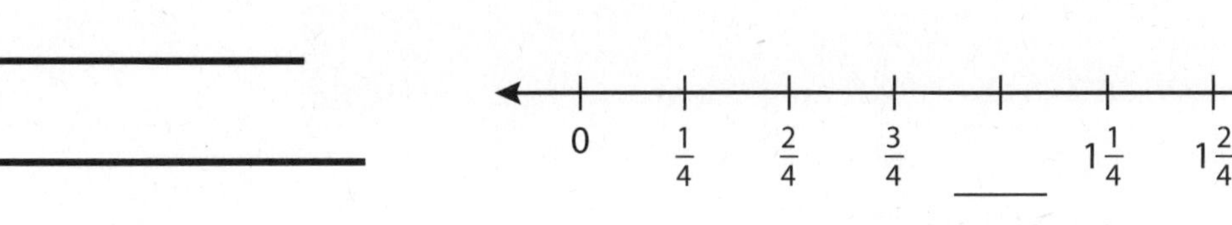

Show and Grow *I can do it!*

1. Measure the length of each line to the nearest quarter inch. Then record each length on the line plot above.

Name ______________________

Apply and Grow: Practice

2. Measure the length of each line to the nearest quarter inch. Record each length on the line plot.

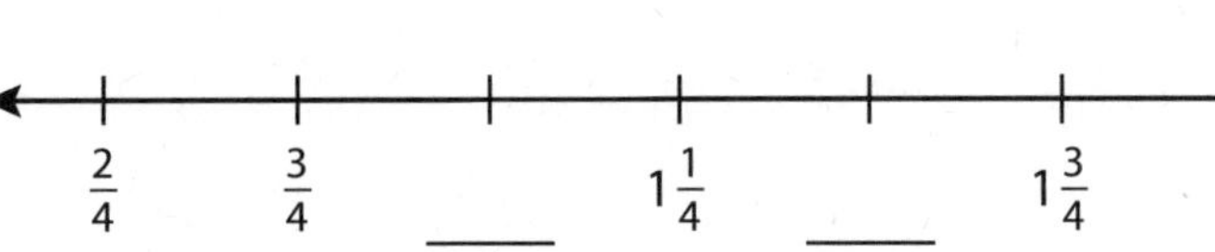

Number of inches

How might the scale change if the two lines below are recorded in the line plot?

3. Measure the length of each eraser to the nearest quarter inch. Then record each length on the line plot.

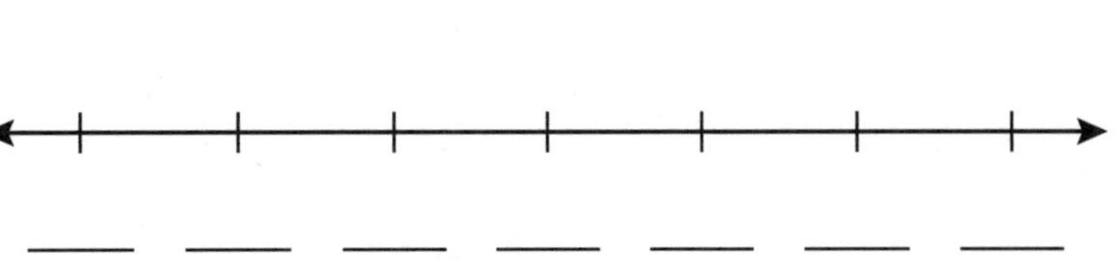

Number of inches

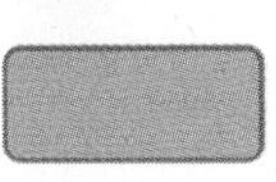

4. MP **Use Math Tools** Draw a line that measures $5\frac{3}{4}$ inches long.

Think and Grow: Modeling Real Life

Measure the lengths of 10 pencils to the nearest quarter inch. Record each length on the line plot.

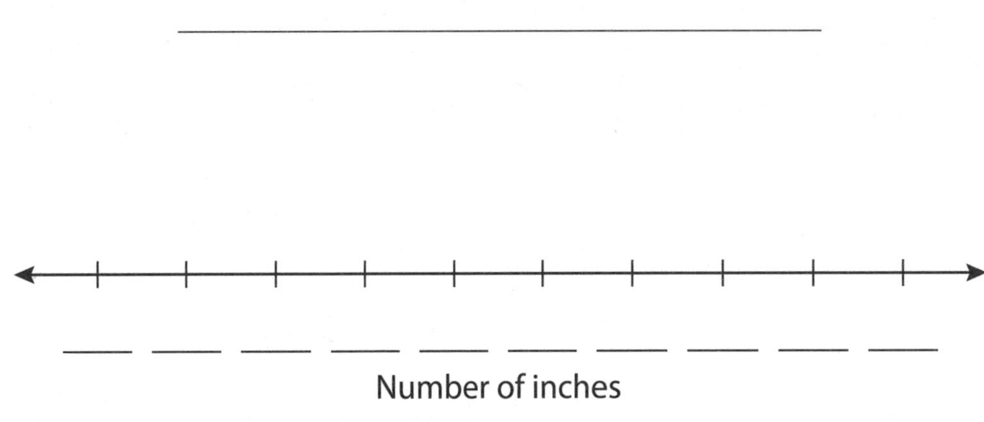

Show and Grow I can think deeper!

5. Measure the heights of 10 books to the nearest quarter inch. Record each length on the line plot.

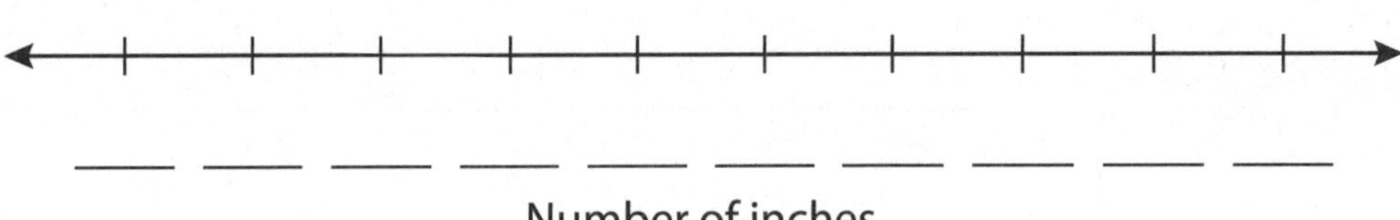

Write and answer a question about your line plot.

Name ______________________

Homework & Practice 14.7

Learning Target: Measure objects to the nearest quarter inch and make line plots.

Example Measure the length of each ribbon to the nearest quarter inch. Then record each length on the line plot.

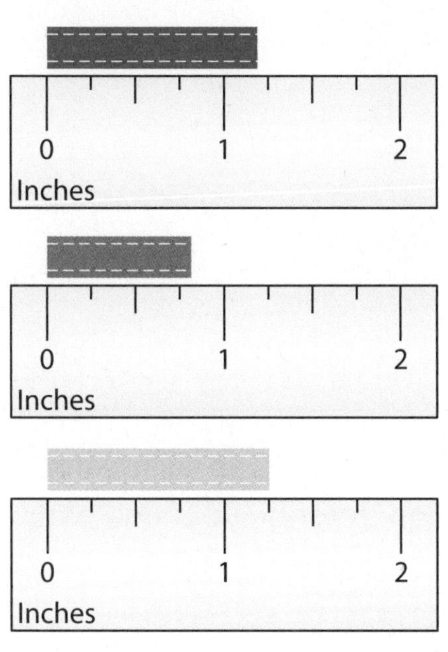

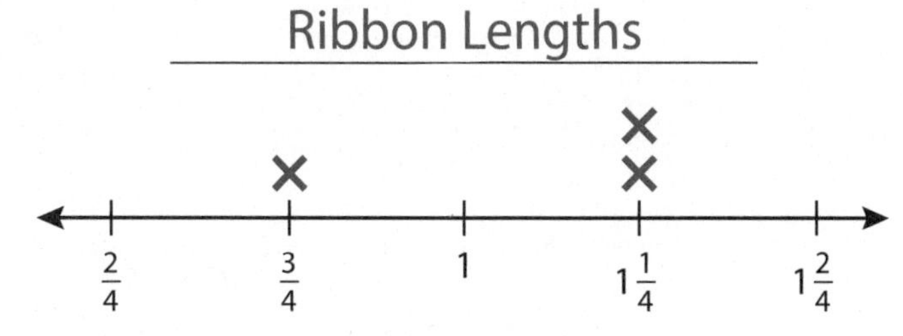

1. Measure the length of each celery stick to the nearest quarter inch. Record each length on the line plot.

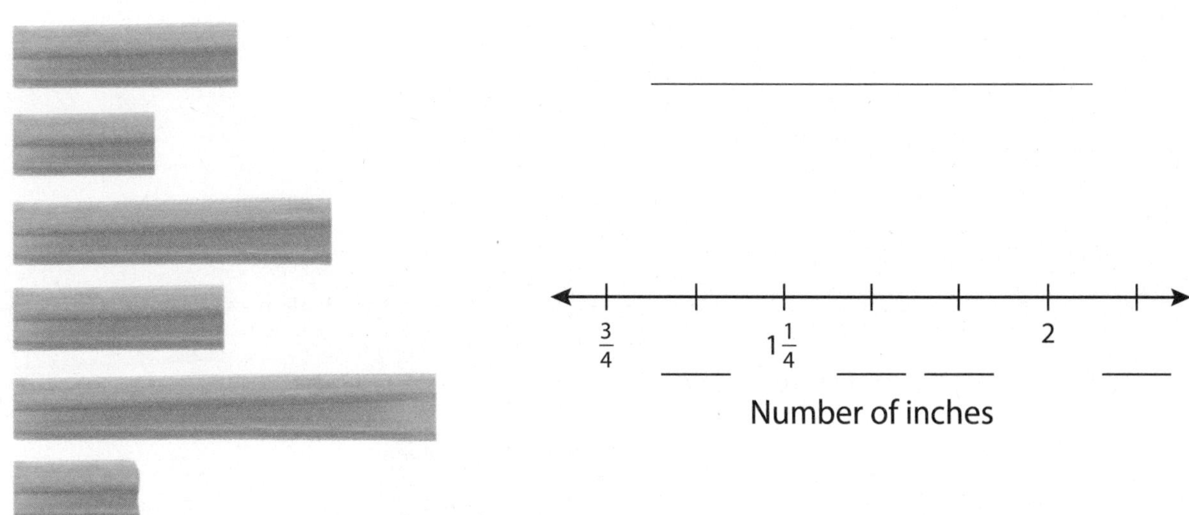

Which celery stick length is the most common?

2. Which One Doesn't Belong? Which does *not* belong with the other three?

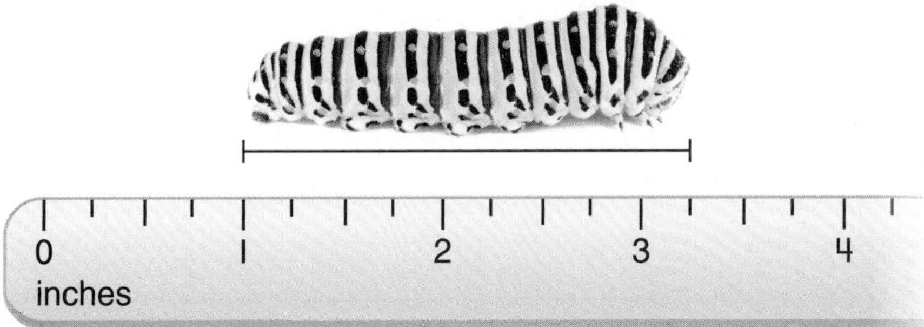

3. MP Precision Find the length of the caterpillar to the nearest quarter inch. Explain.

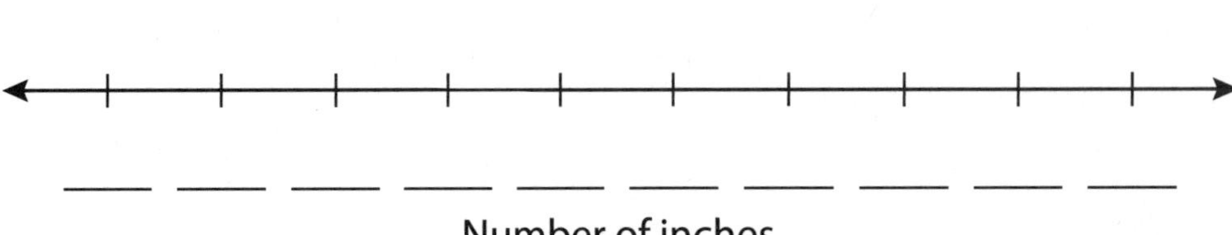

4. MP Modeling Real Life Measure the lengths of your 10 fingers to the nearest quarter inch. Record each length on the line plot. Then describe your line plot.

Number of inches

Make three observations about your line plot.

Review & Refresh

What fraction of the whole is shaded?

5. 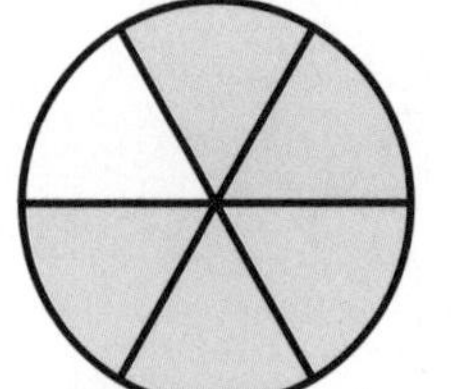

$\frac{\square}{\square}$ is shaded.

6. 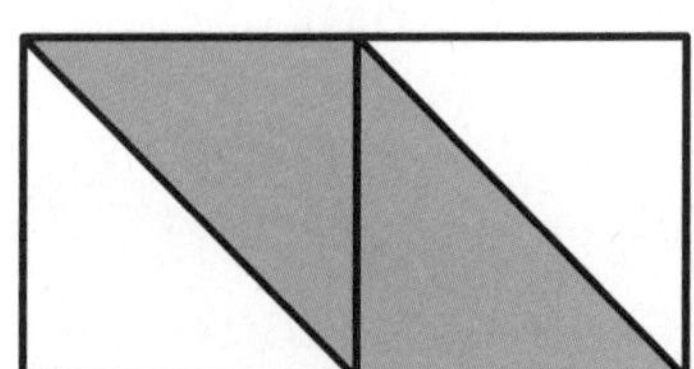

$\frac{\square}{\square}$ is shaded.

Name ___________________________________

Performance Task 14

1. You plant 3 bamboo seeds during the first week. You measure and record the growth of your bamboo plants for the next 3 weeks.

Week 2	
Plant	**Growth**
A	3 in.
B	2 in.
C	4 in.

Week 3	
Plant	**Growth**
A	3 in.
B	3 in.
C	4 in.

Week 4	
Plant	**Growth**
A	4 in.
B	3 in.
C	4 in.

a. Find the height of each plant after the fourth week. Make a bar graph of the plant heights.

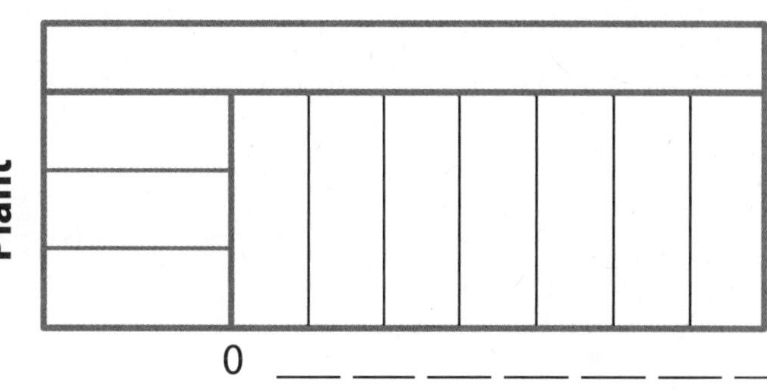

b. **MP Construct an Argument** Do you think any of the plants will be taller than 15 inches after 5 weeks? Explain.

2. a. Measure and record the height of each bamboo plant on Bamboo Growth to the nearest quarter inch.

Bamboo Growth

Number of inches

b. Which height occurs the most?

Roll and Graph

Directions:

1. Players take turns rolling a die.
2. Record each of your rolls on your line plot.
3. The first player to get 10 rolls of one number wins!

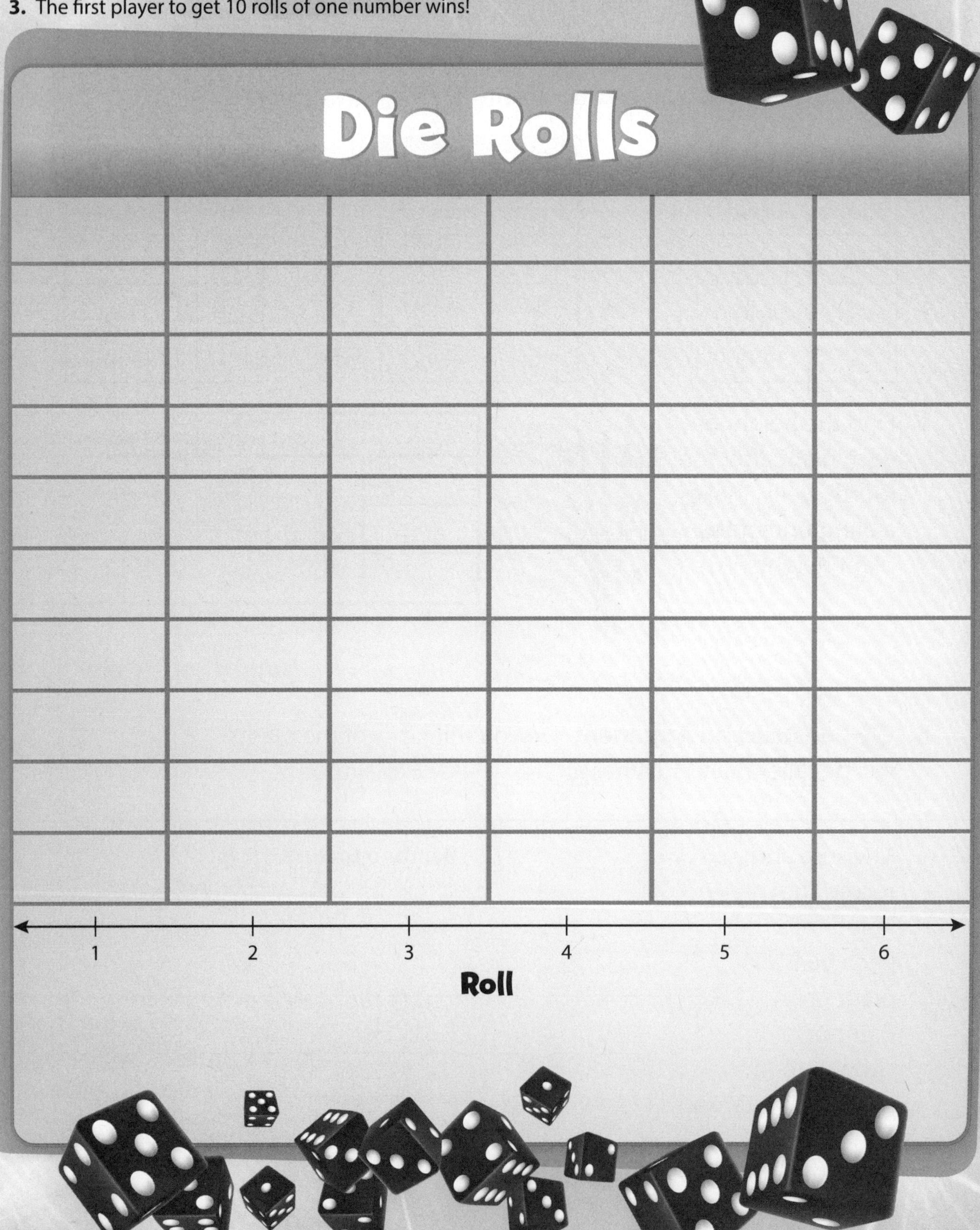

Name ______________________________

Chapter Practice 14

14.1 Read and Interpret Picture Graphs

1. Use the graph to answer the questions. How many tickets were sold in August?

Amusement Park Ticket Sales	
May	Ticket Ticket
June	Ticket Ticket Ticket Tic
July	Ticket Ticket Ticket Ticket Ticket
August	Ticket Ticket Ticket Ticket Tic
September	Ticket Tic

Each Ticket = 20 tickets.

How many more tickets were sold in July or August than in May, June, or September?

Which month had more ticket sales than June, but fewer ticket sales than July? How many tickets were sold this month?

14.2 Make Picture Graphs

2. You collect supplies for an animal shelter. You receive 4 collars, 20 tennis balls, 18 dog bones, and 12 cat toys. Complete the picture graph.

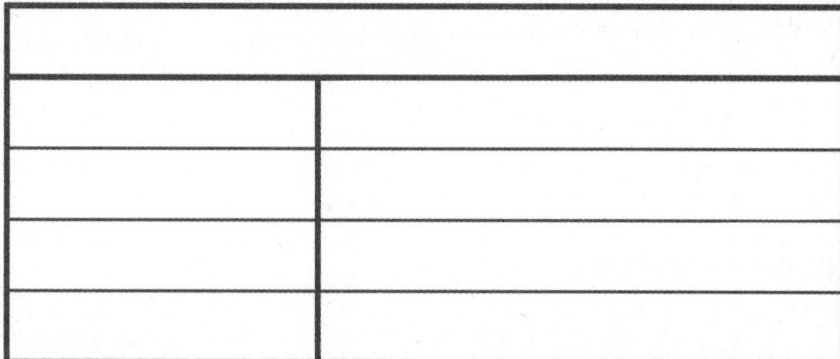

Each ◯ = ______ supplies.

3. A zookeeper takes care of 30 animals. There are 6 monkeys, 12 flamingos, and 9 kangaroos. The rest of the animals are giraffes. Complete the picture graph.

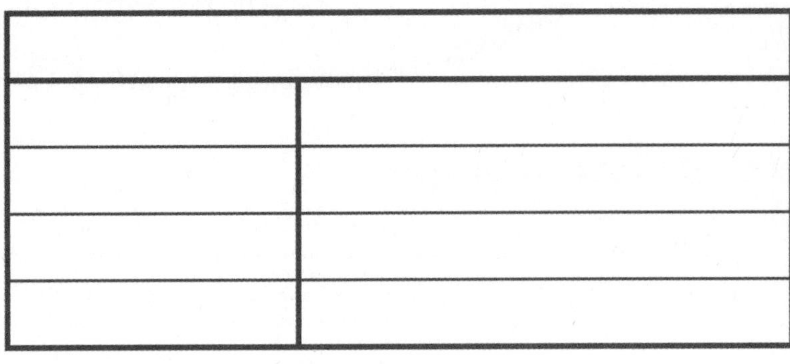

Each ◯ = ______ animals.

14.3 Read and Interpret Bar Graphs

4. Use the graph to answer the questions.

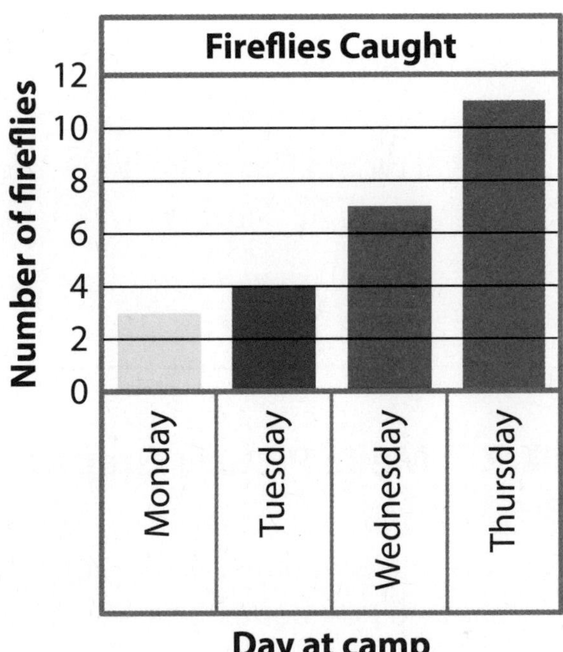

How many more fireflies does your friend catch on Thursday than on Monday?

MP **Patterns** What do you notice about the number of fireflies caught from Monday to Thursday?

On which two days did your friend catch 10 fireflies combined?

You catch 5 fireflies on Monday, 4 fireflies on Tuesday, 8 fireflies on Wednesday, and 7 fireflies on Thursday. Who caught more fireflies at camp?

14.4 Make Bar Graphs

5. Use the frequency table to complete the bar graph.

Trading Cards	
Student A	30
Student B	15
Student C	10
Student D	15

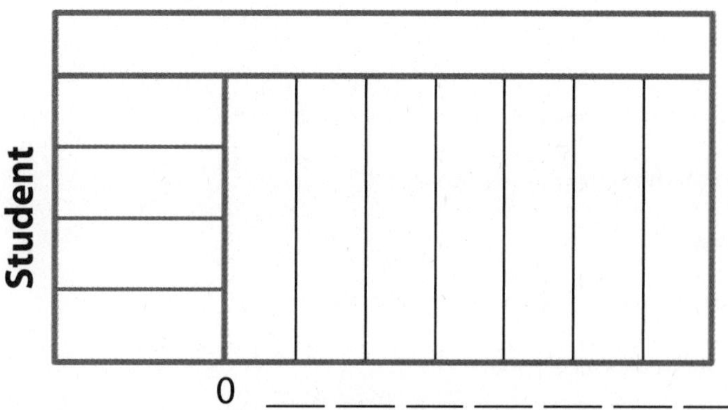

Another student, Student E, has 45 trading cards. How would the bar graph change?

 **Modeling Real Life** Including the number of trading cards of Student E, order the numbers of cards from least to greatest.

14.5 Make Line Plots

6. Use the table to complete the line plot.

Number of meters

Tree Heights (meters)	
23	19
19	24
24	21
21	22
24	21
19	19

14.6 Measure Lengths: Half Inch

7. Measure the length of each snail trail from a snail race to the nearest half inch. Record each length on the line plot.

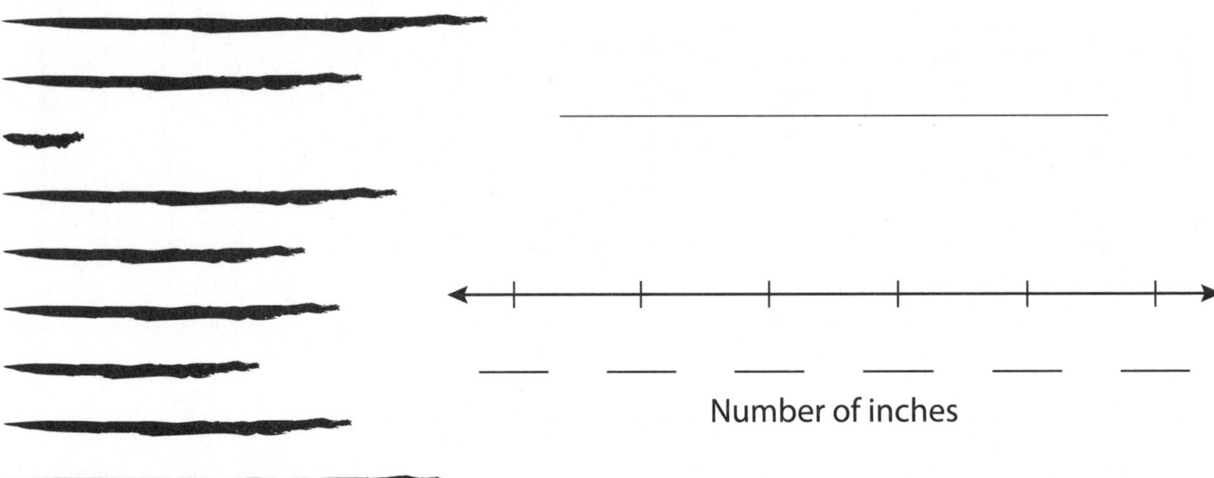

MP Modeling Real Life What is the length of the longest snail trail? What is the length of the shortest snail trail?

14.7 Measure Lengths: Quarter Inch

8. Measure the length of each feather to the nearest quarter inch. Then record each length on the line plot.

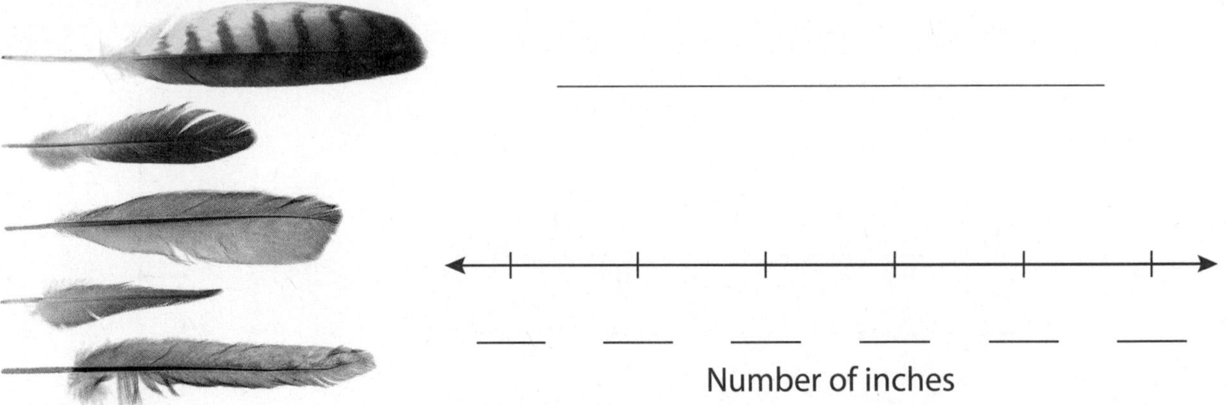

15 Find Perimeter and Area

Chapter Learning Target:
Understand perimeter and area.

Chapter Success Criteria:
- I can identify the perimeter of a shape.
- I can describe the area of a shape.
- I can compare the area and perimeter of a shape.
- I can find the area and perimeter of a shape.

- Imagine you build a tree house. Where would you build it? When would you go to your tree house?
- How can you use math to determine the amount of wood needed to build a tree house? Why is it important to have precise measurements?

Name ______________________________

15 Vocabulary

Review Words

area

square unit

Organize It

Use the review words to complete the graphic organizer.

[ ]

The amount of surface a shape covers

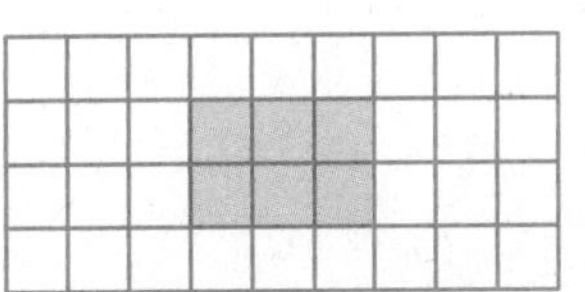 = 1 [ ]

Define It

What am I?

The distance around a figure

$4 \times 2 = M$ $2 \times 2 = R$ $6 \times 2 = E$

$3 \times 2 = I$ $8 \times 2 = T$ $5 \times 2 = P$

10	12	4	6	8	12	16	12	4

Chapter 15 Vocabulary Cards

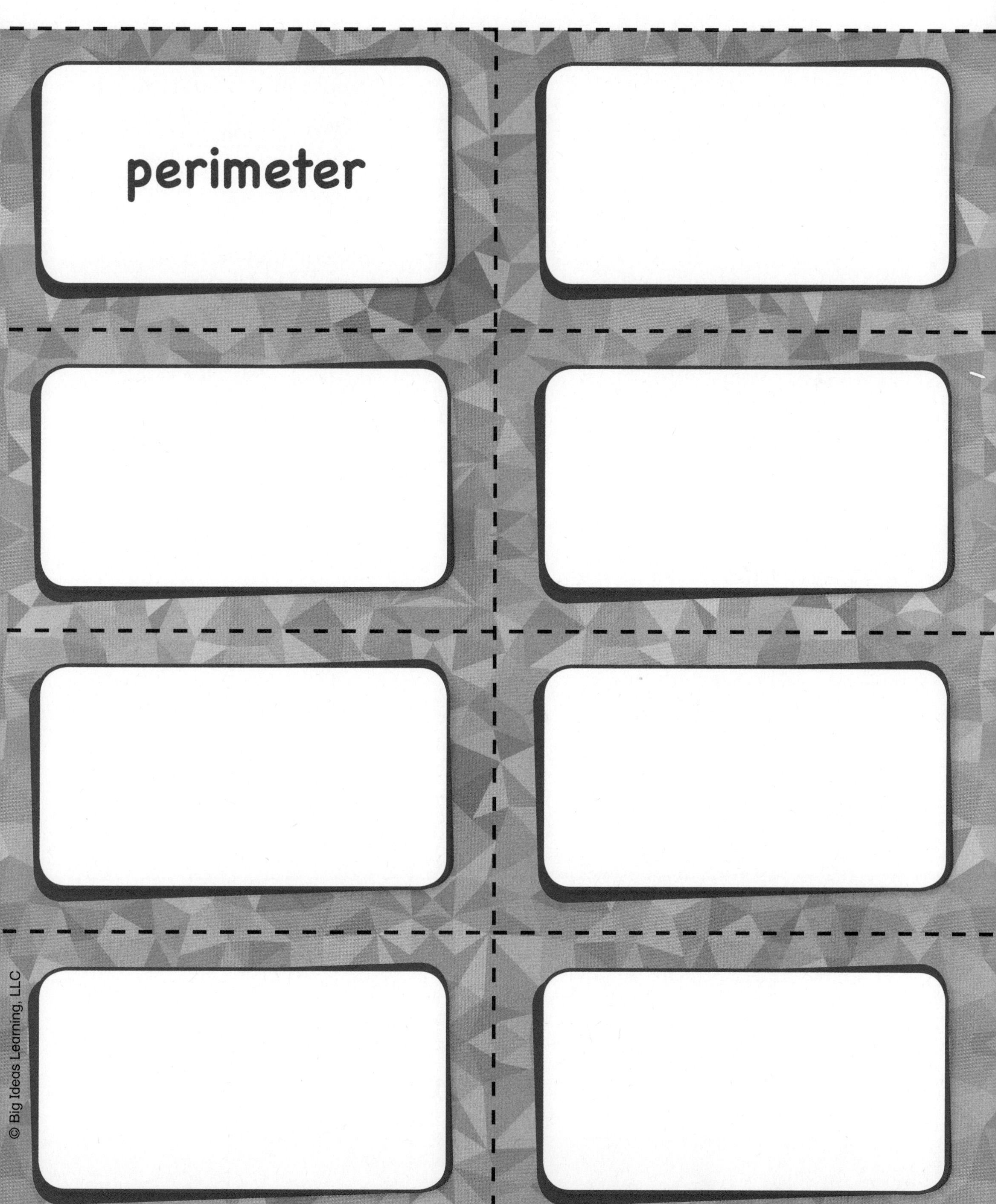

The distance around a figure

The perimeter of the rectangle is 14 inches.

Name ______________________________

Understand Perimeter 15.1

Learning Target: Find perimeters of figures.

Success Criteria:

- I can count the number of units around a figure.
- I can tell the perimeter of a figure using standard units.
- I can use a ruler to find the perimeter of a figure.

Explore and Grow

Model a rectangle on your geoboard. Draw the rectangle and label its side lengths. What is the distance around the rectangle?

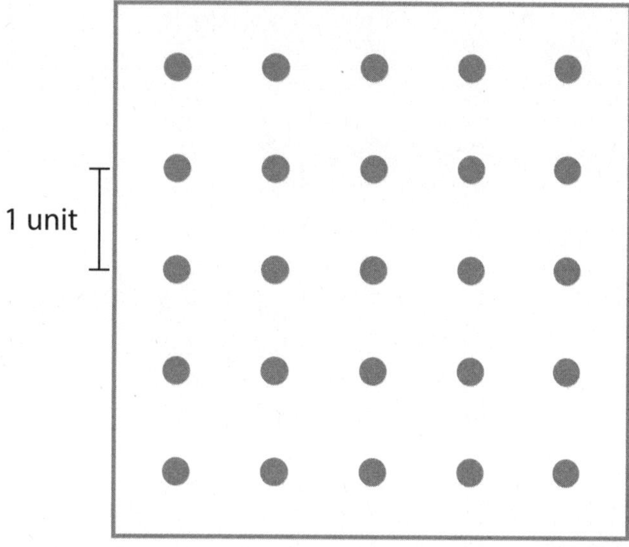

_____ units

Structure Change the side lengths of the rectangle on your geoboard. What do you notice about the distance around your rectangle compared to the distance around the rectangle above? Explain.

Think and Grow: Understand Perimeter

Perimeter is the distance around a figure. You can measure perimeter using standard units, such as inches, feet, centimeters, and meters.

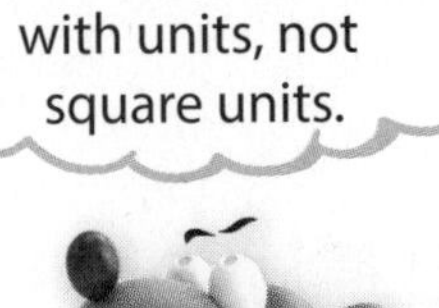

Example Find the perimeter of the rectangle.

Choose a unit to begin counting. Count each unit around the rectangle. →

	1	2	3	4	5	6	7	
20								8
19								9
18								10
	17	16	15	14	13	12	11	

1 in.

Each unit is ________. There are _____ units around the figure.

So, the perimeter is _____ inches.

Show and Grow I can do it!

Find the perimeter of the figure.

1.

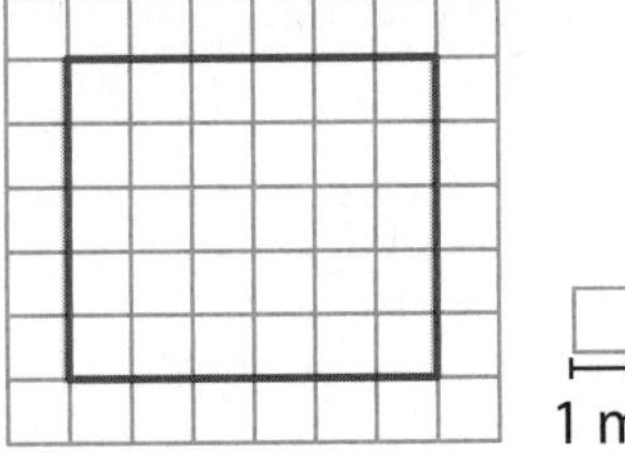

1 m

There are _____ units around the figure.

So, the perimeter is _____ meters.

2.

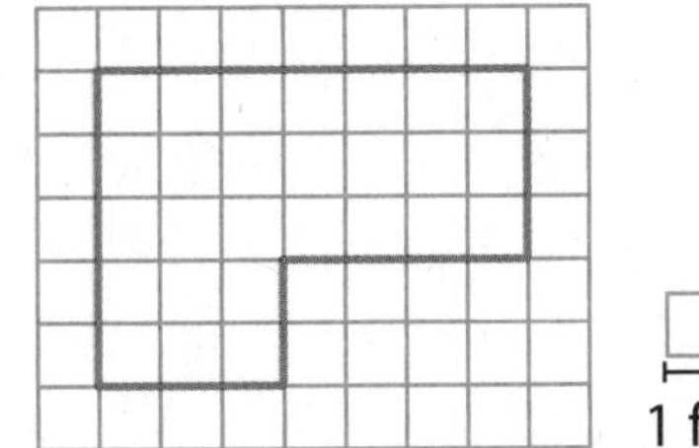

1 ft

There are _____ units around the figure.

So, the perimeter is _____ feet.

3. Draw a figure that has a perimeter of 16 centimeters.

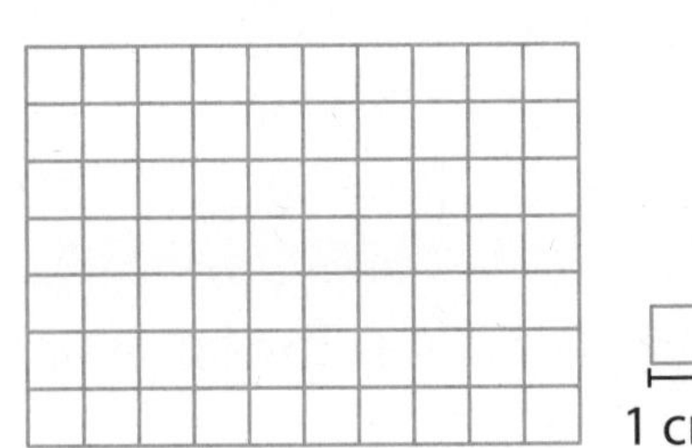

1 cm

Name ______________________________

Apply and Grow: Practice

Find the perimeter of the figure.

4.

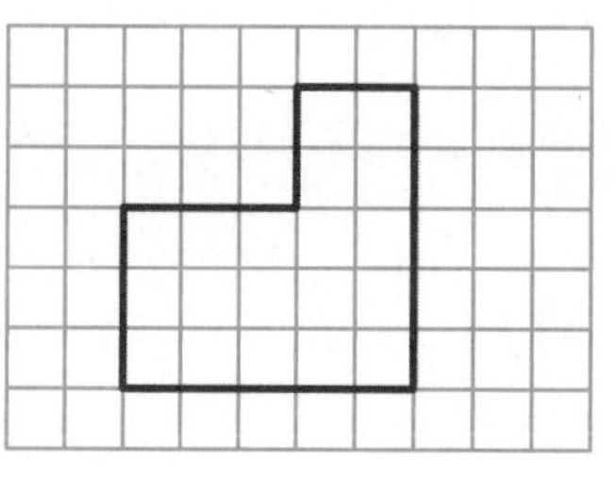

1 cm

There are _____ units around the figure.

So, the perimeter is _______________.

5.

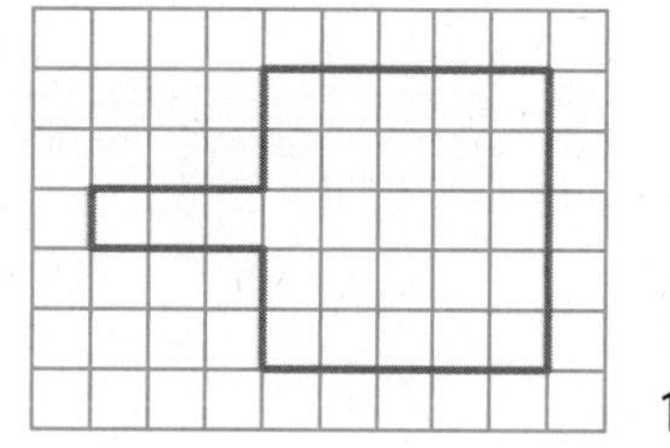

1 ft

There are _____ units around the figure.

So, the perimeter is _______________.

6.

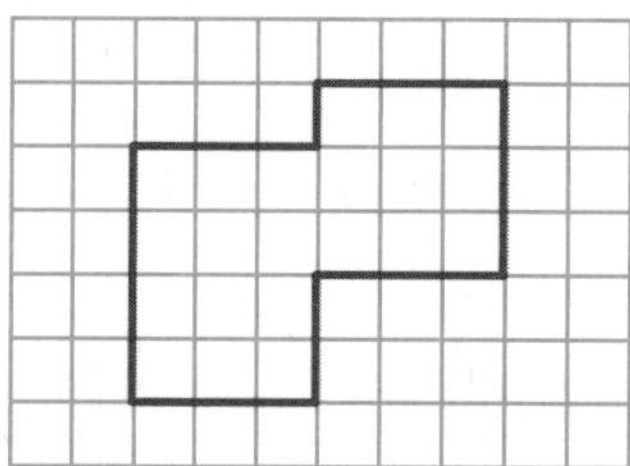

1 in.

Perimeter = _______________

7.

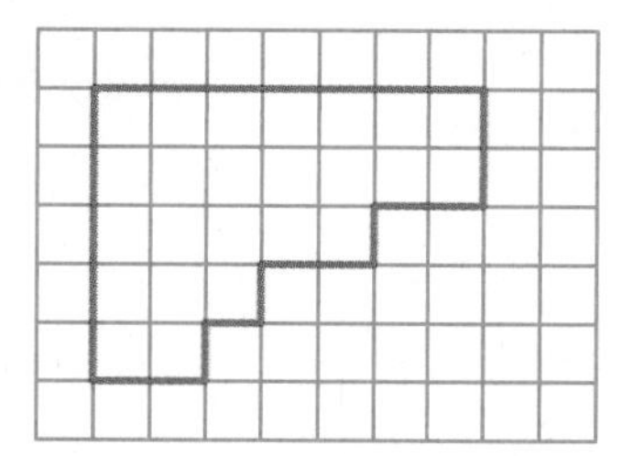

1 m

Perimeter = _______________

8. Draw a figure that has a perimeter of 14 centimeters.

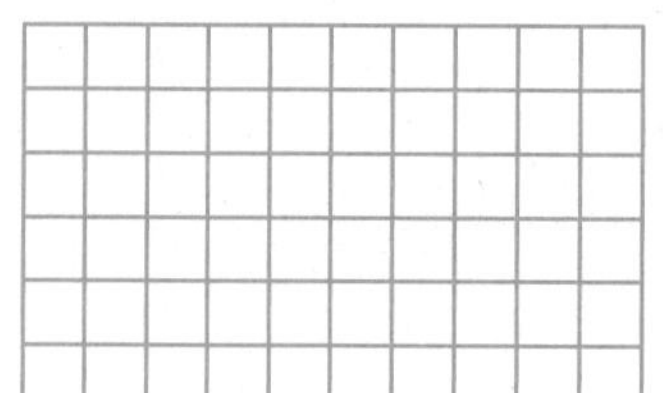

1 cm

9. MP **Does It Make Sense?** Which is the most likely measurement for the perimeter of a photo?

20 inches   100 meters

5 centimeters   2 inches

10. MP **YOU BE THE TEACHER** Your friend counts the units around the figure and says the perimeter is 12 units. Is your friend correct? Explain.

Think and Grow: Modeling Real Life

Use a centimeter ruler to find the perimeter of the bookmark.

_____ cm

_____ cm **I ♥ TO READ** _____ cm

_____ cm

_____ cm

The perimeter is ______________.

Show and Grow *I can think deeper!*

11. Use an inch ruler to find the perimeter of the decal.

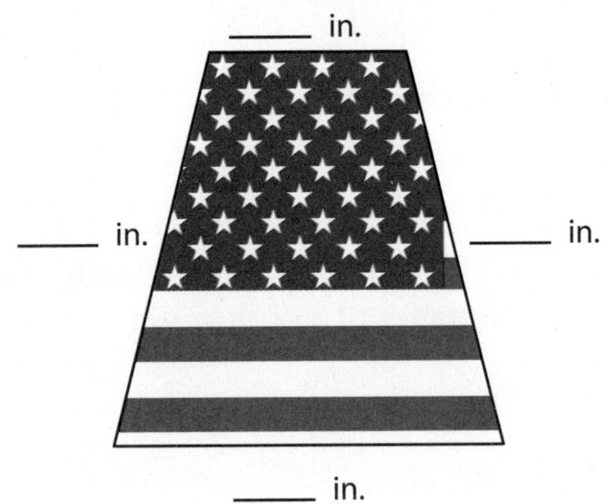

12. How much greater is the perimeter of your friend's desk than the perimeter of your desk?

MP Maintain Accuracy How can you be sure you counted every foot of the perimeter?

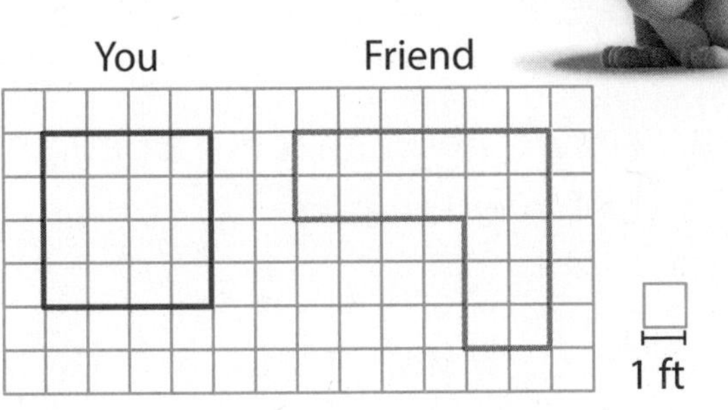

13. **DIG DEEPER!** Explain how you might use a centimeter ruler and string to estimate the perimeter of the photo of the window.

Name ______________________________

Homework & Practice 15.1

Learning Target: Find perimeters of figures.

Example Find the perimeter of the figure.

Choose a unit to begin counting. Count each unit around the figure.

1 2 3 4 5 6 7 8 9 10 11 12 13 14 15 16 17 18 19 20 21 22

1 m

Each unit is 1 meter.

There are 22 units around the figure.

So, the perimeter is 22 meters.

Find the perimeter of the figure.

1.

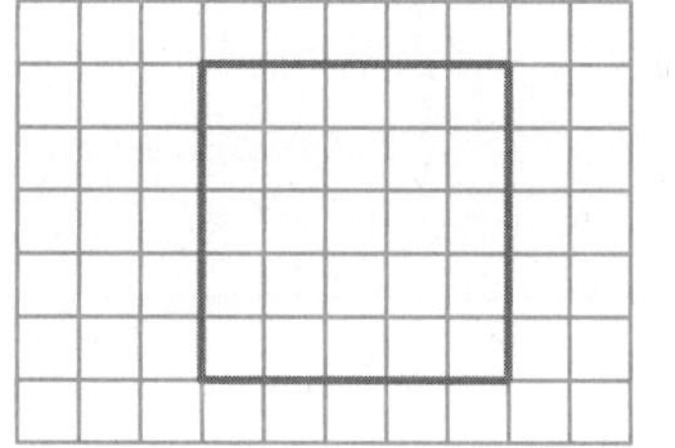

1 in.

There are _____ units around the figure.

So, the perimeter is _____ inches.

2.

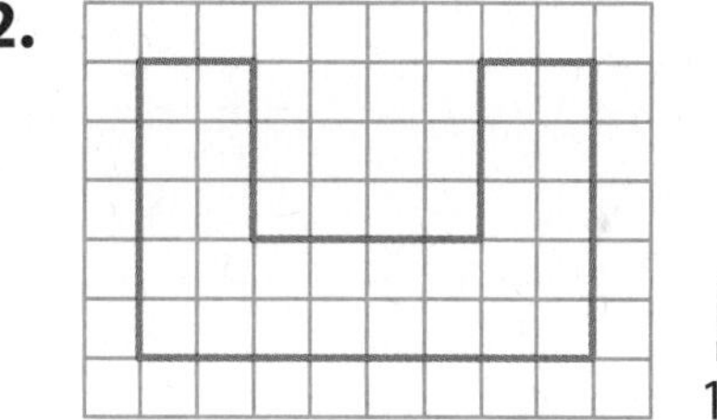

1 ft

There are _____ units around the figure.

So, the perimeter is _____ feet.

3.

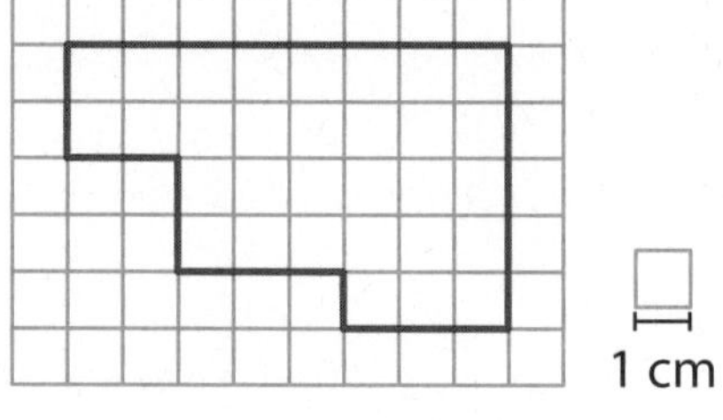

1 cm

Perimeter = ______________

4.

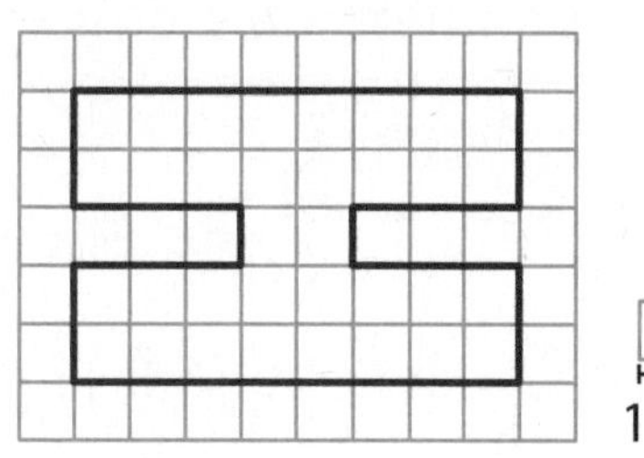

1 m

Perimeter = ______________

5. Draw a figure that has a perimeter of 18 inches.

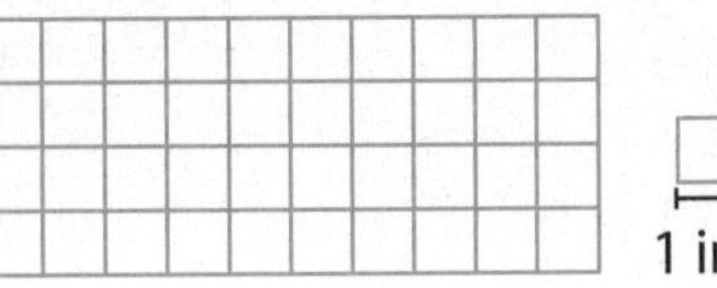

6. MP **Reasoning** Which color represents the perimeter of the rectangle? What does the other color represent?

7. MP **Modeling Real Life** Use a centimeter ruler to find the perimeter of the library card.

8. MP **Modeling Real Life** How much greater is the perimeter of your piece of fabric than the perimeter of your friend's piece of fabric?

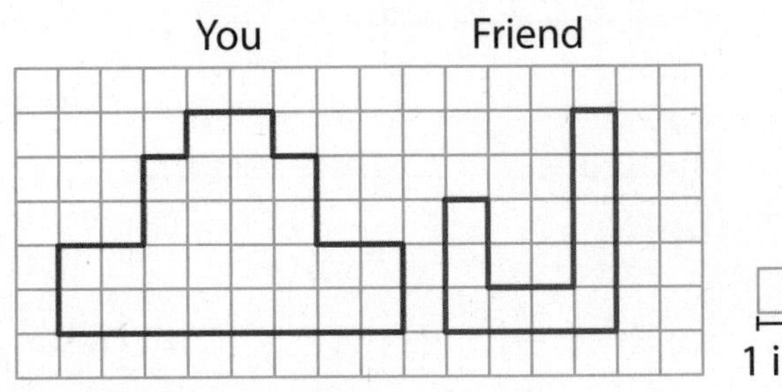

DIG DEEPER! Show how you can add to your friend's piece of fabric so the perimeters are equal.

Review & Refresh

Write two equivalent fractions for the whole number.

9. $1 = \frac{\square}{4} = \frac{\square}{6}$

10. $4 = \frac{\square}{1} = \frac{\square}{2}$

11. $6 = \frac{\square}{4} = \frac{\square}{6}$

Name ______________________________

Find Perimeters of Polygons 15.2

Learning Target: Find perimeters of polygons.

Success Criteria:

- I can add all the side lengths to find the perimeter of a polygon.
- I can multiply to find the perimeter of some polygons.

Model a rectangle on your geoboard. Draw the rectangle and label its side lengths. Then find the perimeter in more than one way.

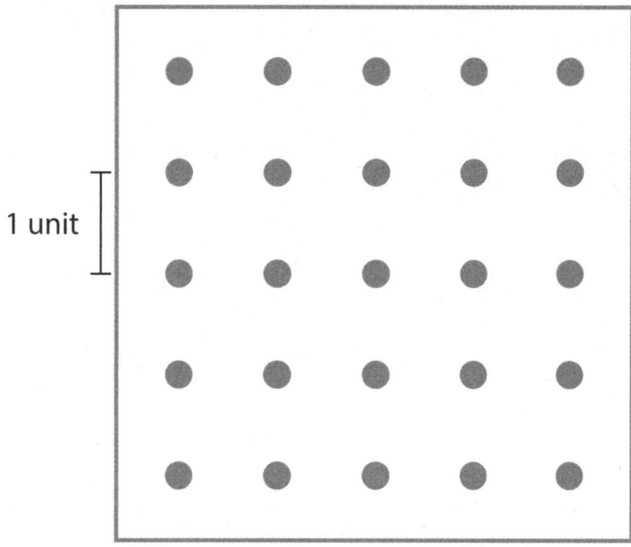

_____ units

Compare Arguments Compare your methods of finding the perimeter to your partner's methods. Explain how they are alike or different.

Think and Grow: Find Perimeter

Example Find the perimeter of the trapezoid.

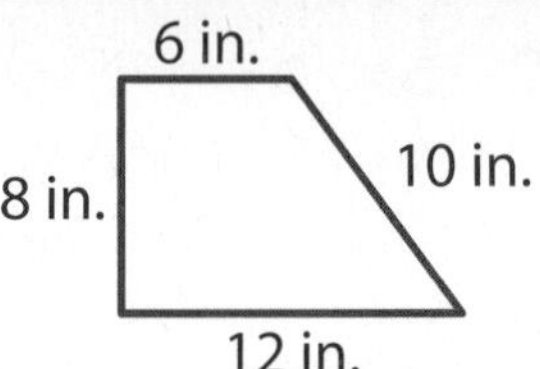

You can find the perimeter of a figure by adding all of the side lengths.

_____ + _____ + _____ + _____ = *P*

_____ = *P*

Write an equation. The letter *P* represents the unknown perimeter. Add the side lengths.

So, the perimeter is ________.

Example Find the perimeter of the rectangle.

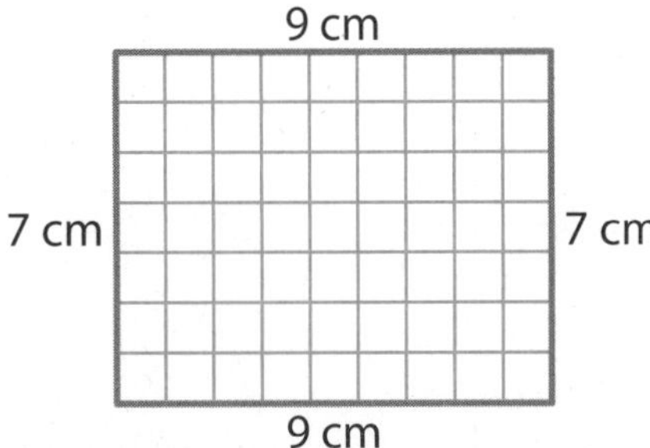

Because a rectangle has two pairs of equal sides, you can also use multiplication to solve.

One Way:

_____ + _____ + _____ + _____ = *P*

_____ = *P*

Another Way:

2 × _____ + 2 × _____ = *P*

_____ + _____ = *P*

_____ = *P*

So, the perimeter is ________.

Show and Grow *I can do it!*

Find the perimeter of the polygon.

1.

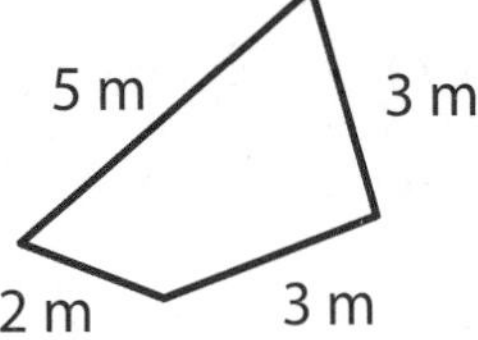

The perimeter is ________.

2.

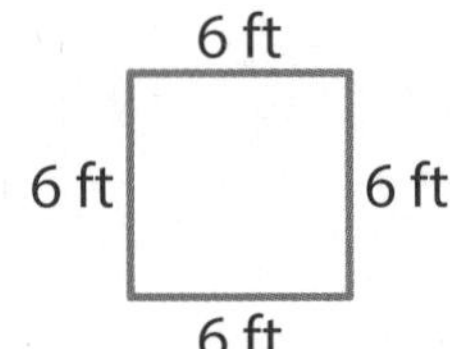

The perimeter is ________.

Name ____________________

Apply and Grow: Practice

Find the perimeter of the polygon.

3.

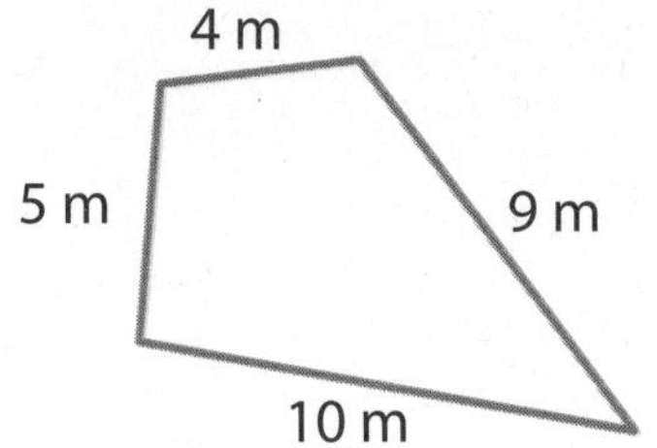

Perimeter = ________

4.

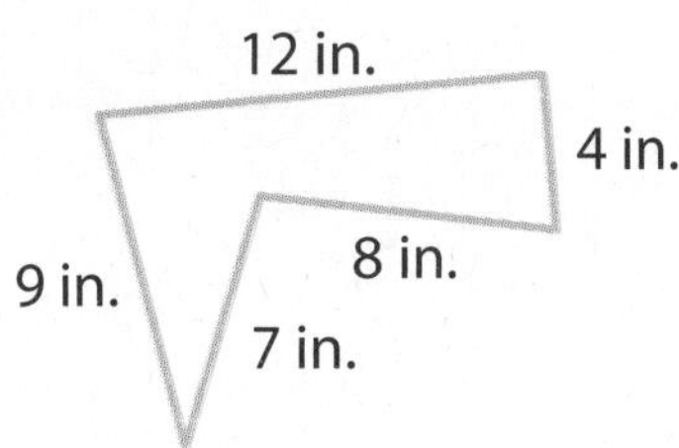

Perimeter = ________

5. Rectangle

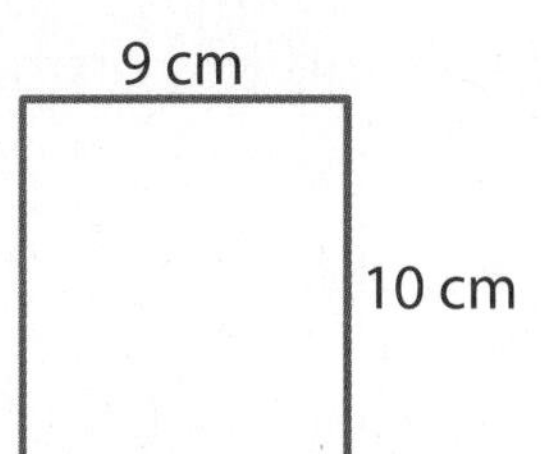

Perimeter = ________

6. Rhombus

Perimeter = ________

7. Parallelogram

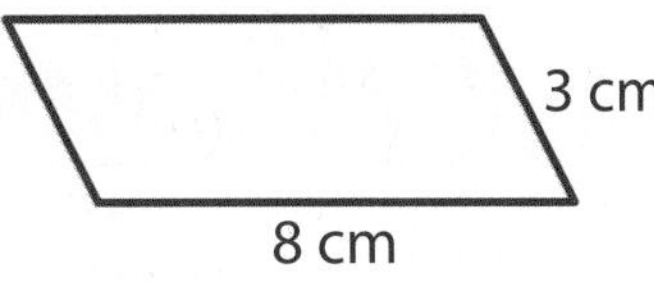

Perimeter = ________

8. Square

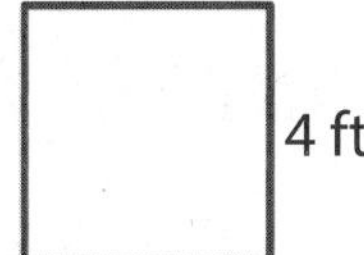

Perimeter = ________

9. You build a pentagon out of wire for a social studies project. Each side is 8 centimeters long. What is the perimeter of the pentagon?

10. MP **Number Sense** The top length of the trapezoid is 4 feet. The bottom length is double the top. The left and right lengths are each 2 feet less than the bottom. Label the side lengths and find the perimeter of the trapezoid.

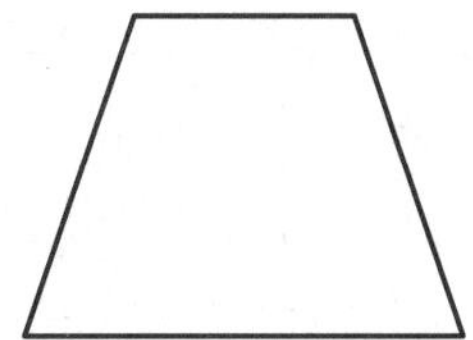

11. **Writing** Explain how finding the perimeter of a rectangle is different from finding its area.

12. **DIG DEEPER!** A rectangle has a perimeter of 12 feet. What could its side lengths be?

Think and Grow: Modeling Real Life

The rectangular sign is 34 feet longer than it is wide. What is the perimeter of the sign?

Understand the problem:

Make a plan:

Solve:

The perimeter is ________.

Show and Grow I can think deeper!

13. A city has a rectangular sidewalk in a park. The sidewalk is 4 feet wide and is 96 feet longer than it is wide. What is the perimeter of the sidewalk?

14. A team jogs around a rectangular field three times. The field is 80 yards long and 60 yards wide. How many yards does the team jog?

15. Each side of the tiles is 8 centimeters long. What is the sum of the perimeters?

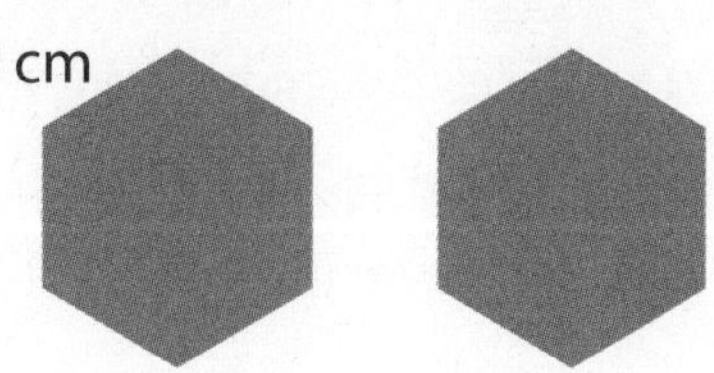

DIG DEEPER! You put the tiles together as shown. Is the perimeter of this new shape the same as the sum of the perimeters above? Explain.

Name ________________________

Learning Target: Find perimeters of polygons.

Example Find the perimeter of the rhombus.

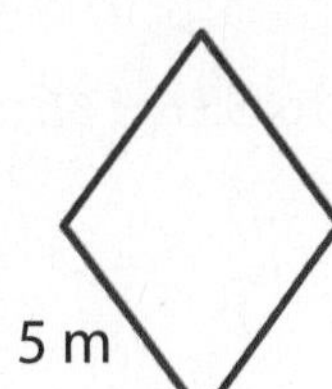

Because a rhombus has four equal sides, you can also use multiplication to solve.

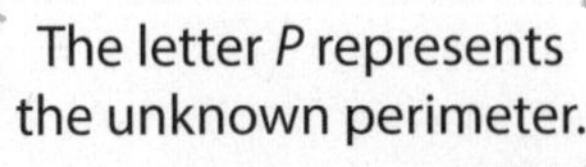

One Way:

$\underline{5} + \underline{5} + \underline{5} + \underline{5} = P$

$\underline{20} = P$

Another Way:

$4 \times \underline{5} = P$

$\underline{20} = P$

So, the perimeter is 20 meters.

Find the perimeter of the polygon.

1.

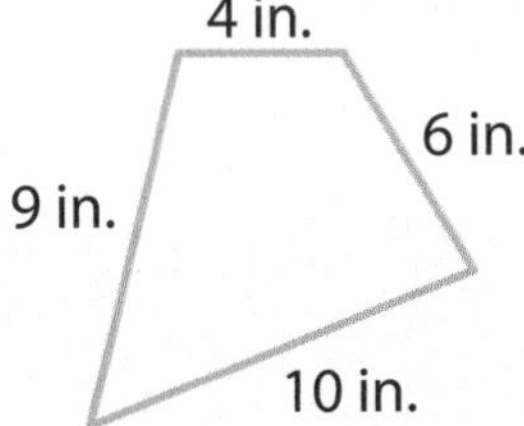

Perimeter = ________

2.

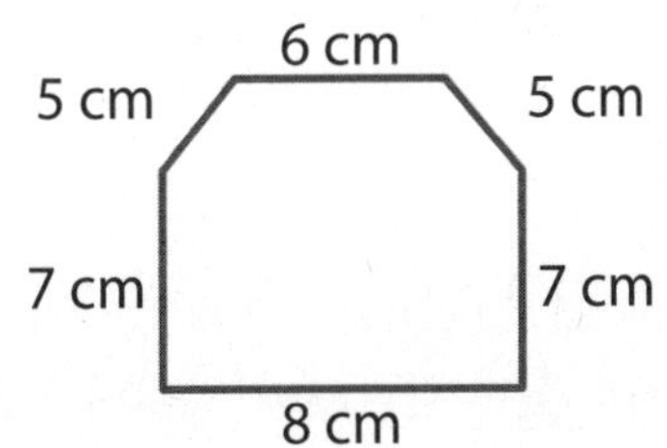

Perimeter = ________

3. Square

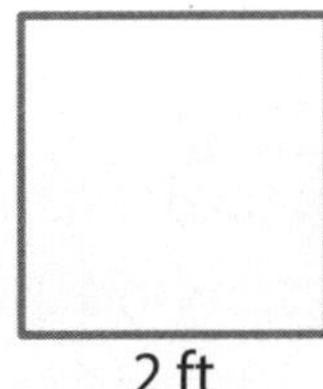

Perimeter = ________

4. Parallelogram

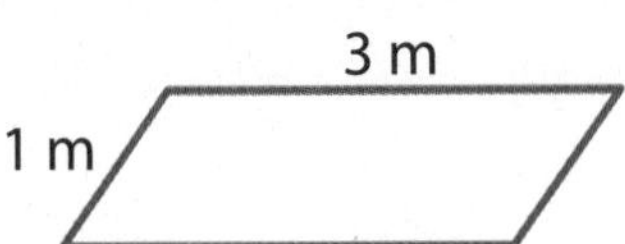

Perimeter = ________

5. Rhombus

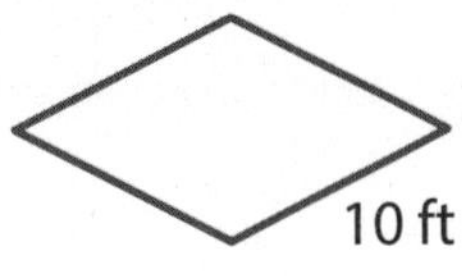

Perimeter = ________

6. Rectangle

Perimeter = ________

7. Each side of a triangle is 5 centimeters long. What is the perimeter of the triangle?

---

8. 

Descartes says that a square will always have a greater perimeter than a triangle because it has more sides. Is he correct? Explain.

9. MP **Structure** Draw a pentagon and label its sides so that it has the same perimeter as the rectangle.

3 m

7 m

---

10. MP **Modeling Real Life** An Olympic swimming pool is 82 feet longer than it is wide. What is the perimeter of the swimming pool?

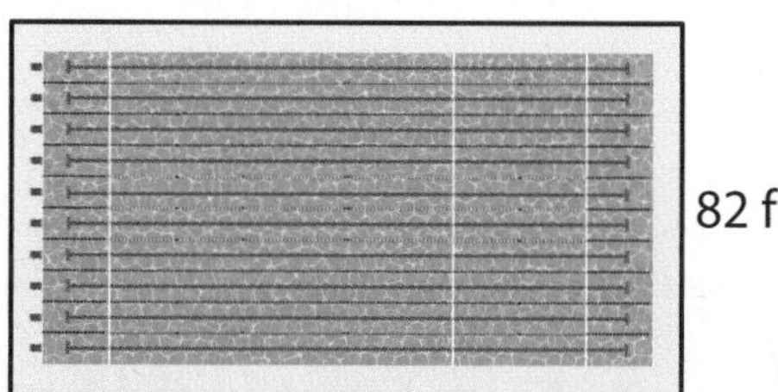

---

11. **DIG DEEPER!** You want to put painter's tape around four tree house windows like the one shown. You have a 30-foot roll of painter's tape. Do you have enough tape? Explain.

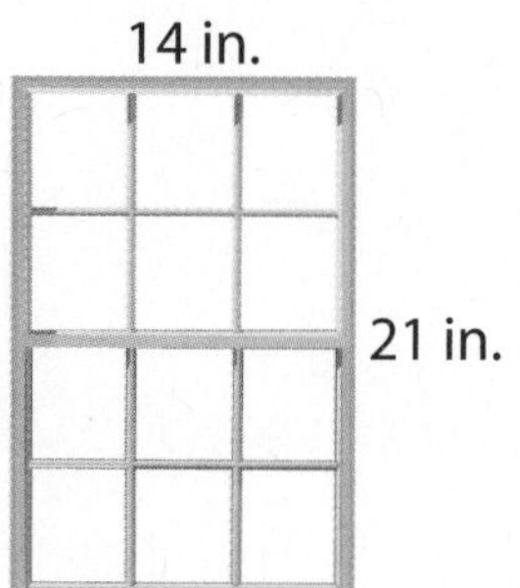

Review & Refresh

Find the sum.

12. $590 + 147$

13. $636 + 258$

14. $476 + 329$

Name ________________________________

Find Unknown Side Lengths 15.3

Learning Target: Use perimeter to find the unknown side lengths of a polygon.

Success Criteria:

- I can use perimeter to find an unknown side length.
- I can use multiplication and the perimeter to find the unknown side length when all sides are equal.

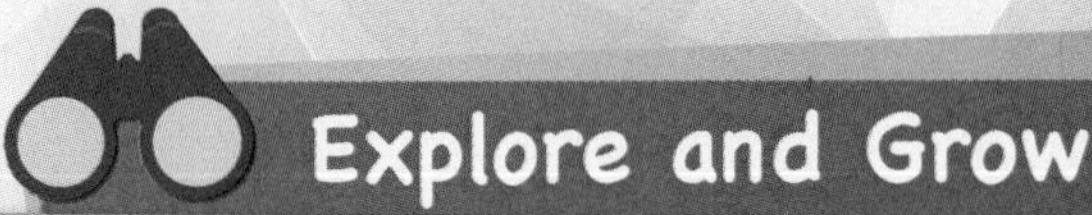

You have a map with the three side lengths shown. The perimeter of the map is 20 feet. Describe how you can find the fourth side length of your map without measuring.

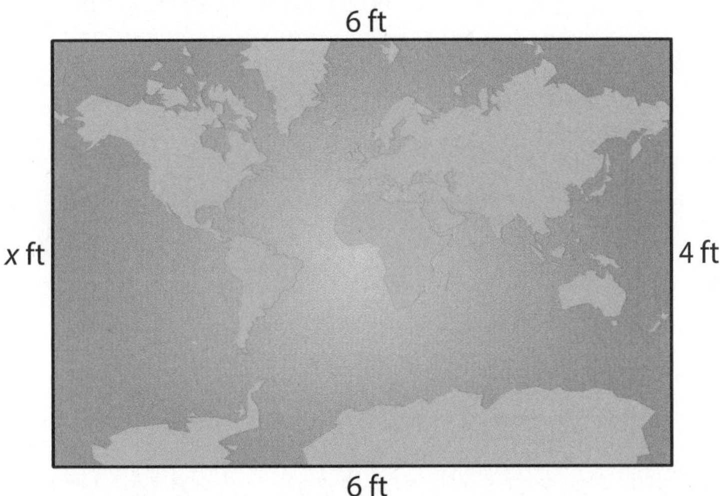

Repeated Reasoning How is finding the unknown side length of a square different from finding the unknown side length of a rectangle?

Think and Grow: Find Unknown Side Lengths

Example The perimeter of the trapezoid is 26 feet. Find the unknown side length.

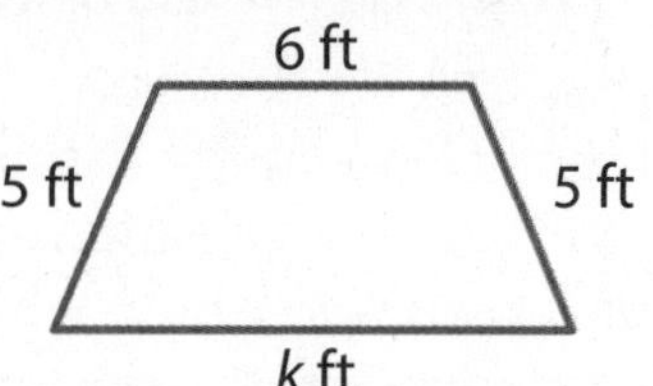

$k +$ ____ $+$ ____ $+$ ____ $= 26$ Write an equation for the perimeter.

$k + 16 = 26$ Add the known side lengths.

____ $+ 16 = 26$ What number plus 16 equals 26?

So, $k =$ ____.

The unknown side length is ________.

Because the square has 4 equal sides, use a multiplication equation to find each unknown side length.

Example The perimeter of the square is 32 centimeters. Find the length of each side of the square.

n cm / n cm / n cm / n cm

$4 \times n = 32$ Write an equation for the perimeter.

$4 \times$ ____ $= 32$ 4 times what number equals 32?

So, $n =$ ____.

So, the length of each side is ________.

Show and Grow I can do it!

Find the unknown side length.

1. Perimeter = 34 inches

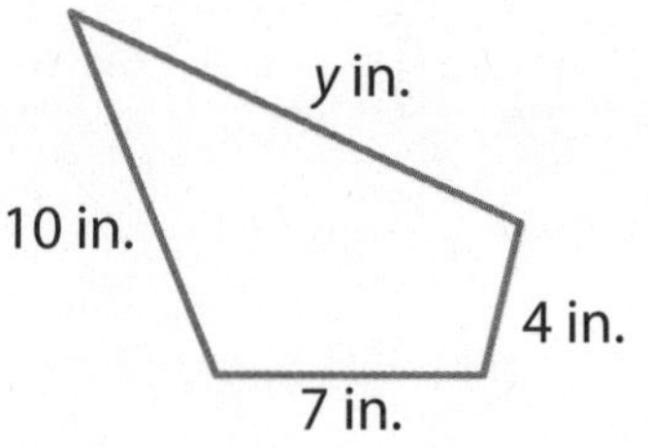

$y =$ ________

2. Perimeter = 20 meters

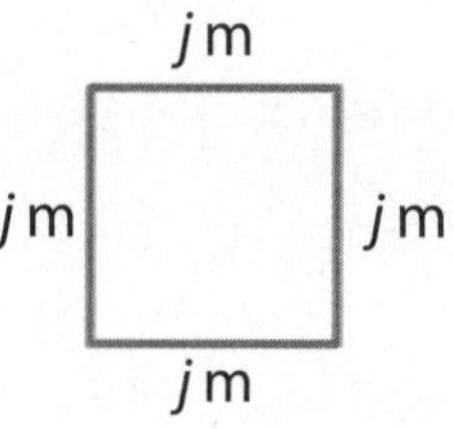

$j =$ ________

Name ____________________

Apply and Grow: Practice

Find the unknown side length.

3. Perimeter = 19 feet

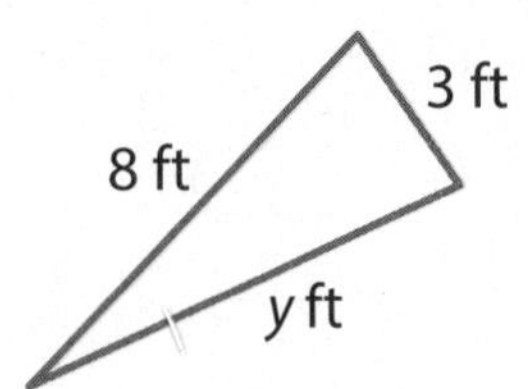

y = ____________

4. Perimeter = 26 centimeters

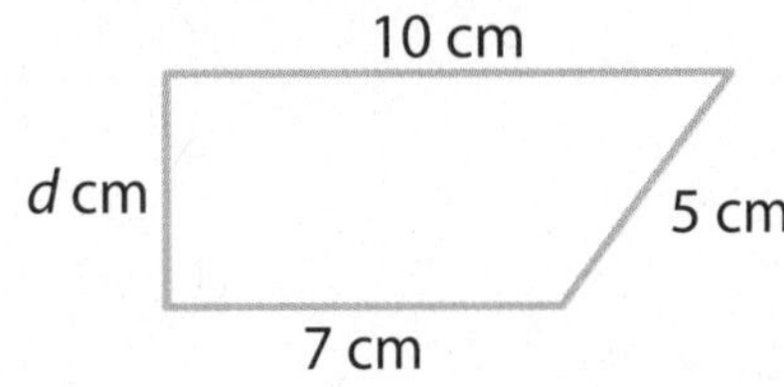

d = ____________

5. Perimeter = 30 feet

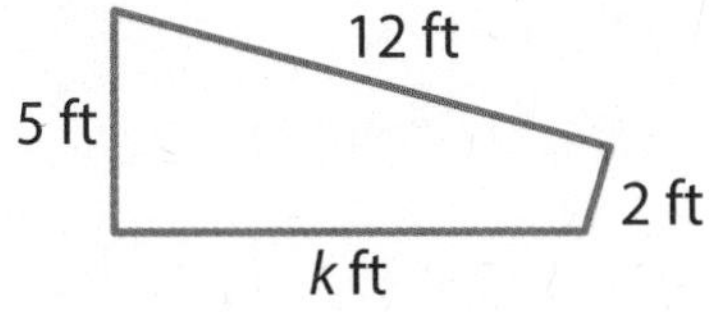

k = ____________

6. Perimeter = 32 inches

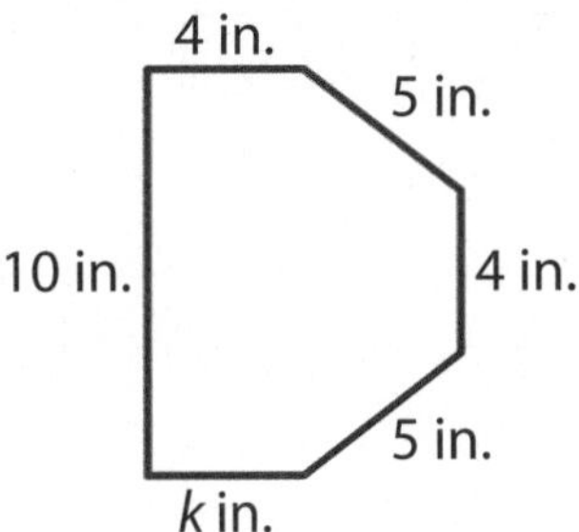

k = ____________

7. Perimeter = 8 meters

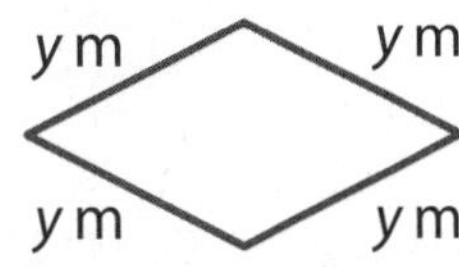

y = ____________

8. Perimeter = 48 inches

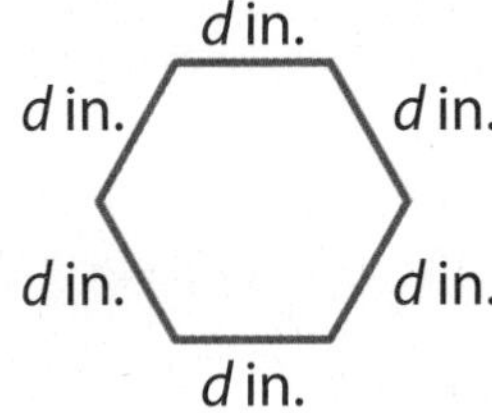

d = ____________

9. MP **Number Sense** A rectangle has a perimeter of 30 centimeters. The left side is 7 centimeters long. What is the length of the top side?

10. **Writing** A triangle has three equal sides and a perimeter of 21 meters. Explain how to use division to find the side lengths.

11. **DIG DEEPER!** Newton draws and labels the square and rectangle below. The perimeter of the combined shape is 36 feet. Find the unknown side length.

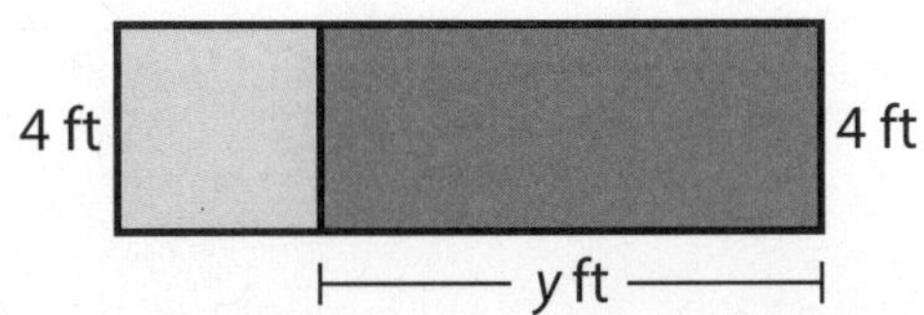

Think and Grow: Modeling Real Life

The perimeter of the rectangular vegetable garden is 30 meters. What are the lengths of the other three sides?

Understand the problem:

Make a plan:

Solve:

The lengths of the other three sides are

__________, __________, and __________.

Show and Grow I can think deeper!

12. The perimeter of the rectangular zoo enclosure is 34 meters. What are the lengths of the other three sides?

13. The floor of an apartment is made of two rectangles. The perimeter is 154 feet. What are the lengths of the other three sides?

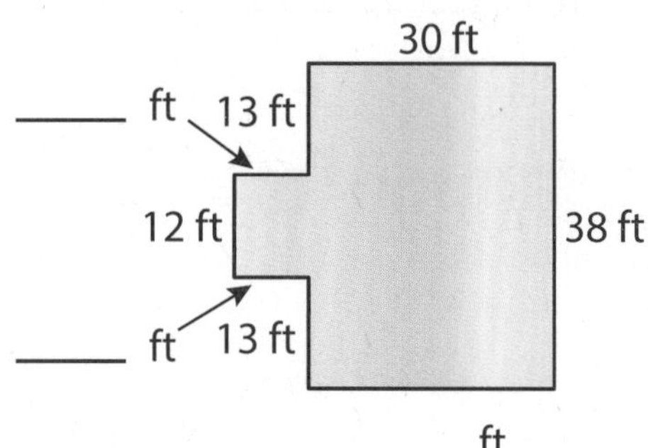

14. DIG DEEPER! You want to make a flower bed in the shape of a pentagon. Two sides of the flower bed are each 7 inches long, and two sides are each 16 inches long. The perimeter is 57 inches. Sketch the flower bed and label all of the side lengths.

Name ____________________

Homework & Practice 15.3

Learning Target: Use perimeter to find the unknown side lengths of a polygon.

Example The perimeter of the quadrilateral is 29 centimeters. Find the unknown side length.

$k +$ __6__ $+$ __10__ $+$ __8__ $= 29$

$k + 24 = 29$

__5__ $+ 24 = 29$

So, $k =$ __5__.

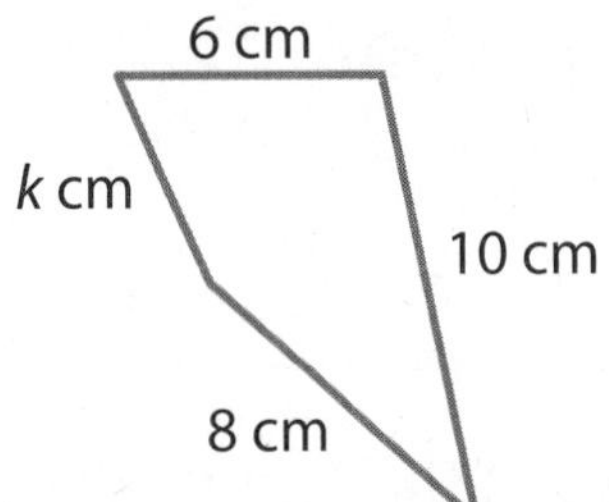

The unknown side length is __5 centimeters__.

Find the unknown side length.

1. Perimeter = 24 feet

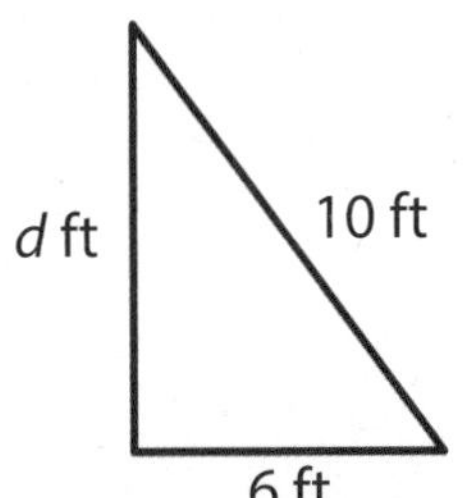

$d =$ ____________

2. Perimeter = 46 inches

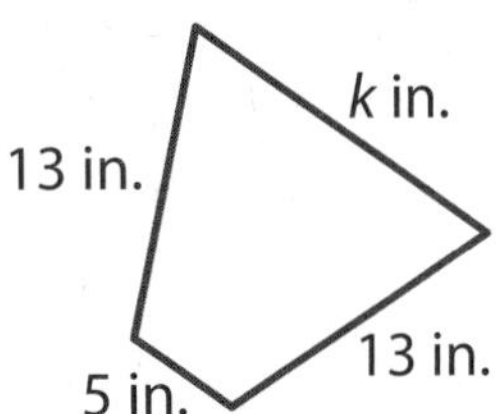

$k =$ ____________

3. Perimeter = 21 centimeters

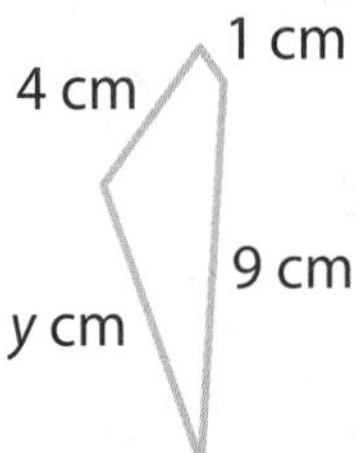

$y =$ ____________

4. Perimeter = 41 meters

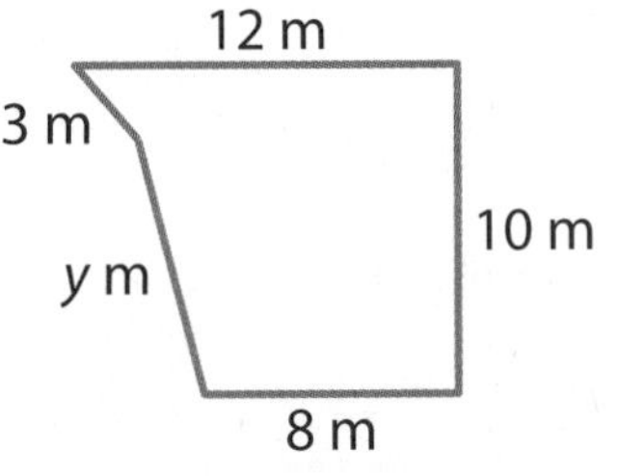

$y =$ ____________

5. Perimeter = 12 feet

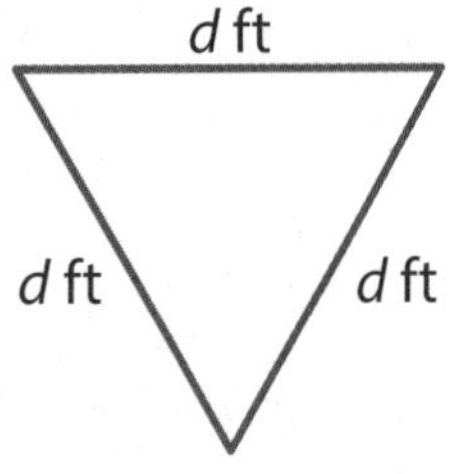

$d =$ ____________

6. Perimeter = 50 inches

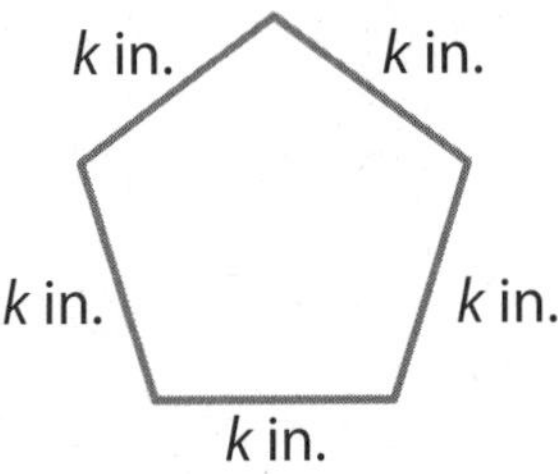

$k =$ ____________

7. **DIG DEEPER!** Each polygon has equal side lengths that are whole numbers. Which polygon could have a perimeter of 16 centimeters? Explain.

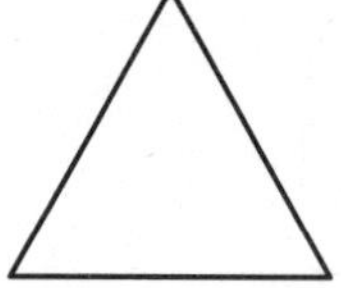
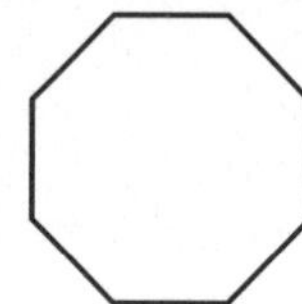
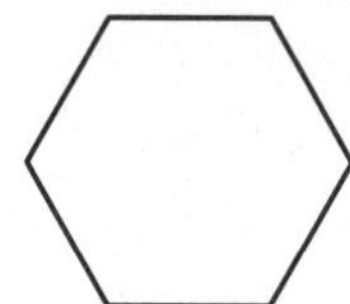

8. **Number Sense** The area of a square is 25 square inches. What is its perimeter?

9. **Modeling Real Life** The perimeter of the rectangular sidewalk is 260 meters. What are the lengths of the other three sides?

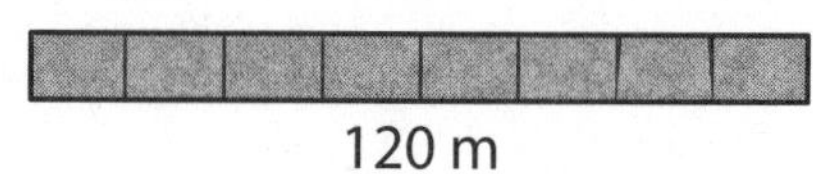

10. **Modeling Real Life** Two rectangular tables are pushed together. The perimeter is 40 feet. What are the lengths of the other three sides?

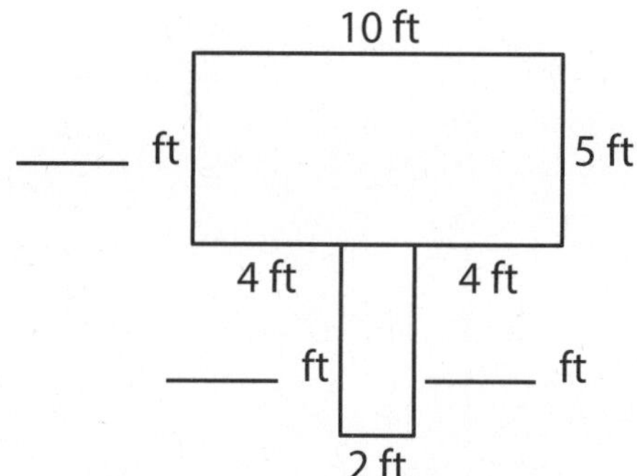

Review & Refresh

Write the time. Write another way to say the time.

11.

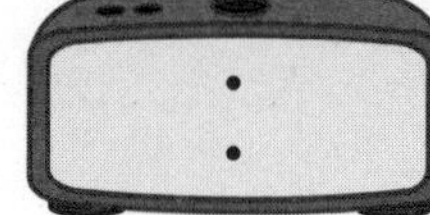

12.

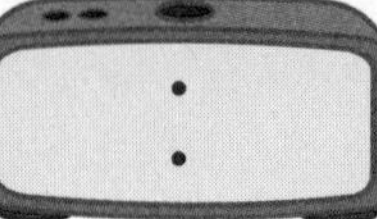

13.

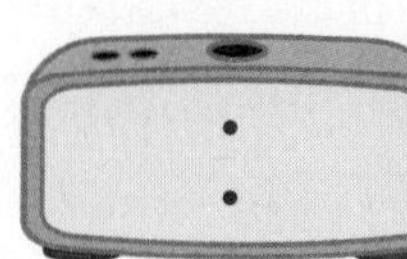

Name ______________________________

Same Perimeter, Different Areas 15.4

Learning Target: Use area to compare rectangles with the same perimeter.

Success Criteria:

- I can find the perimeter and area of a given rectangle.
- I can draw a rectangle with the same perimeter as a given rectangle.
- I can compare the areas of the rectangles.

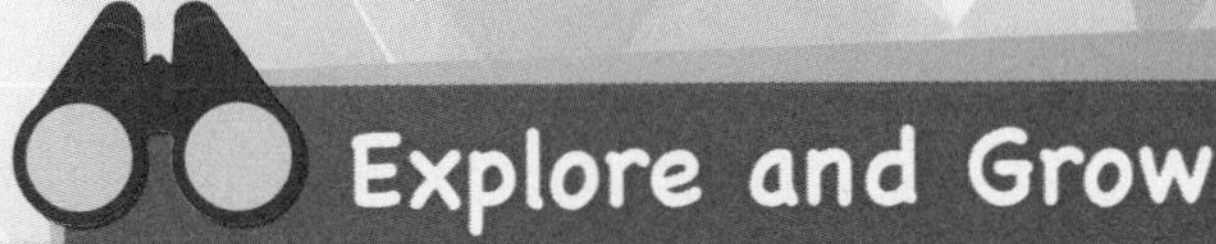

Explore and Grow

Use color tiles to create two different rectangles that each have a perimeter of 16 units. Then draw your rectangles and label their dimensions. Do the rectangles have the same area? Explain how you know.

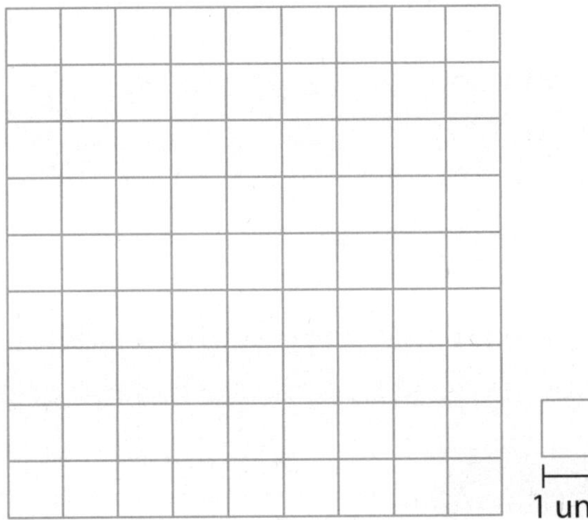

Communicate Clearly Draw another rectangle that has the same perimeter but different dimensions. Compare the area of the new rectangle to the rectangles above. What do you notice?

Think and Grow: Same Perimeter, Different Areas

Example Find the perimeter and the area of Rectangle A. Draw a different rectangle that has the same perimeter. Which rectangle has the greater area?

Rectangle A

Perimeter = 4 + 6 + 4 + 6

= ________

Area = 6 × 4 = ________

Rectangle B

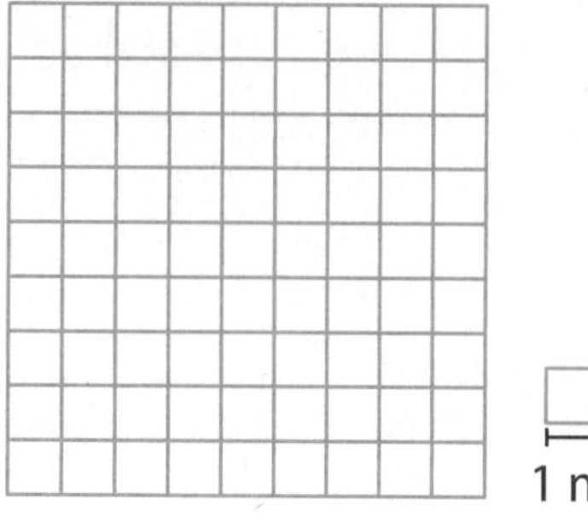

Perimeter = _____ + _____ + _____ + _____

= ________

Area = _____ × _____ = ________

Rectangle _____ has the greater area.

Show and Grow *I can do it!*

1. Find the perimeter and area of Rectangle A. Draw a different rectangle that has the same perimeter. Which rectangle has the greater area?

Rectangle A

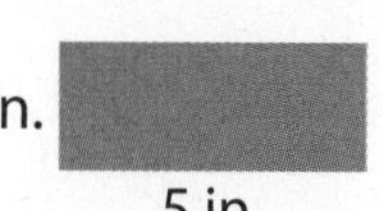

Perimeter = ________

Area = ________

Rectangle B

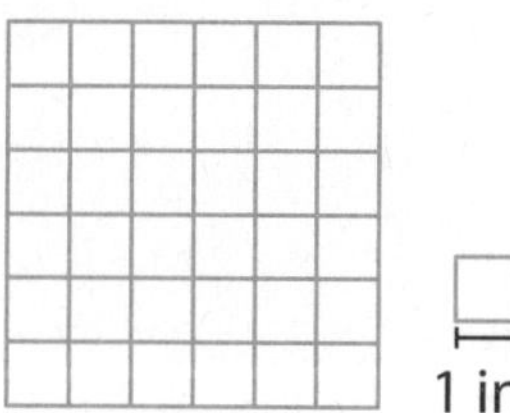

Perimeter = ________

Area = ________

Rectangle _____ has the greater area.

Name ______________________________

Apply and Grow: Practice

Find the perimeter and area of Rectangle A. Draw a different rectangle that has the same perimeter. Which rectangle has the greater area?

2. Rectangle A

10 cm

1 cm

Perimeter = __________

Area = __________

Rectangle B

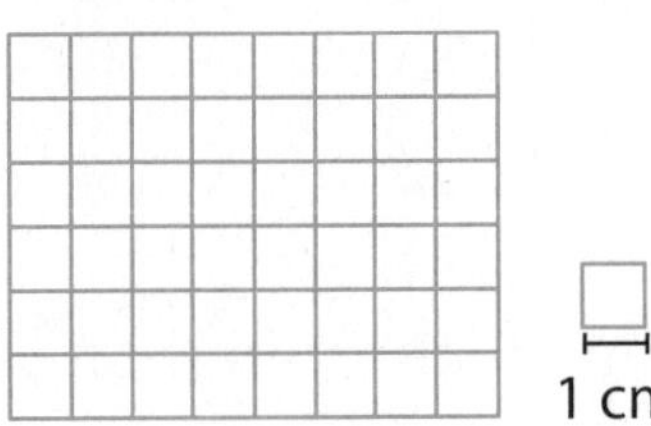

Perimeter = __________

Area = __________

Rectangle ____ has the greater area.

MP Reasoning Describe a different rectangle you could draw.

3. Rectangle A

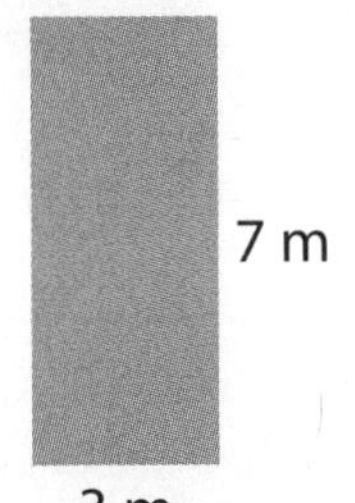

Perimeter = __________

Area = __________

Rectangle B

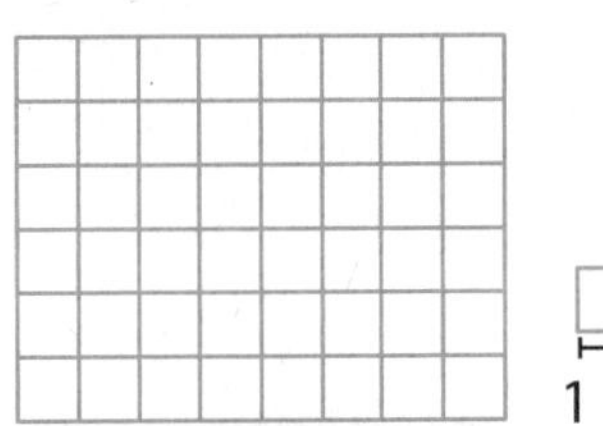

Perimeter = __________

Area = __________

Rectangle ____ has the greater area.

4. **MP Structure** Draw a rectangle that has the same perimeter as the one shown, but with a lesser area. What is the area?

8 ft

5 ft

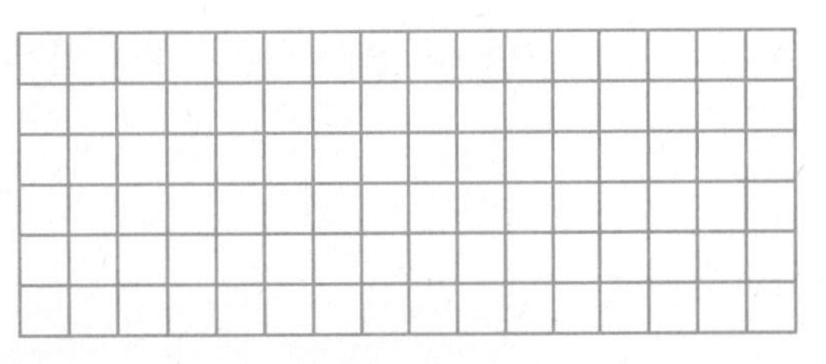

Think and Grow: Modeling Real Life

A paleontologist has 12 meters of twine to rope off a rectangular section of the ground. How long and wide should she make the roped-off section so it has the greatest possible area?

Draw to show:

She should make the roped-off section _____ meters long and _____ meters wide.

Show and Grow I can think deeper!

5. Newton has 16 feet of wood to make a rectangular sandbox. How long and wide should he make the sandbox so it has the greatest possible area?

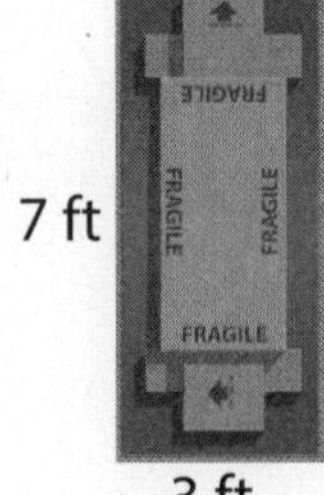

6. **DIG DEEPER!** You and Newton are building forts. You each have the same length of rope to make a rectangular perimeter for the fort on the ground. Your roped-off section is shown. Newton's section has a greater area than yours. Draw one way Newton could rope off his fort.

Descartes also builds a fort. He has the same length of rope as you to make a perimeter around his fort. Descartes's roped-off section has a lesser area than yours. Draw one way Descartes could rope off his fort.

Name ______________________

Homework & Practice 15.4

Learning Target: Use area to compare rectangles with the same perimeter.

Example Find the perimeter and the area of Rectangle A. Draw a different rectangle that has the same perimeter? Which rectangle has the greater area?

Rectangle A

Perimeter = 9 + 2 + 9 + 2

= 22 inches

Area = 9 × 2

= 18 square inches

Rectangle B

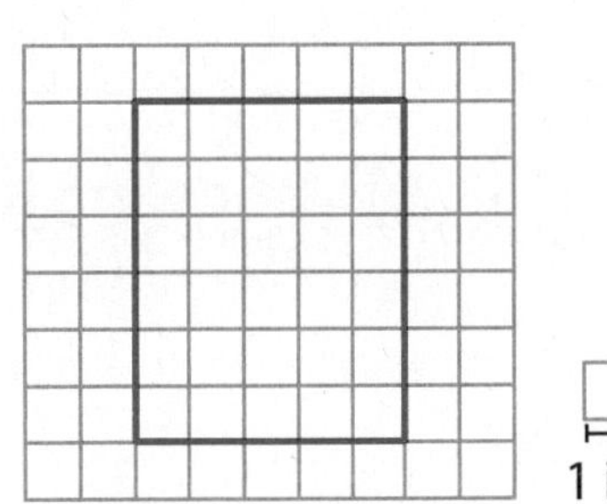

Perimeter = 6 + 5 + 6 + 5

= 22 inches

Area = 6 × 5

= 30 square inches

Rectangle B has the greater area.

1. Find the perimeter and area of Rectangle A. Draw a different rectangle that has the same perimeter. Which rectangle has the greater area?

Rectangle A

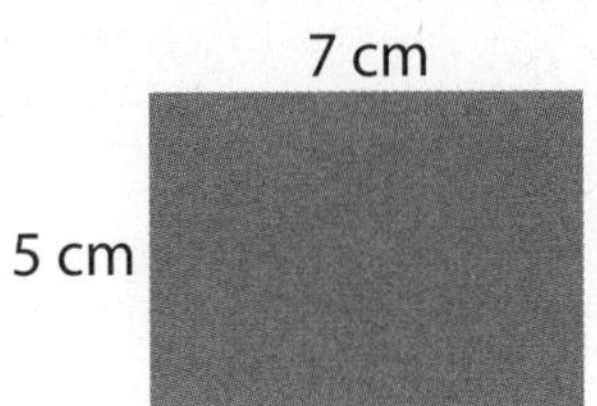

Perimeter = ______

Area = ______

Rectangle B

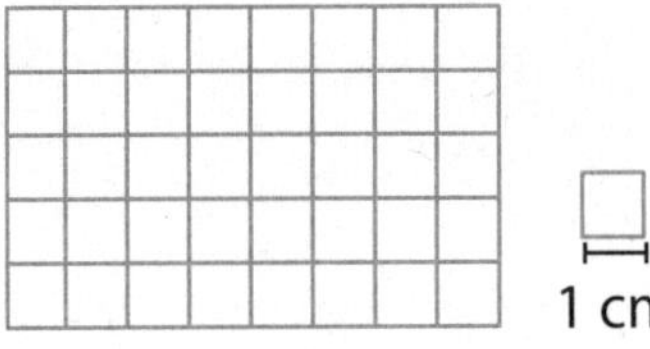

Perimeter = ______

Area = ______

Rectangle _____ has the greater area.

2. **Patterns** Complete the pattern. Find the area of each rectangle.

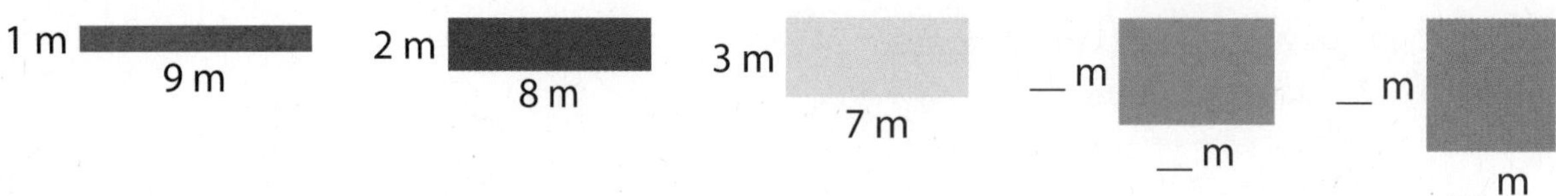

Each rectangle has the same perimeter. As the area increases, what do you notice about the shape of the rectangle?

3. **Modeling Real Life** You are making a card with a 36-centimeter ribbon border. How long and wide should you make the card so you have the greatest possible area to write?

4. **DIG DEEPER!** A school has two rectangular playgrounds that each have the same perimeter. The first playground is shown. The second has a lesser area than the first. Draw one way the second playground could look.

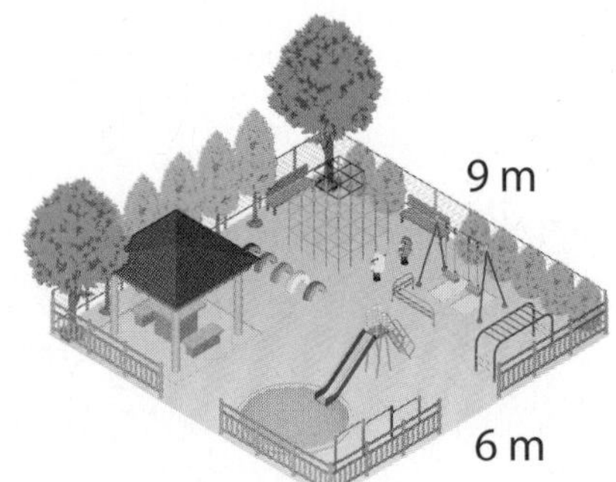

The school builds another playground. It has the same perimeter as the first. The third playground has a greater area than the first. Draw one way the third playground could look.

Review & Refresh

Find the product.

5. $2 \times 30 =$ ______

6. $6 \times 20 =$ ______

7. $3 \times 90 =$ ______

Name ______________________________

Same Area, Different Perimeters 15.5

Learning Target: Use perimeter to compare rectangles with the same area.

Success Criteria:

- I can find the area and perimeter of a given rectangle.
- I can draw a different rectangle with the same area as a given rectangle.
- I can compare the perimeters of the rectangles.

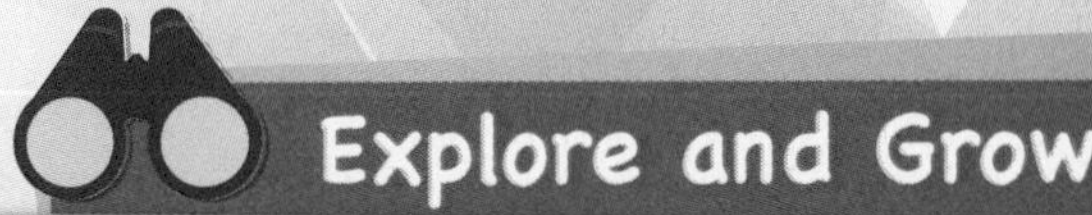

Use color tiles to create two different rectangles that each have an area of 18 square units. Then draw your rectangles and label their dimensions. Do the rectangles have the same perimeter? Explain how you know.

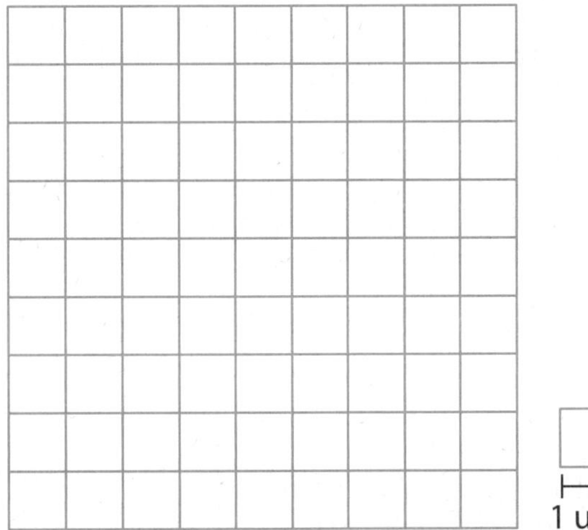

Structure As the perimeter increases and the area stays the same, what do you notice about the shape of the rectangle?

Think and Grow: Same Area, Different Perimeters

Example Find the area and the perimeter of Rectangle A. Draw a different rectangle that has the same area. Which rectangle has the lesser perimeter?

Rectangle A

2 ft

6 ft

Area = 2×6

= ______

Perimeter = $6 + 2 + 6 + 2$

= ______

Rectangle B

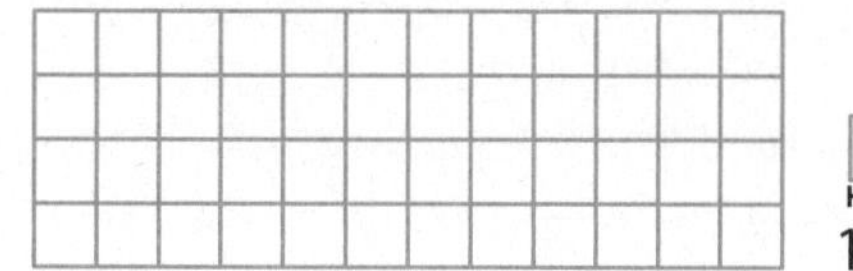

1 ft

Area = ____ × ____

= ______

Perimeter = ____ + ____ + ____ + ____

= ______

Rectangle ____ has the lesser perimeter.

Show and Grow *I can do it!*

1. Find the area and the perimeter of Rectangle A. Draw a different rectangle that has the same area. Which rectangle has the lesser perimeter?

Rectangle A

6 cm

6 cm

Area = ______

Perimeter = ______

Rectangle B

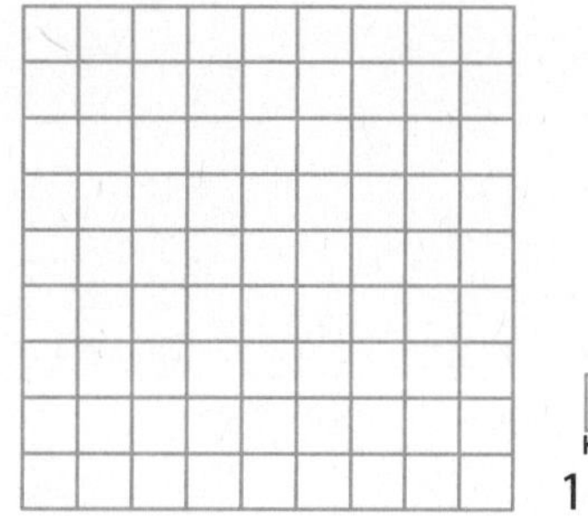

1 cm

Area = ______

Perimeter = ______

Rectangle ____ has the lesser perimeter.

Name ____________________

Apply and Grow: Practice

Find the area and the perimeter of Rectangle A. Draw a different rectangle that has the same area. Which rectangle has the lesser perimeter?

2. Rectangle A

10 in.

2 in.

Area = ____________

Perimeter = ____________

Rectangle B

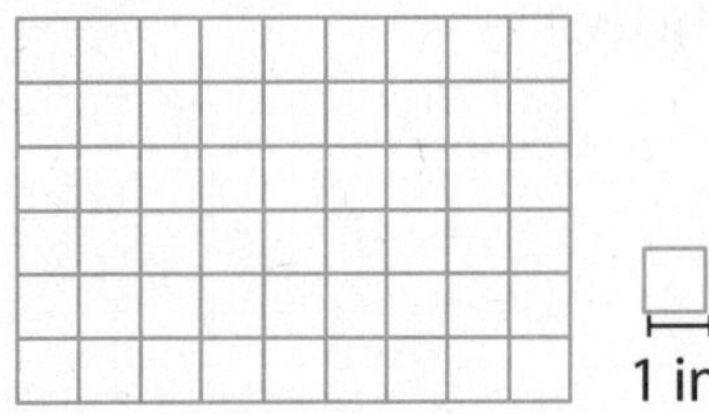

Area = ____________

Perimeter = ____________

Rectangle ____ has the lesser perimeter.

3. Rectangle A

2 m

4 m

Area = ____________

Perimeter = ____________

Rectangle B

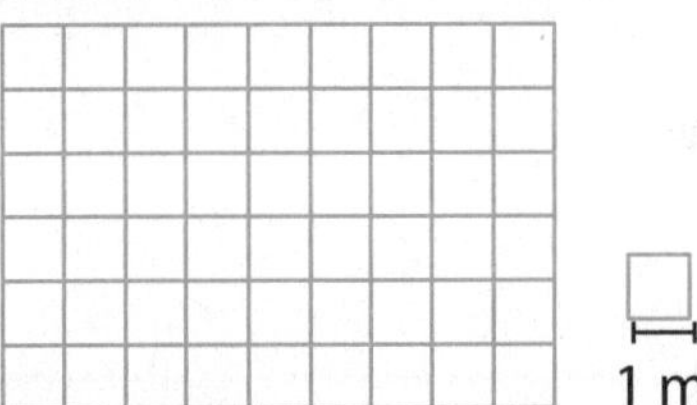

Area = ____________

Perimeter = ____________

Rectangle ____ has the lesser perimeter.

4. **DIG DEEPER!** The perimeter of a blue rectangle is 10 feet. The perimeter of a green rectangle is 14 feet. Both rectangles have the same area. Find the area and the dimensions of each rectangle.

Think and Grow: Modeling Real Life

You have 40 square patio bricks that are each 1 foot long and 1 foot wide. You want to make a rectangular patio with all of the bricks. How long and wide should you make the patio so it has the least possible perimeter?

Draw to show:

You should make the patio _____ feet long and _____ feet wide.

Show and Grow *I can think deeper!*

5. Your friend has 16 square foam tiles that are each 1 foot long and 1 foot wide. He wants to make a rectangular exercise space with all of the tiles. How long and wide should he make the exercise space so it has the least possible perimeter?

---

6. **DIG DEEPER!** You and your friend each use fencing to make a rectangular playpen for a puppy. Each pen has the same area. Your pen is shown. Your friend's pen uses less fencing than yours. Draw one way your friend could make her pen.

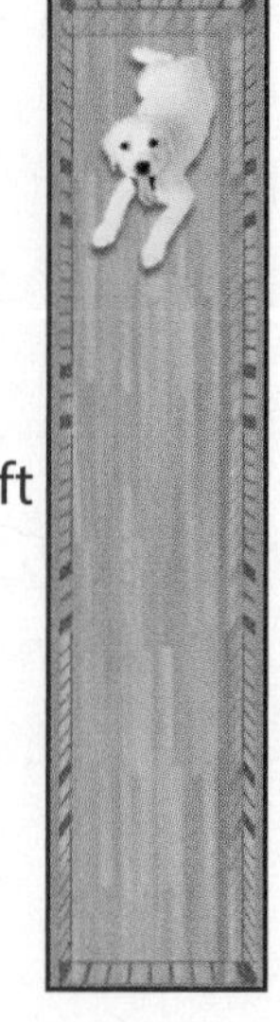

Your cousin makes a playpen for a puppy. His pen has the same area as your pen. Your cousin's pen uses more fencing than yours. Draw one way your cousin could make his pen.

Name ______________________________

Learning Target: Use perimeter to compare rectangles with the same area.

Example Find the area and the perimeter of Rectangle A. Draw a different rectangle that has the same area. Which rectangle has the lesser perimeter?

Rectangle A

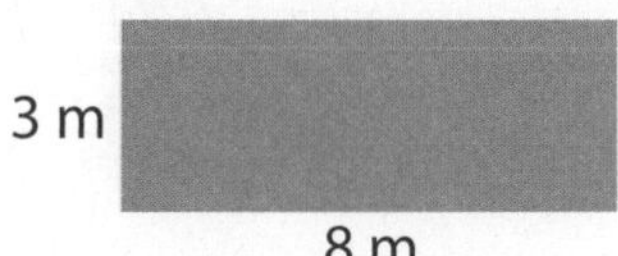

Area = 3 × 8

= 24 square meters

Perimeter = 3 + 8 + 3 + 8

= 22 meters

Rectangle B

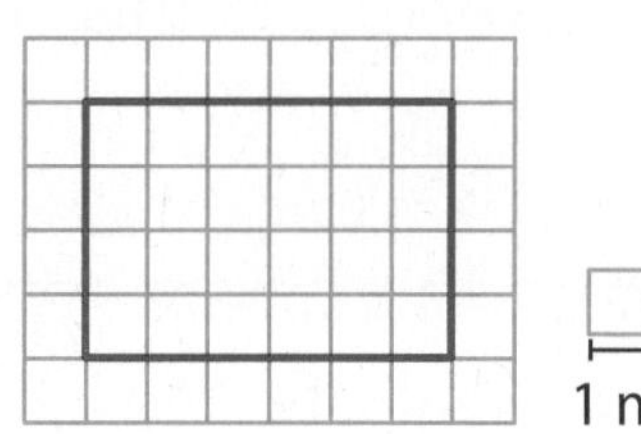

Area = 4 × 6

= 24 square meters

Perimeter = 4 + 6 + 4 + 6

= 20 meters

Rectangle B has the lesser perimeter.

1. Find the area and the perimeter of Rectangle A. Draw a different rectangle that has the same area. Which rectangle has the lesser perimeter?

Rectangle A

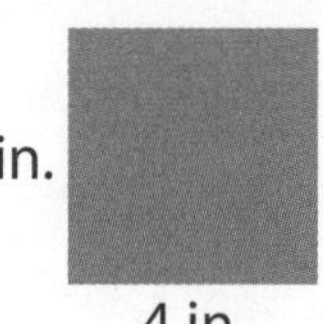

Area = ______________

Perimeter = ______________

Rectangle B

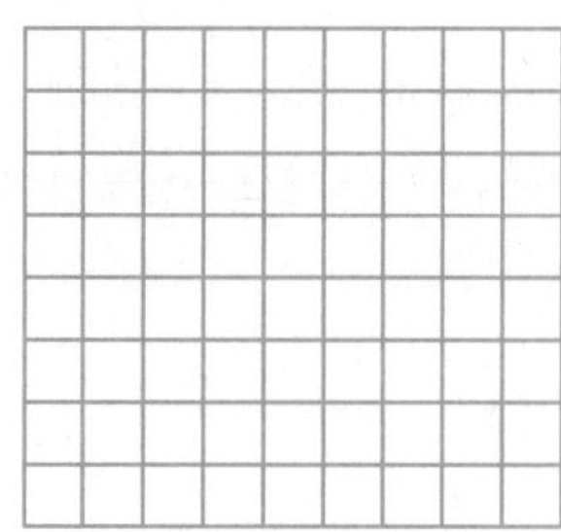

Area = ______________

Perimeter = ______________

Rectangle _____ has the lesser perimeter.

2. **Structure** The dimensions of a rectangle are 4 feet by 10 feet. Which shape has the same area, but a different perimeter?

7 ft

7 ft

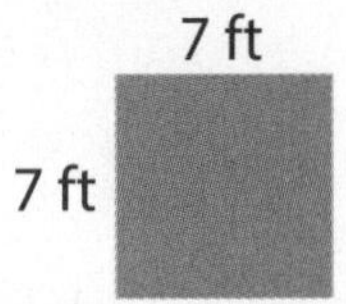

5 ft

8 ft

5 ft

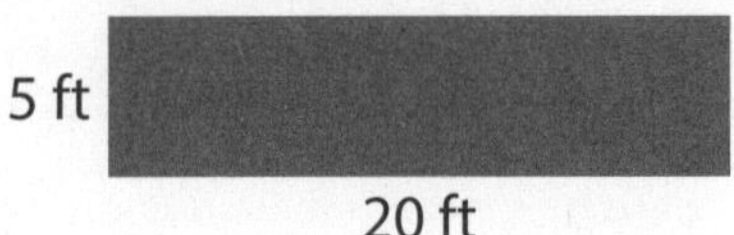

20 ft

---

3. **Construct an Argument** The two fields have the same area. Players run one lap around each field. At which field do the players run farther? Explain.

Field A

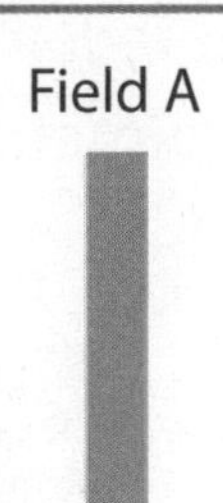

Field B

---

4. **Modeling Real Life** You have 24 square pieces of T-shirt that are each 1 foot long and 1 foot wide. You want to make a rectangular T-shirt quilt with all of the pieces. How long and wide should you make the quilt so it has the least possible perimeter?

---

5. **DIG DEEPER!** You and Descartes each have 40 cobblestone tiles to arrange into a rectangular pathway. Your pathway is shown. Descartes's pathway has a lesser perimeter than yours. Draw one way Descartes could make his pathway.

4 tiles

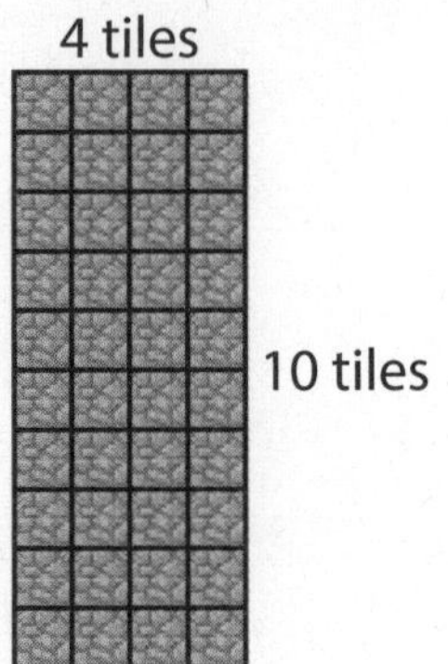

10 tiles

Newton also makes a rectangular pathway with 40 cobblestone tiles. His pathway has a greater perimeter than yours. Draw one way Newton could make his pathway.

Review & Refresh

Identify the number of right angles and pairs of parallel sides.

6. Right angles: _____

Pairs of parallel sides: _____

7. Right angles: _____

Pairs of parallel sides: _____

Name ____________________

Performance Task 15

You and your cousin build a tree house.

1. **Modeling Real Life** The floor of the tree house is in the shape of a quadrilateral with parallel sides that are 4 feet long and 10 feet long. The other 2 sides are equal in length. The perimeter is 24 feet. Sketch the floor and label all of the side lengths.

2. Each rectangular wall of the tree house is 5 feet tall. How many square feet of wood is needed for all of the walls?

3. You cut out a door in the shape of a rectangle with sides that are whole numbers. Its area is 8 square feet. What is the height of the door?

4. You want to paint the floor and walls on the inside of your tree house. The area of the floor is 28 square feet. Each quart of paint covers 100 square feet.

   a. How many quarts of paint do you need to buy?

   b. **Construct an Argument** Do you have enough paint to paint the outside walls of the tree house? Explain.

Perimeter Roll and Conquer

Directions:

1. Players take turns rolling two dice.
2. On your turn, draw a rectangle on the board using the numbers on the dice as the side lengths. Your rectangle cannot cover another rectangle.
3. Write an equation to find the perimeter of the rectangle.
4. If you cannot fit a rectangle on the board, then you lose your turn. Play 10 rounds, if possible.
5. Add all of your rectangles' perimeters together. The player with the greatest sum wins!

Example:

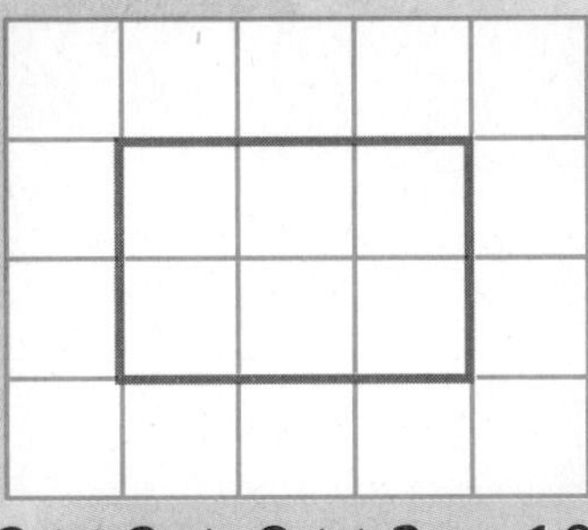

$2 \times 2 + 2 \times 3 = 10$

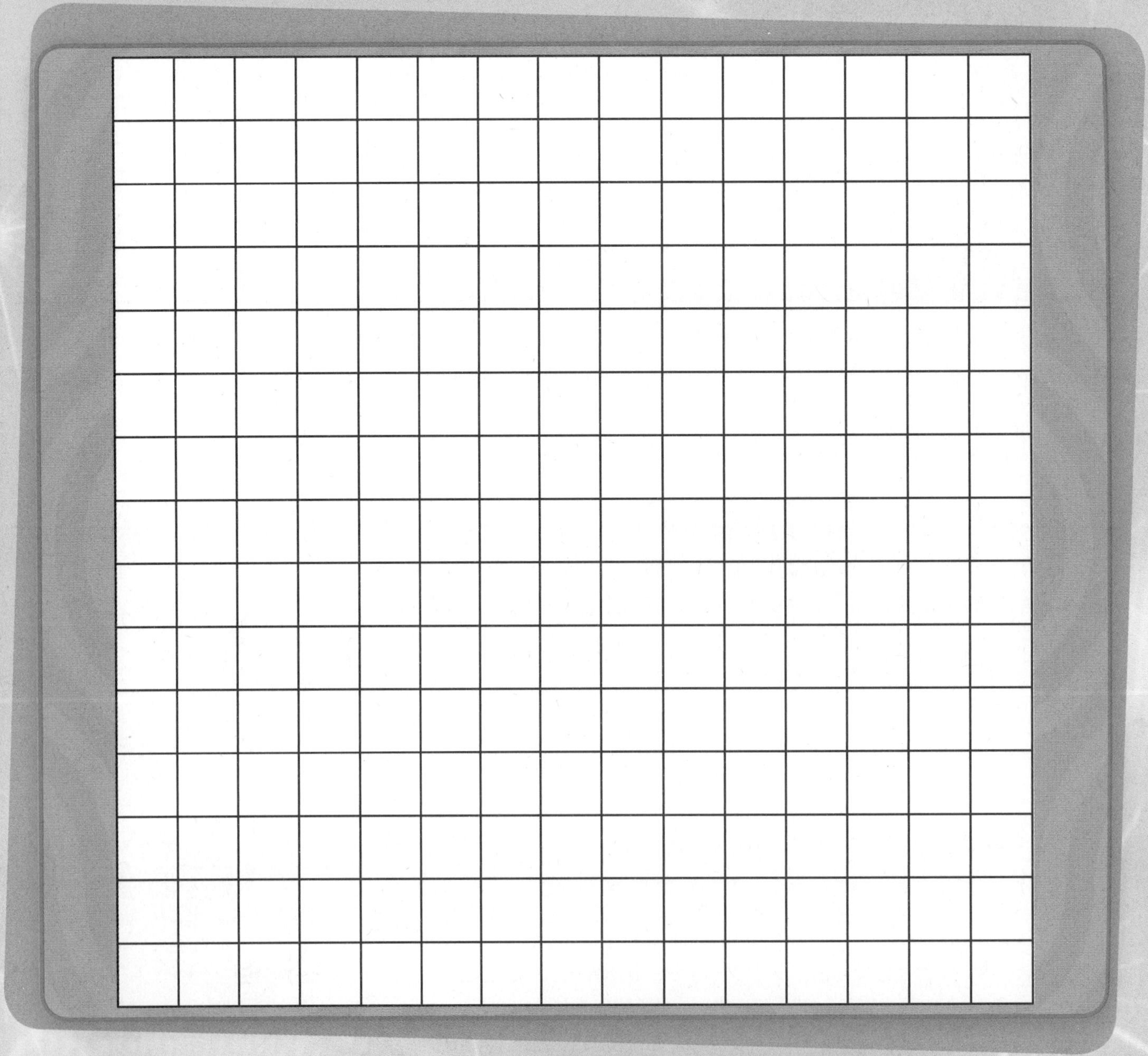

Name ______________________________

Chapter Practice 15

15.1 Understand Perimeter

Find the perimeter of the figure.

1.

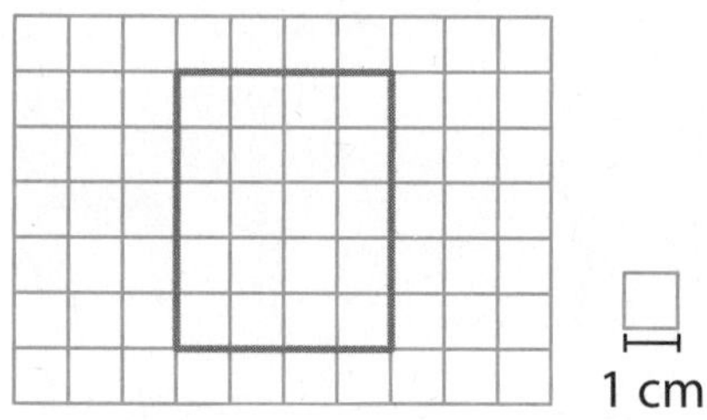

Perimeter = ____________

2.

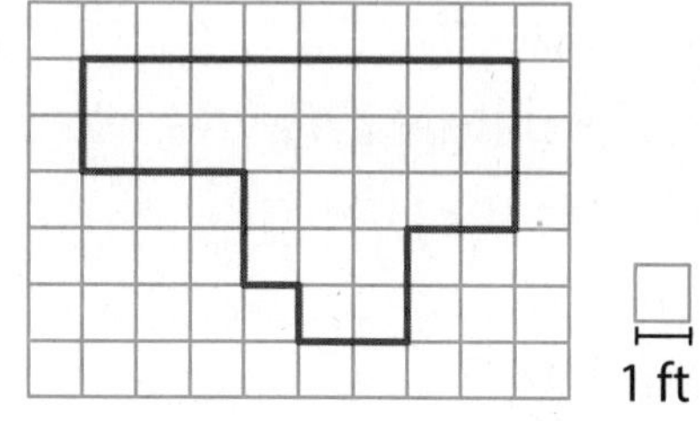

Perimeter = ____________

3. Draw a figure that has a perimeter of 10 inches.

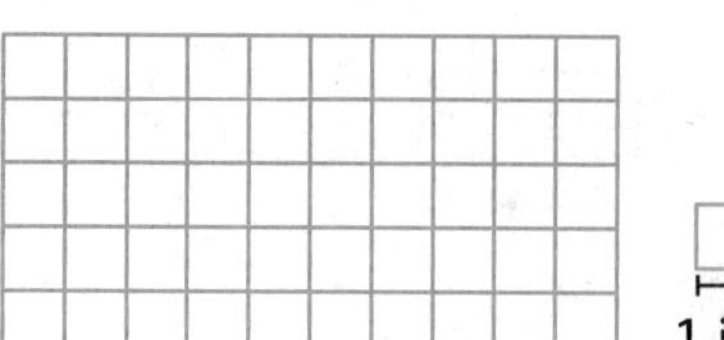

15.2 Find Perimeter of Polygons

Find the perimeter of the polygon.

4.

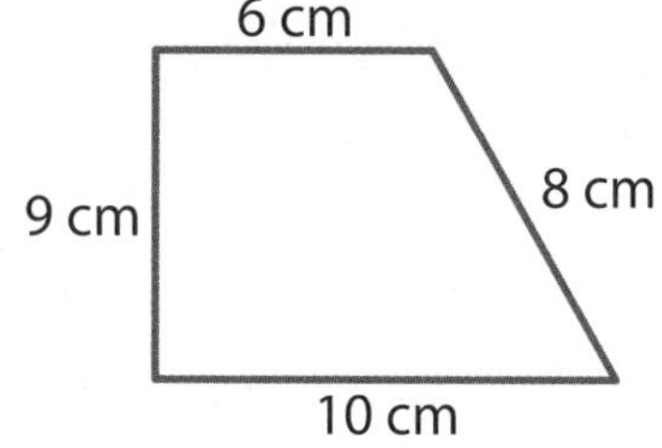

Perimeter = ________

5.

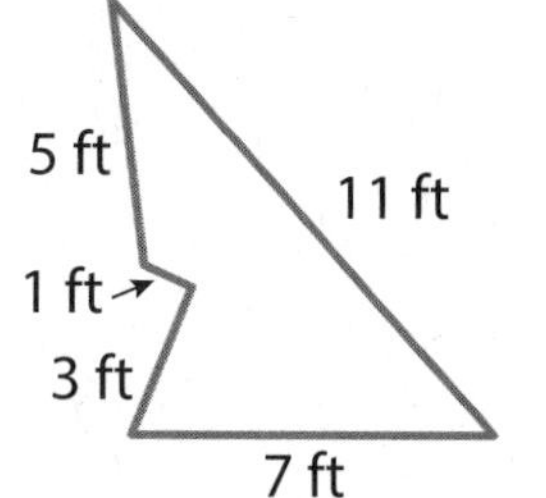

Perimeter = ________

6. Parallelogram

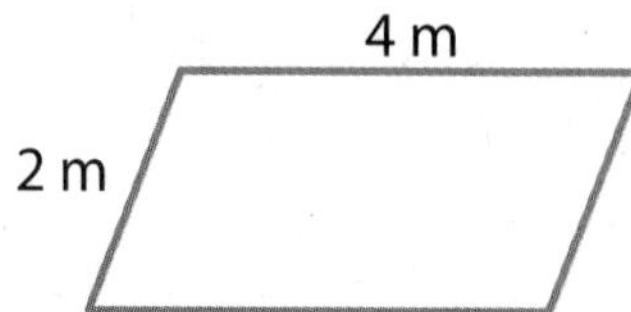

Perimeter = ________

Find the perimeter of the polygon.

7. Rhombus

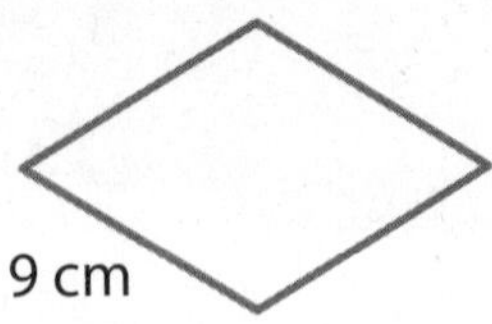

Perimeter = ______

8. Rectangle

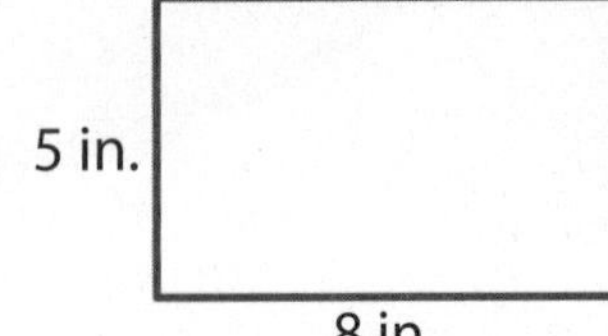

Perimeter = ______

9. Square

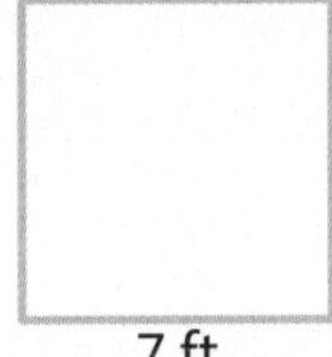

Perimeter = ______

10. MP **Modeling Real Life** You want to put lace around the tops of the two rectangular lampshades. How many centimeters of lace do you need?

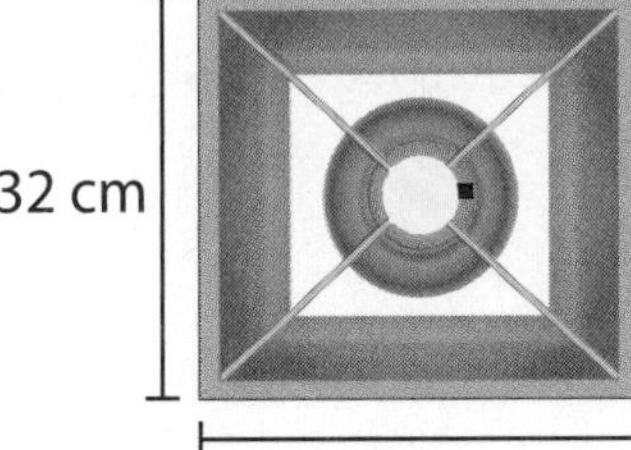

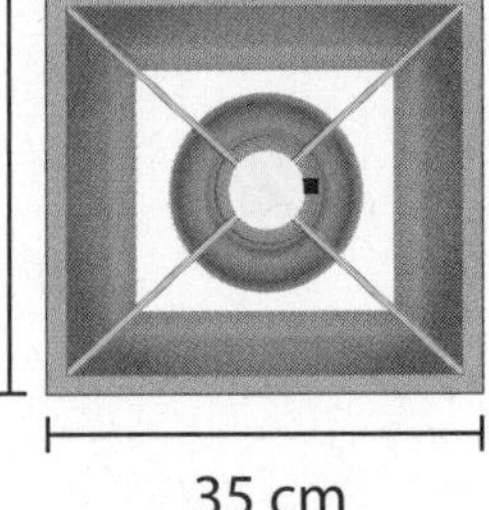

15.3 Find Unknown Side Lengths

Find the unknown side length.

11. Perimeter = 22 feet

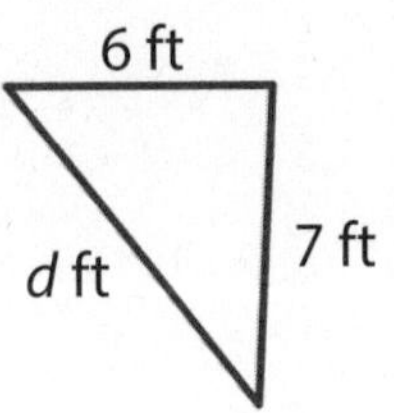

$d =$ ______

12. Perimeter = 31 inches

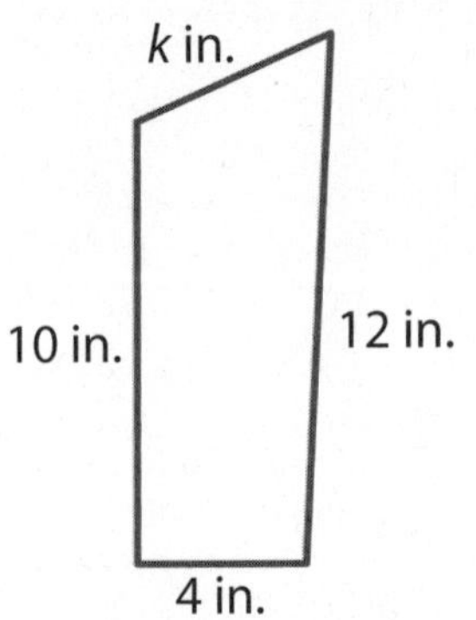

$k =$ ______

13. Perimeter = 34 meters

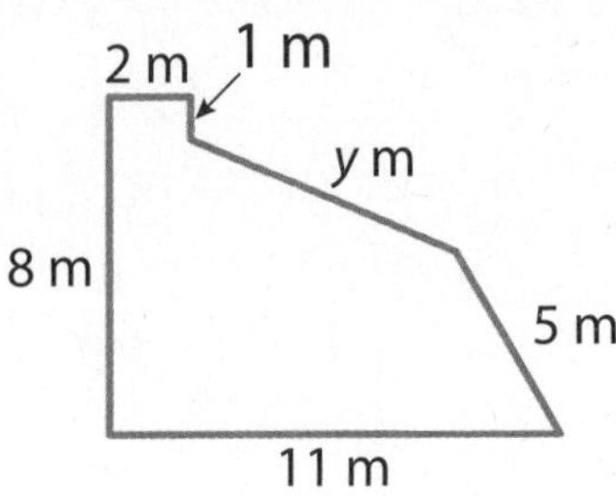

$y =$ ______

Find the unknown side length.

14. Perimeter = 24 feet

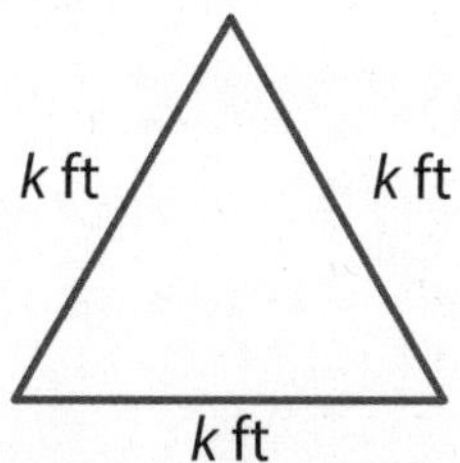

$k =$ ________

15. Perimeter = 16 meters

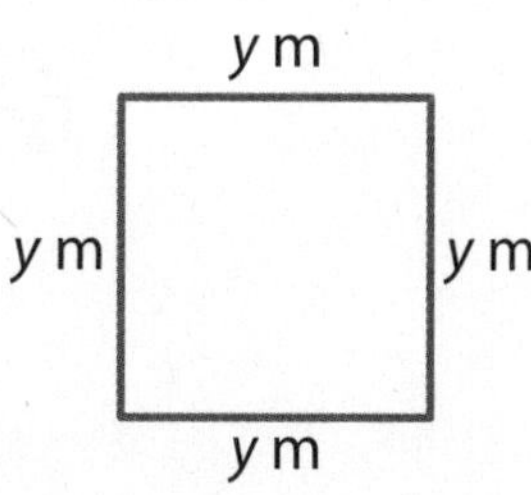

$y =$ ________

16. Perimeter = 30 inches

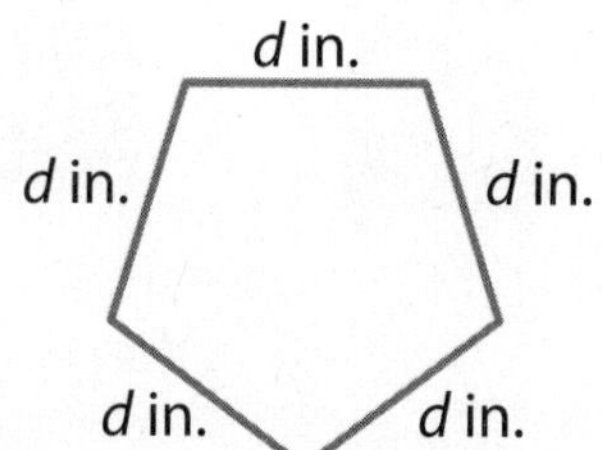

$d =$ ________

17.  **Number Sense** A rectangle has a perimeter of 38 centimeters. The left side length is 10 centimeters. What is the length of the top side?

15.4 Same Perimeter, Different Areas

18. Find the perimeter and area of Rectangle A. Draw a different rectangle that has the same perimeter. Which rectangle has the greater area?

Rectangle A

Perimeter = ________

Area = ________

Rectangle B

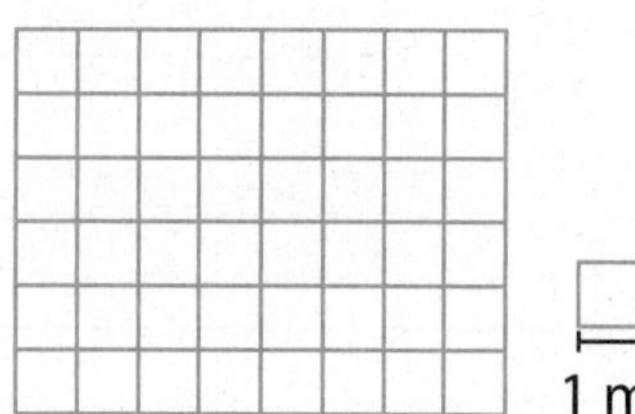

Perimeter = ________

Area = ________

Rectangle ____ has the greater area.

19. MP **Patterns** Each rectangle has the same perimeter. Are the areas increasing or decreasing? Explain.

15.5 Same Area, Different Perimeters

20. Find the area and the perimeter of Rectangle A. Draw a different rectangle that has the same area. Which rectangle has the lesser perimeter?

Rectangle A

Area = ________________

Perimeter = ________________

Rectangle B

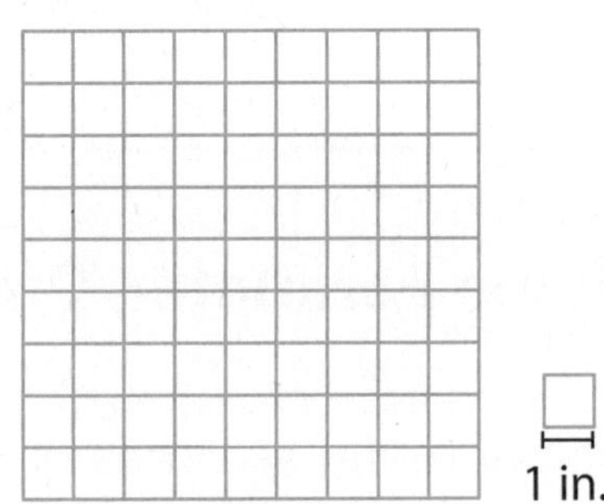

Area = ________________

Perimeter = ________________

Rectangle _____ has the lesser perimeter.

21. MP **Reasoning** The two dirt-bike parks have the same area. Kids ride dirt bikes around the outside of each park. At which park do the kids ride farther? Explain.

Name ___________________________

Cumulative Practice 1–15

1. A mango has a mass that is 369 grams greater than the apple. What is the mass of the mango?

Ⓐ 471 grams
Ⓑ 369 grams
Ⓒ 267 grams
Ⓓ 461 grams

2. Which term describes two of the shapes shown, but *not* all three of the shapes?

Ⓐ polygon
Ⓑ rectangle
Ⓒ square
Ⓓ parallelogram

3. A rectangular note card has an area of 35 square inches. The length of one of its sides is 7 inches. What is the perimeter of the note card?

Ⓐ 5 inches
Ⓑ 24 inches
Ⓒ 84 inches
Ⓓ 12 inches

4. How many minutes are equivalent to 4 hours?

Ⓐ 400 minutes
Ⓑ 240 minutes
Ⓒ 24 minutes
Ⓓ 40 minutes

5. A balloon artist has 108 balloons. He has 72 white balloons, and an equal number of red, blue, green, and purple balloons. How many purple balloons does he have?

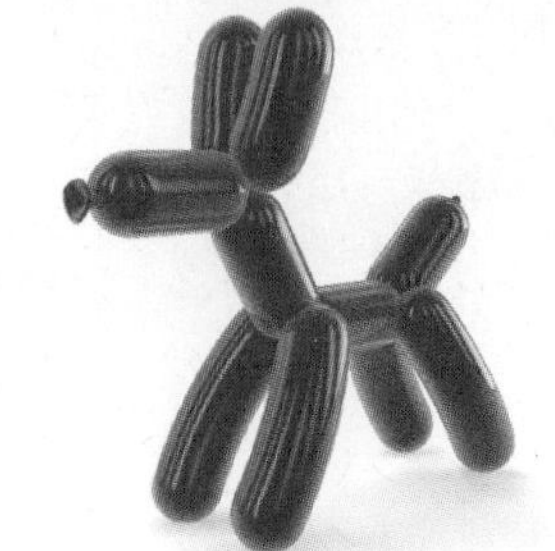

Ⓐ 36 Ⓑ 180 Ⓒ 9 Ⓓ 32

---

6. Which statements about the figures are true?

Square: 6 in.

Rectangle: 4 in., 9 in.

- ☐ The shapes have different perimeters.
- ☐ The shapes have the same areas.
- ☐ The shapes have the same perimeters.
- ☐ The shapes have different areas.

---

7. The graph shows how many students ordered each lunch option.

Lunch Orders	
Grilled chicken	☺ ☺ ☺ ◖
Turkey hot dog	☺ ◖
Peanut butter and jelly sandwich	☺ ☺
Salad bar	☺ ☺ ☺

Each ☺ = 6 students.

Part A How many students ordered lunch?

Part B Choose a lesser value for the key. How will the graph change?

---

8. Find the sum.

$$\begin{array}{r} 354 \\ 297 \\ 156 \\ +\ 128 \\ \hline \end{array}$$

9. What is the perimeter of the figure?

Ⓐ 26 units

Ⓑ 22 units

Ⓒ 20 units

Ⓓ 16 units

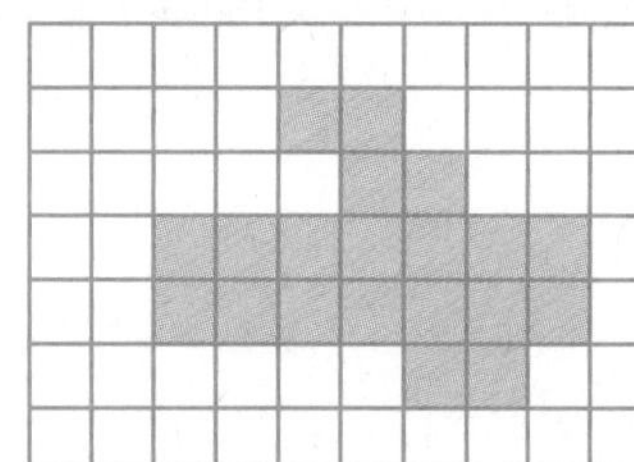

1 unit

---

10. Which bar graph correctly shows the data?

Championship Wins	
Knights	6
Warriors	4
Spartans	3
Wolves	5

Ⓐ

Championship Wins

Team

Knights

Warriors

Spartans

Wolves

0 1 2 3 4

Number of wins

Ⓑ

Championship Wins

Team

Knights

Warriors

Spartans

Wolves

0 2 4 6 8

Number of wins

Ⓒ

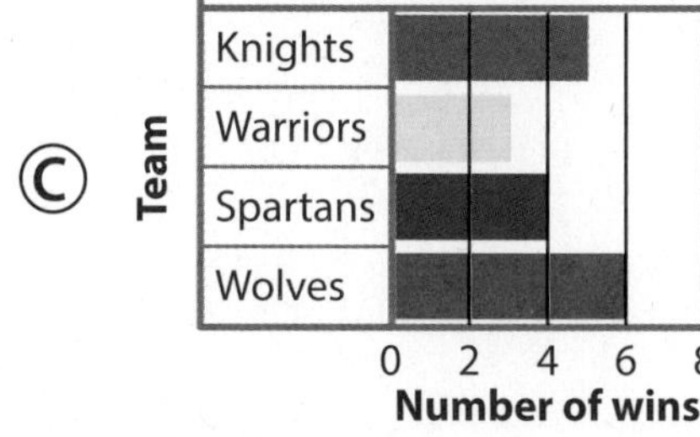

Ⓓ

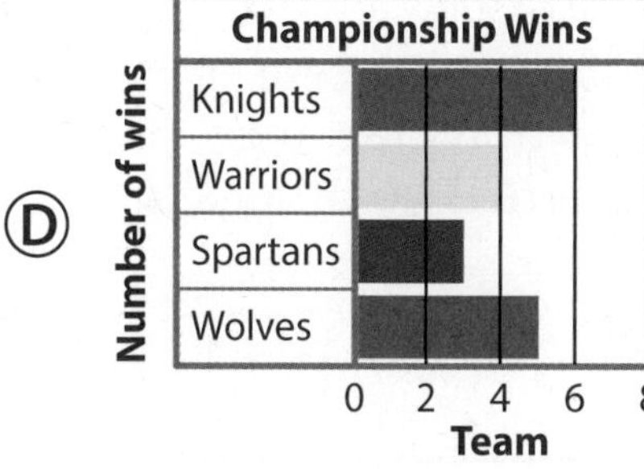

---

11. Which polygons have at least one pair of parallel sides?

☐ 

☐ 

☐ 

☐ 

12. The perimeter of the polygon is 50 yards. What is the missing side length?

Ⓐ 41 yards

Ⓑ 10 yards

Ⓒ 91 yards

Ⓓ 9 yards

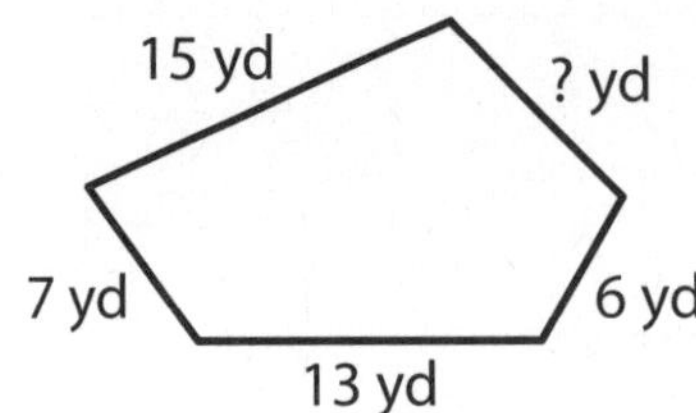

---

13. Which line plot correctly shows the data?

Miami High Temperatures (degrees Fahrenheit)	
Monday	89
Tuesday	92
Wednesday	92
Thursday	92
Friday	93
Saturday	89

Ⓐ **Miami Temperatures**

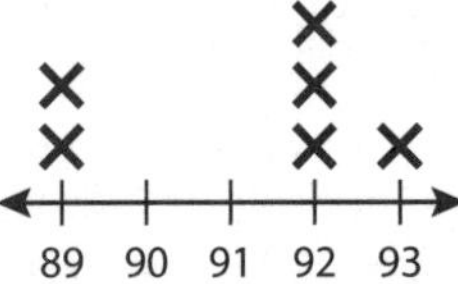

Number of degrees Fahrenheit

Ⓑ **Miami Temperatures**

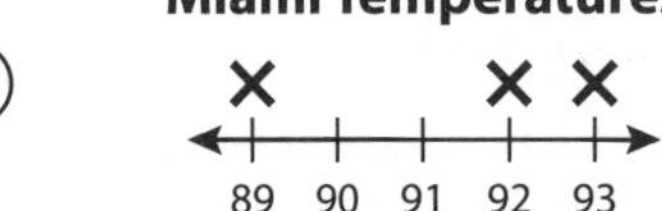

Number of degrees Fahrenheit

Ⓒ **Miami Temperatures**

89 90 91 92 93

Number of degrees Fahrenheit

Ⓓ **Miami Temperatures**

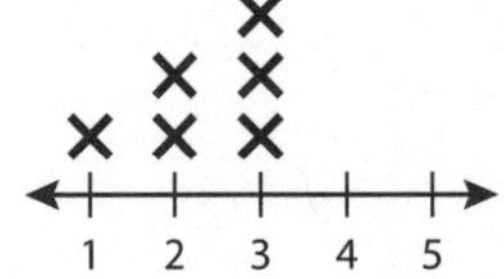

Number of degrees Fahrenheit

---

14. Your friend is asked to draw a quadrilateral with four right angles. She says it can only be a square. Is she correct?

Ⓐ Yes, there is no other shape it can be.

Ⓑ No, it could also be a rectangle.

Ⓒ No, it could also be a hexagon.

Ⓓ No, it could also be a trapezoid.

---

15. Which numbers round to 480 when rounded to the nearest ten?

- ☐ 484
- ☐ 478
- ☐ 472
- ☐ 485
- ☐ 475
- ☐ 489

Name

STEAM Performance Task 1–15

1. **Use Technology** Use the Internet or some other resource to learn more about crested geckos.

   a. Write three interesting facts about geckos.

   b. Geckos need to drink water every day. Is this amount of water measured in *milliliters* or *liters*? Explain.

   c. Geckos can live in a terrarium. Is the capacity of this terrarium measured in *milliliters* or *liters*? Explain.

2. Your class designs a terrarium for a gecko.

   a. The base of the terrarium is a hexagon. Each side of the hexagon is 6 inches long. What is the perimeter of the base?

   b. The terrarium is 20 inches tall. All of the side walls are made of glass. How many square inches of glass is needed for the terrarium?

   c. Another class designs a terrarium with a rectangular base. All of its sides are equal in length. The base has the same perimeter as the base your class designs. What is the perimeter of the base? What is the area?

3. An online store sells crested geckos. The store owner measures the length of each gecko in the store. The results are shown in the table.

The temperature inside a terrarium for a gecko should be between 78 and 82 degrees.

Crested Gecko Lengths (inches)					
$7\frac{1}{2}$	8	$5\frac{1}{4}$	$5\frac{3}{4}$	$6\frac{1}{4}$	$5\frac{1}{2}$
5	$5\frac{1}{4}$	$7\frac{1}{4}$	$6\frac{1}{2}$	7	$6\frac{3}{4}$
$5\frac{1}{2}$	$6\frac{1}{4}$	$5\frac{1}{2}$	6	$5\frac{1}{2}$	$6\frac{1}{2}$
$7\frac{1}{4}$	$6\frac{1}{2}$	5	$5\frac{1}{2}$	$7\frac{1}{2}$	6

MP Maintain Accuracy What strategy did you use to include all values from the table in your line plot?

a. Use the table to complete the line plot.

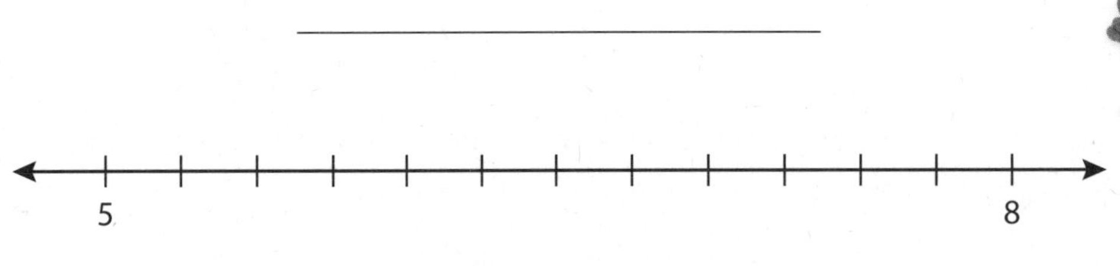

b. How many geckos did the store owner measure?

c. What is the difference in the lengths of the longest gecko and the shortest gecko?

d. How many geckos are shorter than $6\frac{1}{4}$ inches?

e. **MP Structure** The length of a gecko's tail is about 3 inches. How would the line plot change if the store owner measured the length of each gecko without its tail?

Glossary

A

Addition Property of Zero
[propiedad adicional de cero]

The sum of any number and 0 is that number.

$5 + 0 = 5$

$48 + 0 = 48$

$376 + 0 = 376$

---

angle **[ángulo]**

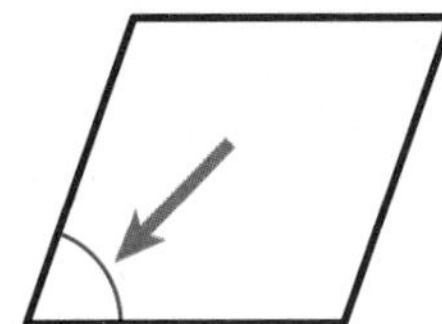

---

area **[área]**

The amount of surface a shape covers

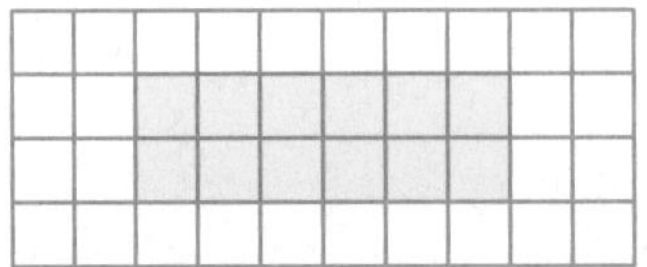

You can measure area by counting the number of unit squares needed to cover a flat surface with no gaps or overlaps.

---

array **[arreglo]**

A group of objects arranged into rows and columns

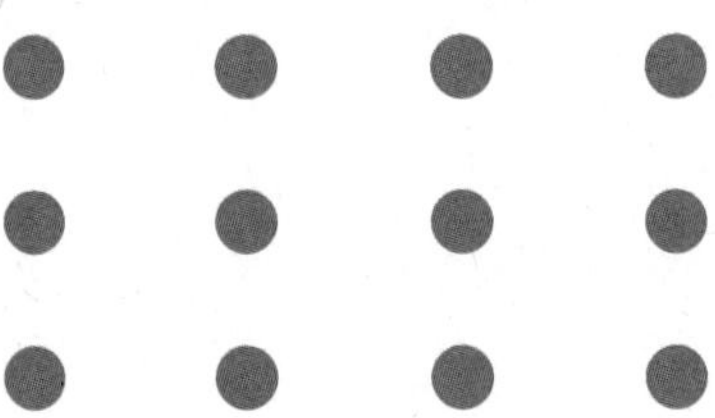

Associative Property of Addition
[propiedad asociativa de la suma]

Changing the grouping of addends does not change the sum.

$7 + (3 + 4) = 14$

$(7 + 3) + 4 = 14$

So, $7 + (3 + 4) = (7 + 3) + 4$.

Associative Property of Multiplication
[propiedad asociativa de la multiplicación]

Changing the grouping of factors does not change the product.

$2 \times (3 \times 4) = 24$

$(2 \times 3) \times 4 = 24$

So, $2 \times (3 \times 4) = (2 \times 3) \times 4$.

B

bar graph **[gráfica de barras]**

A graph that shows data using bars

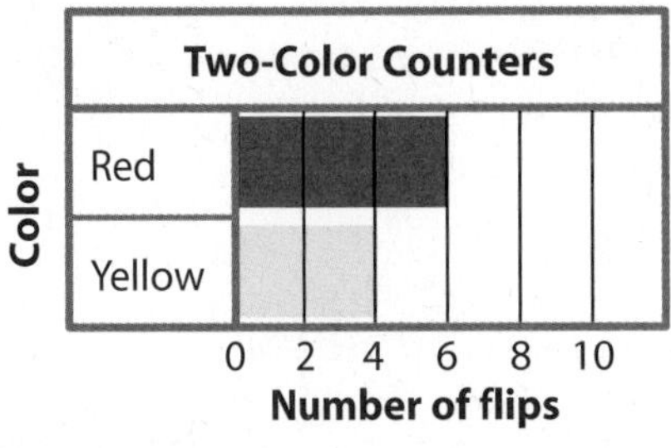

column [columna]

A vertical (up and down) arrangement of objects in an array

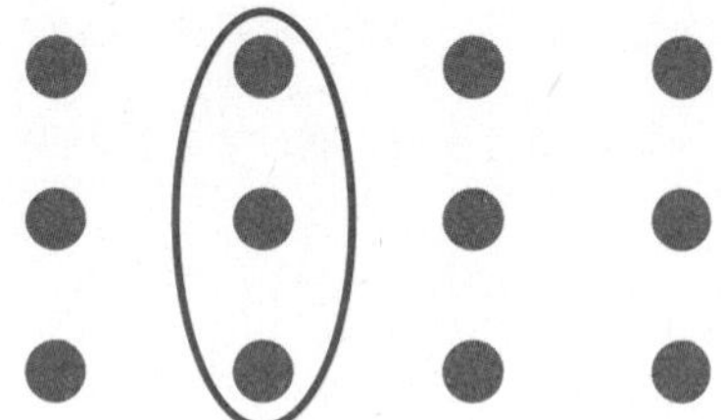

Commutative Property of Addition
[propiedad conmutativa de la suma]

Changing the order of addends does not change the sum.

$6 + 5 = 11$

$5 + 6 = 11$

So, $6 + 5 = 5 + 6$.

Commutative Property of Multiplication
[propiedad conmutativa de la multiplicatión]

Changing the order of factors does not change the product.

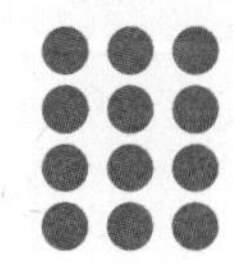

$4 \times 3 = 12$ $3 \times 4 = 12$

So, $4 \times 3 = 3 \times 4$.

compatible numbers
[números compatibles]

Numbers that are easy to add or subtract mentally and are close to the actual numbers

$$\begin{array}{r} 147 \\ +\ 199 \\ \hline \end{array} \longrightarrow \begin{array}{r} 150 \\ +\ 200 \\ \hline \end{array}$$

denominator [denominador]

The part of a fraction that represents how many equal parts are in a whole

$\frac{1}{6} \leftarrow$ denominator

Distributive Property (with addition)
[propiedad distributiva con adición]

$3 \times (5 + 2) = (3 \times 5) + (3 \times 2)$

$(5 + 2) \times 3 = (5 \times 3) + (2 \times 3)$

Distributive Property (with subtraction)
[propiedad distributiva con sustracción]

$3 \times (5 - 2) = (3 \times 5) - (3 \times 2)$

$(5 - 2) \times 3 = (5 \times 3) - (2 \times 3)$

dividend [dividendo]

The number of objects or the amount you want to divide

$$10 \div 2 = 5$$

division [división]

An operation that separates a group of objects into groups of equal size

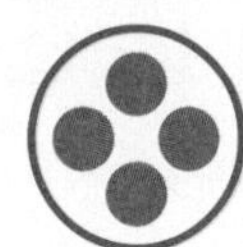 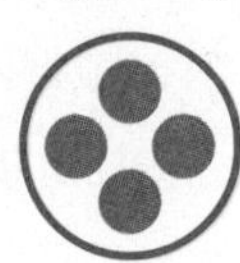 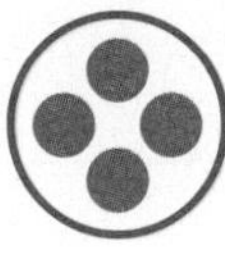

$12 \div 3 = 4$

$12 \div 4 = 3$

division symbol [simbolo de división]

$$12 \div 3 = 4$$

divisor [divisor]

The number by which you divide

$$10 \div 2 = 5$$

E

eighths [octavos]

The whole is divided into eight equal parts, or **eighths**.

elapsed time [tiempo transcurrido]

The amount of time that passes from a starting time to an ending time

The elapsed time is 38 minutes.

equal groups [grupos iguales]

Groups that have the same number of objects

 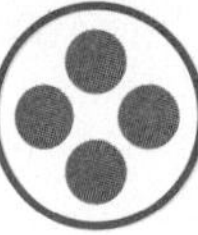 

equation [ecuación]

A mathematical sentence that uses an equal sign, =, to show that two expressions are equal

$4 \times 3 = 12$

$12 \div 4 = 3$

equivalent [equivalente]

Having the same value

$\frac{8}{8} = 1$

$3 = \frac{3}{1}$

$2 = \frac{4}{2} = \frac{6}{3}$

Glossary

equivalent fractions
[fracciones equivalentes]

Two or more fractions that name the same part of a whole

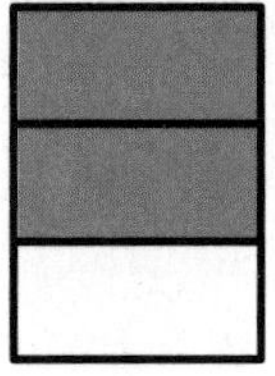
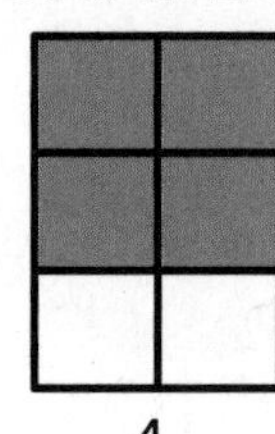

$\frac{2}{3} = \frac{4}{6}$

estimate **[estimar]**

A number that is close to an exact number

18 + 69 = ?

Exact Sum: 87

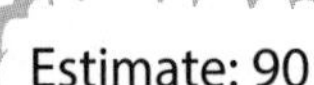

fact family **[familia de hechos]**

A group of related facts that uses the same numbers

$3 \times 2 = 6$

$2 \times 3 = 6$

$6 \div 3 = 2$

$6 \div 2 = 3$

factors **[factor]**

Numbers that are multiplied to get a product

$3 \times 4 = 12$

fraction **[fracción]**

A number that represents part of a whole

$\frac{1}{6}$

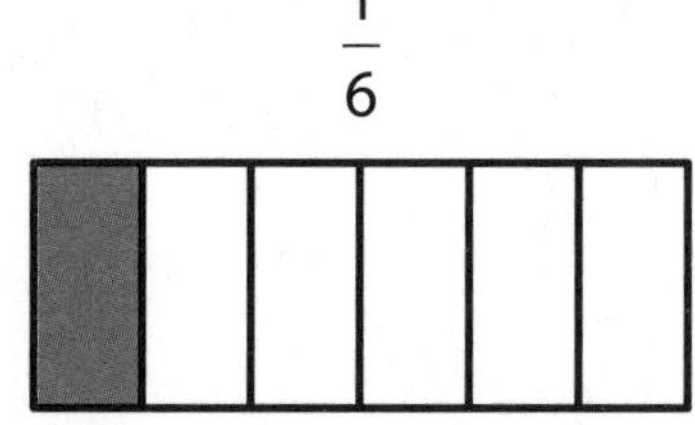

frequency table **[table de frecuencia]**

A table that gives the number of times something occurs

Two-Color Counters	
Red	6
Yellow	4

gram (g) **[gramo]**

The standard metric unit used to measure mass

The mass of a paper clip is about 1 **gram**.

inverse operations
[operaciones inversas]

Operations that "undo" each other, such as addition and subtraction or multiplication and division

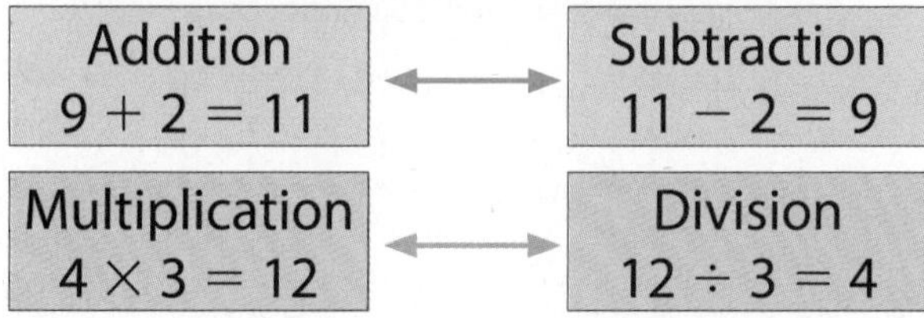

key **[clave]**

The part of a graph that gives the value of one picture or symbol

Two-Color Counters	
Red	○○○
Yellow	○○

Each ○ = 2 flips.

kilogram (kg) **[kilogramo]**

A metric unit used to measure mass

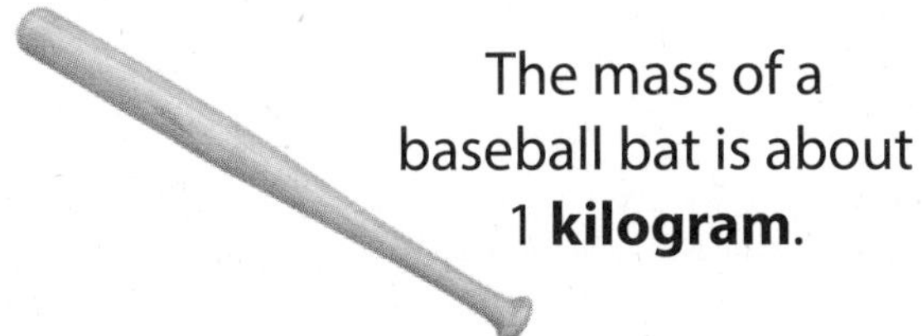

The mass of a baseball bat is about 1 **kilogram**.

line plot **[diagrama líneal]**

A graph that uses marks above a number line to show data values

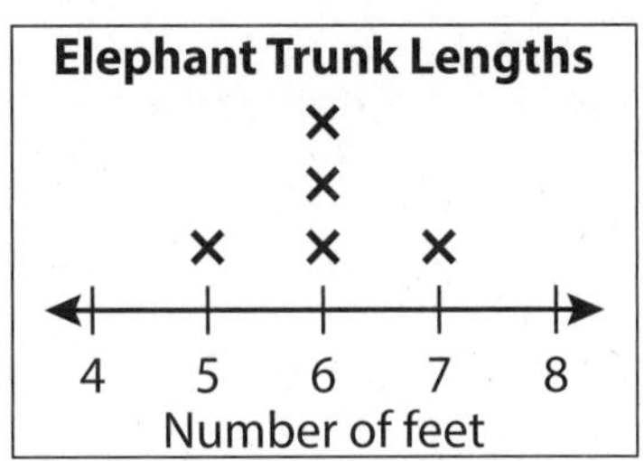

liquid volume **[volumen liquido]**

The amount of liquid in a container

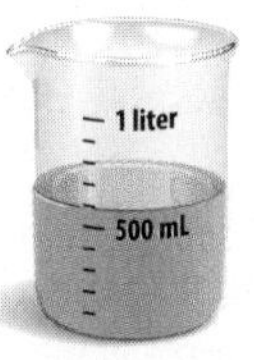

liter (L) **[litro]**

The standard metric unit used to measure liquid volume

There is about 1 **liter** of liquid in the water bottle.

mass **[masa]**

The amount of matter in an object

milliliter (mL) **[mililitro]**

A metric unit used to measure liquid volume

20 drops of liquid from an eyedropper is about 1 **milliliter**.

multiple [múltiplo]

The product of a number and any other counting number

$1 \times 5 = 5$
$2 \times 5 = 10$
$3 \times 5 = 15$
$4 \times 5 = 20$

multiples of 5

multiplication [multiplicación]

An operation that gives the total number of objects when you combine equal groups

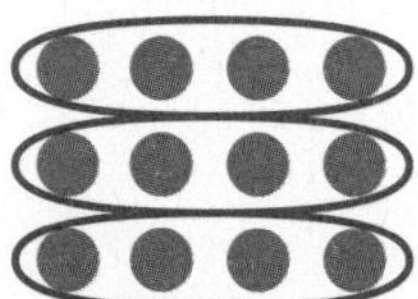

$3 \times 4 = 12$

Multiplication Property of One [propiedad de multiplicación de uno]

The product of any number and 1 is that number.

$10 \times 1 = 10 \quad 1 \times 2 = 2$

Multiplication Property of Zero [propiedad de multiplicación de cero]

The product of any number and 0 is 0.

$5 \times 0 = 0 \quad 0 \times 2 = 0$

multiplication symbol [símbolo de multiplicación]

$3 \times 4 = 12$

numerator [numerador]

The part of a fraction that represents how many equal parts are being counted

$\frac{1}{6}$ ← numerator

parallel sides [lados de paralelos]

Two sides that are always the same distance apart

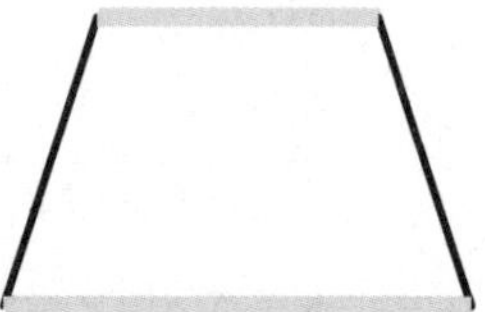

parallelogram [paralelogramo]

A quadrilateral with two pairs of parallel sides

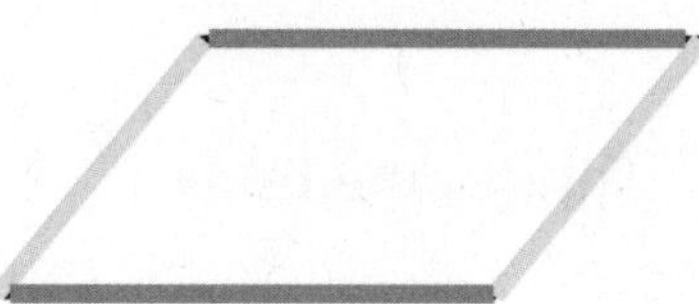

perimeter [perímetro]

The distance around a figure

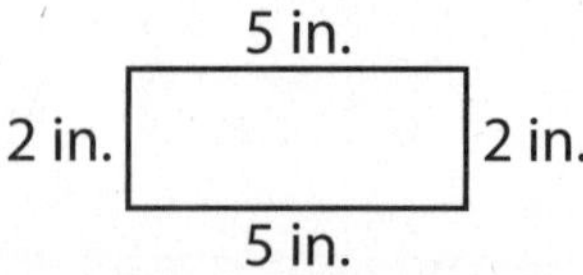

The perimeter of the rectangle is 14 inches.

picture graph [gráfico de imagen]

A graph that shows data using pictures or symbols

Two-Color Counters	
Red	◯◯◯
Yellow	◯◯

Each ◯ = 2 flips.

place value [valor posicional]

The value of the place of a digit in a number

231

↑

The digit 2 has a place value of 100 because it is in the hundreds place.

polygon [polígono]

A closed, two-dimensional shape with three or more sides

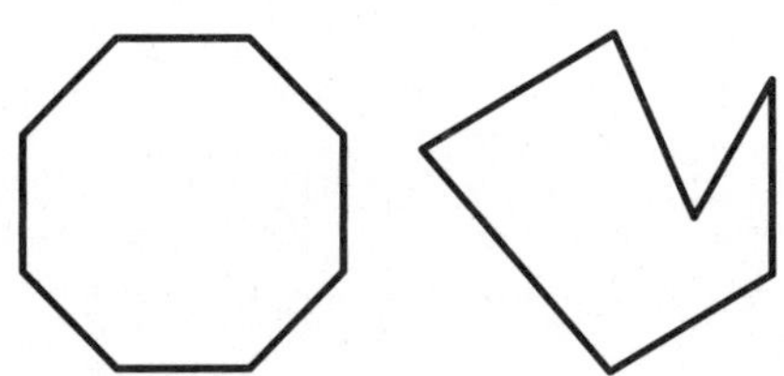

product [producto]

The answer to a multiplication problem

$$3 \times 4 = 12$$

Q

quadrilateral [cuadrilátero]

A polygon with four sides

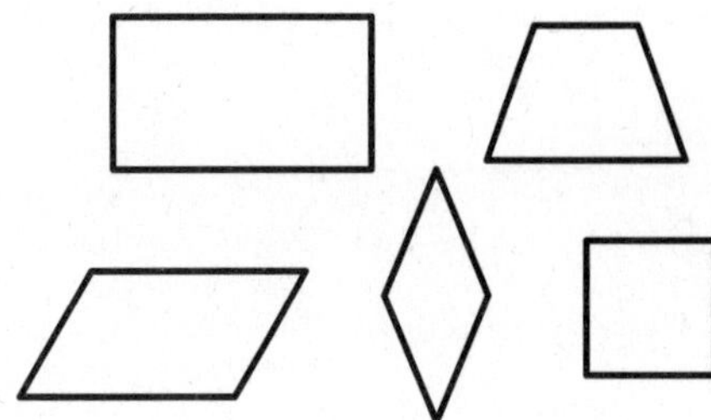

quotient [cociente]

The answer when you divide one number by another number

$$10 \div 2 = 5$$

R

rectangle [rectángulo]

A parallelogram with four right angles

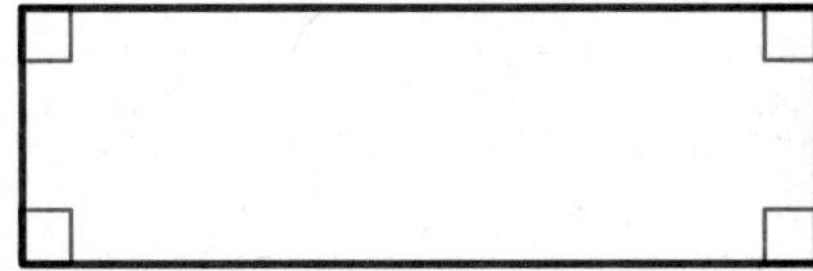

rhombus [rombo]

A parallelogram with four equal sides

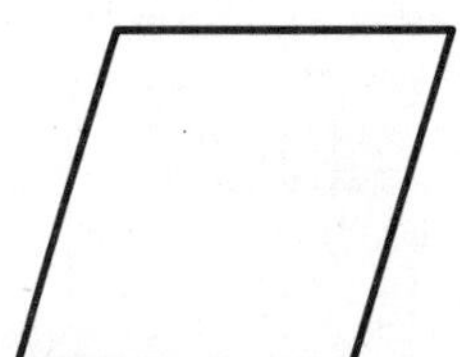

right angle **[ángulo recto]**

An L-shaped angle

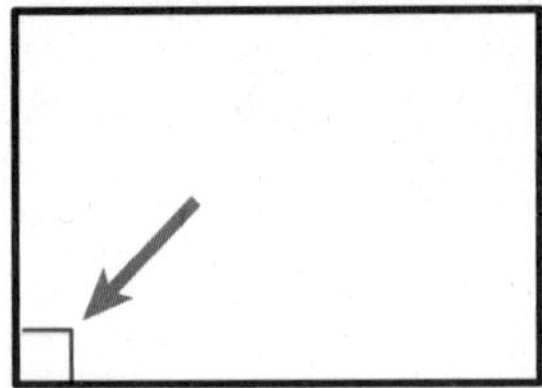

round **[redondear]**

To replace a number with the nearest multiple of ten or hundred

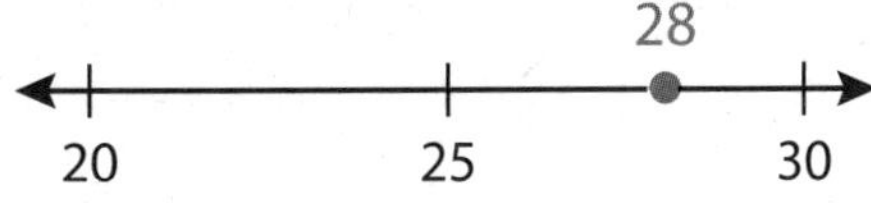

28 **rounded** to the nearest ten is 30.

row **[fila]**

A horizontal (left to right) arrangement of objects in an array

scale **[escala]**

A group of labels that shows the values at equally spaced grid lines

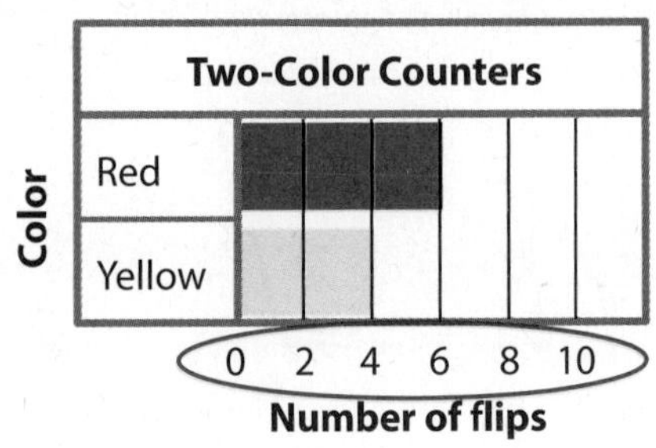

side **[lado]**

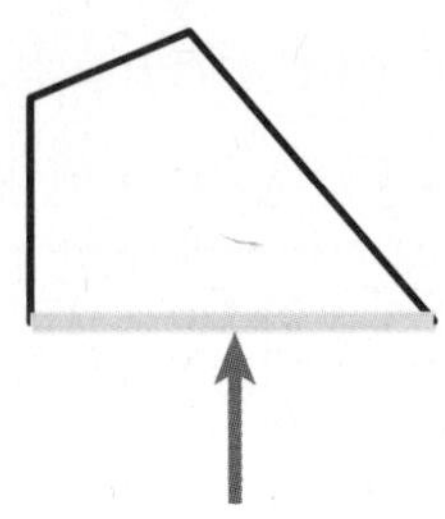

sixths **[sextos]**

The whole is divided into six equal parts, or **sixths**.

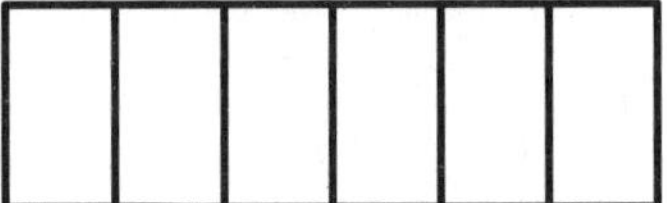

square **[cuadrado]**

A parallelogram with four right angles and four equal sides

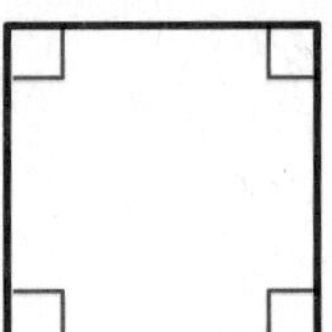

square unit **[unidad cuadrada]**

A unit used to measure area

square centimeter

square meter

square inch

square foot

tape diagram [diagrama de cinta]

A model that shows a whole divided into parts

4	4	4

12

---

time interval [interval de tiempo]

An amount of time

15 minutes

30 minutes

57 minutes

42 minutes

---

trapezoid [trapecio]

A quadrilateral with exactly one pair of parallel sides

unit fraction [fracción unitaria]

Represents one equal part of a whole

The fraction $\frac{1}{6}$ is a unit fraction.

unit square [cuadrado de una unidad]

A square with sides that are each 1 unit long

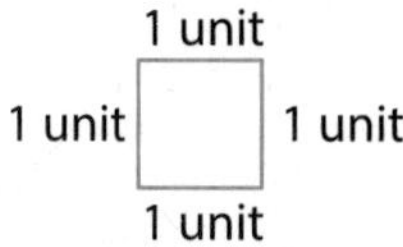

vertex [vértice]

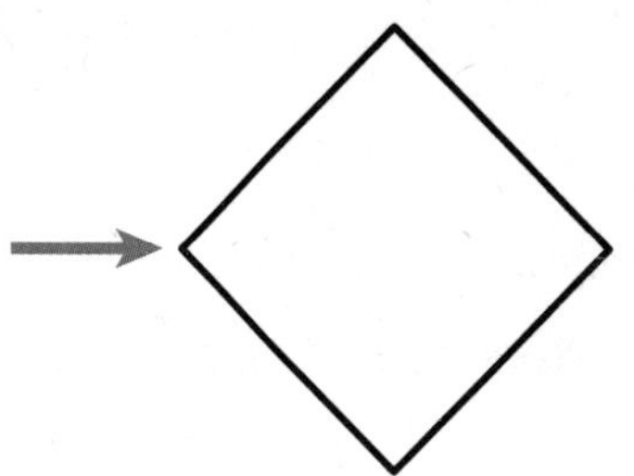

whole [entero]

All of the parts of one shape or group

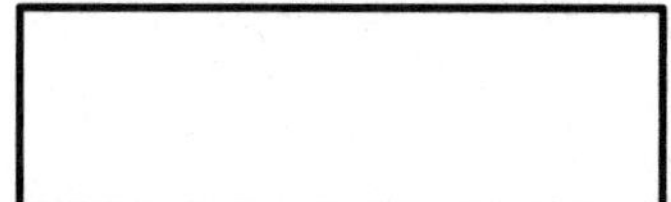

---

whole numbers [números entero]

The numbers 0, 1, 2, 3, and so on

Index

Index

E

F

G

N

O

Index

T

Reference Sheet

Symbols

× multiply ÷ divide = equals > greater than < less than

Equal Shares

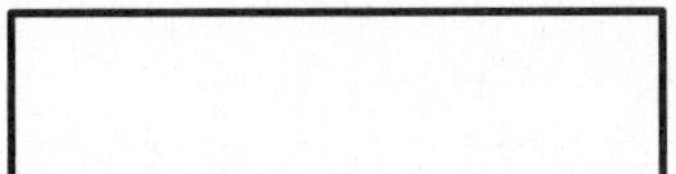

A **whole** is all of the parts of one shape or group.

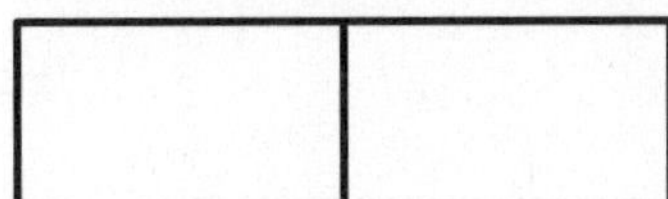

2 equal parts or **halves**

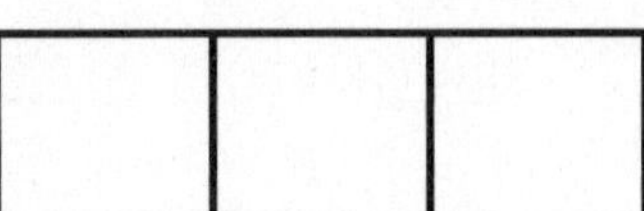

3 equal parts or **thirds**

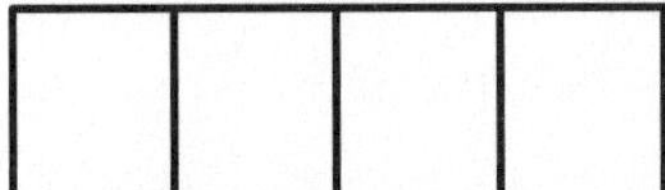

4 equal parts or **fourths**

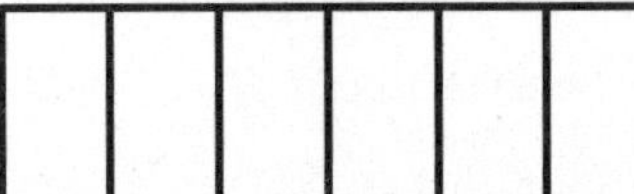

6 equal parts or **sixths**

8 equal parts or **eighths**

Fractions

$\frac{1}{4}$ ← **numerator** (1), ← **denominator** (4)

A **fraction** is a number that represents part of a whole.

Time

1 minute (min) = 60 seconds (sec)

1 hour (h) = 60 minutes

1 day (d) = 24 hours

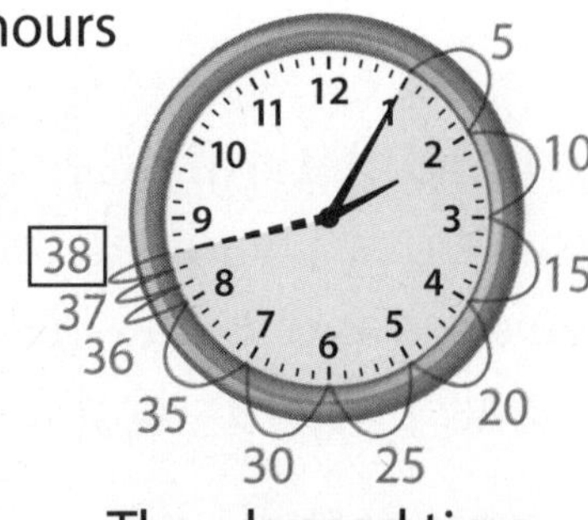

The elapsed time is 38 minutes.

Liquid Volume

1 liter (L) = 1,000 milliliters (mL)

Mass

1 kilogram (kg) = 1,000 grams (g)

Reference Sheet

Length

Half Inch

$\frac{0}{2}$ $\frac{1}{2}$ $\frac{2}{2}$ $\frac{3}{2}$ $\frac{4}{2}$

0 1 2
Inches

Quarter Inch

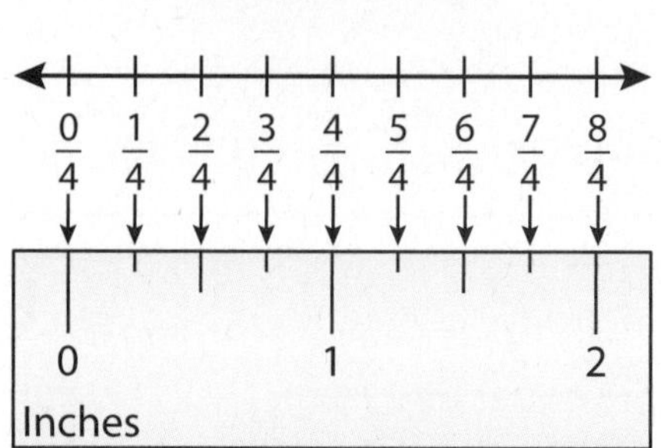

Area and Perimeter

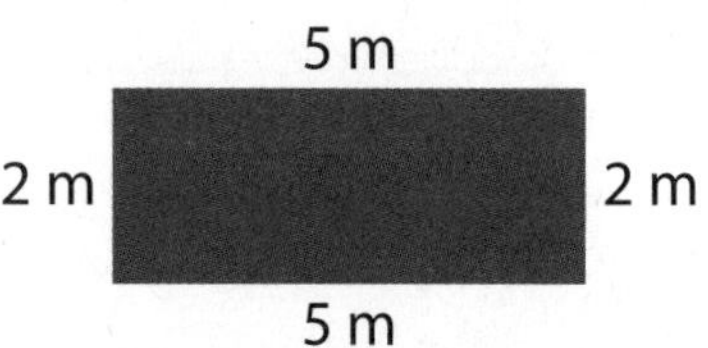

Area $= 5 \times 2 = 10$ square meters

Perimeter $= 2 + 5 + 2 + 5 = 14$ meters

or

Perimeter $= 2 \times 2 + 2 \times 5 = 14$ meters

Shapes

A **polygon** is a closed two-dimensional shape with three or more sides.

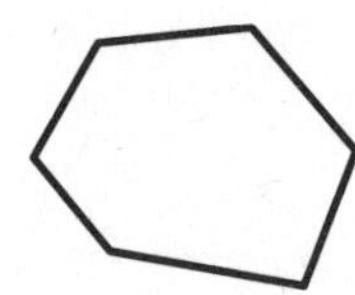

A **quadrilateral** is a polygon with four sides. Quadrilaterals have four vertices and four angles. They can have parallel sides and right angles.

Trapezoid

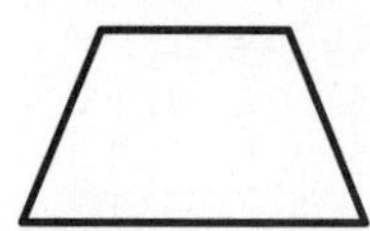

exactly 1 pair of parallel sides

Parallelogram

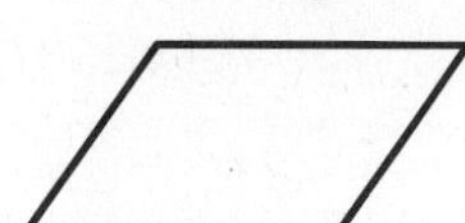

2 pairs of parallel sides

Rectangle

2 pairs of parallel sides
4 right angles

Rhombus

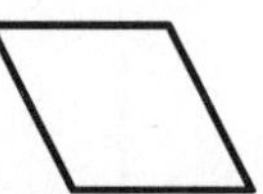

2 pairs of parallel sides
4 equal sides

Square

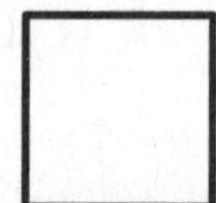

2 pairs of parallel sides
4 equal sides
4 right angles

Credits

Chapter 1

0 AlisonCohenRosa/iStock/Getty Images Plus; **5** Rawpixel/iStock/Getty Images Plus, Floortje/iStock/Getty Images Plus; **6** *right* MikeBraune/Shutterstock.com; *left* Anna Marynenko/Shutterstock.com; **8** hatman12/iStock/Getty Images Plus; **12** GlobalP/iStock/Getty Images Plus; **14** robynmac/iStock/Getty Images Plus; **17** PashaIgnato/iStock/Getty Images Plus; **18** Volosina/iStock/Getty Images Plus; **20** Mark Kostich/iStock/Getty Images Plus; **24** *top* DNY59/E+/Getty Images; *bottom* Alla Maistrenko/Shutterstock.com; **26** Captainflash/E+/Getty Images; **30** efilippou/E+/Getty Images; **32** Anettphoto/Shutterstock.com; **36** bucky_za/E+/Getty Images; **38** traveler1116/iStock/Getty Images Plus; **42** *top* choness/iStock/Getty Images Plus; *bottom* WesAbrams/iStock/Getty Images Plus; **45** *top* joakimbkk/iStock/Getty Images Plus; *bottom* GlobalP/iStock/Getty Images Plus

Chapter 2

51 FatCamera/iStock/Getty Images Plus; **56** *top* ventdusud/iStock/Getty Images; *bottom* Africa Studio/Shutterstock.com; **58** Ivantsov/iStock/Getty Images Plus; **62** *top* Noam Armonn/Shutterstock.com; *bottom* ThamKC/iStock/Getty Images Plus; **64** *top* spxChrome/iStock/Getty Images Plus; *bottom* urbancow/E+/Getty Images; **68** *top* drbueller/iStock/Getty Images Plus; *bottom* scanrail/iStock/Getty Images Plus; **70** 3dalia/iStock/Getty Images Plus; **74** *top* petrovv/iStock/Getty Images Plus; Halfpoint/Shutterstock.com; *bottom* SerrNovik/iStock/Getty Images; **76** Pavel Vakhrushev/Shutterstock.com; **80** ©iStockphoto.comNicolas McComber; **83** Floortje/E+/Getty Images; **84** JenniferPhotographyImaging/E+/Getty Images; **85** *top* farakos/iStock/Getty Images Plus; *bottom* CQYoung/iStock/Getty Images Plus; **86** design56/iStock/Getty Images Plus; **87** timurock/iStock/Getty Images Plus, Andrea Izzotti/iStock/Getty Images Plus; **88** ideabug/Getty Images Plus/iStock/Getty Images Plus; **89** *top* sdominick/iStock/Getty Images Plus; *bottom* MichaelJay/iStock/Getty Images Plus

Chapter 3

93 FotografiaBasica/E+/Getty Images; **98** *top* JackF/iStock/Getty Image Plus; *bottom* SafakOguz/iStock/Getty Images Plus; **100** *top* stockbyte/stockbyte/Getty Images; *bottom* iSashkinw/iStock/Getty Images Plus; **110** *top* t_kimura/E+/Getty Images; *bottom* FotoZlaja/iStock/Getty Images Plus; **112** Sannie32/iStock/Getty Images Plus; **116** *right* Lera-Art/iStock/Getty Images Plus; Pattie Calfy/iStock/Getty Images Plus; *left* Floortje/E+/Getty Images; **118** *left* pixhook/iStock/Getty Images Plus; *right* Oktay Ortakcioglu/E+/Getty Images; **122** © Glenda Powers/Dreamstime.com; **124** cchones/iStock/Getty Images Plus; **127** EHStock/iStock /Getty Images Plus; **128** *top* scanrail/iStock/Getty Images Plus; *bottom* Bet_Noire/iStock/Getty Images Plus; **130** digihelion/E+/Getty Images; **134** khongkotkong/Shutterstock.com; **136** anna1311/iStock/Getty Images Plus; **139** DigitalVues/Alamy Stock Photo; **140** Jiri Vaclavek/Shutterstock.com; **142** *top* blackred/iStock/Getty Images Plus; *bottom* duckycards/E+/Getty Images; **143** Andrey_Popov/Shutterstock.com; **144** TheCrimsonMonkey/iStock/Getty Images Plus; **145** *left* leezsnow/E+/Getty Images; *right* klikk/iStock/Getty Images Plus; **146** squirrel77/iStock/Getty Images Plus; **147** mustafaU/iStock/Getty Images Plus; **148** photo5963/iStock/Getty Images Plus; **149** *left* George_Cislariu/iStock/Getty Images Plus; *right* Dokmaihaeng/iStock/Getty Images Plus; **152** 4kodiak/iStock/Getty Images Plus; **153** *top* ISMODE/iStock/Getty Images Plus; *bottom* nikkytok/iStock/Getty Images Plus; **154** *right* Dole08/iStock/Getty Images Plus; *left* pavlen/iStock/Getty Images Plus

Chapter 4

155 uschools/E+/Getty Images; **160** *right* artcyclone/DigitalVision Vectors/Getty Images; *left* Paul Orr/Shutterstock.com; **162** Garsya/iStock/Getty Images Plus, fotyma/iStock/Getty Images Plus; **166** Professor25/iStock/Getty Images Plus, tashka2000/iStock/Getty Images Plus; **171** margouillatphotos/iStock/Getty Images Plus; **174** Saravn/iStock/Getty Images Plus; **178** *right* XiXinXing/iStock/Getty Images Plus; *left* robynmac/iStock/Getty Images Plus; **180** Neustockimages/E+/Getty Images; **184** jedsadabodin/iStock/Getty Images Plus; **186** Zeljko Bozic/Hemera/Getty Images; **190** BRULOVE/iStock/Getty Images Plus; **195** xxmmxx/E+/Getty Images; **196** targovcom/iStock/Getty Images Plus; **198** Xtremest/iStock/Getty Images Plus; **201** DNY59/E+/Getty Images; **202** *right* DNY59/iStock/Getty Images Plus; *left* Buriy/iStock/Getty Images Plus; **204** eldadcarin/iStock/Getty Images Plus; **205** NatUlrich/Shutterstock.com; **207** *top* trentemoller/Shutterstock.com; *bottom right* Creativeye99/iStock/Getty Images Plus; *bottom left* Andris Tkacenko/Shutterstock.com; **208** *top* Photograpther/iStock/Getty Images Plus; *bottom* alfocome/Shutterstock.com; **210** efilippou/E+/Getty Images; **211** *left* mrhighsky/iStock/Getty Images Plus; *right* Digital Vision/Digital Vision/Getty Images; **212** *top* lilu330/iStock/Getty Images Plus; kbeis/DigitalVision Vectors/Getty Images; *bottom* alex-mit/iStock/Getty Images Plus; **215** cvm/Shutterstock.com; **216** BasSlabbers/iStock Unreleased/Getty Images; **218** pagadesign/E+/Getty Images; **220** ©iStockphoto.com/Santino Ambrogio; **222** *top* Viorika/iStock/Getty Images Plus; *bottom* Creativ/iStock/Getty Images Plus

Chapter 5

223 Peter Weber/Shutterstock.com; **228** Antonel/iStock/Getty Images Plus; **234** laurent/E+/Getty Images; **236** *left* scanrail/iStock/Getty Images Plus; *right* egal/iStock/Getty Images Plus; **240** MentalArt/iStock/Getty Images Plus; **243** Jasmina81/iStock/Getty Images Plus; **245** ChrisGorgio/iStock/Getty Images Plus; **246** PhotoMelon/iStock/Getty Images Plus; **247** hatman12/iStock/Getty Images Plus; **248** bankrx/iStock/Getty Images Plus; **249** Andrey_Popov/Shutterstock.com; **252** Ljupco/iStock/Getty Images Plus

Chapter 6

253 piskunowiczp/iStock/Getty Images Plus; **263** Antagain/iStock/Getty Images Plus; **264** Valengilda/iStock/Getty Images Plus; **270** *top* NASA/Gabriel Fiset; *bottom* Rodrusoleg/iStock/Getty Images Plus; **272** bluecinema/iStock/Getty Images Plus; **278** serezniy/iStock/Getty Images Plus; **284** Spiderplay/E+/Getty Images; **286** 3d_kot/iStock/Getty Images Plus; **288** Andrea Izzotti/iStock/Getty Images Plus

Chapter 7

289 TERADAT SANTIVIVUT/E+/Getty Images; **300** tibor5/E+/Getty Images; **302** *center* Antonel/iStock/Getty Images Plus, Rodrusoleg/iStock/Getty Images Plus; ; *bottom* Hemera Technologies/PhotoObjects.net/Getty Images Plus; **318** ChrisGorgio/iStock/Getty Images Plus, vitacopS/iStock/Getty Images Plus; **320** adempercem/iStock/Getty Images Plus; **321** *right* LongHa2006/E+/Getty Images; *left* narvikk/iStock/Getty Images Plus; **324** *top* grimgram/iStock/Getty Images Plus; *bottom* DrPAS/iStock/Getty Images Plus

Chapter 8

325 Jupiterimages/BananaStock/Getty Images; **330** Olivier Le Queinec/Shutterstock.com; **335** Memitina/iStock/Getty Images Plus; **336** *right* zoom-zoom/iStock/Getty Images Plus; *left* WestLight/iStock/Getty Images Plus; **338** Wavebreakmedia/iStock/Getty Images Plus; **342** *top left* Okea/iStock/Getty Images Plus; *top right* hudiemm/E+/Getty Images; *Exercise 17 left* ZargonDesign/E+/Getty Images; *Exercise 17 center* pioneer111/iStock/Getty Images Plus; *Exercise 17 right* siraanamwong/iStock/Getty Images Plus; **344** *left* anilakkus/iStock/Getty Images Plus; *center* firstpentuer/iStock/Getty Images Plus; *right* Vereshchagin Dmitry/Shutterstock.com; **347** KarenMower/E+/Getty Images; **348** *top left* zokru/iStock/Getty Images Plus; *top right* GlobalP/iStock/Getty Images Plus; *bottom* Arsgera/iStock/Getty Images Plus; **350** joey333/iStock/Getty Images Plus; **354** AJ Adelmari/iStock/Getty Images Plus; **360** gualtiero boffi/Shutterstock.com; **362** KVBPhotos/iStock/Getty Images Plus; **366** olliven/Shutterstock.com; **368** GlobalP/iStock/Getty Images Plus; **371** Nerthuz/iStock/Getty Images Plus; **372** *top left* Quarta_/iStock/Getty Images Plus; *top right* cmannphoto/iStock/Getty Images Plus; *Exercise 18 left* gielmichal/iStock/Getty Images Plus; *Exercise 18 center* pagadesign/E+/Getty Images; **374** *left* esunghee/iStock/Getty Images Plus; *center* wabeno/iStock/Getty Images Plus, brickrena/iStock/Getty Images Plus, vasilypetkov/iStock/Getty Images Plus; *right* cherezoff/iStock/Getty Images Plus; **377** kyoshino/iStock/Getty Images Plus; **378** scanrail/iStock/Getty Images Plus; **380** kreinick/iStock/Getty Images Plus; **384** andrea crisante/Shutterstock.com; **393** *right* fergregory/iStock/Getty Images Plus; *left* paulaphoto/iStock/Getty Images Plus; **396** ChrisGorgio/iStock/Getty Images Plus; **398** RichLegg/E+/Getty Images; **399** tiler84/iStock/Getty Images Plus; **402** ma-k/E+/Getty Images; **403** Africa Studio/Shutterstock.com; **404** SolStock/iStock/Getty Images Plus

Chapter 9

405 WHL/Blend Images/Getty Images; **410** Kadmy/iStock/Getty Images Plus; **412** *Exercise 5* aguirre_mar/iStock/Getty Images Plus; *Exercise 6* Elena Masiutkina/Shutterstock.com; **416** *top* D3Damon/iStock/Getty Images Plus; *bottom* Lisses/Shutterstock.com; **418** luismmolina/E+/Getty Images; **422** *top* Floortje/E+/Getty Images; *bottom* DmitriyKazitsyn/iStock/Getty Images Plus; **427** *left* Photology1971/iStock/Getty Images Plus; *right* Mr. Klein/Shutterstock.com; **428** *right* Givaga/iStock/Getty Images Plus; *left* scanrail/iStock/Getty Images Plus; **429** DNY59/E+/Getty Images; **430** GlobalStock/E+/Getty Images; **432** mbongorus/iStock/Getty Images Plus; **433** *left* Blackzheep/iStock/Getty Images Plus; *right* Rawpixel/iStock/Getty Images Plus; **434** mayakova/iStock/Getty Images Plus; **436** anna1311/iStock/Getty Images Plus; **437** nkbimages/iStock Unreleased/Getty Images Plus; **440** evemilla/E+/Getty Images; **442** *left* winnieapple/iStock/Getty Images Plus; *right* L Barnwell/Shutterstock.com

Chapter 10

443 LightFieldStudios/iStock/Getty Images Plus; **448** *top* Daddybit/iStock/Getty Images Plus; *bottom* iuliia_n/iStock/Getty Images Plus; **450** repinanatoly/iStock/Getty Images Plus; **456** *Exercise 9* Jupiterimages/Stockbyte/Getty Images; *Exercise 10* EM Arts/Shutterstock.com, BWFolsom/iStock/Getty Images Plus, Roman Samokhin/iStock/Getty Images Plus, AlexStar/iStock/Getty Images Plus; **460** barbol88/iStock/Getty Images Plus; **466** *right* Rodrusoleg/iStock/Getty Images Plus; *left* Rfarrarons/iStock Editorial/Getty Images Plus; **468** andrea crisante/Shutterstock.com; **472** keko-ka/iStock/Getty Images Plus; **474** keko-ka/iStock/Getty Images Plus

Chapter 11

481 DGLimages/iStock/Getty Images Plus; **486** yvdavyd/iStock/Getty Images Plus; **488** bmcent1/iStock/Getty Images Plus; **492** VladislavStarozhilov/iStock/Getty Images Plus; **494** 4x6/iStock/Getty Images Plus; **497** MentalArt/iStock/Getty Images Plus; **498** crossroadscreative/iStock/Getty Images Plus; **504** svry/Shutterstock.com; **506** koya79/iStock/Getty Images Plus; **510** kreinick/iStock/Getty Images Plus; **512** ewg3D/iStock/Getty Images Plus; **515** popovaphoto/iStock/Getty Images Plus; **516** IgorDutina/iStock/Getty Images Plus; **418** LauriPatterson/iStock/Getty Images Plus; **521** Maartje van Caspel/iStock/Getty Images Plus; **522** *Exercise 20* bedo/iStock/Getty Images Plus; kaanates/iStock/Getty Images Plus; **524** *right* ET-ARTWORKS/iStock/Getty Images Plus; *left* drewhadley/E+/Getty Images; **528** *right* MicroStockHub/iStock/Getty Images Plus; *left* Henrik_L/iStock/Getty Images Plus; **530** JoyTasa/iStock/Getty Images Plus; Liliboas/E+/Getty Images; **531** alisafarov/iStock/Getty Images Plus; **535** DenisNata/Shutterstock.com; **536** bogonet/iStock/Getty Images Plus

Chapter 12

537 vvvita/iStock/Getty Images Plus; **538** *left* margouillatphotos/iStock/Getty Images Plus; *right* Rose_Carson/iStock/Getty Images Plus; *right center* Toxitz/iStock/Getty Images Plus; amstockphoto/iStock/Getty Images Plus; *left center* Hemera Technologies/PhotoObjects.net/Getty Images Plus; *right bottom* temmuzcan/iStock/Getty Images Plus; **542** den-belitsky/iStock/Getty Images Plus; **544** *left* OcusFocus/iStock/Getty Images Plus; *right* TinnaPong/Shutterstock.com; **548** *top right* Ljupco/iStock/Getty Images Plus; *bottom left* SchulteProductions/E+/Getty Images; *bottom right* antpkr/iStock/Getty Images Plus; **550** Daniel Cole/Hemer/Getty Images Plus, urfinguss/iStock/Getty Images Plus; **554** *top right* ithinksky/iStock/Getty Images Plus; *center* ronstik/iStock/Getty Images Plus; *bottom right* Image Source/Photodisc/Getty Images; **556** Mary Wandler/iStock/Getty Images Plus; **558** jgroup/iStock/Getty Images Plus; **559** *top* emholk/iStock/Getty Images Plus; *bottom* Ron Chapple studios/Hemera/Getty Images; **560** evemilla/E+/Getty Images; **563** *left* F-91/iStock/Getty Images Plus; *right* GaryAlvis/E+/Getty Images; **564** *top left* temmuzcan/iStock/Getty Images Plus; *top right* Toxitz/iStock/Getty Images Plus; *center left* Rose_Carson/iStock/Getty Images Plus; *center right* Savany/iStock/Getty Images Plus; *bottom left* clubfoto/E+/Getty Images; *bottom right* savageultralight/iStock/Getty Images Plus; **565** *top left* ECummings00/iStock/Getty Images Plus; *top right* Mallivan/iStock/Getty Images Plus; *center left* ttatty/iStock/Getty Images Plus; *center right* design56/iStock/Getty Images Plus; *bottom right* Jose manuel Gelpi diaz/Hemera/Getty Images Plus; *bottom right and Exercise 9 left* Hemera Technologies/PhotoObjects.net/Getty Images Plus; *Exercise 9 center* kbwills/iStock/Getty Images Plus; arammiri/Stock/Getty Images Plus; *Exercise 9 right* TokenPhoto/E+/Getty Images; **566** *top right* NatalyaAksenova/iStock/Getty Images Plus; *center* Turnervisual/ iStock/Getty Images Plus; *bottom* DonNichols/E+/Getty Images; **567** *top* Talaj/iStock/Getty Images Plus; *Exercise 1* GSPictures/iStock/Getty Images Plus; *Exercise 2* Odua Images/Shutterstock.com; *Exercise 3* timquo/Shutterstock.com; *Exercise 4* 1001holiday/Shutterstock.com, michaeljung/iStock/Getty Images Plus; *Exercise 5* OcusFocus/iStock/Getty Images Plus; *Exercise 6* Big Ideas Learning; **568** *top right* wdstock/iStock/Getty Images Plus; *bottom right* Sonia Dubois/Shutterstock.com; **570** *top left* paseven/iStock/Getty Images Plus; *top right* bortonia/DigitalVision Vectors/Getty Images; *center left* Winai_Tepsuttinun/iStock/Getty Images Plus; *center right* urfinguss/iStock/Getty Images Plus; **571** sunstock/iStock/Getty Images Plus; **572** *top* Talaj/iStock/Getty Images Plus; *center* kbwills/iStock/Getty Images Plus; *bottom left* Colonel/iStock/Getty Images Plus; *bottom right* hadasit/Shutterstock.com; **573** *top left* arthobbit/iStock/Getty Images Plus; *top right* mariaflaya/iStock/Getty Images Plus; *center left* sceka/DigitalVision Vectors/Getty Images; *center right* Kseniia_Designer/iStock/Getty Images Plus; **574** *left* trigga/E+/Getty Images; *right* Spantomoda/iStock/Getty Images Plus; **575** *top left* iSashkinw/Stock/Getty Images Plus; *top right* anna1311/iStock/Getty Images Plus; *center* Alexandre Nunes/Hemera/Getty Images Plus; *center left* Fotoplanner/iStock/Getty Images Plus; *bottom left* Ivantsov/iStock/Getty Images Plus; *bottom right* JoyTasa/iStock/Getty Images Plus; **576** *top right* amstockphoto/iStock/Getty Images Plus; *center left* Dmytro_Skorobogatov/iStock/Getty Images Plus; *center right* bergamont/iStock/Getty Images Plus; *bottom left* nuwatphoto/iStock/Getty Images Plus; *bottom right* lucielang/iStock/Getty Images Plus; **577** *Exercise 3* andrea crisante/Shutterstock.com; *Exercise 4* vikif/iStock/Getty Images Plus; *Exercise 5* goir/iStock/ Getty Images Plus; *Exercise 6* alvarez/iStock/Getty Images Plus; *bottom left* pictafolio/E+/Getty Images; *bottom right* _jure/iStock/Getty Images Plus; **578** *top* Okea/iStock/Getty Images Plus, Suzifoo/iStock/Getty Images Plus; *center* harmpeti/iStock/Getty Images Plus, DNY59/E+/Getty Images; *bottom* GaryAlvis/iStock/Getty Images Plus; **579** *top* TokenPhoto/E+/Getty Images; *Exercise 1* Robert Kirk/iStock/Getty Images Plus; *Exercise 2* Dima Moroz/Shutterstock.com; *Exercise 3* design56/iStock/Getty Images Plus; *Exercise 4* Sergiy1975/iStock/Getty Images Plus; *Exercise 5* AnthonyRosenberg/iStock/Getty Images Plus; *Exercise 6* ra3rn/iStock/Getty Images Plus; **580** *top* GlobalP/iStock/Getty Images Plus; *bottom* ipopba/iStock/Getty Images Plus; **584** *left* hudiemm/E+/Getty Images; *right* mdmilliman/iStock/Getty Images Plus; **586** NonChanon/iStock/Getty Images Plus; **587** scanrail/iStock/Getty Images Plus; **589** PhotoMelon/iStock/Getty Images Plus; **590** *left* Nuarevik/iStock/GettyImages Plus; *right* AndreaAgrati/iStock/Getty Images Plus; **591** *top left* MileA/iStock/Getty Images Plus; *top right* akova/iStock/Getty Images Plus; *center left* Hemera Technologies/PhotoObjects.net/Getty Images Plus; *center right* Ryan McVay/Photodisc; **592** *top left* popovaphoto/iStock/Getty Images Plus; *top right* Creativeye99/iStock/Getty Images Plus; *center left* Dixi_/iStock/Getty Images Plus; *center right* DNY59/E+/Getty Images; **593** scanrail/iStock/Getty Images Plus; **594** Tsekhmister/iStock/Getty Images Plus; **595** pagadesign/E+/Getty Images; **596** eskymaks/iStock/Getty Images Plus; **597** Steve Collender/Shutterstock.com; ronniechua/iStock/Getty Images Plus, Denis Vrublevski/Shutterstock.com, amstockphoto/iStock/Getty Images Plus; **598** didesign021/iStock/Getty Images Plus

Chapter 13

599 drduey/iStock/Getty Images Plus; **610** mariusFM77/E+/Getty Images; **622** nikkytok/iStock/Getty Images Plus; **625** Pobytov/E+/Getty Images

Chapter 14

629 oxico/iStock/Getty Images Plus; **638** ChrisGorgio/iStock/Getty Images Plus; **640** snvv/iStock/Getty Images Plus; **650** AndreyPopov/iStock/Getty Images Plus; **652** elinedesignservices/iStock/Getty Images Plus; **656** GlobalP/iStock/Getty Images Plus; **658** Maxiphoto/iStock/Getty Images Plus; **659** *top* narvikk/E+/Getty Images; *bottom* GlobalP/iStock/Getty Images Plus; **663** *top* HeinzTeh/Shutterstock.com; *center* slobo/iStock/Getty Images Plus; *bottom* Tatiana Popova/Shutterstock.com; **664** *top* Photograpther/iStock/Getty Images Plus; *bottom* VadimPO/iStock/Getty Images Plus; **665** pioneer111/iStock/Getty Images Plus; **670** hatman12/iStock/Getty Images Plus; **671** BWFolsom/iStock/Getty Images Plus; **672** arlindo71/iStock/Getty Images Plus; **673** pixhook/E+/Getty Images; **678** *top* aristotoo/E+/Getty Images; *bottom* DrPAS/iStock/Getty Images Plus;

Chapter 15

679 JITD/Shutterstock.com; **684** Ida Jarosova/iStock/Getty Images Plus; **692** Dvougao/iStock/Getty Images Plus; **696** shalamov/iStock/Getty Images Plus; **702** Philipp83/iStock /Getty Images Plus; **704** keko-ka/iStock/Getty Images Plus; **708** *left* Phatthanit/Shutterstock.com; *right* GlobalP/iStock/Getty Images Plus; **711** *top* Ben-Schonewille/iStock/Getty Images Plus; *bottom* YvanDube/E+/Getty Images; **717** iDymax/iStock/Getty Images Plus; **718** emarto/iStock/Getty Images Plus; **721** *top* Cavvy01/iStock/Getty Images Plus; *bottom* kikkerdirk/iStock/Getty Images Plus

Cartoon Illustrations: MoreFrames Animation
Design Elements: oksanika/Shutterstock.com; icolourful/Shutterstock.com; Valdis Torms